Re-reading Foucault: On Law, Power and Righ

Re-reading Foucault: On Law, Power and Rights is the first collection in English fully to address the relevance of Michel Foucault's thought for law. Foucault is the best known and most cited of the late twentieth century's 'theory' academics. His work continues to animate a range of different critical work across intellectual disciplines in the arts, humanities and social sciences. There has, however, been comparatively little examination of the legal implications and applications of Foucault's work. This collection helps to fill that gap, providing an in-depth analysis of Foucault's thought as it pertains to a range of different legal themes, such as: the opposition between 'law' and 'the juridical'; the problem of moral and legal judgment; the historical basis of rights; and the political dimensions (and limitations) of contemporary human rights discourse. Including contributions from acknowledged experts on Foucault's work, as well as pieces by emerging scholars, *Re-reading Foucault: On Law, Power and Rights* will be of considerable interest across a range of disciplines, including law, philosophy, political theory, sociology, social theory and criminology.

Ben Golder is a Senior Lecturer in the Faculty of Law at the University of New South Wales.

Re-reading Foucault: On Law, Power and Rights

Edited by
Ben Golder

Routledge
Taylor & Francis Group
a GlassHouse Book

First published 2013
by Routledge
2 Park Square, Milton Park, Abingdon, Oxon OX14 4RN

Simultaneously published in the USA and Canada
by Routledge
711 Third Avenue, New York, NY 10017

A GlassHouse Book

Routledge is an imprint of the Taylor & Francis Group, an informa business

British Library Cataloguing in Publication Data
A catalogue record for this book is available from the British Library

Library of Congress Cataloging in Publication Data
Re-reading foucault : on law, power and rights / Edited by Ben Golder.
p. cm.
1. Law–Philosophy. 2. Foucault, Michel, 1926–1984. I. Golder, Ben.
K230.F682R47 2012
340'.1–dc23

2012012571

ISBN: 978-0-415-67353-2 (hbk)
ISBN: 978-0-415-63413-7 (pbk)
ISBN: 978-0-203-09456-3 (ebk)

Typeset in Baskerville
by Graphicraft Limited, Hong Kong

Contents

Acknowledgements

I would like first to thank each of the contributors to this collection, and especially Colin Gordon for agreeing to translate Philippe Chevallier's chapter. On this score, I would also like to record my thanks to Patrick Savidan and *Raison Publique* for permission to publish in English the chapter that appears translated here as 'Michel Foucault and the question of right' (and which first appeared in volume 13, issue 1 of *Raison Publique* in 2010 as 'Michel Foucault et la question du droit'). Work on this collection was supported by the Gilbert + Tobin Centre of Public Law at the University of New South Wales (my thanks there especially go to Andrew Lynch), and I benefited greatly from the assistance of several research assistants (law students at the University of New South Wales) in preparing the manuscript: Fiona Chong, Angela Kintominas and Mabel Koo. Thank you also to the editorial staff at Routledge for their support of and help with this project, especially Colin Perrin and Melanie Fortmann-Brown. Lastly, thank you to the Melbourne artist, Emily Mierisch, for the use of her original artwork in the cover design of this book.

Notes on contributors

Philippe Chevallier, PhD, is the author of *Michel Foucault. Le pouvoir et la bataille* (Pleins Feux, 2004), and *Michel Foucault et le Christianisme* (ENS editions, 2001), and the co-editor, with Tim Greacen, of the collection *Folie et justice: relire Foucault* (Erès, 2009). He is currently working at the Bibliothèque nationale de France.

Peter Fitzpatrick is currently Anniversary Professor of Law at Birkbeck, University of London and Honorary Professor of Law in the University of Kent. In 2007 he was given the James Boyd White Award by the Association for the Study of Law, Culture and the Humanities. He has taught at universities in Europe, North America and Papua New Guinea, and published many books on legal philosophy, law and social theory, law and racism, and imperialism, the latest ones being *Law as Resistance: Modernism, Imperialism, Legalism* (Ashgate, 2008) and, with Ben Golder, *Foucault's Law* (Routledge, 2009). Outside the academy he has been in an international legal practice and was also in the Prime Minister's Office in Papua New Guinea for several years.

Ben Golder is a Senior Lecturer in the Faculty of Law at the University of New South Wales (UNSW). He holds undergraduate law and English literature degrees from UNSW and a doctorate in legal theory from the University of London. Prior to joining the faculty, Ben taught law at the University of East London, University College London, Birkbeck College and New York University in London. With Peter Fitzpatrick he is the author and editor, respectively, of *Foucault's Law* (Routledge, 2009) and *Foucault and Law* (Ashgate, 2010), and is currently at work on a manuscript on Foucault's politics of rights in the late work.

Colin Gordon has been translating, editing and writing about Michel Foucault's work since the 1970s, alongside a career in health informatics. He edited *Power/Knowledge: Selected Interviews and Other Writings, 1972–1977* by Michel Foucault (Harvester, 1980), co-edited and co-authored *The Foucault Effect: Studies in Governmentality* (Harvester Wheatsheaf, 1991), selected the contents and wrote the introduction to *Power: Essential Works of Foucault, 1954–1984, Volume 3* (New Press, 2000) and co-organized the conference *The Foucault Effect 1991–2011* at Birkbeck College in June 2011.

Alan Hunt is Chancellor's Professor of Law and Sociology at Carleton University in Ottawa. He has published on the sociology of law, on Foucault and law, on governmentality and many fields of moral regulation.

Lissa Lincoln joined the American University of Paris after completing her doctoral work in French theory and literature at McGill University. Her dissertation, entitled *Albert Camus et la question du juste*, presents a Foucaultian reading of normative language in Camus's fiction, specifically the language of judgment, and its (de)construction through legal discourse. She also holds an MA in French literature from the University of Alberta, the focus of her Master's thesis being a comparative study of seventeenth-century French moralists. She teaches courses in law and literature, critical legal theory, literary scandal and censorship, critical theory, French literature, and composition, and her research interests focus upon law, jurisprudence, legal theory and discourse, particularly in their interrelationship with literature, philosophy and critical theory. Lissa is currently preparing for publication her book, *Albert Camus: Legal Discourse and the Problem of Judgment.*

Pat O'Malley is Professorial Research Fellow in Law at the University of Sydney. Most of his writing in the past 20 years has focused on risk as a technology of government, especially in criminal justice. Recent books on the topic include *Crime and Risk* (Sage, 2010), *The Currency of Justice: Fines and Damages in Consumer Societies* (Routledge, 2009) and, with Kelly Hannah Moffatt, *Gendered Risks* (Cavendish, 2006). A more general book on *Risk, Uncertainty and Government* was published in 2004 (Cavendish). Current work is exploring the role of fire prevention as a critical domain of urban security; also in preparation is a monograph on *Crime, Excitement and Risk*, exploring the place of risk-taking and excitement in contemporary crime and consumer culture, and their correlates in the apparatus of criminal justice.

Paul Patton is Professor of Philosophy at the University of New South Wales in Sydney, Australia. He is the author of *Deleuze and the Political* (Routledge, 2000) and *Deleuzian Concepts: Philosophy, Colonization, Politics* (Stanford, 2010). He is editor of *Deleuze: A Critical Reader* (Blackwell, 1996), with Duncan Ivison and Will Sanders of *Political Theory and the Rights of Indigenous Peoples* (Cambridge, 2000), with John Protevi of *Between Deleuze and Derrida* (Continuum, 2003) and with Simone Bignall of *Deleuze and the Postcolonial* (Edinburgh, 2010). He has translated work by Deleuze, Foucault, Nancy and Baudrillard. His publications deal with aspects of French poststructuralist philosophy and a variety of topics in contemporary political philosophy. He is a member of the Editorial Board ('Contemporary-Critical Continental') for the Sage *Encyclopedia of Political Theory* (General Editor: Mark Bevir), and a member of the Editorial Boards of *Philosophy Compass* (Continental), *Deleuze Studies* and *Derrida Today.*

George Pavlich is a Professor of Law and Sociology at the University of Alberta. He has published on law, legal theory, sociology and criminology. Much of his work has centred on Foucault, such as the collection, co-edited with Gary Wickham, *Rethinking Law, Society and Governance: Foucault's Bequest* (Hart, 2001). Recent work includes the collection *After Sovereignty* (Routledge, 2010) and *Law and Society Redefined* (Oxford University Press, 2011).

Bal Sokhi-Bulley is a Lecturer in Law at Queen's University Belfast. She has a PhD from the University of Nottingham, where she also obtained an LLM in International Human Rights Law, and an LLB in European Law from the University of Warwick. Her research interests lie in critical theory and human rights. She has recently published in *Law & Critique*, *Social & Legal Studies*, and the *Human Rights Law Review* on the theme of using Michel Foucault's concept of 'governmentality' to understand the regulatory and governing potential of the European Union's rights discourse.

Véronique Voruz is Senior Lecturer in Law and Criminology at the University of Leicester, and in Foucaultian Perspectives in Criminology at the School of Criminology of the Université Catholique de Louvain-la-Neuve in Belgium. She is currently writing a book on Foucault and criminology for Routledge as well as writing the introduction for, and translating from French into English, with Dr Suzanne Yang, Dr Biagi-Chai's book, *Serial Killers: Criminology, Psychiatry, Responsibility*.

Jessica Whyte is a Lecturer in Cultural and Social Analysis at the University of Western Sydney, Australia. She has published widely on contemporary continental philosophy (Agamben, Foucault, Rancière), theories of sovereignty and biopolitics, critical legal theory and critiques of human rights. She is a co-editor of the *Theory and Event* symposium 'Form of Life: Giorgio Agamben, Ontology, Politics' (2010), of the *Australian Feminist Law Journal* special edition 'Law, Crisis, Revolution' (2010) and of the *Agamben Dictionary* (Edinburgh University Press, 2011). She completed her doctorate on the political thought of Giorgio Agamben in the Centre for Comparative Literature and Cultural Studies, Monash University, in 2010. Her current research is on the emergence of the 'right to intervene' in the practices of the new activist humanitarian NGOs of the 1970s, and its transformation into a legitimising discourse for state militarism.

Introduction

Re-reading Foucault on law, power and rights

Ben Golder

What is the place of law in Foucault's various and varied accounts of modernity? What does Foucault have to say about law and what importance does he accord it in the social and political order of things? Has he omitted or excluded it illegitimately? Of course, these opening questions themselves betray a certain *methodological legalism* which Foucault's oft-canvassed theoretical opposition to juridical styles of thought would seek fundamentally to put into question. Rather than problematizing the category of law, these ways of posing the question of Foucault's relationship to law tend arguably to accept the stability and legitimacy of law. They assume the utility of law as a grid of intelligibility for the operation of power and take law as a starting point for analysis rather than as that which is itself in need of problematization. Alternatively, then: Can one even speak of 'law' outside of the rationalities and technologies of power operative in a given social formation? In speaking of law (and thus necessarily *speaking the law*) what does the theorist enable (and, more to the point, occlude)? Must not one rather ask how it came to be, and with what effects, that (a certain form of) law itself furnished the premises of political and social analysis and critique? Who speaks when law speaks, and who and what gets silenced? How might we think law *autrement*, as Lissa Lincoln asks perceptively in her contribution to this collection?

These, no doubt, represent some of the methodological counter-questions and analytical detours whereby Foucault seeks to displace the theoretical privilege, the sovereignty even, of the 'juridico-discursive' theory of power (for example, see Foucault 1979: 83). But remaining for a while within the orbit of my opening set of questions and their juridical entailments – Where is the law in Foucault and what has he done with it? – it is fair to say both that these questions have (tellingly) structured much of the extant debate within legal scholarship on Foucault's relationship to law *and* that, according to their terms, the judgment entered has been, on the whole, a negative one. As several of the contributors to this collection begin by discussing, Foucault's alleged failure to take proper account of law in his analyses of modernity has been a significant cause of concern, castigation and critique in the literature on Foucault and law. Colin Gordon puts the matter in the following way in his chapter, entitled 'Expelled questions: Foucault, the Left and the law'. He writes:

> A discussion of Foucault and law is almost routinely obliged, very much in the same way as a discussion of Foucault and gender, Foucault and geography or Foucault and post-colonial studies, to begin by acknowledging a widely held opinion that his work can be criticized for saying too little about law, or for belittling and disparaging the historical importance of law, its function in the constitution of modernity, and its constitutive and normative presence in social reality.
>
> (see Chapter 1, p. 13)

In Anglophone legal scholarship the best-known exponent of the view that Foucault downplayed the significance of law in modernity is the work, either sole-authored or in collaboration, of Alan Hunt (1992, 2004) and Gary Wickham (2002, 2006).[1] Their 1994 book, *Foucault and Law: Towards a Sociology of Law as Governance* (Hunt and Wickham 1994), articulated what subsequently came to be popularized as the 'expulsion thesis' – namely that Foucault had expelled law from any significant role in modernity. As Philippe Chevallier makes clear in his chapter (Chapter 8), citing French sources, this interpretation has by no means been confined to the Anglophone reception of the French thinker (see, also, Lincoln's chapter, Chapter 4). Indeed, Chevallier opens his chapter with what can stand as a succinct statement of the 'expulsion thesis':

> Is law the poor relation among the topics of Foucault's work? There has been widespread complaint to this effect, often with the suggestion that the philosopher remained limited here to a narrow, statist view of law and right, a viewpoint largely guided by the Napoleonic Codes, which fails to take account of contemporary developments which multiply the possibilities for individuals of legal recourse, including against the state. Foucault, it is claimed, neglected the virtues of political justice, which he discounted as an abstract, transcendental doctrine of traditional political thought, ill-suited for grasping the real functioning of modern power in its two principal forms, 'disciplinary power' and 'biopower'. For this French philosopher, starting with the early modern 'classical age', political power over the bodies of individuals operated principally through a *physis*, as a science of the growth and multiplication of beings, relegating juridical fictions to the prop room.
>
> (see Chapter 8, p. 171)

This dominant interpretation of Foucault – a 'widely held opinion', as Gordon has it in the above quotation – has recently been contested, revised, supplemented, extended and problematized along a number of different fronts.[2] It is to this interpretive work of re-imagining law in, and through, Foucault's work that the present collection, *Re-reading Foucault: Law, Power and Rights*, is dedicated. As I have been discussing, the common approach to assessing the legal theoretical import of Foucault's work has been to examine what he has had to say about law in a number of places – often restricted to a fairly circumscribed range of texts from the mid- to late-1970s that are felt to have a more directly 'political' bearing – and then, on the basis of such a survey, often to conclude either that he did not have a great deal to say about the matter or that what little he did have to say was not particularly edifying – and this often in line with the 'expulsion thesis'. By contrast, the chapters in this collection take a range of different methodological approaches. By no means all of the contributors take the 'expulsion thesis' as their starting point, nor even the place and function of law in Foucault's work as an orienting frame of reference, nor indeed even law *per se* as their explicit object of inquiry. Some *do* return to the question of law in Foucault's work and seek thereby to articulate a different understanding of law (indeed an 'other law', as Peter Fitzpatrick has it (Chapter 2)) in his work. Others approach the question of Foucault's relation to law differently, discerning in his work the critical, methodological resources for thinking law and its functions in a different register (for example, Lincoln's chapter on judgment (Chapter 4)). Yet others perform this very work themselves, deploying Foucaultian insights in order to theorize legal and political formations, whether they be historical (as, for example, in George Pavlich's analysis of colonial sovereignty (Chapter 5)) or contemporary (as, for example, in Bal Sokhi-Bulley's use of 'governmentality' to expose the regulatory dimension of human rights discourse (Chapter 11)). What links these various chapters, in sum, is a concern to re-read Foucault in order to draw out the legal implications of his work – either directly or via some application of his work.[3] The following chapters hence confront a range of questions surrounding the place and function of law and legal concepts (the juridical, judgment, sovereignty, right, rights, normativity) in Foucault's work *and* also, crucially, of how Foucault's work helps us to think of these very categories differently.

The chapters

Colin Gordon (Chapter 1) begins by problematizing the very question with which I opened this introductory chapter, namely the question of the place of law in Foucault's thought. Rather than assuming that law is somehow lacking in Foucault's account of modernity, Gordon proceeds by questioning why it is that the very presence or absence of law comes to assume such theoretical and political importance in engagements with Foucault. Gordon poses himself what he calls a 'maliciously genealogical' (see p. 14) question along the following lines: 'What may be at stake in our politico-intellectual culture, and what interests, struggles or stratagems can potentially be involved, when a thinker such as Foucault is accused from various directions of insufficient attention or respect for law?' (see p. 14). What is essentially at stake for him is the response within contemporary Left politics to the question of legality – and that both the concerns, and the style, of the discourse around Foucault and law are to be understood as refracted through these questions. Whilst the first half of Gordon's chapter pursues this question by situating Foucault in regards to the contemporary Left and its own engagement with questions of legality, the second half of his chapter picks up on a range of different 'legal themes and strands in Foucault's work' (see p. 25ff.). This survey then opens on to the remainder of the collection, as many of the contributors subsequently pick up, and reflect upon, these very themes in their engagements with Foucault.

The following two chapters, by Peter Fitzpatrick (Chapter 2) and Alan Hunt (Chapter 3), both take up the question of alternative understandings of law in Foucault's work, and both do so, at least initially, through the series of lectures 'Truth and Juridical Forms' which Foucault delivered in Brazil in 1973 (2000). For Fitzpatrick, developing an argument explored in the book *Foucault's Law* (Golder and Fitzpatrick 2009), this series of lectures provides the opening (and the structural motif) for a discussion of law's 'nested halves' – being its two, aporetic, dimensions of determinacy and responsiveness – which is layered throughout the chapter. Fitzpatrick here extends this argument about law to Foucault's constituting of the individual, and of society, and, finally, to theory itself – engaging here explicitly with questions of whether Foucault 'had' a theory of law. For his part, Hunt takes the Brazil lectures as an occasion to revisit a question previously posed – and answered – in his 1994 book, with Gary Wickham, *Foucault and Law*, namely 'whether Foucault's stimulating and original account of the place of law in modern society excludes or marginalizes the role played by the expansion and diversification of legal mechanisms in constituting modernity' (see Chapter 3, p. 64). Here the answer is somewhat different, taking account as it necessarily must for Hunt of 'an important dimension of Foucault's discussion, . . . [that is,] the nature and role of the "juridical", [which] did not receive the attention it deserve[d]' in his previous account of Foucault due in part to the delayed availability of Foucault's Rio de Janeiro lectures in English translation (p. 64). Hunt's chapter begins with a survey and a critique of these lectures. Ultimately finding Foucault's account deficient in several respects, Hunt nevertheless finds the lectures revealing for how they 'open[ed] up the field of the juridical' (see Chapter 3, p. 71) in Foucaultian analysis. Hunt's chapter draws upon this idea in advancing 'an understanding of law as a "juridical assemblage"' (see Chapter 3, p. 71) – a contingent, aleatory, non-systemic field characterized by 'the coexistence of different combinations of legal, judicial, and normative elements' (see Chapter 3, p. 80). Hunt concludes thus:

> The deployment of the concept of the assemblage makes it possible to bring together some of the disparate elements found in Foucault's engagement with the juridical field. We no longer need to castigate him for his narrow emphasis on the imperative dimensions of law. We can appreciate that his focus on the interaction between different fields of power, knowledge and governance manifested itself in his substantive preoccupation with the ways in which forms of law interact with mechanisms of discipline and with strategies and techniques of governance.
>
> (see Chapter 3, p. 81)

In Chapter 4, Lissa Lincoln approaches the question of the juridical – and more particularly of the modalities of legitimation and judgment – through a reading of both Foucault and Camus. As with Gordon's chapter, which methodologically displaces the standard questions of whether there is an adequate theoretical account of law in Foucault's work in favour of a problematization of the legal privilege in contemporary readings of Foucault, Lincoln herself approaches the question of judgment through asking after how the problem of judgment is itself constructed. As we shall see, she does this through a reading of Camus and Foucault. Whilst Camus the moralizing humanist would at first blush seem very much opposed to Foucault the critic of humanism (and, indeed, of philosophy understood as the legislation of values and the prescription of the good), Lincoln's chapter uncovers 'an interesting, if unexpected, connection' between the two thinkers (see Chapter 4, p. 87) the two thinkers. For her, what in fact unites both thinkers is precisely their shared problematization of the modality of judgment. Her chapter explains both how a reading of Foucault allows one to understand the Camusian project *autrement* but also how Foucault's analytic approach itself productively opens up the problem of legal judgment.

The next three chapters engage with law and legal issues from a different direction – that is, via a series of reflections which take particular power relations well-theorized by Foucault (sovereignty, surveillance and biopolitics) as their focus, before then relating this analysis to law or introducing legal questions in light of the analysis. In Chapter 5, George Pavlich deploys Foucault's reading of Hobbes in the lecture course '*Society Must be Defended*' (Foucault 2003b) in order to theorize a historical example of what he calls colonial sovereignty politics. The example that Pavlich focuses upon is the administration and governance of the Cape of Good Hope at the turn of the nineteenth century. Pavlich draws upon Foucault's 'perceptive interpretation of Hobbes' (see Chapter 5, p. 109) in '*Society Must be Defended*' in order to demonstrate how the maintenance of sovereign control actually relies upon a range of different political technologies (including law). As he puts it:

> Drawing on a 'softer' version of Hobbes, colonial sovereignty might equally be understood less as a top-down imposition following conquest, and more as an ongoing achievement of local power relations that seek to fashion legitimate and effective legal or governmental forms. In other words, by returning to Foucault's interpretation of Hobbes, this chapter draws attention to de Mist's emphasis on the ongoing, dynamic, and always-volatile bottom-up political relations that must be harnessed for effective juridical and sovereign governance to emerge.
>
> (see Chapter 5, p. 109)

In Chapter 6, Véronique Voruz conducts 'a reflection on the status of the gaze in our societies, often called control . . . or surveillance societies' (see Chapter 6, p. 127). Distancing herself from current and popular approaches in criminology and surveillance studies that seek to deploy Foucault's understanding of 'panopticism' as some kind of Weberian ideal type to the study of society, Voruz returns to Foucault's work in order 'to map what Foucault says of the gaze at different times' (see Chapter 6, p. 128). This rich textual study of the various articulations of the gaze in Foucault's work has a range of possible applications for legal and criminological thinking. As Voruz foreshadows them:

> A close scrutiny of the gaze, and of what the gaze is made to perform in Foucault's own work, may help us fruitfully to elucidate whether it is truly the *visual* which is at stake in our closed-circuit television . . . culture, but also in multi-factorial risk registers, DNA databases and the current tendency to introduce practices bypassing subjective responsibility in criminal justice via neuro-scientific visibilization of the operation of the brain in the emergent field of neuro-law.
>
> (see Chapter 6, p. 128)

Finally, in Chapter 7, Pat O'Malley reconstructs, with and (in part) against Foucault, a genealogy of what he calls 'biopolitical justice'. Focusing on questions of punishment, O'Malley retraces the shift from a disciplinary anthropology of the offender to a biopolitical and environmental modulation of the population via apparatuses of security. For O'Malley, Foucault's own account of this transition underplays key connections between Benthamite penology and the neoliberal penological imagination of the 1970s. Central to this process, a fact also unexplored by Foucault, was the fine (which was of central importance to the late Bentham's thinking on punishment). The genealogy offered by O'Malley in this chapter both points backwards to the Benthamite lineages of contemporary practices and also illuminates the contours of our contemporary, commodified biopolitical 'domain of governance [which is] policed primarily at the margins by risk, within which there is a "floating" of the moral order, [and] in which the market and money optimize all circulations, good and bad' (see Chapter 7, p. 165).

The last four chapters each concern rights and, once again, the different engagements approach the question of rights in (and through) Foucault's work in a variety of ways. Each of the chapters, however, refuses a simplistic and summary judgment of Foucault – that, for example, he was simply a negative critic of rights discourse and that he had nothing constructive to add to debates around rights, that he failed to develop a theory of rights, and that his work is consequently of no real use for thinking through the juridical or political dimensions of contemporary rights regimes. To the contrary, each of the final four authors locates in Foucault's work either a much richer consideration of rights or the methodological possibility of deploying Foucault's insights in order productively to (re)theorize rights. A number of shared concerns circulate through these chapters, albeit addressed in different ways by the authors – the possible modern grounds, or normative bases, of rights once they are detached from metaphysical claims about human nature or essence; the connection between (current and novel) rights claims and pre-existing political formations; and the extent to which rights can effectively pose themselves against those extant political formations (within which they are embedded) in the name of counter-conduct, critique, or even revolutionary change.

In Chapter 8, Chevallier returns to both Foucault's lecture courses at the *Collège de France* and a series of political and journalistic interventions contemporary with these lectures in order to outline a new understanding of rights in Foucault's work. Beyond Foucault's well-known critique of sovereign right, indeed even beyond his occasional 'strategic' or 'instrumental' deployments of given juridical rights for particular political purposes, Chevallier argues that in these sources it is 'possible to find premises for a more positive and non-disciplinary approach to right' (see Chapter 8, p. 178) – recalling here the cryptic 'new right' that Foucault had tantalizingly alluded to towards the end of the second lecture of '*Society Must be Defended*' in 1976 (Foucault 2003b: 40). Chevallier discerns, and elaborates upon, this possibility in Foucault's development of the concept of the 'rights of the governed' from 1977 onwards and his chapter here proceeds to situate it within Foucault's then current genealogies of liberal (and neoliberal) modes of governmentality in the lecture courses of 1977 and 1978: *Security, Territory, Population* (Foucault 2007) and *The Birth of Biopolitics* (Foucault 2008a).

Similarly, Paul Patton in Chapter 9 returns to this work of Foucault's on different forms of modern governmental reason in order to help construct what he calls a 'naturalistic' account of rights, by which he means an account which 'grounds [rights] in existing forms of political normativity and legal practice . . . [which] does not depend on any transcendent conception of the moral basis of rights, or of the human nature in which they are grounded, and in which rights are an important part of the social world in which we live' (see Chapter 9, p. 188). For Patton, then, Foucault's work provides theoretical support for the proposition, and itself helps empirically to illuminate and substantiate the different ways in which 'criticism of the exercise of power, often in the name of particular rights, invariably draws upon rationalities of government that are available in the prevailing political culture' (see Chapter 9, p. 199).

Jessica Whyte's critical examination in Chapter 10 of Foucault's own turn to rights discourse in his late work proceeds from this very proposition; namely, as she puts it, 'Foucault's argument that counter-conducts share a set of elements with the governmental rationality they oppose' (see Chapter 10, p. 213). Accepting this premise, and in line with recent revisionist histories of human rights that understand the hypertrophic rise of the discourse of human rights in the late 1970s as being connected to the deemed exhaustion of existing forms of (communist, socialist, revolutionary) political utopia (see especially Moyn 2010), Whyte situates Foucault's deployment of 'rights talk' in this particular historical juncture characterized by the ascent both of the discourse of human rights and, concomitantly, of neoliberal global capitalism. Are we then to understand human rights as the counter-conduct proper to neoliberalism, and, if so, what limitations might this import for the critical and contestatory possibilities claimed on behalf of human rights? The question for Whyte then becomes: '[I]f counter-conducts always engage in a game, attempting to open up new spaces of freedom, it is worth asking after the possibilities that exist in the present to refuse to play within the pre-determined rules of that game, and to open up a new crisis of governmentality that could subvert and re-orient those rules' (see Chapter 10, p. 225). Or, put in a different way, itself a motif for her chapter: 'Is revolution desirable?'

The final chapter in the collection, Chapter 11, by Bal Sokhi-Bulley, also engages with the politics of rights and the limits of critique. Sokhi-Bulley's chapter addresses the contemporary rights discourse of the European Union (EU) and, more specifically, the EU's Fundamental Rights Agency (FRA). Whilst clothed in the bland and seemingly apolitical rhetoric of 'new governance', the FRA's rights discourse, argues Sokhi-Bulley, is actually a highly *governmentalised* practice which engenders and regulates subject positions through a range of different mechanisms. Human rights emerge in Sokhi-Bulley's account not as a discourse of liberation nor even as protective of the individual, but rather as the enlistment of the individual within a certain normative ideal of EU citizenship. To be the subject of rights in this Foucaultian account is precisely to be *subjectified* in and by the power relations of rights.

Notes

1 Hunt and Wickham's work on Foucault and law, singly or in collaboration, is the most extensive development of this interpretation in the Anglophone literature but they were by no means the first to make this critique of Foucault. This critique was ventilated in the 1980s before the publication of *Foucault and Law* – see Gordon's chapter in the present collection for discussion (Chapter 1).

2 As I mention in the text, above, this collection is itself conceived as forming a part of an ongoing attempt to re-read Foucault from the perspective of law and legal theory. Recent book-length attempts either to retrieve an alternative understanding of law in Foucault's work, or to apply his work to a study of legal phenomena, include: Golder and Fitzpatrick 2009, and Sharpe 2009. Whilst these texts, and others, have recently been published, there has also been an ongoing critical response to the 'expulsion thesis' in the literature from mid-1990s onwards. For examples, see Tadros 1998 and Munro 2001.

3 This *re-reading* of Foucault is, as the reader of this collection will encounter, often motivated by an explicit concern to return to underappreciated (or hitherto unpublished or untranslated) sources in order to revise or supplement the extant Foucaultian record. As the project of publishing and translating Foucault's annual lecture courses at the *Collège de France* proceeds apace, for example, it is clear (and has been for some time) that many of his observations in that context contain a pointed relevance for theorizing law and legal questions. Rather obviously, Foucault's discussions of sovereignty and biopolitics in the lecture course '*Society Must be Defended*' (Foucault 2003b) have proved to offer fertile ground for legal reflection, as indeed have the lecture courses on governmentality and neoliberalism for the following two years, *Security, Territory, Population* (Foucault 2007) and *The Birth of Biopolitics* (Foucault 2008a). Yet contributors to the present collection also refer here to earlier and later courses in elucidating

Foucault's different positions on law and rights, from *Abnormal* (Foucault 2003a) and *Psychiatric Power* (Foucault 2008b) through to *The Hermeneutics of the Subject* (Foucault 2005) and *The Government of Self and Others* (Foucault 2010). In addition, many of the contributors here engage with the set of lectures Foucault gave in Brazil in 1973, and which were published in English in 2000 under the title 'Truth and Juridical Forms' (Foucault 2000) as well as two other series of lectures roughly contemporary with these: Foucault's lectures at Louvain (Foucault forthcoming) and his first lecture course at the *Collège de France* (Foucault 2011).

References

Foucault, M. (1979) *The Will to Knowledge: The History of Sexuality, Vol. 1*, trans. R. Hurley, Harmondsworth: Penguin

___ (2000) 'Truth and Juridical Forms', in J. D. Faubion (ed.) *Essential Works of Foucault 1954–1984 Vol. 3: Power*, New York, NY: The New Press

___ (2003a) *Abnormal: Lectures at the Collège de France, 1974–75*, trans. G. Burchell, London: Verso

___ (2003b) *'Society Must be Defended': Lectures at the Collège de France, 1975–76*, trans. D. Macey, London: Allen Lane

___ (2005) *The Hermeneutics of the Subject: Lectures at the Collège de France, 1981–82*, trans. G. Burchell, New York, NY: Palgrave Macmillan

___ (2007) *Security, Territory, Population: Lectures at the Collège de France, 1977–78*, trans. G. Burchell, New York, NY: Palgrave Macmillan

___ (2008a) *The Birth of Biopolitics: Lectures at the Collège de France, 1978–79*, trans. G. Burchell, New York, NY: Palgrave Macmillan

___ (2008b) *Psychiatric Power: Lectures at the Collège de France, 1973–74*, trans. G. Burchell, New York, NY: Palgrave Macmillan

___ (2010) *The Government of Self and Others: Lectures at the Collège de France 1982–83*, trans. G. Burchell, Houndmills: Palgrave Macmillan

___ (2011) *Leçons sur la volonté de savoir: Cours au Collège de France (1970–1971) suivi de Le savoir d'Oedipe*, Paris: Gallimard/Seuil

___ (forthcoming), *Mal faire, dire vrai: fonctions de l'aveu*, Louvain and Chicago, IL: Louvain University Press/University of Chicago Press

Golder, B. and Fitzpatrick, P. (2009) *Foucault's Law*, Abingdon: Routledge

Hunt, A. (1992) 'Foucault's Expulsion of Law: Toward a Retrieval', *Law & Social Inquiry*, 17: 1–38

___ (2004) 'Getting Marx and Foucault into Bed Together!', *Journal of Law and Society*, 31: 592–609

Hunt, A. and Wickham, G. (1994) *Foucault and Law: Towards a Sociology of Law as Governance*, London: Pluto Press

Moyn, S. (2010) *The Last Utopia: Human Rights in History*, Cambridge, MA: Harvard University Press

Munro, V. (2001) 'Legal Feminism and Foucault – A Critique of the Expulsion of Law', *Journal of Law and Society*, 28: 546–67

Sharpe, A. (2009) *Foucault's Monsters and the Challenge of Law*, Abingdon: Routledge

Tadros, V. (1998) 'Between Governance and Discipline: The Law and Michel Foucault', *Oxford Journal of Legal Studies*, 18: 75–103

Wickham, G. (2002) 'Foucault and Law', in R. Banakar and M. Travers (eds) *An Introduction to Law and Social Theory*, Oxford: Hart

___ (2006) 'Foucault, Law, and Power: A Reassessment', *Journal of Law and Society*, 33: 596–614

Part 1

Law, judgment and the juridical

Chapter 1

Expelled questions: Foucault, the Left and the law

Colin Gordon

The law is one of a number of domains of reality and study concerning which it has been customary since Foucault's death (if not already in his lifetime) to discuss, deplore, excuse, diagnose, or endeavour to make good, his failure to devote a degree of attention sufficient to satisfy the expectations of a certain audience. A discussion of Foucault and law is almost routinely obliged, very much in the same way as a discussion of Foucault and gender, Foucault and geography or Foucault and post-colonial studies, to begin by acknowledging a widely held opinion that his work can be criticized for saying too little about law, or for belittling and disparaging the historical importance of law, its function in the constitution of modernity, and its constitutive and normative presence in social reality.

A few doubts and reservations suggest themselves about this customary framework of discussion. One of these concerns the widespread and automatic assumption that Foucault, in what was after all an academic career cut short in mid-span, ought – putting the matter as simply and naïvely as possible – to have written everything about everything, and was not eligible for the usual permission allowed by the academic division of labour to focus and concentrate a personal programme of research on a delimited and specialized range of topics. The status which Foucault has acquired or been accorded in contemporary public space seems to carry with it an implicit obligation, subject to public accountability, and in case of default to rebuke, to have something adequate to say about every topic. To a remarkable, and remarkably unnoticed, extent Foucault is evaluated and judged as a universal intellectual whose thought is expected to provide an encyclopaedic compendium of illumination, explanation, inspiration and orientation. On reading his younger commentators, one often had the impression that Foucault had placed himself under an obligation to write not only the books he wrote, the books he had said he would write and the books he failed to live to write, but also the books, or at least the founding intellectual groundwork of the books, which some of his readers and critics have themselves desired to write, and in some cases, despite his inadequate assistance, succeeded in writing.

The contention that Foucault neglects, disparages or undervalues law has been widely canvassed and has in the process been subjected to a degree of critical challenge. I agree with those[1] who argue that Foucault's work somewhat obviously has considerably more of interest to say about law, and about rights, than those who have most loudly voiced their disappointment at his contribution on these matters have found fit to notice. On the other hand, it is as well to acknowledge frankly, and before deciding whether apologies are in order, that law is not the central theme of Foucault's work. This bare fact still leaves open to us the option of whether we choose to consider it a problem. It might appear less of a problem if one notices what many critical commentators, in the face of readily available evidence, choose to ignore, namely that (as was already extensively illustrated by the contents of *The Foucault Effect* (see Burchell, Gordon and Miller 1991 – much of which had already been available in journal publication for a decade), Foucault did not work alone, and that some of his closest collaborators, notably François Ewald, carried out research under his inspiration which had a strong and central concern with legal themes.[2]

Two other interesting questions remain. One is whether, regardless of the contingencies of Foucault's own choices and constraints – including the not insignificant constraint of early death – Foucault's work could be used, or continued, in order to produce a genealogy (or a genealogical history) of law in various periods of Western – or indeed non-Western – history. The other (with some supplementaries) is about our own critical requirements and expectations. If we think Foucault did not rate law as important enough, how much is enough? And where can we turn for guidance on the correct estimate of this matter? If his relative silence about law is held in some sense to be a culpable silence, what was it that he should have said and why was it important and necessary that he should have said it? And who else has said the things which Foucault should have said? If the proper status of law is not satisfactorily recognized by Foucault, what is it, and what would constitute its satisfactory recognition?

Along with these, perhaps naïve, but surely admissible queries (not all of which I shall undertake to answer here), another, perhaps more maliciously genealogical, question could also be posed about the terms of this discussion, which I shall try to explore here a little: what may be at stake in our politico-intellectual culture, and what interests, struggles or stratagems can potentially be involved, when a thinker such as Foucault is accused from various directions of insufficient attention or respect for law? What should one make, indeed, of the very style of polemical discourse in which some at least of this discussion has been conducted? The part I refer to is that which can appear on occasion to have the mode and style of an ideological inquisition, and where one seems liable to encounter a degree of pervasive confusion of the doxological and epistemological modes; that is to say, of rectitude in terms of belief and faith as distinct from rectitude in terms of truth-telling. This is likewise as area of discussion where the underlying stakes can appear to concern the acceptability of certain topics of discussion from the point of view of certain systems of belief and faith. *Discipline and Punish* was received in various quarters as a problematic book, and its impact as a cause of disquiet, because, among other things, of the ways in which it represented the exercise of power in liberal societies as vastly exceeding the bounds of its legitimating foundations in law. This is one of the very well-known and undeniable sources in Foucault's work for what, in the wording due to Alan Hunt and developed in his 1994 book with Gary Wickham, is known as the 'expulsion thesis'; namely, the thesis of the 'expulsion' of law in Foucault's analyses as a principal explanatory or analytic category from the study of modernity (Hunt 1992b; Hunt and Wickham 1994). But it remains hard in reading much of the literature – including parts of the recent book by Ben Golder and Peter Fitzpatrick (2009) which focuses on a critical reassessment of Hunt and Wickham – to establish clearly whether the perceived offence in *Discipline and Punish* is more an offence against fact (or historical veracity) or against doxa (the right-minded way in which things should be seen, said or thought – or left unseen, unsaid and unthought).

This chapter will proceed in two parts. In the first part, I want to begin to answer the genealogical question I have just raised; namely whether the situation of Foucault within a particular politico-intellectual culture can help explain the problematization of his approach to law and rights in much of the literature. In brief, I argue that it *can* and that the source of much of the disquiet concerning Foucault's engagements with law is to be found in intellectual moves being made within the contemporary Left intellectual *milieu* concerning law and legality. I also want myself, as foreshadowed above, to problematize some of the polemical structure of this discourse and some of its presuppositions. In the second part of the chapter, having proposed an explanation of why Foucault's approach to law supposedly falls short, I change tack somewhat and offer a brief tour of some of Foucault's important and seminal remarks on law which the negligence of critics has so far helped to deny the attention and utilization they might properly have merited.

Foucault, law and the contemporary Left scene

It was not apparent to all readers of Foucault's work during his lifetime that the sufficiency of its respect for law would become a major preoccupation in its subsequent discussion, notably among those of a left-leaning or 'critical' persuasion. This degree of concern can seem hard to account for on the basis of Foucault's own work and opinions (indeed, even more so with the increasing availability of new sources). If one wishes to explain it, one needs to place this preoccupation within a wider context of politico-academic anxieties and contentions: a field of forces in political culture which Foucault's interventions may have had, and may still have, a capacity to affect, to disrupt and to provoke.

The notion I would like to explore in this first part of the chapter is that the theme of law for Foucault (to the limited extent that it features as a continuing and distinct theme in his thought), and the significance for others of Foucault's treatment (or lack of treatment) of that theme, have something to do with the question of the changing and contested limits of the politically sayable, and the positions from which, and conditions under which, free public utterance is an effective political possibility. What we choose to make of the continuing relevance of Foucault's thought is a separate matter from what continuing interest we may take in his public career as an intellectual (innovative, exemplary or otherwise), and interpretations of either in terms of the other are, properly and often deservedly, contestable. But there are times when a connection seems worth making for other than hagiographic or demagogic purposes.[3] The quite brief period, barely a decade and a half, in which Foucault was an engaged actor and an audible voice in the public sphere (and a professor at the *Collège de France*) is framed by two struggles to achieve and retain a position of autonomy – initially, in relation to the organized forces and structures of an insurgent and revolutionary Left, and later in relation to a governing socialist-communist coalition which included both his allies and his adversaries. It is perhaps not fanciful to link these respective struggles to the terms in which Foucault formulated the themes of his initial and final lectures at the *Collège* – the order of discourse and the courage of truth.

The period after 1968 when Foucault made his public debut as a prominent politically engaged intellectual involved some crucial issues, choices and moves concerning the relation between justice, politics and the political role. The role which Foucault, Sartre and others were called upon to play was, as Daniel Defert (2003) describes it, a traditional and well-understood one at the time: universally recognized figures in literary, cultural and academic life would be called on at a time of political confrontation to appeal, from the high ground of their neutral eminence, in defence of victims of arbitrary or exceptional measures of state repression – victims who might themselves include revolutionaries engaged in forms of struggle which spanned the limits of legality. The standard term in revolutionary parlance for such personalities was 'democrats', and a common rubric for such interventions was 'justice and truth'. This was precisely the model of the 'universal intellectual', as 'master of justice and truth', against which Foucault formulated, via his widely cited dialogues with Deleuze, Pasquino and Fontana (Foucault 1977b, 1980b) the alternative model of a 'specific intellectual'. An important element in Defert's account is that the term 'democrats' in the revolutionary parlance, if not exactly interchangeable with the other Leninist category of 'useful idiots', was a double-edged epithet of faint praise, involving the implicit awareness of a transaction in which the intellectual served an instrumental purpose for the revolutionary movement which needed to remain unavowed on both sides. In the context of the quasi-revolutionary atmosphere and political movements of the post-1968 years – the *Gauche Prolétaire* in particular, whose leaders were arrested and imprisoned in 1969-70 – Foucault represented a high-value potential asset in the 'democrat' category: a newly established, bestselling intellectual star with a novel generational brand-identity, a progressive image uncomplicated by recent political involvements. This same period around 1968 was, coincidentally or otherwise, the moment when Foucault's academic career made its decisive breakthrough, from modest provincial obscurity in the psychology department at Clermont-Ferrand, via a brief adventure at the leftist experimental campus at Vincennes, to election to the summit of national academic prestige, a chair at the *Collège de France*.

Foucault seems to have responded to this situation – perhaps with the significant prompting of Daniel Defert among others – with lucid adroitness and efficacy, in two key respects. First, he was invited to co-sign a public appeal on behalf of the imprisoned Maoists, seeking either their release or the recognition of their status as political prisoners. Foucault instead proposed a campaign focused on the French prison system in general, and the condition of all of its prisoners. On being then asked to help set up this initiative in the form – favoured by the revolutionary groups – of a tribunal of inquiry, Foucault instead proposed an alternative form of intervention, the *Groupe d'Information sur les Prisons* (*GIP*). The *GIP* was an information-gathering group, which worked by distributing questionnaires to prisoners and their relatives, intended to empower them – together with some professionals employed in the prison system who had the courage to speak out, at the risk and sometimes price of their careers – to communicate to the public their own direct knowledge and experience of prison conditions. The *GIP* thus took the form of a focused action to produce a modification in the order of discourse, and to contribute towards an 'insurrection of subjected knowledges' – to use the terms he himself used respectively in 1970 and 1976 (see Foucault 1981, 2003b: 7).

Not long afterwards (as François Ewald has recounted), Foucault declined a further invitation to join a leftist tribunal of inquiry into the alleged rape of a female worker by a factory-owner in the northern mining town of Bruay-en-Artois (Ewald 2011). It is worth recalling that the model of the independent tribunal had a prominent international visibility during these same years, under the auspices of one of the most universal of twentieth-century intellectuals: the Russell Tribunal (also known as the Russell-Sartre tribunal) into the war in Vietnam, and its successor investigations (the second into the Chilean military coup and the third into West German *berufsverbote*), one of which (into Palestine) is in course at the present time. An initiative (whose designation, at least, might not have met with Foucault's blessing), the 'Foucault Tribunal on the State of Psychiatry', was organized as a four-day event in Berlin in 1998, with the participation of Thomas Szasz, Kate Millett and Daniel Defert, among others, to be then followed in June–July 2001 by a Russell Tribunal on Human Rights in Psychiatry and '*Geist Gegen Genes*', also in Berlin.[4]

Such was part of the tactical and strategic context which underlay Foucault's debates at this time around notions of rights and resistance with the young French Maoist leaders Benny Lévy and André Glucksmann,[5] and with the American linguist and anti-war polemicist Noam Chomsky (Chomsky and Foucault 1997). These experiences and encounters also prepared and foreshadowed the political analysis of *Discipline and Punish* and the first volume of *The History of Sexuality*. It perhaps helps to explain something of the challenge Foucault posed at the time, and can still pose, to Marxist brands of revolutionary politics and their latter-day successors and surrogates, as well as the sources of the countervailing critique of his work from these and allied directions, in which the theme of law has had an interesting persistence. These tensions are captured in one of the iconic photos of the time (a detail of which appears on the cover of the posthumous edition of the Berkeley lecture series *Fearless Speech*) (Foucault 2001). The photo shows Foucault, megaphone in hand, speaking alongside Sartre at an anti-racist demonstration in the Parisian immigrant area of Goutte d'Or, under the watchful supervision of a cadre of the *Gauche Prolétaire*.[6] (We can now expand and refresh our view of some of this period iconography, with the help of a major document from this exact period, newly published under the editorial care of Daniel Defert himself: the edition of Foucault's first annual *Collège de France* lecture series, delivered in 1971 under the title *La volonté de savoir*, and comprising a vigorously Nietzschean genealogy of truth, justice and philosophy in the setting of class struggles in pre-classical and classical Greece – Foucault 2011b).

In bald summary, some of the key points at issue between Foucault and the leftist currents of this time included the following:

1 Foucault was an ex-member of the French Communist Party, the *Parti Commnuiste Française* (*PCF*), who left the party in 1952 at the time of one of the last Stalinist show trials: the anti-Semitic affair of the 'doctors' plot'. He had completed his first major work, *Histoire de la folie*, with its history of an earlier 'great internment', while working in Poland – at that time a communist people's democracy (Foucault 2006). Moreover, Foucault was not unobservant of the ways in which the post-1968 revolutionary movement was capable of replicating, albeit in miniature, ludic and provisional forms, the mechanisms of revolutionary demagogy and terror – perhaps especially at those times when a revolutionary movement appropriated, as a weapon against its enemies, the formal procedures of popular justice.[7] The *PCF* itself, unequivocally subordinate throughout its existence to Soviet control, was until 1978 the largest Left political party in France. The increasingly hostile reaction to Foucault's *Histoire de la folie* on the part of French psychiatrists, including the Marxist-leaning and reformist post-war wing of the profession, during the years around 1970 and after the book's Gallimard reprint in 1972, made Foucault aware that his linkage of psychiatry's origins to the background of a great internment evoked specific and unwelcome historical and contemporary resonances for Marxists as well as for psychiatrists – relating not only to the continued existence of the Gulag archipelago as a massive institution of Soviet power, but also to the extended use of psychiatric internment (enabled by the complicity of a psychiatric profession) for the repression and persecution of political dissent.[8]

2 Part of the relevant contemporary political background was the Chinese Great Cultural Revolution of 1967, welcomed and celebrated at the time by Sartre, Beauvoir, Godard and many other intellectual figures.[9] Foucault was at this time as uninformed as most Western observers of the nature and extent of the Maoist terror, but, until clearer evidence emerged in the later 1970s, he at least had the prudence on most occasions cautiously to acknowledge this ignorance as a reason to abstain from comment.

3 Foucault's interest in prisons pre-dated 1968, and like Defert he observed that the 1968 movement, for all its intolerance of the antiquated tyrannies of the educational system, initially bypassed and ignored the parallel disciplinary universe of the prison. Far from feeling an instant solidarity with the experience of prisoners, the immediate leftist response to the imprisonment of its leaders was to demand recognition of their political status, denouncing their degrading assimilation to the status of common-law criminals.

4 Daniel Defert's recollections (in his Chronology for *Dits et écrits*) of Foucault's response to the Bruay-en-Artois episode indicated that Foucault detected a strand of quasi-racist class-war demagogy in a leftist media campaign against the crimes of the accused factory-owner (Defert 1994). This preoccupation re-emerges in the discussion (infrequently examined by his commentators) in Foucault's 1975–6 lectures, '*Society Must be Defended*', of the strand of anti-Semitic racism in French nineteenth-century socialism, at least up to the time of the Dreyfus affair (Foucault 2003b: 262–3).[10]

Writing some time ago about some of these issues, in *The Foucault Effect*, I drew attention to a specific line of anti-communist analysis, sometimes explicit and sometimes implicit in Foucault's work of the 1970s, of which *Discipline and Punish* is the most prominent point (Gordon 1991). The key points of this line of analysis include Foucault's remark that the Panopticon works equally well irrespective of whomever occupies its central tower (Foucault 1977a: 207). This observation points forward historically to the readiness of socialist regimes to take over *en bloc*, for the control of the faithful and elimination of enemies, the disciplinary and penal apparatuses of capitalism. Furthermore, for Foucault, Marxism lacks a critical analysis of disciplinary power in part because it embraces discipline as historically indispensable to the making of the working class as revolutionary agent of history. Marxism is the part-product of a successful nineteenth-century tactic of bourgeois class struggle, in which the prison serves as a crucial instrument serving to divide sources of popular resistances to capitalism into mutually hostile strata: a respectable, law abiding proletariat and a *lumpen*, criminal, subproletariat (see Foucault 1980a).

The last of these points is echoed in Foucault's 1983–4 lecture course, where the style of living of the revolutionary is introduced as one of the modern avatars of the Cynic philosophical life, assuming as such two contrasted forms: one avowedly libertarian or anti-conformist; and the other – which Foucault associated explicitly with the *PCF* – making a deliberate lifestyle choice in favour of conformism and respectability, as an affirmation of proletarian moral superiority over the decadence of the bourgeoisie (Foucault 2011a: 186).[11]

A certain insistence here on the theme of law and rights among Left intellectuals of this generation could indeed be seen as of a piece with other ideological moves of this time such as the Trotskyist embrace of Jürgen Habermas's dogmatic reworking of the Frankfurt-school critical *Aufklärung*. The point of the exercise is stated fairly candidly in a review essay (of Christine Sypnowich's *The Concept of*

Socialist Law) published by Alan Hunt in the *New Left Review* in 1992: 'I take one of the lessons of the demise of "actually no longer existing socialism" to be the necessity for any defensible socialism to provide, and to guarantee, individual rights against the state and bureaucracy' (Hunt 1992a: 112). The commitment to law acts as a permanent statement that the errors of socialist regimes have been understood, and will not be repeated. But it also serves, and this may be its function in the staged denunciations of Foucault's 'expulsion thesis', that these errors have been so well understood that no further analysis is called for.

This background may be helpful in reading some of the motives and forces at work in critiques produced by post-Althusserian and Trotskyist theoreticians of the period such as Hunt and Wickham, Bob Fine (1984: 200) and Paul Hirst (1986: 49), with respect to Foucault's inadequate treatment of law or, more colourfully, Foucault's 'expulsion' of law from the analysis of modernity. The 1970s and, to a diminishing extent, the 1980s were a period of leftist political aspiration and accompanying ventures of Left intellectual reconstruction, reformulation and redefinition, some under the rubrics of Western Marxism and Eurocommunism. Attempts to conceive in new terms of the possible form of existence of a democratic and socialist economy and society, and of a democratic and legal transition from liberal capitalism to such a polity, were frequently accompanied by attempts to manage an orderly intellectual evacuation from doctrinaire Marxist-Leninist orthodoxy to revised and more tenable positions. The rediscovery and/or revival of a Marxist theory of law (the same 1979 issue of the journal *Ideology & Consciousness* in which we translated Foucault's lecture on governmentality contained a review by Roger Cotterell of a new translation of Evgeny Pashukanis's *Law and Marxism: A General Theory*) had immediate potential relevance in relation to efforts to define new forms of collective economic ownership and workers' control, sometimes extending to the reconsideration of older strands of native socialist tradition such as guild socialism.

While Leninist/Trotskyist, and indeed Marxist, axioms were in this way being cautiously and experimentally amended, the abandonment of untenable dogmatic positions was conducted with a conspicuous and matching concern for ideological order, and – it would appear – a willingness to retain some of the traditional weaponry of socialist polemic to discipline unacceptable deviations. The revived popularity of Durkheim (accelerated by the greatly expanded and fashionable sociology faculties of the post-1960s universities) serviced the heightened demand in this conjunction for a sociological metaphysic of order applicable to the design of a future socialist regime whose socialist essence was at this time open to an unaccustomed degree of uncertainty.

All of these factors meant that the idea of supplementing or of correcting classic Marxist doctrine through the addition of a socialist and sociological theory of law was an idea whose time was widely judged to have come (although whether such a theory actually existed or could be created appears to have been a matter of less concern). Members of this constituency may have felt a certain sense of gratifying superiority and *schadenfreude* on finding that the unsettling bundle of innovations and challenges presented by Foucault's work did not include any discernible interest in providing a version of the said desideratum: these challenges were likely to be less troubling if Foucault's enterprise was shown to have failed to have attempted a topic which was now being judged to be compulsory for any thinker with a serious claim to advise Left political forces aspiring to the legitimate acquisition of sovereign power.

It is interesting to compare the treatment of this point by Hunt and Wickham in their 1994 book, *Foucault and Law*, with the abovementioned review article by Hunt in the *NLR* some two years previously. The book portrays Foucault as overlooking theoretical developments in the 1960s and 1970s when Western Marxism was undergoing 'its most fertile development and breaking, among other things, with a narrow equation of power, state and repression' (Hunt and Wickham 1994: 33). As for Foucault's treatment of Marxism's founders and founding texts, they write that: 'statism there is in Marx, but this provides no justification for ignoring the much more developed analysis that Marx provides of economic power that is dramatically and revealingly absent from Foucault's own work' (Hunt and Wickham 1994: 18). The *NLR* article, on the other hand, acknowledges candidly and categorically something which is left unsaid in the course of these rousing observations, namely that the founding texts of Marxism contain virtually no elements or basis for a specifically socialist treatment of law or a theory of the role of law under socialism and communism. Citing Engels's thesis on the withering away of the state under socialism Hunt comments: 'It is perhaps not too severe to insist that Engels formulation is simply nonsense' (Hunt 1992a: 110). As Hunt states:

> The consequences of the line of political thought that developed from this famous thesis have been severe: a complete absence or void in the socialist politics of law, administration and constitution. . . . This absence is no mere gap, ready to be filled, but rather a yawning void which has led most Marxists, past and present, to deny and ridicule the idea that such an issue has any proper place amongst the concerns of socialists.
>
> (Hunt 1992a: 110–11)

If Hunt does not choose to refer here by the precise word to an expulsion of law by most Marxists, past and present, this is indubitably what he is talking about.[12] There is a total and discreet silence about this problem in *Foucault and Law*.

Hunt and Wickham's book is a late blossom of a peculiar and now (apparently) largely extinct ideological culture, a work designed to offer pietist-catechistic reassurance for the perplexed in an age of doubt, and it might be said that the subdiscipline of critical legal studies has served over the past two decades, among other things, as the medium through which an obsolete polemic has conditioned the background assumptions of younger, postmodern generations. In its inquisitorial – and, on occasion, demagogic and pruriently defamatory – forensic style, it has a fair amount in common with other exercises in the defence of a late-leftist, dialectically enlightened orthodoxy against alleged postmodernist betrayal, such as the works of Peter Dews (1987), or the book-length dissection by Afary and Anderson of Foucault's writings on Iran (Afary and Anderson 2005). This was, for a long time, down to the appearance of *Foucault's Law* in 2009, the only book to be devoted specifically to the discussion of Foucault and law.

'Law is not important'

Theory, at least in the left-academic understanding of the term over the past two generations, is of course a notion with distinct juridical and normative affinities. Theory may detect culpabilities and deviations; it may investigate suspect silences; it may call for auto-critique, the theoretical version of the confessional. It involves, of course, the use and handling of evidence. I shall look briefly at some handling performed in the process by which Hunt and Wickham construct their reading of Foucault's 'expulsion' of law. The methods by which Hunt and Wickham establish the existence of an 'expulsion thesis' in Foucault's texts include an element of manipulation. They cite from the 'Governmentality' lecture the following extract (taken from p. 13 of my 1979 translation):

> [T]he instruments of government, instead of being laws, now come to be a range of multiform tactics. Within the perspective of government, *law is not what is important.*
>
> (Hunt and Wickham 1994: 53, emphasis added by the authors)

By the following page, Hunt and Wickham are writing (referencing the identical source):

> Recall that Foucault asserts that 'law is not important'.
>
> (Hunt and Wickham 1994: 54)

It is difficult here not to admire the use of the didactic 'recall that . . .'. It may be useful now to recall the full paragraph in the translation from which the above quotation is taken:

> I believe we have here an important turning-point: whereas the end of sovereignty is internal to itself and possesses its own intrinsic instruments in the shape of its laws, the finality of government resides in the things it manages and in the pursuit of the perfection and intensification of the processes which it directs, and the instruments of government, instead of being laws, now come to be a range of multiform tactics. *Within the perspective of government,* law is not what is important: this theme is very frequent right through the 17th century, *and it is explicit in the 18th in the texts of the Physiocrats which explain that it is not through the law that the aims of government are to be reached.*
>
> (Foucault 1979: 13, emphasis added)

In the words which Hunt and Wickham quote – and indeed in the rest of his work – Foucault is not, as their analysis appears regularly to assume, subdividing universal socio-historical categories into two classes, the important and the unimportant, and assigning certain of these – law, the state, sovereignty – to the category of the unimportant. Rather, he is reconstructing the conceptual framework of a strand of early modern governmental thought dating from the sixteenth century on, illustrated by citation from the French humanist Guilllaume de La Perrière's *Le miroir politique*. Foucault is not stating in his own name (or, as Hunt and Wickham put it, 'asserting') a proposition about the unimportance of law. He is reporting a view held within a historical strand of thought whose impact on practice his account shows to have been far from unimpeded.

Nor does he claim to be describing a trend of thought which irresistibly shapes our subsequent modernity. It related to a specific temporal context, and, as is well known from innumerable commentaries, the same lecture indicates that the disjunction which Foucault detects within this period between the instrumentalities of sovereignty and government is succeeded by a phase of synthesis and integration, the '"governmentalization" of the State' (Foucault 2007: 109), in which the function and value of legislative mechanisms, contrary to the opinions of the Physiocrats, was acknowledged. Foucault further comments on this in the summary of his 1978–9 course, *The Birth of Biopolitics*:

> In the search for a liberal technology of government, it emerged that the juridical form was a far more effective instrument of regulation than the wisdom or moderation of governors. (Due to their mistrust of law and the juridical institution, the physiocrats were more inclined to seek this regulation in the recognition, by a despot with institutionally unlimited powers, of the 'natural' laws of the economy which are imposed on him as evident truth.)
>
> (Foucault 2008: 321)

'Imperative to resist'

Some of Hunt and Wickham's most striking comments on Foucault occur not in their chapters of direct exposition and critique of his views on law, but in their chapter proposing a theory and a methodology, assisted by the parts they find useful to adapt from Foucault's analyses, of a 'sociology of law as governance'. This consists in large part of a faithfully Durkheimian metaphysics of the social bond and the essential role of law in its production and reproduction – the notion of governance serving here as a receptacle for transposing some of Foucault's accounts of power and government into a form where it is possible to eliminate direct reference to notions of either power or resistance. Where the topic of resistance is mentioned, it is in order for it to be dismissed, along with Foucault's preoccupation with the question. Hunt and Wickham here indicate – with remarkable and revelatory candour – that resistance is a quasi-pathological social phenomenon, linked to the (even more evidently pathological) notion of an 'imperative to resist', which they suggest – somewhat in the manner of the 'Ubu-esque' experts in criminal psychiatry whose court testimonies Foucault cites in *Abnormal* (Foucault 2003a: 11–12) – is in turn an object of perverse and obsessive preoccupation and attraction on the part of Foucault (Hunt and Wickham 1994: 85).[13] Their sources for this reading are: first, the speculations on Foucault's personal erotic tastes contained in James Miller's biography of Foucault (Miller 2000), which Hunt and Wickham adopt and endorse as 'well-documented' (Hunt and Wickham 1994: 86); and, secondly, the documentary dossier which Foucault edited and co-authored, *I, Pierre Rivière* – from which any reference by Foucault to the notion of a compulsion to resist is, of course, entirely absent (Foucault 1975). Among the further publications of the past decade, we do, on the other hand, have Foucault's lectures on the *Abnornmal* which trace the early emergence in nineteenth-century European psychiatry of an anthropological and psychological evaluation of revolutionaries, classifying them into the 'good' and 'bad' categories of respectively advanced and degenerate human specimens (Foucault 2003a: 152–5). This topic had been foreshadowed much earlier, in *Histoire de la folie*, which retold the nineteenth-century psychiatric hagiographies representing the heroic founder-figure Philippe Pinel as liberating the chained mad men and women of Bicêtre in the face of the enraged opposition of a representative of the Jacobin Terror (see, generally, Foucault 2006: 463–511).

Given the primary subject-matter of Foucault's best-known book, one other noteworthy feature of the socialist discussion of Foucault and law by Hunt and Wickham is shared by Hunt's *NLR* article and a significant amount of the discussion it has promoted (including, to a large extent, the recent book by Ben Golder and Peter Fitzpatrick), namely an almost complete absence of discussion of criminal law and penal justice, either under capitalism or under socialism – including notably those aspects of these topics to which Foucault devoted some specific attention, namely the engagements of psychiatry with penal justice, and the death penalty. As far as a socialist future is concerned, Hunt's *NLR* paper audaciously acknowledges that conflicts will continue to arise under socialism which an apparatus of law will be required to regulate and resolve, but does not mention the continued requirement for the sanctioning and punishment of crime. As far as the socialist past is concerned (a past which was still very much present, of course, during the period of the intellectual flowering of Western Marxism), the use of judicial and penal procedures and means by communist governments leading to the punishment by internment, forced labour and death of tens of millions, does not generally qualify for mention, let alone analysis. It may be that it is what Foucault's work has been capable of contributing to that particular analysis – among others – which has largely and silently motivated the noisy condemnations from certain quarters of his inability to say anything useful about law in general. Be that as it may, there remains, outside of a few well-trampled *loci*, a lot of very interesting and sparsely utilized thinking about law in Foucault's *oeuvre*, some highlights of which I devote the rest of this chapter to reviewing briefly.

Legal themes and strands in Foucault's work

Foucault has a good deal, and a number of different and interesting things, to say about law in the course of his publications and public interventions. It is just that, whether one likes it or not, he does not have a master theory or thesis about law. Foucault is not a foundationalist thinker and his analyses tend not to posit any historical agency or layer of being as causally primal or deterministic in the last instance. Nothing is dominant or subordinate, active or passive, creative or constraining, good or bad, in all places and in all circumstances. This generalization is well illustrated in the case of Foucault's treatment, or treatments, of legal themes and topics. Foucault does not have one thing to say about law. He has several things to say. Many of the very interesting things he has to say have been overlooked or ignored as a result of the widely disseminated impression, one of whose enabling contexts I endeavoured to sketch in the first part of the chapter, that Foucault 'expelled' or removed law from his analyses. In the second part of this chapter I shall now present some brief reminders of some of the more neglected strands – some, but not all, of which have become more accessible through posthumous publications since the early 1990s.

The genealogy of the inquest and the examination

Discipline and Punish deals with the transformation of criminal and penal justice around and during the early nineteenth century (Foucault 1977a). This includes a rather short (and little discussed) genealogical section dealing with the longer-range emergence of legal rationality in the Christian West. The publication in *Dits et écrits* (and later in the 'Essential Works' volume of selected translations, entitled *Power*) of Foucault's 1973 lectures in Brazil on 'Truth and Juridical Forms' (themselves drawing on lecture courses delivered in France over the previous three years, two of which remain to be published), provide a fuller development of this genealogy, centring on the interweaving roles of two procedures of power-knowledge: the inquiry or inquest (*enquête*) and the examination (*examen*) (see Foucault 2000c). This complex analysis has not yet received the attention which it merits. Among its interesting features are: (a) that the *enquête* is a Western Christian rediscovery or reinvention of a form of empirical inquiry established in classical Hellenistic culture and systematized by Aristotle; (b) that the *enquête*, as a practice of secular and royal justice, drew significantly upon a model originating in the administrative and spiritual government of the Church, called the 'visitation'; and (c) that this juridical model of crime, guilt and correction owes an essential and lasting debt to the Christian model of sin, confession and penance. With the royal appropriation and monopolization of the institution of justice, the Christian model of crime as disobedient fault serves as a precedent for the attribution to every crime of the status of an offence against the king. The long-term interplays between the histories of the confession (*aveu*) and justice subsequently form the key theme of Foucault's 1980–1 Louvain lectures, entitled *Mal faire, dire vrai: fonctions de l'aveu* (see Foucault forthcoming), which complements the analysis of *Discipline and Punishment* by examining the link between penal regimes and technologies of the self, and parallels *The History of Sexuality* by examining the link between *aveu* and the formation of the penal and criminal, as distinct from the sexual, subject.[14]

Not only do the Brazil lectures contain a substantive and original, if rapidly sketched, genealogical treatment of law, something barely imaginable if one had lent credence to the expulsion-theorists' representation of Foucault; but, far from (as Hunt and Wickham would have it) relegating legal rationality to an archaic and essentially pre-modern historical stratum, they characterize the juridical form of the *enquête* as the epistemological matrix of the Western empirical and physical sciences from the Renaissance down to the present day. Then, from the period of the Enlightenment onwards, the *enquête*, in the second main stage of Foucault's judicial genealogy which forms the focus of *Discipline and Punish*, undergoes further admixture and hybridization, in theory, science and practice, with the different rationality which Foucault considers (itself conjoined with the other Christian legacy of the *aveu*) to be the epistemological matrix of the human and 'psy' sciences, namely the *examen*.

Law and liberalism

Bentham's utilitarian doctrine of legislation and the agenda and non-agenda of government has almost as prominent a place in Foucault's account of liberal governmental rationality as his Panopticon has in *Discipline and Punish*. The summary of the 1978–9 course describes its objective with some care and exactitude, particularly in terms of Foucault's specific use of the notion of liberalism (which he does not attempt to impose on others), and its precise relation to, and distinction from, considerations of liberalism in terms (which he again does not seek to marginalize) of law and constitution (see, generally, Foucault 2008: 317–25). As he puts it there:

> Undoubtedly liberalism does not derive from juridical thought any more than it does from an economic analysis. Neither is it born from the idea of a political society founded upon a contractual bond. Rather, in the search for a liberal technology of government, it emerged that the juridical form was a far more effective instrument of regulation than the wisdom or moderation of governors. Regulation through law was not sought for because of the supposedly natural legalism of liberalism, but because the law defines forms of general intervention excluding particular, individual and exceptional measures, and because participation of the governed in drawing up the law in a parliamentary system is the most effective system of governmental economy.
> (Foucault 2008: 321)

As he then points out, it does follow from this instrumental affinity that liberal government, the rule of law (or juridical liberalism) and representative government (or political liberalism) are invariably found to coexist (Foucault 2008: 321). In the 2004 French edition of the course, Michel Senellart reproduces a section of Foucault's lecture notes dealing further with the role attributed in liberal government to the process and functioning of legislative and public deliberation. Of four senses which he proposes to attribute here to the term 'liberalism', the last is:

> the organization of specific methods of transaction for defining the limitation of government practices:
> – constitution, parliament,
> – opinion, the press
> – commissions, enquiries.
>
> (Foucault 2004: 21)

A further important dimension of the juridical implications of liberalism discussed in the 1978–9 lectures concerns international European and global order. Foucault here explains that the liberal transformation of governmentality also implies a transformation in the model of international order, and of the balance of Europe prevalent in the period of mercantilism and the *Police* state. Instead of an economic zero-sum competition between states where rivalry can only be stabilized by the game of alliances which prevents any one player from outright domination, the liberal regime of domestic and international market exchange allows a process in which all parties optimize their gains – that is, the enrichment of each player tends to enrich the others – and there is no limit on the sum of potential growth. However, and crucially, this possibility of unlimited and – in principle – peaceful and parallel growth of the several national players in the European space can only be assured if Europe itself is assured of the external availability of an unlimited global market. The availability to European commerce of this market becomes a condition for progress, through the mutually and benignly supportive growth of national economies, towards universal perpetual peace, but also, for that reason, a teleological necessity for ensuring the regional international order of European states. Distinguishing this key development both from the prior beginnings of European colonizations, and from the subsequent full development of colonial imperialism, Foucault illustrates this linkage through comments on the evolving law of the sea, on new schemes for perpetual peace such as those of Immanuel Kant (with its account of the natural foundations of cosmopolitan or commercial law), and on the different hybrids of *Police* and liberal schemes of international order embodied by the Napoleonic empire and, after its defeat, the Congress of Vienna of 1815 (see, generally, Foucault 2008: 51–73).

The later nineteenth century: social law, risk, criminology

Foucault organized and took part in a number of collaborations and discussions focusing on problems and transformations in legal rationality during the late nineteenth century. These included at least two seminar series at the *Collège de France* (one in 1976, focused on criminal psychiatry and the dangerous individual and another in 1979, on the crisis of late nineteenth-century juridical thought); an international conference at Toronto in 1977, whose proceedings were published in full in the first issue of the *International Journal of Law and Psychiatry*; and, a seminar series at Louvain which was chaired by Foucault and subsequently published as a book edited by the distinguished Belgian jurist and judge Françoise Tulkens (1986, 1988). This work and these discussions are reflected in the contributions to *The Foucault Effect* by Pasquino, Donzelot and Ewald (Pasquino 1991; Donzelot 1991a, 1991b; Ewald 1991), and their interconnections discussed there in my introduction (Gordon 1991). Foucault's paper at the Toronto conference, entitled 'About the Concept of the "Dangerous Individual" in Nineteenth-Century Legal Psychiatry' (Foucault 2000a), has been described by Daniel Defert as a resume of the 1976 Paris seminars, which ran alongside the lectures entitled 'Society Must be Defended' (Defert 1994: 52). This is an extremely important and wide-ranging paper. One of Foucault's few texts to be published directly in English during his lifetime, it figures in the bibliography of Hunt and Wickham's *Foucault and Law*, but is nowhere cited or discussed in that volume. It outlines the history of a profound and wide-ranging mutation in fundamental conceptions of criminal law, shifting attention from criminal acts to criminal actors and the sanctioning of offences to the detection and treatment or elimination of dangerous individuals. One important consequence of this mutation which emerges in Foucault's commentaries on contemporary criminal trials and the role of criminologists is the greatly enhanced demand for confession (*aveu*), not so much in order to confirm the commission of a crime but in order to allow assessment of the criminal subject.

Of particular interest is the linkage which Foucault detects here between this mutation and concurrent changes in the jurisprudence of civil liability for accidents – itself closely linked to the emergence of systems of accident insurance and compensation, in which the state was eventually to become a principal actor, thereby also acquiring for itself a new role. New notions of social law, related to conceptions of social risk and solidarity, and linked in close synergy with the metaphysics of the social bond which was being concurrently developed within the new science of sociology – key elements in the invention of a welfare state – here interacted with the social evolutionism of the Italian school of criminology (focused on the detection and neutralization of a dangerous and degenerate underclass),[15] and the Belgian criminological school of 'social defence', led by Adolph Prins, which is among the phenomena alluded to in the closing lecture of Foucault's 1975–6 series *'Society Must be Defended'* (whose title, in line with the promise made at the end of the previous year's lectures, indicates that this theme might originally have been intended to figure more centrally in this course of lectures) (Foucault 2003b: 258).

These conceptions and rationalities were to profoundly mark Western, and other, societies during the twentieth century, and remain central to politico-juridical choices which Foucault frequently addressed in his own public interventions. Indeed, they pose continuing unresolved challenges in our societies today while their legacy has left deep traces in the history of the past century. In a couple of his round table discussions in 1978 (one of which was translated in *Power/Knowledge* – see Foucault 1980c: 224 ff.), Foucault cited the intervention of a French expert at the St Petersburg International Conference of Criminologists, held in 1890, who invited his Russian colleagues to make use of the vast undeveloped spaces of Siberia to establish a new system of penal labour colonies. Thus the elite of Western juridical science may have provided a fateful intellectual input for a major and terrible institution of what Alan Hunt, writing in 1992, was to refer to as 'actually no longer existing socialism' (Hunt 1992a: 112).

Legal constructivism: neoliberalism, law and criminal justice

In my introduction to *The Foucault Effect*, I tried within a narrow compass to draw due attention to the interesting and distinctive law-related developments in Foucault's treatments of both the German and the American schools of twentieth-century neoliberalism in his then unpublished 1978–9 series lectures, entitled *The Birth of Biopolitics* (Gordon 1991). That summary seems valid in the light of Michel Senellart's excellent edition of these deservedly acclaimed lectures. Serious reflection on neoliberal thought was virtually unknown in the New Left of 1979. Indeed even today, a recent history by the Marxist geographer David Harvey scarcely takes cognizance of any politically influential neoliberal thought before the governments of Reagan and Thatcher (Harvey 2005). The points I noted in *The Foucault Effect* can be very briefly restated.

Foucault shows the case of post-1945 Germany to be an example of the ways and occasions in which respective problems of sovereignty and governmental rationality, between which he had been so careful at the level of a history of concepts and systems of thought to differentiate, can interact in critical and decisive ways. Policies for economic regeneration, and specifically the capability to recreate an economic market order as an engine of material survival, followed by prosperity, served in turn as the motor for the gradual re-establishment of a legitimate political sovereignty (Foucault 2008: 81–95). In turn, one of the ideas driving these policies and emanating from a group of Austro-German economists and jurists was the distinctive idea that the free competitive market is not a natural order, but an artificial reality, a 'juridico economic order', which has to be actively brought into being and sustained (in the face of countervailing economic forces and social factors) by a continuing process of governmental intervention and legislative regulation (Foucault 2008: 133–5, 167 ff.). Austro-German neoliberalism, on Foucault's account, is characteristically a philosophy of government understood as a continuous juridical constructivism, in which 'law and order' – the economic order and the rule of law (*état de droit*, *Rechtsstaat*) – are interdependent and inseparable.[16]

In American neoliberalism, what Foucault's analysis tends to suggest is that it is the reverse which is the case. Foucault focused his attention on a limited set of works by the Chicago school which propose a new economic theory of human behaviour, crime and legislation. In 1979 this analysis yielded, on Foucault's account, two apparent positives and at least one negative. On the positive side, Gary Becker's economic model of crime and punishment required that the costs of punishing and preventing crime should not exceed their benefits: zero tolerance is not economical, good penal policy does not aim at the extinction of crime, but at a balance between the curves of the supply of crime and negative demand. Or again: society does not have a limitless demand for compliance. Society does not need to conform to an exhaustive disciplinary system. A society finds that it has a certain level of illegality and it would find it very difficult to have this rate indefinitely reduced (Foucault 2008: 256). Secondly, there is an 'anthropological erasure of the criminal', meaning that the subspecies of *Homo criminalis* is reabsorbed into the universal analytical framework of *Homo oeconomicus*: the interests and motivations of the criminal are not (or do not need to be understood as) different from those of the law-abiding citizen (Foucault 2008: 258). According to Foucault, this results in a move from disciplinary penal technologies to new techniques of risk assessment, environmental technology and behavioural psychology (which, however, in these lectures he does not go on to describe further): an environmental type of intervention instead of the subjugation of individuals. However, while he recounts, as an example, the neoliberal arguments against aggressively punitive measures against drug use and addiction, on the other hand Foucault also (briefly) acknowledges here the existence of a neoliberal economic argument for the deterrent effectiveness of the death penalty. Moreover it is clear from his comments here and elsewhere that he recognizes in the new repertoires of techniques a serious range of potential new menaces.[17]

This analysis is neither a prophecy nor a prediction. The actual course of penal policy in the USA over the past 30 years – including 'zero tolerance', 'three strikes', life without parole and the colossal expansion of the carceral population – evidently does not reflect the triumph of the arguments Foucault discerned in Gary Becker, while Becker himself has meanwhile joined the economist advocates of the continued retention of the death penalty. The developments since Foucault's time are (needless to say) not simply explicable on the basis of Foucault's analyses, though these, if aptly applied and supplemented, may still play their part.Bernard Harcourt has argued both that pro-market economic ideology is intrinsically and historically conjoined to a demand for aggressive law enforcement, and that there is a latent neoliberal economic rationale for the long-term exclusion from society of its surplus and unproductive population (Harcourt 2011a, 2011b). Foucault prefaces his analysis of American developments by noting the unbroken thread of liberal critique running through the history of American society and politics – the constant questioning and challenging of the legitimate scope of governmental action and intervention. David Garland's study of the American death penalty points to the decisive influence of an equally distinctive, long-term and converse populist and demagogic factor in American democracy: the powerful demand for local control of justice as a major stake in politics at the grassroots community level, and – with historically varying degrees of overtness – as a continuing tool of racial hegemony (Garland 2010). Also, Jonathan Simon's *Governing though Crime* (2007), meanwhile presents a coherent narrative of the penal and policing policy developments of the backlash decades as forming a consistent new rationality of government.

Public law and political intervention

The set of Foucault's shorter writings and interviews which I selected from *Dits et écrits* for translation in the volume entitled *Power* was intended to offer a representative selection of investigations and interventions touching on power and the political, including both previously known and translated, as well as newer, materials.[18] A very significant proportion of its content can be seen to explicitly address juridical, criminal and penal issues. These include commentaries on specific legal cases whose conduct or procedure (and consequent outcome) appeared to Foucault to pose a specific problem – for example, a recent capital murder trial in which hypothetical psychiatric testimony on a suspect's potential motivations had been accepted as evidence indicative of guilt (Foucault 2000d). One strand in these commentaries – not irrelevant to the American circumstances discussed above – related to demagogic factors in denials of executive clemency by two French presidents, and the symbolic deployment of an archaic juridical and penal authority as a prerogative of the sovereign state: when the death penalty was abolished in 1981, Foucault commented that the distance between state and society had been reduced 'by a head' (Foucault 2000b: 459).

There has been a welcome and growing recent attentiveness (exampled in this collection in the chapter by Philippe Chevallier, Chapter 8) to the creative and inventive political potential contained in Foucault's thoughts on new forms of rights: anti-disciplinary rights, relational rights, the right to suicide, the rights of the governed; not forgetting his concern for the protection of threatened rights no longer convenient to reason of state, such as the right to asylum. With the passage of time, less credence appears to be given to the argument – popular among some elements of the Trotskyist and liberal academia – that Foucault's theoretical positions precluded him from any capacity for meaningful or constructive public intervention, and as a result there may be fewer takers for sectarian falsification and caricature of the actual content of these interventions.

Foucault's work was unfinished and important parts of it – touching directly on themes discussed here – remain to be published over the next few years. Our picture of the overall and final goals of his work, originally based on his last publications and interviews, is likely to be significantly modified once the final five lecture courses are all available. Looking back at the period of the early 1970s, in the light of his most recently published lectures, it would appear that he was open at certain times (partly influenced at this point by the structuralist-Marxist classical scholars, Jean-Pierre Vernant and Marcel Detienne) to a reading of the Greek origins of law as a 'bourgeois' or proto-bourgeois invention serving the dual purposes of civil peace and class inequality. Foucault certainly declared, in a famous 1971 debate with Noam Chomsky, and on other occasions, that demands for rights were not the only nor necessarily the most appropriate form in which political struggles should be conducted (Chomsky and Foucault 1997).

These comments neither anticipate nor invalidate Foucault's further thinking, from 1976 on, about possible other and new kinds of rights. It would be idle to suggest that Foucault's political analysis does not evolve significantly between 1970 and 1980. With hindsight it is, nevertheless, reasonable to read the sharpest edge of critique and warning in Foucault's comments at this time as addressing the dangerous inclination (already mentioned in my preliminary comments above) of Left revolutionary parties to appropriate to themselves the function of dispensing popular justice.

A simple reading to which I myself used to subscribe is that Foucault's *démarche* essentially consisted of bypassing the classical political themes of the forms and foundations of legitimate power, in order to uncover the actual operations of the mechanisms which this dignified and decorous discourse had clothed and occluded – the mechanisms which he successively analysed under the headings of 'power-knowledge' and 'governmentality'. It would then perhaps have been a thesis of what in Italian political culture is known as *dietrismo*, which might literally be translated as 'behind-ism' – the idea that the reality of things is always secret and hidden, a covert operation behind the arras, concealed behind the scenery of public appearances which Pasquale Pasquino called the *theatrum politicum* (Pasquino 1991). In his (shortly to be published) 1980 *Collège de France* lectures, *Le gouvernement des vivants*, Foucault effectively distances himself, and moves on, from this approach by bringing the history of legitimation and its subjective acceptance into the framework of analysis. In the 1980 lectures (and again shortly later at Louvain), Foucault proposes a politico-philosophical reading of Sophocles' *Oedipus Rex* which, in almost all but one point, repeats an analysis presented in 1971 (and again in Rio de Janeiro in 1973). The essential difference is in the 'take-home' message. In 1971, the tragedy enacts the moment of public discredit, disqualification and repudiation of the tyrant who gains and wields power through knowledge which is his peculiar possession: in the West, from this point on, power/knowledge will subsist only as a hidden and disavowed reality. In 1980, the accent shifts from the repression of power/knowledge to the discovery and positing of an essential relationship between hegemony and *aletourgia*, between the exercise of legitimate sovereignty and the manifestation of truth. Foucault set for himself here the new task of writing the history of this relationship. He says explicitly that this means moving on from the narrower analytical framework of power/knowledge, but not from the framework of governmentality. He also says here explicitly that the framework of power/knowledge has marked a progress beyond an attempt to analyse political legitimation and subjective political assent in terms of ideology. I have argued elsewhere (Gordon 2011) that Foucault's work had a longer-term, unfulfilled, agenda to create a genealogy of political culture, part of which would involve the analysis – as a positive reality – of the constitution of a public political consciousness. As early as the 1975–6 lectures, Foucault characterizes Athenian and early modern political theatre as having a shared and essential concern with the didactic exposition of public law (Foucault 2003b: 174 ff.). In the 1977–8 lectures, he gives an alternative characterization of early modern theatre as an exposition and exploration of the *coup d'état* (Foucault 2007: 265 ff.). In 1980 he may well have wanted to say that these two characterizations are opposite sides of the same coin, or matching parts of the same *symbolon*. Whether or not it proves possible for Foucault's agenda to be continued or completed by other hands, it is likely that both of these perspectives will merit retention, and also that the role of law in the unending interplay between power, truth and subjectivity will, for the foreseeable future, remain an essential, if not necessarily hegemonic, component.

The above might be a neat enough conclusion, if our subject lent itself to a conclusion: it does not. Foucault's work was unfinished, his engagement with questions of law and penal justice far from being either resolved or abandoned. When, after lecturing in Paris on the patristic doctrines of baptism and penitence, Foucault travelled in late 1980 to teach and direct seminars at the Catholic University of Louvain, Fabienne Brion and Bernard Harcourt describe his stay in Louvain as 'the trace of a militant engagement, the fruit of an alliance with radical jurists and critical criminologists . . . at the time of the planned revision of the Belgian Penal Code' (in Foucault forthcoming). In February 1984, while he was lecturing in Paris on the interpretation of the last words of Socrates, Foucault revised the text of an interview with the Brussels magistrate Foulek Ringelheim, entitled 'Qu'appelle-t-on punir?', whose theme was precisely our continuing disarray in regard to giving sense or meaning to practices of punishment, and the challenges of devising more acceptable forms of punishment than those currently imposed.[19] It remains something of a scandal that a thinker who did more than anyone of his generation to place these issues before our attention could be represented (by others of a 'critical' persuasion) as uninterested in law. One should instead ask – and here I have allowed myself some licence to speculate – why those who are interested in law find it possible or expedient to bracket this question and its treatment by Foucault. Foucault took up and expanded on the Nietzschean insight that punishment is one of those things in human affairs which over time can change, and lose, its meaning, means and motive. Honesty compels us to admit that in the years since 1984, we have not advanced many steps beyond the recognition of this uncertainty – if indeed we have even retained this much. Here if anywhere is an occasion to practise the art of reflected problematization which has been one of Foucault's justly valued intellectual legacies, while also practising the vigilance he taught and practised against the opportunisms of expertise and demagogy.

Acknowledgement

I am deeply grateful to Ben Golder for his generous, tireless and exceptionally helpful editorial assistance.

Notes

1 Notably Ben Golder and Peter Fitzpatrick (2009), who provide a survey of earlier comments.

2 I cite some of this collaborative work in later sections of this chapter. François Ewald's major work is *L'état providence* (see Ewald 1986a). An abridged edition was released in 1996 but neither version has yet been translated into English. The chapter 'Insurance and Risk' in *The Foucault Effect* (see Ewald 1991) is an extract from an earlier unpublished research paper. At the time of his death Foucault was discussing with Robert Badinter (the Minister of Justice who had abolished the death penalty in 1981, and who periodically called on the philosopher for his advice) a plan for the creation of a research centre in the philosophy of law, associated with the *Collège de France*, in which Ewald might have been likely to play a key role. Ewald was Foucault's research assistant from the mid-1970s, and collaborated at Foucault's invitation in research on nineteenth-century mutations in conceptions of accident, risk, crime and danger. Ewald comments in a recent interview:

> The project allowed me to continue my earlier work [on the genealogy of legislation on industrial accidents] in a new perspective, focussing on juridical materials. Thus there was a sort of division of labour with Foucault's research. My doctoral thesis was inscribed in a field he had determined, complementary to his own work, but which he did not want to directly take on himself.
>
> (Ewald 2011)

This complementarity undoubtedly existed and Ewald's genealogical work of this period is of very high quality and enduring interest. I am not so sure that its philosophical superstructure is of entirely equal interest, or a necessary corollary of Foucault's investigative perspective. Ewald occasionally tends to overstate the extent of the division of labour between himself and Foucault, as in his remark that: 'Nulle part, dans son oeuvre, Michel Foucault ne traite du droit' (Nowhere in his work does Michel Foucault deal with law): Ewald 1986b.

3 There have been, roughly, two ways of dealing with Foucault's record of public intervention. One has been the Habermasian formula of pragmatic or performative self-contradiction: if his actions make apparent ethical and rational sense, they are to be discounted because his theory makes such actions impossible. The other is used by Hunt and Wickham: to draw a merciful veil over the interventions in order to see what can be usefully recycled from the theoretical equipment. They write:

> We suggest that there is no embarrassment in holding that some of Foucault's own political stances, such as his naïve 'abolitionist' views about criminal justice or his ill-advised enthusiasm for the regime of the mullahs in Iran, are frankly silly and barely worth debating . . . [A]ny serious assessment of Foucault depends not on the causes he espouses but on what those who read him can do with his enormously fertile leads and suggestions.
>
> (Hunt and Wickham 1994: 36)

4 On this period of the *GIP* and *Gauche Prolétaire*, see a well-documented summary in the 'Course context' by Fabienne Brion and Bernard Harcourt (in Foucault forthcoming).

5 See the discussion by Brion and Harcourt in the 'Situation du cours' in Foucault (forthcoming).

6 See http://www.michel-foucault.com/gallery/pictures/foucaulta31.html (accessed 26 April 2012).

7 Foucault used the argument in his debate with the Maoists that class struggle should not rely on the biased instruments and pseudo-neutrality of bourgeois justice (see Foucault 1980a). His more serious point – which may have been heeded – was, I suspect, that party justice is the shortest of roads to terror. He commented in a later interview that the notion of 'popular justice' was more a mentality of war than a mentality of justice (see Foucault 2000f: 402). The *Gauche Prolétaire* quietly disbanded itself in late 1973. France in the following decades was largely free of political terrorism. Foucault may deserve some share of credit for this.

8 Among the least discussed texts by Foucault in the post-Marxist critical canon is the incisive analysis (Foucault 1980d: 134–7) of methods in Left discourse for avoiding or closing the question of the Gulag.

9 Foucault's *Les mots et les choses* was mocked and execrated by Parisian red guards in Godard's 1967 film, *La Chinoise*.

10 I asked Foucault, in 1980 or 1981, to confirm that he perceived significant vestiges of Pétainism in French political culture, and he replied: 'Yes, and especially in the case of the Communist Party.'

11 The *New Left Review*'s reviewer of this volume, Michael Hardt, somewhat nervously describes these comments relating to what might be called the sumptuary laws of revolutionary movements, as 'polemical' (Hardt 2010: 159). (This is, if I am not mistaken, the first review of a work by Foucault in the pages of the *NLR*. Hardt seems to be feeling his way to establish an appropriate tone.)

12 Evgeny Pashukanis was, as Hunt mentions in his *NLR* article, the doyen of Bolshevik jurists and a principal theoretical exponent of the primitive Marx-Engels line on the withering away of law and state. It is perhaps worth recalling here that this doctrine was officially discarded soon after the start of Stalin's period of rule, some time in advance of the flowering of Western Marxism. Pashukanis, having published a series of obligatory public recantations, was denounced as a 'Trotskyite saboteur' and executed in 1937, the year of the promulgation of the Soviet constitution.

13 'Stir crazy', to quote the title of Clifford Geertz's review of *Discipline and Punish* (see Geertz 1978).

14 As Fabienne Brion and Bernard Harcourt describe in their 'Course context' for these lectures, *Mal faire, dire vrai* is an axial text between the analyses of power/knowledge and governmentality and the analyses of veridiction and techniques of self. This publication will change our perspective on Foucault – as, no doubt, will the following publications of the remaining Paris lecture courses, with their strong focus on juridical, penal and penitential themes.

15 Enrico Ferri, the younger of the two major figures in the Italian school, was a prominent intellectual, alongside Mussolini, in a faction of the Italian Socialist Party, and later in the Fascist Party.

16 Attention should be drawn to the short genealogy of these concepts provided here, their linkage to evolving practices of administrative law, and the differing UK and French perspectives on the role of the state in administrative law (see Foucault 2008: 168–78). Foucault was keenly interested in policy debates on the rule of law and law reform. In 1977 he attended the annual conference of the *Syndicat de la Magistrature*, itself one of the most important legacies of 1968. In his invited talk, he gave a polite but critical review of the Socialist Party's recent policy dossier, *Liberté, Libertés*, in which he discerned an inflationary tendency towards the 'juridification' of social relations through the implantation of new, judicially staffed regulatory entities. As Foucault puts it in this lecture (promising a further detailed discussion which he did not then deliver), 'justice tends to become, and must become, an omnipresent public service' (Foucault 2008: 176; 180, n. 37; see also Foucault 1984). One of Foucault's research co-authors of *I, Pierre Rivière*, the historian and political scientist Blandine Barret-Kriegel, was

commissioned by the socialist president of France, François Mitterrand, to write the report *L'état et la démocratie* (1985), in which the concept and question of the *état de droit* is central.

17 Castel (1981), in a work praised by Foucault, analyses the emergence of new, quantitative, informatics-based techniques of risk management; Harcourt (2007) describes the developed American practices of actuarial sentencing, a generation later.

18 My 'Introduction' to that volume (somewhat abridged by the editor) included an attempt to summarise Foucault's politics, the themes of his public interventions, and his position and concerns in relation to law. Most of that account seems valid in the light of subsequent publications, but the following section of this chapter seeks to indicate significant nuances that can now be added. Foucault's 'attitude' to law could perhaps be condensed to five points: (a) law is an indispensable defence against power; (b) we (and the law itself) can be required to choose between law and order; (c) law and democracy are genealogical siblings in terms of the accountability of power through truth; (d) the rule of law is a coherent idea, but the empire of the 'judiciable' should not be limitless; and (e) every legal regime generates an accompanying economy of illegality, and the modern penal apparatus is one of the most intense centres of such an economy.

19 Foucault 2000e; see also Foucault 2000f. Two years before he put forward a now famous proposal to define critique as the will not to be governed in a certain way, he posed the question in an electrifying and undeservedly forgotten paper delivered in 1976 to a Montreal conference on prisoners' rights, of 'whether we want to be punished'. This talk develops the (now largely forgotten) theme of *Discipline and Punish* that penal policy is explicable only in the framework of a political economy of illegalities (see Foucault 2009).

References

Afary, J. and Anderson, K. B. (2005) *Foucault and the Iranian Revolution: Gender and the Seductions of Islamism*, Chicago, IL: University of Chicago Press

Burchell, G., Gordon, C. and Miller, P. (eds) (1991) *The Foucault Effect: Studies in Governmentality*, Chicago, IL: University of Chicago Press

Castel, R. (1981) *La gestion des risques. De l'anti-psychiatrie à l'après-psychanalyse*, Paris: Éditions de Minuit

Chomsky, N. and Foucault, M. (1997) 'Human Nature: Justice versus Power', in A. I. Davidson (ed.) *Foucault and his Interlocutors*, Chicago, IL: University of Chicago Press

Defert, D. (1994) 'Chronologie', in D. Defert and F. Ewald (eds) *Dits et écrits*, Paris: Gallimard

___ (2003) 'L'emergence d'un nouveau front: les prisons', in P. Artières, L. Quéro and M. Zancarini-Fournel (eds) *Le Groupe d'Information sur les Prisons. Archives d'une lutte 1970–1972*, Paris: Éditions de l'IMEC

Dews, P. (1987) *Logics of Disintegration: Post-structuralist Thought and the Claims of Critical Theory*, London: Verso

Donzelot, J. (1991a) 'The Mobilization of Society', in G. Burchell, C. Gordon and P. Miller (eds) *The Foucault Effect: Studies in Governmentality*, Chicago, IL: University of Chicago Press

___ (1991b) 'Pleasure in Work', in G. Burchell, C. Gordon and P. Miller (eds) *The Foucault Effect: Studies in Governmentality*, Chicago, IL: University of Chicago Press

Ewald, F. (1986a) *L'état providence*, Paris: Grasset

___ (1986b) 'Pour un positivisme critique: Michel Foucault et la philosophie du droit', *Droits: revue française de théorie juridique*, 3: 137–42

___ (1991) 'Insurance and Risk', in G. Burchell, C. Gordon and P. Miller (eds) *The Foucault Effect: Studies in Governmentality*, Chicago, IL: University of Chicago Press
___ (2011) 'Au Collège de France. Entretien avec François Ewald', in P. Artieres *et al.* (eds) *Michel Foucault*, Paris: Éditions de l'Herne
Fine, B. (1984) *Democracy and the Rule of Law: Liberal Ideals and Marxist Critiques*, London and Sydney: Pluto Press
Foucault, M. (ed.) (1975) *I, Pierre Rivière, Having Slaughtered my Mother, my Sister, and my Brother . . . : A Case of Parricide in the 19th Century*, trans. F. Jelinek, New York, NY: Pantheon
___ (1977a) *Discipline and Punish*, trans. A. Sheridan, London: Allen Lane/Penguin
___ (1977b) 'Intellectuals and Power: A Conversation between Michel Foucault and Gilles Deleuze', trans. D. F. Bouchard and S. Simon, in D. F. Bouchard (ed.) *Language, Counter-Memory, Practice: Selected Essays and Interviews*, Ithaca, NY: Cornell University Press
___ (1979) 'Governmentality', trans. C. Gordon, *Ideology & Consciousness*, 6: 5–21
___ (1980a) 'On Popular Justice: A Discussion with Maoists', in C. Gordon (ed.) *Power/Knowledge: Selected Interviews and Other Writings 1972–1977*, Brighton: Harvester Press
___ (1980b) 'Truth and Power', in C. Gordon (ed.) *Power/Knowledge: Selected Interviews and Other Writings 1972–1977*, Brighton: Harvester Press.
___ (1980c) 'The Confession of the Flesh', in C. Gordon (ed.) *Power/Knowledge: Selected Interviews and Other Writings 1972–1977*, Brighton: Harvester Press
___ (1980d) 'Powers and Strategies', in C. Gordon (ed.) *Power/Knowledge: Selected Interviews and Other Writings 1972–1977*, Brighton: Harvester Press
___ (1981) 'The Order of Discourse', in R. Young (ed.) *Untying the Text: A Post-Structuralist Reader*, London: Routledge
___ (1984) 'Michel Foucault à Goutelas: la redéfinition du "judiciable"', *Justice*, 115: 36–9
___ (2000a) 'About the Concept of the "Dangerous Individual" in Nineteenth-Century Legal Psychiatry', in J. D. Faubion (ed.) *Essential Works of Foucault 1954–1984 Vol. 3: Power*, New York, NY: The New Press
___ (2000b) 'Against Replacement Penalties', in J. D. Faubion (ed.) *Essential Works of Foucault 1954–1984 Vol. 3: Power*, New York, NY: The New Press
___ (2000c) 'Truth and Juridical Forms', in J. D. Faubion (ed.) *Essential Works of Foucault 1954–1984 Vol. 3: Power*, New York, NY: The New Press
___ (2000d) 'The Proper Use of Criminals', in J. D. Faubion (ed.) *Essential Works of Foucault 1954–1984 Vol. 3: Power*, New York, NY: The New Press
___ (2000e) 'What is Called "Punishing"?', in J. D. Faubion (ed.) *Essential Works of Foucault 1954–1984 Vol. 3: Power*, New York, NY: The New Press
___ (2000f) 'Interview with *Actes*', in J. D. Faubion (ed.) *Essential Works of Foucault 1954–1984 Vol. 3: Power*, New York, NY: The New Press
___ (2001) *Fearless Speech*, New York, NY: Semiotext(e)
___ (2003a) *Abnormal: Lectures at the Collège de France 1974–75*, trans. G. Burchell, London: Verso
___ (2003b) *'Society Must be Defended': Lectures at the Collège de France, 1975–76*, trans. D. Macey, London: Allen Lane
___ (2004) *La naissance de la biopolitique: Cours au Collège de France, 1978–79*, Paris: Gallimard/Seuil
___ (2006) *History of Madness*, trans. J. Murphy and J. Khalfa, Abingdon: Routledge
___ (2007) *Security, Territory, Population: Lectures at the Collège de France 1977–78*, trans. G. Burchell, Houndmills: Palgrave Macmillan
___ (2008) *The Birth of Biopolitics: Lectures at the Collège de France, 1978–79*, trans. G. Burchell, New York, NY: Palgrave Macmillan

___ (2009) 'Alternatives to the Prison: Dissemination or Decline of Social Control?', *Theory, Culture and Society*, 26: 12–24

___ (2011a) *The Courage of Truth: Lectures at the Collège de France, 1983–84*, trans. G. Burchell, London: Palgrave Macmillan

___ (2011b) *Leçons sur la volonté de savoir: Cours au Collège de France (1970–1971) suivi de Le savoir d'Oedipe*, Paris: Gallimard/Seuil

___ (forthcoming), *Mal faire, dire vrai: fonctions de l'Aveu*, Louvain and Chicago, IL: Louvain University Press/University of Chicago Press

Garland, D. (2010) *Peculiar Institution: America's Death Penalty in an Age of Abolition*, Cambridge, MA: Harvard University Press

Geertz, C. (1978) 'Stir Crazy', *The New York Review of Books*, 21/22: 3–6

Golder, B. and Fitzpatrick, P. (2009) *Foucault's Law*, Abingdon: Routledge

Gordon, C. (1991) 'Governmental Rationality: An Introduction', in G. Burchell, C. Gordon and P. Miller (eds) *The Foucault Effect: Studies in Governmentality*, Chicago, IL: University of Chicago Press

___ (2011) 'Governmentality and the Genealogy of Politics', paper presented at *The Foucault Effect, 1991–2011* Conference at Birkbeck College, June 2011, http://backdoorbroadcasting.net/2011/06/colin-gordon-governmentality-and-the-genealogy-of-politics/ (accessed 12 March 2012)

Harcourt, B. (2007) *Against Prediction: Profiling, Policing, and Punishing in an Actuarial Age*, Chicago, IL: University of Chicago Press

___ (2011a) *The Illusion of Free Markets: Punishment and the Myth of Natural Order*, Cambridge, MA: Harvard University Press

___ (2011b) 'The Punitive Order: Free Markets, Neoliberalism, and Mass Incarceration in the United States', paper presented at *The Foucault Effect, 1991–2011* Conference at Birkbeck College, June 2011, http://backdoorbroadcasting.net/2011/06/bernard-harcourt-the-punitive-order-free-markets-neoliberalism-and-mass-incarceration-in-the-united-states/ (accessed 12 March 2012)

Hardt, M. (2010) 'Militant Life', *New Left Review*, 64: 151–60

Harvey, D. (2005) *A Brief History of Neoliberalism*, Oxford: Oxford University Press

Hirst, P. Q. (1986) *Law, Socialism and Democracy*, London: Allen & Unwin

Hunt, A. (1992a) 'A Socialist Interest in Law', *New Left Review*, 192: 105–19

___ (1992b) 'Foucault's Expulsion of Law: Toward a Retrieval', *Law & Social Inquiry*, 17: 1–38

Hunt, A. and Wickham, G. (1994) *Foucault and Law: Towards a Sociology of Law as Governance*, London: Pluto Press

Miller, J. (2000) *The Passion of Michel Foucault*, Cambridge, MA: Harvard University Press

Pasquino, P. (1991) 'Theatrum Politicum: The Genealogy of Capital – Police and the State of Prosperity', in G. Burchell, C. Gordon and P. Miller (eds) *The Foucault Effect: Studies in Governmentality*, Chicago, IL: University of Chicago Press

Simon, J. (2007) *Governing Through Crime: How the War on Crime Transformed American Democracy and Created a Culture of Fear*, New York, NY: Oxford University Press

Tulkens, F. (1986) 'Généalogie de la défense sociale en Belgique (1880–1914)', *Actes*, 54: 38–41

___ (1988) *Généalogie de la défense sociale en Belgique (1880–1914). Travaux de séminaire M. Foucault (Louvain-la-Neuve, 1981)*, Brussels: Story-Scientia

Chapter 2

Foucault's other law

Peter Fitzpatrick

> *When the Lord Apollo gave ambiguous voice he was indicating the essence of right understanding. We who come into the world of being seem one; but in potential we are many. So the words in which the divine truth was revealed had to embrace, as best they could, the diverse possibilities coiled into any one moment. Choices which might point different ways.*
>
> (Tiresias in Vickers 2007: 57)

Introduction I

To begin with a beginning: in 'Truth and Juridical Forms' Foucault seeks an 'origin', no less, for certain 'social practices whose historical analysis enables one to locate the emergence of new forms of subjectivity', among which it seemed to him 'the most important ones are juridical practices' (2001a: 4 – references without the author's name are to Foucault).[1] And he would begin with classical Greek instances of 'judicial practices that gave rise to models of truth which still circulate in our society', the main instance being Sophocles' *Oedipus* (2001a: 15). To cut to the crux, Foucault finds that the play and its tragedy unfold in 'a series of nested halves that fit together', producing 'a unique object whose overall configuration is the manifest form of power' (2001a: 22). The 'figure' and even meaning of these conjoint parts is to be found in 'the famous technique of the *symbolon*, the Greek symbol', a technique that is at once 'juridical, political, and religious' (2001a: 22). The pervasive joinder in *Oedipus* is that between an oracular and incomplete pronouncement by Apollo and its completion in the earthly and inescapable revelation of Oedipus' parricide by 'the most hidden herdsman of the forest' (2001a: 23). The mediating connection between these two halves is 'the prophet Tiresias' – 'Tiresias, though blind, throbbing between two lives', Tiresias 'who, like Apollo, is someone divine, . . . but he is mortal in truth, the double the light god projects as a shadow on the surface of the earth' (2001a: 20; Eliot 1974a: 71). And it is Tiresias who reveals initially to Oedipus that he is the one who killed his father.

Yet Tiresias is not the carrier of a 'blind' fate. With this revelation Oedipus could have acted in ways, pursued possibilities, that could have rendered matters otherwise (2001a: 24). And it is Oedipus the king wanting to hold on to power exclusively, the 'tyrant' who 'attaches no importance to the laws and who replaces them with his whims and his orders', who becomes a figure of power 'whom the *Oedipus* story was meant to expel finally from history' (2001a: 24, 28).[2]

Introduction 2

The response to reviews is not the most alluring of genres, and in Foucault's company it is something especially precarious. But before coming to the dangers, first the cause or causes of contention. The most frequently advanced criticism of Golder and Fitzpatrick of *Foucault's Law* (Golder and Fitzpatrick 2009) is that the authors attribute to Foucault a theory of law and he did not have any such theory. The book is seen, aptly in a way, as the polar opposite of 'the expulsion thesis' so-called. As is fairly well known, this thesis says that with the advent of modernity Foucault expelled law from its erstwhile significance and relegated it to a position of utter and instrumental subordination to, and dependence on, disciplinary modes of power, among other contenders (see, especially, Hunt and Wickham 1994). And indeed if a label were to be given to our overall argument, it would be 'the inclusion thesis', this argument being that in modern society law is not expelled from a prime positioning but, rather, law is for Foucault at the constituent core of such society. This law is not, or not just, the contained creature of the expulsion thesis, but a surpassing law illimitably responsive to alterity – 'Foucault's other law' (Golder and Fitzpatrick 2009: chapter 2). Yet, far from wanting to expel the expulsion thesis, we wanted to adopt it. It was key and integral to the overall argument. And this argument was that Foucault's law is 'made up' of the constituent antinomy in which it is both utterly dependent yet still surpassingly responsive. More abruptly, we do not read Foucault in a way that would expel anything.

The critical riposte comes in two strands. The main strand agrees that Foucault did advance these two ideas of law but adds that he did not combine them into a theory of law (for example, Norrie 2009). The more benign of these criticisms would tolerate our presumption to the extent that Foucault did frequently call for his work to be used as a toolkit and such (as to which see Golder and Fitzpatrick 2009: 131, n. 4) – and so much so that we were justified in creatively bringing the two dimensions of law together, but not in attributing the result to Foucault. The idea that Foucault's views of law are essentially divergent could be bolstered in his frequent injunctions against asking him 'to remain the same' (1974: 17). And that idea is further bolstered in Foucault's just as frequently objecting to what he would call totalitarian theories, all-subsuming theories (for example, see 1977a: 208; and see Golder and Fitzpatrick 2009: 3–4). Unities, continuities, objects of theoretical elaboration are continually 'disturbed' and 'dispersed' by what inexorably challenges their existent determinacy (1974: 25–6, 71). Foucault would, furthermore, add a wry prescription to this process by advocating legislation which would 'prohibit the use of the author's name more than once, with the additional right to anonymity and the use of pseudonyms in order that each book might be read for itself' (1989a: 315).

This modest proposal would chime with the minor strand of criticism which, like the major, would recognize that, even if Foucault did adopt two notions of law, law's responsive dimension was advanced in a work on literature, or in a distinct and marginal slice of Foucault's *oeuvre*, or both, none of which 'count' sufficiently when set against the force and frequency of his advancing the expulsion thesis (for example, see Minkkinen 2011: 119). Yet this variety of relegation falls prey to Foucault's objection enforcing any unity of 'the author', a unity achieved by just such a type of relegation, among other means (1977b: 127–9). Still, Foucault was frequently and conspicuously concerned with the overall coherence of his work, and especially with justifying the seeming shifts between what are usually seen as its distinct phases (for example, see 1989b: 293). What, in sum, seems to be involved here is an explicit alternation in Foucault's regard for the author's *oeuvre*, an alternation between its multiple diffusions (as written and as read) and its being a set construction (for example, see 1974: 23–5). So, whilst Foucault's author is not the figure of an ultimately determinate limitation, still the author remains a focusing, a focusing for the time being, on a precipitate of the practical infinity of its times, 'of all possible readings' (1977b: 138; and for the quotation 1988: 52).

It would be premature to extend this reading of Foucault on Foucault to theory since that extension will be reflected in the rest of this chapter where the constituent dimensions of law will be found to match the vexed category of theory conceived in Foucault's terms. The steps along the way are made up of concatenate aporias, 'nested halves', to do with the constituting of the individual, of society, and of law – and finally of theory. 'Aporia' throughout will, in terms of its Greek derivation, import the idea of no road, no already assured passage, between its separate 'halves'. Taking law for now as the instance, the dimensions of law proposed in *Foucault's Law* emerge in the present exercise as aporetic. There could then be ground for agreement with the critics' charge that Foucault did not combine these dimensions of law into anything like a theory of law. But that ground would be seeded with a sinuous irony since the 'halves' of the aporetic separation combine inseparately. Law is thence found to be constituted in and as the appositive and force-filled relation between the separation and the combining of the 'halves' of aporia. The aporia is generative.

Individual I

Like the contained law of the expulsion thesis, Foucault's individual is usually seen as a creature comprehensively bound, the product of something else. Wearisome as it will be to the *cognoscenti*, some instances have to be offered. This is the individual rendered as a subject cast against 'the subject in its unity and its sovereignty' (2001a: 10). The modern subject would, rather, be various and bound within 'the human sciences' (1970: 144–5). And when focusing on the productivity of power Foucault finds that the 'individual is in fact a power-effect, . . . a relay: power passes through the individuals it has constituted' (2003a: 30). The resulting 'man' is bound in his very 'soul' – 'in himself the effect of a subjection much more profound than himself' (1979a: 30).

Yet the very diversity of individuals produced may somewhat restrain the claim to a comprehensiveness of that production, and there are at least as many differentiated types of subjects or individuals as there are distinct sites of productive power. And whilst this diversity entails 'a multiplicity of individual elements' (1979a: 170), a distinctness of constituent sites of power coming from below can in itself provide no unified subject, but such a subject provides the prime locus for the cohering and operative effect of disciplinary power. To order the diversity of powers brought to bear on it, the subject cannot simply be an effect of those powers but would require some standing apart from them, some being outside them. Yet it may be that there are techniques of power, such as surveillance and examination, through which the diversity coheres into 'the singularization of individuals' so that nonetheless and ultimately 'the individual is converted into an element for the exercise of power' (2007a: 147–8).

Individual 2

Foucault often scorned all-determining claims of power, or indeed of anything else (for example, see 2001b: 432; 2008: 256–7). And in seemingly stark contrast to the individual as the soul-seized carrier of other dispositions he (also) saw the individual unbound. But there are differences to be observed.

When relegating power as his abiding concern, Foucault found that his goal had been 'to create a history of the different modes by which, in our culture, human beings are made subjects' (1982: 208). This refurbished project extended to 'the forms and modalities of the relation to self by which the individual constitutes and recognises himself *qua* subject' (1987a: 6). That could signal, again, the individual's being 'in himself the effect of a subjection much more profound than himself' – a situation in which 'he becomes the principle of his own subjection' (1979a: 30). Even the individual's or the subject's vaunted ability to resist the encompassing reach of power can still leave resistance in a subordinate 'role of adversary, target, support or handle in power relations': resistance 'is never in a position of [mere] exteriority in relation to power' (1981: 95). And even whilst acknowledging the multiplicity of powers coming from below, Foucault would still accord power 'dense' concentrations around which one finds a resistant plurality – 'the swarm of points of resistance' (1981: 96). So completely can resistance be absorbed into 'power relations' that these can consist 'in taking the forms of resistance against different forms of power as a starting point' (1982: 211).

The culminating containment, along with its dissipation, comes in the modernist and positivist conceiving of 'man' distinct and supposedly entire – conceived, however and precariously, within an 'analytic of finitude' where 'man appears in his ambiguous position as an object of knowledge and as a subject that knows: enslaved sovereign' (1970: 312). Yet this is a saving ambiguity, even if an ultimately unresolved or irresolvable one. The very delimitation of 'man' in finitude impels relation to what is ever beyond it. So, whilst such a 'man' is 'a source of order for the totality', that source is ever beyond, ever outside of, a 'finitude . . . always designated on the basis of man as a concrete being' (1970: 313, 318). In all, '[m]an, in the analytic of finitude, is a strange empirico-transcendental doublet, since he is a being such that knowledge will be attained in him of what renders all knowledge possible' (1970: 318). Thence, 'finitude was conceived in an interminable cross-reference with itself' (1970: 318), and this 'man' finds himself, so to speak, in and as a finitude which divides from yet 'promises that very infinity it refuses', a finitude 'outlined in the paradoxical form of the endless' (1970: 314). And that is the paradoxical compounded since, to repeat somewhat, this infinite finitude is embedded in 'man as a concrete being', a 'man' bound by the very forces 'he' has somehow to encompass and make 'subject to total clarification' (1970: 310, 318).

Foucault provides many other resonant combinations. Most compendiously, 'men's subjection' is described in *The History of Sexuality, Vol. 1* as 'their constitution as subjects in both senses of the word' (1981: 60).[3] The individual is not only an effect of power, but also effects power. There is something of a similar alternation disturbing the constrained notion of resistance outlined earlier. The role of resistance is also advanced by Foucault as one on which the 'existence' of 'power relationships depends', a resistance that 'relied . . . on life and man as a living being' (1981: 95, 144). Not only that, the 'plurality of resistances' is not something 'doomed to perpetual defeat' but is, rather, 'inscribed in' relations of power 'as an irreducible opposite' (1981: 96). Furthermore, it is not just the case that power for Foucault ultimately encompasses resistance. Power can also be encompassed by resistance. It can be a 'strategic codification of . . . points of resistance that makes a revolution possible'; and something always remains impelling resistance within power, thus making possible 'an insurrection of subjugated knowledges' and 'anti-authority struggles' (1982: 211; 2003a: 7).

The tie to power is not one that binds ultimately. Resistance for Foucault was (also) an unconfineable 'power of life' (Deleuze 2006: 77, and see 74 and 76). This counter-power was, moreover, tied to an ultimate autonomy of the individual. 'I believe', Foucault avowed more than once, 'in the freedom of people', a freedom that was incapable of being 'limited at certain frontiers' (1988: 14–15). The ethics of the concern for the self was for Foucault a practice of freedom, where that concern involves a self-distancing 'exercise of the self on the self by which one attempts to develop and transform oneself, and to attain to a certain mode of being' (1997a: 282).[4]

The engagement between the self and varieties of power involves 'the relationships we have to others through those . . . power relationships' (1988: 15). Casting that connection more intimately, the very 'care of the self . . . implies a relationship with the other', a relation 'to others and for others' (1997a: 287). In the same vein, Foucault saw modern philosophy as a practice the exercise of which entails 'the transformation of the subject by himself and of the subject by the other' and this practice 'tests its reality in its relationship to politics' (2010: 353–4). As befits its being a practice, 'one of the poles of modern philosophy' became, for Foucault, the 'technologies of the self' (2001c: 403). Through these technologies 'the individual could be integrated into the social totality' (2001c: 410). Or, put another way, such integration is 'obtained' in a 'new political rationality' (2001c: 409). The 'main characteristic of our political rationality is the fact that this integration of the individuals into a community or in a totality results from a constant correlation between an increasing individualization and the reinforcement of this totality' (2001c: 417).[5] And for that 'correlation' the individual has to be the individual positioned against 'the technology of domination', the individual unbound, individual freedom being a 'condition' and a 'precondition . . . for the exercise of power': '[p]ower is exercised only over free subjects, and only insofar as they are free' (1982: 221). More pointedly, 'thought' for Foucault is an insistent mode through which subjects in their freedom affirmatively and continuously constitute their delimited being (1970: 327).

This by now may be very close to the obvious, but the free subject does not produce some surpassing settlement of an infinite finitude. The subject is a combination of a delimited finitude and the imperative ability to 'step back' from the delimited into 'its' alterity (1997b: 117). This uncomfortably unbound sovereign makes several appearances in Foucault's cast of characters, a compendious one being the *Homo oeconomicus* of neoliberalism as 'an entrepreneur of himself' (2008: 226).

Pause I

All of which leaves us with a conundrum. The free, the unbound individual is utterly singular yet subsists integrally bound in a 'relation to others', a relation which goes to constitute a 'social totality', a 'community'. But if, without more, singular individuals are to exist in common, then the only available commonality would be one where they were the same as each other and singularity would be lost. So a condition of their singularity, of the singularity of each in being-together, would seem to be an ability to effect a determinate, a finite commonality which, if they are to remain singular, must somehow be apart from them. Yet unless we resurrect the transcendent or surpassingly elevate some primal immanence, that commonality cannot be apart in the sense that its constituent force is separately and ultimately beyond them. To be their commonality it must connect and relate to them, and in that relation the commonality has to be able to respond illimitably – respond to the practical infinity that could be the life of singular individuals being-together. All of which leads us to what seems to be an aporetic divide similar to that found in being-individual. And such proves, with Foucault's guidance, to be the case.

Society I

Taking the modern rendition of 'society' as shorthand for Foucault's 'social totality' and 'community', and like the individual innately bound, we find a 'manage[d] . . . society' subsumed in varieties of comprehensive arrogation (2008: 296). The most draconic instances come with Foucault's version of a 'biopower' along with that power's sustaining scientism and its appropriation of a compliant 'nature', all of which subsists in conjunction with a comprehensive and constituent 'science of government' of whole 'populations' – in a 'governmentality' (2007b: 104, 108–9; 2008: 15–16). In sum, all these together 'took charge of men's existence' performing their 'highest function' in 'invest[ing] life through and through' (2007b: 55, 66). As Foucault says of 'apparatuses of security' as the 'essential mechanism' of such governing: 'the essential function of security . . . is to respond to a reality in such a way that this response cancels out the reality to which it responds – nullifies it, or limits, checks or regulates it' – 'the delimitation of phenomena within acceptable limits' (2007b: 47, 108; 2003a: 246, 249). Disciplinary power in its formative effect on the individual is factored into this scenario. The 'new' power cast as co-extensive with 'life' and operating 'in a different scale' to 'individualizing' disciplinary power does nonetheless 'dovetail into' it so that, in all, '[t]he disciplines of the body and the regulations of the population constituted the two poles around which the organization of power over life was deployed' (1981: 139; 2003a: 242–3).[6] Biopower, furthermore, goes to mark off and to constitute the subject of disciplinary power (2008: 184, 194). And there are sites, substantial as well as modal, integrating both such as madness and sexuality, the norm and governmentality (1980c: 125; 1981: 26; 2001c: 225).

The comprehensive claims made for biopower and such raise an obvious problem of plausibility. To borrow Asad's summary: '[s]cientific practices, techniques, knowledges, permeate and create the very fibers of social life in ways that religion no longer does' (1993: 49), yet the very claims of science are intrinsically incomplete and provisional. Adding to the uncertainty, Foucault was frequently disparaging of the claims of 'sciences' and 'scientificity', and often saw them as providing but the 'respectable face' of overweening powers (for example, see 1979a: 23, 223, 296). Yet something more than a façade would seem to be called for to sustain the disciplines as well as biopower and such, something that will embed their universal constituent claims in some plausibility, if they are to provide the formative force of modern society as Foucault sees it. And he does indicate for that purpose three connected, or connectible, strategies.

The first and preliminary strategy would enclose the scientifically incomplete and provisional within a universalized determinacy. That determinacy, in turn, incorporates a comprehensive competence. The 'power' that ensues is thence autonomous, self-evident, and self-generating (for example, see 1979a: 129, 232–3). So, taking a notable instance: 'there is nothing in human conduct that cannot, in one way or another, be questioned by psychiatry', by psychiatry with its 'almost indefinite opening' enabling it 'to become the medical jurisdiction for any conduct whatsoever' (2003b: 160).

That accomplishment is, coming now to the second strategy, assiduously inculcated into the individual in various disciplinary practices, and this so thoroughly that the individual, as we saw, becomes their 'effect' as they seep into and even constitute 'his' very 'soul' (1979a: 30; 2003a: 30). Presumably the operatives of science would also have to have, in that capacity, some self-subsuming commitment to it. Taking for now the earlier quasi-religious invocation of the soul as telling, we find Foucault adding that 'scientificity has become sacred' (2003a: 39). More expansively, what power has deifically to combine is a determinate ipseity and an illimitable reach, a reach 'without limit' (for example, see 1979a: 227; 2008: 276–7, 294–7).[7] The 'solution', invoking now the earlier account of the first strategy, is to make the illimitable immanent to the determinate, thence ramping the determinate up to the status of the transcendent (see Deleuze and Guattari 1994: 45). It is then hardly surprising that disciplinary imperatives should be equated with religion or that Foucault would dub a key operative as a thaumaturge (1979a: 242; 2009: 507, 509).[8] Yet, Foucault immediately adds, even as such operatives become 'miracle workers in the eyes of patients, to their own eyes they could never be anything other than positivist physicians' (2009: 509). And as Asad pithily indicated, the '[s]cientific practices, techniques, knowledges, [that] permeate and create the very fibers of social life' supposedly displace a like reliance on religion (1993: 49). This is the cued entry for the third and culminating strategy, one generated in racism, and one needing more extended consideration.

Racism for Foucault could be several different things (for example, see 2003a: 87–9, 257–8). Abruptly choosing the one to which he devotes most attention, we find that its occidental emergence in the late eighteenth and the nineteenth centuries was for Foucault 'something very different' to the racial division preceding it yet also a continuation of the division, a 'reworking', 'no more than an episode, a phase' within it (2003a: 65, 239). That encompassing racial division was 'the first, historico-political discourse on society' (2003a: 49). It was and remains 'ultimately . . . a way of normalizing society' (2003a: 61). Still, there was a break. A 'revolutionary . . . actual racism . . . takes over' in distinct 'sociobiological terms', takes over as biopower (2003a: 65, 80–1). As opposed to the preceding division between races, this racism is 'biologically monist' encompassing, as it does, a single 'species' and protecting, as it does, the 'racial purity' of that species (2003a: 80–81, 255). This, more expansively, is a protection of 'the integrity, the superiority, and the purity of the race' (2003a: 81). Such superiority imports division within the unity, and a division as somehow primary: '[t]hat is the first function of racism: to fragment, to create caesuras within the biological continuum addressed by biopower' (2003a: 255). It may reveal more of that seeming contradiction if this racism is now situated.

Overwhelmingly, Foucault identified racism with a 'State racism' (2003a: 239 ff.). This was and is a racism the 'activation' of which stems from the persistence of 'the old sovereign power' in its 'national universality' together with 'the way biopower functions through it' (2003a: 239, 258). 'State racism' became 'the basic mechanism of power, as it is exercised in modern States' (2003a: 254).[9]

A resulting puzzle: 'How can the power of death, the function of death, be exercised in a political system centred on biopower?' since 'this power's objective is essentially to make live' (2003a: 254). It is 'at this point that racism intervenes' (2003a: 254). Whereas '[i]n a normalizing society, race or racism is the precondition that makes killing acceptable', 'killing' for Foucault does 'not mean simply murder as such: but also every form of indirect murder: the fact of exposing someone to death, increasing the risk of death for some people. Or, quite simply, political death, expulsion, rejection, and so on' (2003a: 256). At this extreme, then, it is racism that endows biopower and its allied 'power of normalization' with the ability to 'kill' and ostensibly to surpass and contain what is its 'objective . . . essentially to make live' (2003a: 254, 256). These powers, along with their sustaining scientism, are self-endowed with the means to encompass life by way of the mediation of racism.

How then might a superior 'member of a race or a population' exist integrally 'insofar as one is an element in a unitary living plurality' (2003a: 258)? The question could be refined by asking further how any 'member' might exist integrally when faced with the fragmentation of that infinite finitude within which 'man as a concrete being' was bound by illimitable forces 'he' has nonetheless to encompass and make 'subject to total clarification' (1970: 310, 318; and see my discussion, above). Racism was and is a response to the combining of this concrete determinacy with an accommodating responsiveness to the illimitable beyond it. This combining is effected in what could be called a negative universal reference. That reference enables such a combining without its having to assume an essentially positive and ultimately delimited content, a content incompatible with the universalist claims of bio- and disciplinary powers and their sustaining scientism.

The negative universal reference forms in four fused stages. The first has already been observed in the unity of the species. This makes possible the comparison of the 'superior element' and the inferior (2003a: 258). For present purposes, the second stage is intimated in Foucault's finding in that fertile nineteenth century a new 'knowledge of man', 'a knowledge of individuality, of the normal or abnormal, conforming or nonconforming individual' (2001a: 2). This normal individual inhabiting a 'normalizing society' is constituently distinguished from the 'abnormal', 'the evil, . . . the non-normal' (2003b: 316–17). More pointedly, the abnormal is ascribed a positive content in the negation of which the normal acquires its content. And this negative assumption of content absorptively accommodates the illimitablity of the constituent claims of bio- and disciplinary powers.

The third and, finally, fourth stages in constituting the negative universal reference are the seeming obverse of the second. With its putatively pervasive control of life and the living, '[t]he universally disciplinary and regulatory society' of racial exclusion would exclude completely (2003a: 259). What is excluded from the universal can only be utterly excluded. Yet the universal has to be all-inclusive. So the universal negative reference generates an antithesis but then has to be able to include that antithesis within itself, within its integral self. That imperative has two consequences. With one, and this is the third stage, the utterly excluded are nonetheless bidden to progress, or reform, or in some other way achieve inclusion. With the other and the fourth stage, along with its potential now to enter the universal, the antithesis resides always potentially within the bearers of the universal. 'We' were once savages and may regress, or 'we' may fail a constantly demanding disciplinary norm of 'our' society. Or 'we' may simply and of necessity be incorporated within some biopolitical determination.

The negative universal reference provides, then, a bridge to the further reaches that make up Foucault's expansive idea of racism. The initial expansion is not exceptional. The biological has at times been regulated through biopower in explicitly racist terms, such as with eugenics. And for Foucault eclipsing all else, there is 'the paroxysmal development' of biopower in 'the Nazi regime' (1981: 54, 148–50; 2003a: 255–6, 260). Also, in the overlapping periods during which Foucault traced the emergence of biopower and of disciplinary power and for some time after, racist discourse was used to incorporate and regulate the insane, the working class, women, sexuality, children and criminals (for example, see 1981: 147–50; 2003a: 258). And it is not unusual to find with Foucault that various sites of power have generated racism – sexuality, medicine, class and psychiatry (1981: 119, 124–5, 147–50; 2003a: 83, 252, 272; 2003b: 317). Yet most remarkably, for Foucault racism characterizes such sites and others centrally, including criminality, even without its explicit presence (2003a: 257). As with the negative universal reference and racism 'proper', these sites of biopower and discipline create the 'abnormal' and the 'anomaly' as the formative force of their created content (for example, see 1979a: 299). An instance: '[t]he gesture that divides madness is', for Foucault, 'the constitutive one, not the science that grows up in the calm that returns after the division has been made. The caesura that establishes the distance between reason and non-reason is the origin' (2009: xxviii; and see 1970: xxiv, 378–81). Thence 'Reason and Madness' become 'foreign to each other, deaf to any exchange, almost dead to each other' (2009: xxvii). And so, 'men . . . communicate and recognise each other in the merciless language of non-madness' (2009: xxvii; cf. 1970: 379).[10]

The abnormal thence become 'another people within the same people' (see 1979a: 253). They are both 'interior and foreign', subjected to 'an inclusion through exclusion' (1970: xxiv; 2001a: 78). That condition is then inflected towards and inhabits an uneasy normality:

> [T]he child is more individualized than the adult, the patient more than the healthy man, the madman and the delinquent more than the normal and the non-delinquent. . . . [W]hen one wishes to individualize the healthy, normal and law-abiding adult, it is always by asking him how much of the

> child he has in him, what secret madness lies within him, what fundamental crime he has dreamt of committing.
>
> (1979a: 193)

Society 2

Foucault's concern with normality and the norm, both in its 'disciplinary' manifestation and in 'the growing importance assumed by the action of the norm' with the advent of biopower (1981: 144), can begin to unravel the pretension of this 'normalizing society'. With Foucault the norm ends up being something of a combination of opposites (cf. Hume 1985: 521 [III, I, I]). In one sense the norm depicts or describes what is normally so – an activity that extends to characterizing and classifying and to the taking on of a 'positive' and 'technical' quality (1979a: 223; 2003b: 50). In that guise, the norm is opposed to law and rule (for example, see 1981: 144; 2007b: 56; 2008: 30). But that opposition is soon nuanced. For a start, literally, 'there is an originally prescriptive character of the norm' (2007b: 57). As such the norm goes beyond being 'a principle of intelligibility', and is found to be 'a political concept' – 'an element on the basis of which a certain exercise of power is founded and legitimized' (2003b: 50). This involves judgment, a 'normalizing judgement' (1979a: 177, 183). And that judgment operatively combines law and the purely 'positive' norm, an 'asymptotic' combination rendered as, for example, a 'scientifico-legal complex' (1979a: 19, 227; and see Golder 2007: 163, n. 16). Law and judgment enable the extension of the norm in an orientation that surpasses any finality, any determinacy, and that remains ultimately open and indefinite (1979a: 227). Here, against the backdrop of infinity, the thaumaturge re-enters, the doctor who 'could only exert his absolute authority over the world of the asylum insofar as he was . . . Father and Judge, Family and Law' (2009: 506). In a like vein, Foucault observes that '[t]he agent of punishment must exercise a total power' (1979a: 129).

There does remain a determinate cohesion of society supposedly secured by an encompassing sovereignty, at least in the manifest pretensions of national sovereignty. Despite something of a reputation to the contrary, Foucault did reserve a significant and compatible role for sovereignty in a normalizing society. This does not, however, leave a sovereign monism predominate. Foucault did go so far as to see 'the science of government', his 'governmentality', with its incorporation of biopower, as oriented towards 'pre-eminence over all other types of power', including sovereignty (2007b: 104, 108–9). Sovereignty remained weakened on the 'outside' of this 'science of government' (2007b: 104).

The contrary role Foucault assigned to state sovereignty was less residual and less precarious than all this may suggest. Not only was governmentality in its origins accompanied by a heightened 'state centralization', but also with its ensuing realization 'the problem of sovereignty was never more sharply posed' (2007b: 89, 106). This imports a sustained significance for sovereignty in its conjunction with other powers, such as its fused operation with biopower considered in the last section. It is also the case that 'power relations have come more and more under state control' as they have become 'progressively governmentalized' (1982: 224). What 'we have', in sum, is 'a triangle: sovereignty, discipline, and governmental management, which has population as its main target' (2007b: 107–8). The key consequence for present purposes is that anything resembling a sovereign monism is displaced and the domain of state sovereignty rendered partial. Partiality was also, to repeat somewhat, intrinsic to 'discipline, and governmental management' – a partiality heightened by racism with its ineradicable exclusions becoming 'the basic mechanism of power, as it is exercised in modern States' (2003a: 254).

In all, the constituent claim of the normalizing society to encompass and regulate life confronts a productive failure. Again to repeat somewhat, the objective of power enabling this claim 'is essentially to make live' (2003a: 254). So, even though the term biopower would 'designate what brought life and its mechanisms into the realm of explicit calculations' still '[i]t is not that life has been totally integrated into techniques that govern and administer it; it constantly escapes them' (1981: 143). One avenue of escape that we have already visited is resistance: '[w]hen power becomes bio-power, resistance becomes the power of life, a vital power that cannot be confined' (Deleuze 2006: 77). For Foucault then, illimitable life necessarily takes on a certain vitalist force – 'a way of living in complete mobility and not of immobilizing life' (1980a: 60):

> [T]here is indeed always something in the social body, in classes, groups and individuals themselves which in some sense escapes relations of power, something which is by no means a more or less docile or reactive primal matter, but rather a centrifugal movement, an inverse energy, a discharge.
>
> (1980b: 138; cf. 145)

This energy can be sensed in the disasters ensuing from its denial. Nazism provides the most comprehensive attempt at denial – the attempt at a total containment of life or of the social body. With 'the Nazi State' biopower becomes 'absolutely coextensive with the sovereign right to kill anyone, meaning not only other people but also its own people' (2003a: 260). Thence '[w]e have an absolutely racist State, an absolutely murderous State, and an absolutely suicidal State' (2003a: 260). This inexorable logic would extend to the attempt at some determinate containment less than total, containment as a quasi-transcendent sovereignty for example. The holding of life in part would still require a totalized comprehension both to hold the part in an ungiving stasis and to predetermine its relation, or possible relation, to anything else (see Derrida 1979: 125).

It would seem to be time for another contemplative pause. Pause 1 advanced a match between the aporetic divide in the composition of the singular individual in its finitude and the aporetic divide in the life of singular individuals being-together. That divide was then pursued and now confirmed in the exploration of society. But with society of the variety involved here, a constitutional issue remains. The individual had the ability, the jurisdiction as it were, to effect a generative determination resolving the aporetic divide 'for the time being' – a sovereign 'enslaved' but sovereign nonetheless (1970: 312), whereas this society conspicuously falls short. Not only do the available modes of resolution considered so far, variations of normalizing power and state sovereignty, fall short radically of their universal range, their very claim to that universality, and thence their claim to encapsulate or effect society, is founded on particularity and exclusion.

Pause 2

The inability of life or the social body to subsist in or as a set or containing determinacy provides an opening, in a couple of senses, to Foucault's 'thought from the outside' – to this outside in its enabling the coming together of the seemingly disparate dimensions of society and the individual (1987b: 16). To borrow from Deleuze:

> The inside as an operation of the outside: in all his work Foucault seems haunted by this theme of an inside which is merely the fold of the outside, as if the ship were a folding of the sea.
>
> (Deleuze 2006: 81)

Then as something of a corollary there is '[t]he appeal to the outside', which is also 'a constant theme in Foucault' (Deleuze 2006: 72). This haunting pervasion is much noted by others and its significance in his work tended to be confirmed by Foucault (for example, see 2001d: 241; Saghafi 1996: 81, 89; Pelbart 2000: 202). The inside, 'as an operation of the outside', is a 'double' of the outside – the double also being 'the theme that has always haunted Foucault': 'the double is never a projection of the interior; on the contrary, it is an interiorization of the outside' (Deleuze 2006: 81; and see 1977b: 182). The interior 'caught in the form of limitation' is not, cannot be, a set determinacy but in its very continuity remains 'free for a new beginning' (Eliot 1974b: 195; 1987b: 22).

All of which may seem to overplay the dependency of the inside, seeing it as merely 'constituent of the outside' (Deleuze 2006: 87). Something of a contrary emphasis was advanced earlier with 'the analytic of finitude' where the very delimitation of 'man' in finitude emerged in constituent relation to 'the very infinity it refuses', in constituent relation to 'the endless' (1970: 312, 314; and see Deleuze 2006: 73, 105). Thence '"the thought from the outside" . . . stands at the threshold of all positivity' (1987b: 16; and see 1974: 125). And 'as long as the outside is folded' within the inside 'an inside is coextensive with it' (Deleuze 2006: 81).

All that, in turn, may underlie the outside's dependency on the inside for its efficacy. Even though a 'form of the outside' would be 'always undone' and 'the outside never yields its essence', still the outside can be endowed as an amplitude, as an 'ultimate spatiality' or a 'conditioned' temporality, or as 'moving matter'

(1987b: 23, 28, 57; Deleuze 2006: 80, 89).[11] There are two modes through which the 'matter' of the outside is realized. One is, in a sense, internal to the outside. Resistance would seem to be the prime contender – the 'resistances' which 'necessarily operate in a direct relation with the outside', and in so doing 'modify and overturn . . . relations between forces' (Deleuze 2006: 74, 100). Such resistance 'puts itself on the side of life, and turns life against power' – life as the 'capacity to resist force' (Deleuze 2006: 76–7). Foucault's 'transgression' also relates integrally to the outside (1977c: 47–8). In its illimitability, transgression 'affirms limited being – affirms the limitlessness into which it leaps as it opens this zone to existence for the first time' (1977c: 35). And with this affirmation and re-affirmation '[t]ransgression carries the limit right to the limit of its being; transgression forces the limit to face the fact of its imminent disappearance, to find itself in what it excludes' (1977c: 34).

The other mode effecting the outside operates somewhat apart from it – Foucault's 'relations' or 'field' of exteriority (1974: 45, 125). These are relations 'established between' a collection of 'institutions, economic and social processes, behavioural patterns, systems of norms, techniques, types of classification, modes of characterization' (1974: 45). Exteriority, then, is the mediate matter in-between the outside and this collection inside. As such, exteriority channels the illimitable 'force' or 'forces' of the outside not only into the making and varying of the specific 'forms' assumed by these entities in the collection, but also into those formative and transforming 'combinations' of the entities that go to make up the specific forms.[12]

The composing of exteriority, then, merges the inside with the outside. To do this, exteriority must conjoin, in and as itself, its seemingly contrary connections to the outside and the inside. Its constituent relation to an illimitable outside, an outside always 'farther away' from it (Deleuze 2006: 72, 100), orients exteriority itself illimitably. Yet, if its constituent relation were solely to the outside, exteriority would become a mere dissipation. So, we find that exteriority takes on a certain 'positivity', an 'incorporeal materiality' in manifesting itself by delimiting and marking out the content of the inside in its relation to the outside (1974: 125; 1977b: 169). In so doing, exteriority invests and constantly refounds the inside by drawing in the force of the outside, thence rendering the inside as an 'interiorization' of the outside and endowing it with such a range of receptivity that it becomes 'completely co-present' with the outside (Deleuze 2006: 81, 97).[13]

This 'oscillation' of exteriority between the outside and the inside has been captured in terms of an iterable 'wave of extremely short duration' or, even more graphically, in terms of 'peristaltic movements' (1977b: 169; 1977c: 34; Deleuze 2006: 80). That capture, inevitably uneasy, does at least intimate the dependence of exteriority on the poles between which it oscillates – the outside and the inside. Yet, to repeat somewhat, exteriority cannot depend on the outside to the point of its becoming entirely dissipated. Neither can exteriority respond illimitably to the outside yet depend on the inside to the point of being entirely bound to it. Exteriority, in sum, is 'a practical domain that is autonomous (although dependent), and which can be described at its own level (although it must be articulated on something other than itself)' (1974: 121–2).

Law

Law assumes its 'incorporeal materiality' as exteriority. At one stage in his beautiful homage, 'Maurice Blanchot: The Thought from Outside', Foucault evokes transgression almost abruptly and then continues with an answer to the questions posed in that chapter title: 'Where Is the Law/And What Does It Do?' (1987b: 33):

> And of transgression. How could one know the law and truly experience it, how could one force it to come into view, to exercise its powers clearly, to speak, without provoking it, without pursuing it into its recesses, without resolutely going ever farther into the outside into which it is always receding?
> (1987b: 34)

Along with its 'going ever farther into the outside' there is 'the silent and infinitely accommodating welcome of the law' in which law becomes of 'the outside that envelops conduct, thereby removing it from all interiority' (1987b: 34, 38). Yet there is also a counter-movement, as it were. This infinitely trajected law is 'placed under restraint', put 'beside itself' as it separates itself 'via the very separation that institutes it as form, in the very movement by which it formulates . . . exteriority as law', whence 'the law takes place (has found its place)' (1987b: 35, 36; Blanchot 1993: 434). As self-separating and emplaced, law assumes its unitary if 'impalpable substance' as exteriority (1987b: 35). Yet again, in taking on its formed content 'beside itself', 'the presence of the law' is still 'its concealment', and that elusive presence 'haunts cities, institutions, conduct, and gestures' (1987b: 33). As exteriority then, the law is necessarily 'articulated on something other than itself' (1974: 122). It is not 'self-evident' (1987b: 33). It 'has no existence on its own' (Savigny in Rahmatian 2007: 6).

Law as exteriority could, then, be evoked in three fused dimensions. One would 'locate' it within the inside, another would relate it integrally to the outside, and yet another would discern it in-between the two. Taking the location inside first, the law of the inside could bear some resemblance to that abject law often put in positivist terms or, in a usage Foucault often adopts, put in terms of the 'juridical' (for example, see 1979a: 222; 1979b: 16, 21; 1981: 144). We find this law being ever more subjected to 'colonizing' by 'normalizing procedures', find it ever more instrumentally contained in a 'perpetual reference to something other than itself' (1979a: 22; 2003a: 38–9). Yet the reference is perpetual, the subjection never complete and, as Foucault indicated, law still escapes (1979a: 223; 1981: 144).

The escape route goes by way of that further dimension of law in which the exteriority 'finds itself' in-between the inside and the outside. Law's supposed subjection to varieties of power was often set by Foucault in an overdrawn contrast between the powers characteristic of a normalizing society and the unitary 'Law-and-Sovereign' characterizing 'Western societies since the Middle Ages' – societies in which an emerging sovereign power was formulated, manifested and justified as law (1981: 87–9, 97). Yet the escape of law, its continuing as a general reference in the normalizing society, is not confined to an encompassing 'sovereign' connection. Foucault's frequent setting of disciplinary power in contrast to law was to a law 'that makes rules a product of the will of the sovereign' (2003a: 38). But just as often as the contrast was drawn, Foucault observed that the varieties of discipline had their own laws and were themselves even similar to law:

> In appearance, the disciplines constitute nothing more than an infra-law. They seem to extend the general forms defined by law to the infinitesimal level of individual lives; or they appear as methods of training that enable individuals to become integrated into these general demands. They seem to constitute the same type of law on a different scale, thereby making it more meticulous and more indulgent. The disciplines should be regarded as a sort of counter-law.
>
> (1979a: 222)

In a like vein, Foucault cautions, '[t]he minor court that seems to sit permanently in the buildings of discipline, and which sometimes assumes the theatrical form of the great legal apparatus, must not mislead us' (1979a: 183). Still, the language of deception and semblance is more than balanced by numerous straightforward instances such the observation of the disciplinary 'microcourt', of 'the emergence of a new form of "law": a mixture of legality and nature', of our being 'in the society of the teacher-judge, the doctor-judge, the educator-judge, the "social worker"-judge', of the asylum doctor whom we encountered earlier being 'Father and Judge, Family and Law', and the observation that '[t]he psychiatrist really becomes a judge', as well as the observation of much more which we now come to (1979a: 304; 2001a: 83; 2009: 506).

Continuing with this judiciary by many other names, Foucault finds that '[a]t the heart of all disciplinary systems functions a small penal mechanism. It enjoys a kind of judicial privilege with its own laws, its specific offenses, its particular forms of judgement', and with 'its experts in normality, who continue and multiply the functions of the judge' (1979a: 177–8, 228). Our earlier journey through the norm found its normality tied to 'an originally prescriptive character of the norm', a prescription made operative through 'normalizing judgement' (1979a: 177; 2007b: 57). In this way the hold of the norm becomes indefinitely extensive, not only in its enforceability but in its rendering 'individuals' as 'instruments' of its effectiveness (1979a: 170).

The imperative quality of this judging and judgment, of this situated law, is not simply intrinsic to itself but pervades and overreaches the norm as 'factual', as what is normally so. This surpassing through legal judgment can be discerned by looking at the issue of recalcitrance. Not only is the factual, even 'scientific' assertion of normality powerless in the face of recalcitrance, but the recalcitrance, or the figure of incipient recalcitrance, constitutes the norm, and that norm is unconfined by any set 'factual' depiction of it. It is, rather, a norm prolific with 'possibility', ever open to the prospect of legal judgment (see 1979a: 227; 2001a: 40). The judgment called for by this possibility, by the 'freedom' concentrated in recalcitrance, is not something added on to a supposed 'scientific' sufficiency of the norm but is something inherently sustaining of the norm, otherwise the operative limits and ineffectiveness of its scientific pretension would be evident: 'without the possibility of recalcitrance, power would be equivalent to a physical determination', and its limits and inabilities as that starkly exposed (1982: 221).

This same surpassing law is (also) an 'infra-law' or a 'counter-law', a law within, a law of the inside, and a law which in its very exteriority 'must be articulated on something other than itself' (1974: 122; 1979a: 222). Despite that dependence for its articulate content, such law cannot be contained by any content. Its relation to content derived from various powers of normalizing society remains 'asymptotic' (1979a: 227). Even as law retains its mediated dependence on powers of normalization and even as the 'counter-law' of such powers 'becomes the effective and institutionalized content of the juridical forms' (1979a: 224), law and powers of normalization 'find themselves' in a mutually generative complex (see Golder and Fitzpatrick 2009: 26–9, 63–71).

Aptly enough, the pursuit here of law's three fused dimensions has been one increasingly oriented towards the outside – a 'going ever farther into the outside into which [law] is always receding' (1987b: 34). This affinity with the outside was always 'there', always within and generative of the other two dimensions – of the inside and of the exteriority in-between the inside and the outside. At this point the whole exercise is revealed as one in tautology. Like the structuring of *Oedipus*, its end was in its beginning. The decretal revelation of the god which impels the play's beginning is 'essentially' what the shepherd finally revealed, thereby setting off the events that lead to the play's end (2001a: 24). The 'authenticity' of the god's pronouncement from outside is affirmed '[b]y fitting these two parts together', the 'nested halves' (2001a: 22). That joinder, for Foucault, instanced a 'juridical . . . technique' as well as 'judicial practices that gave rise to models of truth which still circulate in our society' (2001a: 15, 22).

There is however, and for 'our society', a difference of overwhelming obviousness which Foucault signals in an inevitable reference to Nietzsche: 'When will all these shadows of god no longer darken us? When will we have completely de-deified nature?' (2001a: 10).[14] The much visited scene of the death of God still draws us back to it, not just because of the questions left by the demise of an ultimate reference, and not only because for Nietzsche we have yet to comprehend '[t]his tremendous event [which] is still on its way', but because, returning to Foucault, 'this death should be understood . . . as the now constant space of our experience' (1977c: 32 and Nietzsche 2001: 120 [125]). So for Nietzsche's wonderfully sane madman, our killing of God is a deed still not 'seen and heard', a deed 'more remote than the remotest stars' (Nietzsche 2001: 120 [125]). And for Foucault it is infinitely remote and endows 'a limitless reign', yet a reign tied to a realization of 'the limit' (1977c: 32).

Between the limitlessness and the limit, bringing what is outside into the world, is Tiresias, the figure of law's exteriority – Tiresias who is 'mortal in truth' but mediates between the mortal and the divine becoming Apollo's 'mortal shadow', 'the double the light god projects as a shadow on the surface of the earth' (2001a: 20). Yet despite, or because of, its divine antecedent, Tiresias' revelation of the parricide, if it is to be effective, 'must be articulated on something other than itself' – on the situated revelation of the shepherd (1974: 122 for the quotation). It is the shadowing illimitability of the law which Oedipus as king would counter, in his doom-laden 'attach[ing] no importance to the laws', by 'replac[ing] them with his whims and his orders' (2001a: 28).[15] Nietzsche's 'shadows of god' also portend a like arrogation of the outside (Nietzsche 2001: 109–10 [108], 199 [343]).[16]

An adequate regard to law in its illimitability begins to look imperative for the sustaining of rule. According law its illimitability is to adopt the rule of law in its fullest sense. This law is not only the 'Rule of Law' which Foucault would aptly set in varieties of 'liberal' society. There are aptitudes of that Rule of Law shared with the rule of law in its fullest sense – aptitudes enabling the realization of possibility and the bringing of irresolution and conflict within the incipience of rule, rather than attempting completely to contain or eliminate them (for example, see 2008: 171–6; Deleuze 2006: 26–7). Of course the rule of law in its modern occidental variation is usually typified in terms of an enduring determinacy, in terms of providing some assured stability of expectation, some definite normative hold on futurity. But to hold a determinacy invariant is impossible since that would entail a totalized comprehension of all that may ever come to and affect it. So for law to rule, it has also to be quite contrary to those standard attributes. It must be utterly responsive and ever capable of being other than what it determinately is. If it failed to be so capable, it would cease to rule situations inexorably changing around it.

This 'infinitely accommodating welcome of the law' is not simply a matter of law's abjection (1987b: 38; and cf. 1977d: 150–1). With law being of the outside, its illimitability secures its autonomy. Even though law is not 'self-evident' and is thence necessarily 'articulated on something other than itself' (1974: 122; 1987b: 33), it still self-generatively extends in its illimitability beyond the 'evident' and the 'something other than itself' and in this way is able to adopt or to regulate them in its own terms. So, for example, the same kind of confidently complete evidence from the 'human sciences' will in the making of law be at times readily accepted but just as readily rejected.[17] In all, whilst being of the outside opens law to the void, there is still a 'fullness of the void, something one cannot silence' (1987b: 23). And whilst law's illimitability cannot be compromised if law is to rule, still the rule of law has to sustain an element of determinacy that grounds some assured stability of expectation, some definite normative hold on futurity, and to do so it has to secure some immunity from its insistent illimitability. For law to rule then, it must generate some determinacy 'for the time being'. Yet that very determinacy of content, the law of the inside, to be itself sustained must remain integrated with the outside – the outside of which it is 'a double' (Deleuze 2006: 81). The standard borrowing from Lampedusa: 'If we want things to stay as they are, things will have to change' (2007: 19).

Conclusion

It is law as exteriority that brings together yet holds necessarily apart law of the inside and law of the outside. As such, this law matches the disparate yet conjoint dimensions of society – society as determinate and as illimitable – giving them an ultimate effect beyond the delimited and delimiting range of both normalizing society and sovereign assertion. These dimensions of society were prefigured in imperatives intrinsic to the commonality of singular individuals being-together. Those imperatives in turn matched the constituent dimensions of the individual – again dimensions of determinacy and illimitability. As determinate entities the individual, society and law are distinct, but the 'nesting' of the determinate inside of each with the illimitable outside, an outside that itself cannot be partitioned, opens them to each other in the plenitude of possible relation.

One more item of business remains, and that is the response to those engaging reviews which provided openings pursued in this chapter. Such a response has been implicit throughout, but perhaps the charge that Foucault did not have a theory of law calls for a more pointed engagement. The specifics of the charge would concede that Foucault did have an 'other law' apart from the contained and instrumentally subordinated variety, but that he did not combine the two types into something that could be seen as his unified theory of law. Whether theory of such a proprietary cast would accord with Foucault's idea of theory is something that will now be questioned, not so much to provide a resounding answer but more to show, by way of a conclusion, what law may be 'in theory'.

For someone who wrote and said such a great deal about law and so profoundly, and for someone who devoted a series of lectures to law (2001a), it may seem at first improbable that Foucault did not 'have' a theory of law. And in this chapter situations have been extracted from what Foucault wrote and said about law which integrate the types of law, the contained and the 'other', into something of a unity. And that integration was itself found to be aligned with some of Foucault's key and abiding concerns. Still, the critic could riposte, all this does not amount to a theory of law distinct and entire.

Whether theory of that kind would be theory for Foucault may be doubted when one regards the ostensibly modest demands Foucault made on theory. Foucault adopted '[t]he notion of theory as a toolkit' (1980b: 145). This is not, or not just, the equivalent of Foucault's gregarious call to use his work as a toolkit, but more a matter of Foucault's seeing theory as 'a practice', something 'local and regional', an 'instrument' brought to bear on 'given situations' (1977e: 208; 1980b: 145). 'Practice' does have a situated solidity to it. It is what is commonly, actively, palpably done. To put something into practice is to commit it to an operatively immediate and secure domain. 'Practice' contrasts in all this with an ethereal, attenuated, conjectural, impractical 'theory'. 'Practice', however, may not be so practically amenable.

Whilst theory is 'an instrument, a *logic* of the specificity of power relations' that same logic extends to 'struggles around' and 'against' such power – to theory as resistance (1980b: emphasis in original, then 1977d: 208). Theory, then, if it is to go on being theory, if it is to remain 'good theory' as it is put, must, like any enduring practice, be receptively self-transforming. Insisting yet more on the obvious, such theory is pursued 'on the basis of reflection', through reflection 'always directed outside itself', with the 'knower . . . straying afield of himself' through 'think[ing] differently' (1980b: 145; 1987a: 8–9; 1987b: 24). This is the same as the knower encountered near the outset, the knower bound in a 'finitude' projected beyond itself, a finitude promising 'that very infinity it refuses' (1970: 314). In this fusion of a situated inside and an outside ever 'free for a new beginning' (1987b: 22), theory joins law as a denizen of exteriority.[18]

That similarity and connection coming at the staged end of this chapter now returns us to its beginning. The generous meaning of 'theory' accommodates 'theor', a legation sent to perform some religious rite or to consult an oracle, including the Delphic oracle who conveyed the pronouncements of the god before and at the beginning of *Oedipus the King*.[19] The compounded connection of events flowing from those pronouncements was effected, for Foucault and as we saw, by a technique that was at once 'juridical, political, and religious' and that reflected, even manifested, 'juridical practices' that included 'judicial practices' generative of 'new forms of subjectivity' and 'models of truth that still circulate in our society' (2001a: 4, 15, 22). What the play offers overall is 'a unique object whose configuration is the manifest form of power' (2001a: 22). Within something of a prospectus to his engagement, Foucault said:

> If there is no relation between knowledge and the things to be known, if the relation between knowledge and known things is arbitrary, if it is a relation of power and violence, the existence of God at the center of the system of knowledge is no longer indispensable.
>
> (2001a: 10)

With theory, that lack and arbitrariness of relation become the contained completeness of theoreticism, to borrow Bakhtin's usage (Bakhtin 1993: 12–13), as against a relation that was for theory, in Foucault's conceiving of it, both a continual opening beyond any containment by power and a resistance to power. With law, that lack and arbitrariness of relation become law as the dependent and violent instrument of power. And yet whilst law is in thrall to its 'articulat[ion] on something other than itself' (1974: 122), it maintains inextricably an illimitable openness, a receptive regard to what is ever beyond power. In giving way to, and giving a way to, what is ever beyond, law is necessarily and also non-violent.

Even as law may not be able to act as a comprised deific substitute 'at the center of the system of knowledge' (2001a: 10), still for Blanchot law 'affirms itself . . . without reference to anything higher: to it alone pure transcendence' (Blanchot 1992: 25; cf. 1989c: 79). In its purity law does not take on a content that is deifically assured, but that same purity inclines it towards the perfectly unbound god of revelation, or even to the voided god of apophatic theology. This is the law that counters the Oedipus 'who joined his knowledge and his power in a certain reprehensible way and whom the *Oedipus* story was meant to expel finally from history' (2001a: 24; cf. 2011: 153).

Acknowledgements

Politic and accurate as it would be to acknowledge editorial kindness, my gratitude to Ben Golder is even more for sustained and sustaining intellectual companionship – and that includes my gratitude for an abundance of references and insight. And my thanks to Marc de Wilde and to Colin Gordon for the provocations.

Notes

1 The slightly arch note sounded with 'origin' reflects Foucault's starting these lectures with a rejection of the idea of the origin by way of distinguishing it from Nietzsche's 'invention', yet he proceeds to commit to a search for 'origins' (2001a: 6–7, 31, 69). This chapter follows the Foucault of 'invention'.

2 This is not merely a retrospective attribution. The performance of the tragedies at 'the festival of the god Dionysus' was 'truly a civic event', an event promoting debate and demotic participation in political life (Goldhill 2007: 120, 123–4). And cf. Foucault (2011: 123) and the emphasis there on '[t]he institution of *nomos*, of the written law, which is not simply political constitution but the very discourse of the social order' (and see 2011: 220–1).

3 Both senses are pointedly imported in the original by 'l'assujettissement des hommes' (1976a: 81).

4 The assiduous near-omission in the story so far of 'periods' of Foucault's work will have to be suspended here to mention the not uncommon charge that Foucault in his 'later' work espoused the liberal subject and saw the care of the self as something simply individualistic. For a cogent rebuttal, see Golder 2010.

5 Skeletal accounts of the kind offered here can appear to be aridly doctrinal. Foucault often situates such things historically in the pieces referred to and at times more expansively (for example, see 2007b).

6 Foucault's famed notion of power as coming 'from below' and as such issuing from a multiplicity of sites can also be squeezed into this scene when he ties that notion to power as generality in such terms as structure, strategy, convergence and hegemonic effects (for example, see 1981: 99–100).

7 This reference is to an ideal. It will, as the argument proceeds here, become increasingly evident that the ideal is an operative or 'actual' one.

8 The translation in the reference here is 'worker of miracles' (2009: 506).

9 Foucault has been much criticised for the narrow focus of his racism, especially with colonial and imperial pathologies receiving at best passing mention. For a criticism that mirrors the analysis of Foucault's expanded idea of racism shortly to come in the text, see Spivak (1988: 290–1). Criticism has extended also to Foucault's ideas of race

and racism generally. My perspective here on both counts would be one gratefully borrowed from Mader (2011: 98–9).

10 An apt editorial caution would impel me to mention that it was only somewhat belatedly that Foucault included madness within the category of productive power as opposed to the simply repressive (for example, see 1993: 204; 2001a: 78, 81–2).

11 An alternative to this attribution of content may be Deleuze's question: 'What tells us that this outside is not a terrifying void and that this life, which seems to put up a resistance, is not just the simple distribution within the void of "slow, partial and progressive" deaths?' (Deleuze 2006: 79). (The quotation seems to be a compression of Foucault (1976: 144).) For Deleuze, Foucault provides something of an answer congruent with what now follows in the text (see Deleuze 2006: 97).

12 The quoted terms, if not quite his sense, come from Deleuze (2006: 49, 93, 100).

13 The appropriation of this dimension of the inside could be seen as enabling the negative universal reference described earlier – enabling the encompassing extraversion of an occidental determinacy (see Blanchot 1993: 196).

14 This is a different translation from that used in this reference (see Nietzsche 2001: 110 [109]).

15 Nietzsche's kinder, if still compatible, interpretation would see Oedipus as the individual who, like 'the suffering Dionysos' in 'his paternal descent from Apollo, god of individuation and just boundaries', 'experiences in his own person the pains of individuation', and that line of interpretation then extends to the loosening of 'the legal knot of the Oedipus fable' in the 'transcendent serenity' of *Oedipus at Colonus* (Nietzsche 1956: 60–1, 65–6).

16 Brought to bear for example on the deviant caught in 'the small captive shadows' that are the prisoners backlit in the Panopticon as prison (1979a: 200; see also 17–18).

17 Compare for instance *Brown v. Board of Education* (1954) and *McCleskey v. Kemp* (1987) in the US Supreme Court. And as the editor has mentioned (personal email communication of 13 November 2011), when engaging with 'the dangerous individual', Foucault 'talks about the ways in which the kinds of predictive evidence going to dangerousness were both welcomed and resisted by the judiciary' (see 2001e: 185–6). To which Dr Golder would add the striking updated instantiation provided by Freiberg (2000).

18 Cf. philosophy as exteriority and the link with theory mediated by 'thought' and 'practice' (in Foucault 1987a: 9 and 2010: 353–4; and see also 1970: 327).

19 *Oxford English Dictionary*, 2nd edn, CD-ROM v 1.3, Oxford: Oxford University Press, 2004, 'theory' meaning 2 and 'theor'. Strictly, only one of the two visits to Delphi involved a legation.

References

Asad, T. (1993) *Genealogies of Religion: Discipline and Reasons of Power in Christianity and Islam*, Baltimore, MD: Johns Hopkins University Press

Bakhtin, M. M. (1993) *Toward a Philosophy of the Act*, trans. V. Liapunov, Austin, TX: University of Texas Press

Blanchot, M. (1992) *The Step Not Beyond*, trans. L. Nelson, Albany, NY: State University of New York Press

___ (1993) *The Infinite Conversation*, trans. S. Hanson, Minneapolis, MN: University of Minnesota Press

Deleuze, G. (2006) *Foucault*, trans. S. Hand, London: Continuum

Deleuze, G. and Guattari, F. (1994) *What is Philosophy?*, trans. H. Tomlinson and G. Burchell, London: Verso

Derrida, J. (1979) *Spurs: Nietzsche's Styles*, trans. B. Harlow, Chicago, IL: University of Chicago Press
Eliot, T. S. (1974a) 'The Waste Land', in *Collected Poems 1909–1962*, London: Faber and Faber
___ (1974b) 'Burnt Norton', in *Collected Poems 1909–1962*, London: Faber and Faber
Foucault, M. (1970) *The Order of Things: An Archaeology of the Human Sciences*, London: Tavistock
___ (1974) *The Archaeology of Knowledge*, trans. A. M. Sheridan Smith, London: Tavistock
___ (1976a) *Histoire de la sexualité: La volonté de savoir*, Paris: Gallimard
___ (1976b) *The Birth of the Clinic: An Archaeology of Medical Perception*, trans. A. M. Sheridan, London: Tavistock
___ (1977a) 'What is an Author?', trans. D. F. Bouchard and S. Simon, in D. F. Bouchard (ed.) *Language, Counter-Memory, Practice: Selected Essays and Interviews*, Ithaca, NY: Cornell University Press
___ (1977b) 'Theatrum Philosophicum', trans. D. F. Bouchard and S. Simon, in D. F. Bouchard (ed.) *Language, Counter-Memory, Practice: Selected Essays and Interviews*, Ithaca, NY: Cornell University Press
___ (1977c) 'Preface to Transgression', trans. D. F. Bouchard and S. Simon, in D. F. Bouchard (ed.) *Language, Counter-Memory, Practice: Selected Essays and Interviews*, Ithaca, NY: Cornell University Press
___ (1977d) 'Nietzsche, Genealogy, History', trans. D. F. Bouchard and S. Simon, in D. F. Bouchard (ed.) *Language, Counter-Memory, Practice: Selected Essays and Interviews*, Ithaca, NY: Cornell University Press
___ (1977e) 'Intellectuals and Power: A Conversation Between Michel Foucault and Gilles Deleuze', trans. D. F. Bouchard and S. Simon, in D. F. Bouchard (ed.) *Language, Counter-Memory, Practice: Selected Essays and Interviews*, Ithaca, NY: Cornell University Press
___ (1979a) *Discipline and Punish: The Birth of the Prison*, trans. A. Sheridan, Harmondsworth: Penguin
___ (1979b) 'My Body, This Paper, This Fire', trans. G. Bennington, *Oxford Literary Review*, 4: 9–28
___ (1980a) 'Georges Canguilhem: Philosopher of Error', *Ideology & Consciousness*, 7: 51–62
___ (1980b) 'Power and Strategies', in C. Gordon (ed.) *Power/Knowledge: Selected Interviews and Other Writings 1972–1977*, Brighton: Harvester Press
___ (1980c) 'Truth and Power', in C. Gordon (ed.) *Power/Knowledge: Selected Interviews and Other Writings 1972–1977*, Brighton: Harvester Press
___ (1981) *The History of Sexuality, Vol. 1: An Introduction*, trans. R. Hurley, Harmondsworth: Penguin
___ (1982) 'Afterword: The Subject and Power', trans. L. Sawyer (of second part, first part written by Foucault in English), in H. L. Dreyfus and P. Rabinow, *Michael Foucault: Beyond Structuralism and Hermeneutics*, Chicago, NY: University of Chicago Press
___ (1987a) *The Use of Pleasure: The History of Sexuality, Vol. 2*, London: Penguin
___ (1987b) 'Maurice Blanchot: The Thought from Outside', trans. B. Massumi, in M. Foucault and M. Blanchot, *Foucault/Blanchot*, New York, NY: Zone Books
___ (1988) 'Truth, Power, Self: An Interview with Michel Foucault', in L. H. Martin *et al.* (eds) *Technologies of the Self: A Seminar with Michel Foucault*, London: Tavistock
___ (1989a) 'An Aesthetics of Existence', trans. J. Johnston, in S. Lotringer (ed.) *Foucault Live (Interviews, 1966–84)*, New York, NY: Semiotext(e)

___ (1989b) 'The Concern for Truth', trans. J. Johnston, in S. Lotringer (ed.) *Foucault Live (Interviews, 1966–84)*, New York, NY: Semiotext(e)
___ (1989c) 'An Historian of Culture', trans. J. Johnston, in S. Lotringer (ed.) *Foucault Live (Interviews, 1966–84)*, New York, NY: Semiotext(e)
___ (1993) 'About the Beginning of the Hermeneutics of the Self', *Political Theory*, 21: 198–227
___ (1997a) 'The Ethics of the Concern of the Self as a Practice of Freedom', trans. P. Aranov and D. McGrawth, in P. Rabinow (ed.) *Essential Works of Foucault 1954–1984 Vol. 1: Ethics*, London: Penguin
___ (1997b) 'Polemics, Politics, and Problematizations', trans. L. Davis, in P. Rabinow (ed.) *Essential Works of Foucault 1954–1984 Vol. 1: Ethics*, London: Penguin
___ (2001a) 'Truth and Juridical Forms', in J. D. Faubion (ed.) *Essential Works of Foucault 1954–1984 Vol. 3: Power*, London: Penguin
___ (2001b) 'The Proper Use of Criminals', in J. D. Faubion (ed.) *Essential Works of Foucault 1954–1984 Vol. 3: Power*, London: Penguin
___ (2001c) 'The Political Technology of Individuals', in J. D. Faubion (ed.) *Essential Works of Foucault 1954–1984 Vol. 3: Power*, London: Penguin
___ (2001d) 'Interview with Michel Foucault', in J. D. Faubion (ed.) *Essential Works of Foucault 1954–1984 Vol. 3: Power*, London: Penguin
___ (2001e) 'About the Concept of the "Dangerous Individual" in Nineteenth-Century Legal Psychiatry', in J. D. Faubion (ed.) *Essential Works of Foucault 1954–1984 Vol. 3: Power*, London: Penguin
___ (2003a) *'Society Must be Defended': Lectures at the Collège de France 1975–76*, trans. D. Macey, London: Allen Lane
___ (2003b) *Abnormal: Lectures at the Collège de France 1974–75*, trans. G. Burchell, New York, NY: Picador
___ (2007a) 'The Incorporation of the Hospital into Modern Technology', trans. E. Knowlton Jr. *et al.*, in J. W. Crampton and S. Elden (eds) *Space, Knowledge and Power: Foucault and Geography*, Aldershot: Ashgate
___ (2007b) *Security, Territory, Population: Lectures at the Collège de France 1977–78*, trans. G. Burchell, Houndmills: Palgrave Macmillan
___ (2008) *The Birth of Biopolitics: Lectures at the Collège de France 1978–1979*, trans. G. Burchell, Houndmills: Palgrave Macmillan
___ (2009) *History of Madness*, trans. J. Murphy and J. Khalfa, Abingdon: Routledge
___ (2010) *The Government of Self and Others: Lectures at the Collège de France 1982–83*, trans. G. Burchell, Houndmills: Palgrave Macmillan
___ (2011) *Leçons sur la volonté de savoir: Cours au Collège de France (1970–1971) suivi de Le savoir d'Oedipe*, Paris: Gallimard/Seuil
Freiberg, A. (2000) 'Guerrillas in our Midst? Judicial Responses to Governing the Dangerous', in M. Brown and J. Pratt (eds) *Dangerous Offenders: Punishment and Social Order*, London: Routledge
Golder, B. (2007) 'Foucault and the Genealogy of Pastoral Power', *Radical Philosophy Review*, 10: 157–76
___ (2010) 'Foucault and the Unfinished Human of Rights', *Law, Culture and the Humanities*, 6: 354–74
Golder, B. and Fitzpatrick, P. (2009) *Foucault's Law*, Abingdon: Routledge
Goldhill, S. (2007) *How to Stage Greek Tragedy Today*, Chicago, IL: The University of Chicago Press

Hume, D. (1985) *A Treatise of Human Nature*, London: Penguin
Hunt, A. and Wickham, G. (1994) *Foucault and Law: Towards a Sociology of Law as Governance*, London: Pluto Press
Lampedusa, G. T. di (2007) *The Leopard*, trans. A. Colquhoun, London: Vintage Books
Mader, M. B. (2011) 'Modern Living and Vital Race: Foucault and the Science of Life', *Foucault Studies*, 12: 97–112
Minkkinen, P. (2011) 'Book Review of Ben Golder and Peter Fitzpatrick *Foucault's Law*', *Social & Legal Studies*, 20: 117–20
Nietzsche, F. (1956) 'The Birth of Tragedy', in F. Nietzsche, *The Birth of Tragedy and the Genealogy of Morals*, trans. F. Golffing, New York, NY: Doubleday
___ (2001) *The Gay Science*, trans. J. Nauckhoff, Cambridge: Cambridge University Press
Norrie, A. (2009) '*Foucault's Law*: Review Commentary', *Law, Social Justice & Global Development*, 14, http://www2.warwick.ac.uk/fac/soc/law/elj/lgd/2009_2 (accessed 1 November 2011)
Pelbart P. P. (2000) 'The Thought of the Outside, the Outside of Thought', *Angelaki: Journal of the Theoretical Humanities*, 5: 201–7
Rahmatian, A. (2007) 'Friedrich Carl von Savigny's *Beruf* and *Volksgeistlehre*', *The Journal of Legal History*, 28: 1–29
Saghafi, K. (1996) 'The "Passion for the Outside": Foucault, Blanchot, and Exteriority', *International Studies in Philosophy*, 28: 79–92
Spivak, G. C. (1988) 'Can the Subaltern Speak?', in C. Nelson and L. Grossberg (eds) *Marxism and the Interpretation of Culture*, Urbana, IL: University of Illinois Press
Vickers, S. (2007) *Where Three Roads Meet*, Edinburgh: Canongate

References to primary sources of law

Brown v. Board of Education 347 US 483 (1954)
McCleskey v. Kemp 481 US 279 (1987)

Chapter 3

Encounters with juridical assemblages: reflections on Foucault, law and the juridical

Alan Hunt

Introduction

This chapter addresses the question of whether Foucault's stimulating and original account of the place of law in modern society excludes or marginalizes the role played by the expansion and diversification of legal mechanisms in constituting modernity. I have addressed related questions previously (Hunt 1992; Hunt and Wickham 1994). My reason for revisiting these issues is that, as my title suggests, what now seems an important dimension of Foucault's discussion, namely the nature and role of the 'juridical', did not receive the attention it deserves. This was largely because his important series of lectures, entitled 'Truth and Juridical Forms' and delivered in Rio de Janeiro in 1973, did not become available in English until 2000 (Foucault 2000). In these lectures, he sets out to outline some working hypotheses 'with a view to a future work' (2000: 1). As was often the case with Foucault's fertile mind, he never pursued this project. I wish to make it clear that I make no pretence of undertaking his unrealized project.

Rather, in this chapter my project will be to draw attention to some suggestive leads that Foucault advanced in those early lectures. This will enable me to put forward some suggestions as to how to advance a sociological approach to conceptualizing juridical forms. I should first explain my interest in the concept of the juridical. Intellectual disciplines not uncommonly proceed for long periods of time with only occasional attention to their domain concepts. For much of the time the core concepts appear self-evident, but then a challenge is mounted to the taken-for-granted conceptualization. Law is just such a self-evident concept; its institutional and professional forms render law a readily visible structure. Every now and then this self-evidence is shaken. Probably the most significant challenge during the last century was that initiated by H. L. A. Hart who refused the previously dominant imperative paradigm in which law had been conceived as a system of prohibitory commands exemplified by the criminal law. Hart's alternative conception produced a model that drew much more heavily on the civil law of legal relations entered into by private citizens typified by contracts and property transactions (Hart 1961). More recently, the ambitions of socio-legal studies have sought to displace this self-evident unitary entity of 'the Law'. One of the ways to facilitate such a project is to deploy the concept of the juridical on the clear understanding that 'the Law' and 'the juridical' are not identical. I shall adopt a conception of the juridical that designates social relations and practices that involve the application of rules by prescribed processes and procedures through which decision-making occurs that involves a determination of the rights of the participants.

The term 'juridical', in most contexts, and in the English language at least, plays a humble adjectival role meaning 'of or pertaining to law or legal proceedings' (*Shorter Oxford English Dictionary*). It is frequently used in academic writing to give a boost to the humble term 'legal' such that 'legal relations' and 'juridical relations' mean pretty much the same thing. I confess to not having bothered too much about the term and plead guilty to occasionally using 'juridical' where I could probably equally well have used 'legal'. But I have become aware of the need to take the term more seriously and of the need to think through the ramifications of the two concepts of the legal and the juridical.

My purpose in exploring Foucault's account of the place of law in modernity is to pay careful attention to the terms in which his formulations are cast and, in particular, to take the concept of the juridical seriously. However, I hasten to insist that this is not merely a definitional issue. And in the present case definitional solutions are rendered virtually impossible by the linguistic complexity of the field, the most obvious example of which is the distinction available in French between 'loi' and 'droit' for which English has to make do with 'law' (roughly, law-as-rules and law-as-rights). In what follows I engage with Foucault's Rio de Janeiro lectures and pick up on some key themes; in particular, I develop the concept of juridical assemblages and use this to explore a number of different treatments of the juridical.

Foucault's Rio de Janeiro lectures

This set of five lectures from 1973, which was delivered before the publication of *Discipline and Punish* (Foucault 1977), exhibits only a loose coherence. Some lectures, especially the fourth and the fifth lectures, are close to the themes developed in that book, but significantly include themes that were not subsequently treated in either *Discipline and Punish* or *The History of Sexuality* (Foucault 1978). It will be these novel themes on which I shall focus my attention in this section of my chapter.

The Rio lectures start with an important linkage to Foucault's earlier writings, in particular to *The Order of Things* (Foucault 1970). His concern is with how the emergence of legal processes is linked to the invention of new fields of knowledge. His emphasis is on the invention of different types of inquiry. The specific interest in juridical practices focuses on practices which define types of subjectivity, forms of knowledge, and relations between man and truth. He identified his specific project as being concerned with 'juridical forms and their evolution in the field of penal law as the generative locus for a given number of forms of truth' (Foucault 2000: 4). He suggests, unfortunately without providing any examples or details, that the knowledge practices originating in the juridical field came to have important implications for the knowledge practices of the natural sciences. It seems evident that it is the invention of 'the inquiry' in the juridical realm that is important for science, but he does nothing even to sketch that connection.

The second lecture pursues an extended commentary on Sophocles' play, *Oedipus Rex*, which is very much part of his power-knowledge explorations of the essays of 1976–8 that are collected in *Power/Knowledge* (Foucault 1980). There are the beginnings of a concern with forms of juridical evidence – in particular, as to what constitutes appropriate testimony in order to establish the cause of the death of the king.

It is only in the third lecture that Foucault takes up an analysis of the transformations in the techniques by which disputes were handled from ancient Greece through to the Renaissance. Early procedure involved a kind of duel or war between individuals, families or tribes by means of oath-swearing. He mentions, but pays little attention to, the conventional thesis that these procedures arose as alternatives to feuding or private vengeance, or as a specific form of feuding. 'Law was thus a regulated way of making war' or a 'ritual form of war', he writes (Foucault 2000: 35): 'Thereafter individuals would no longer have the right to resolve their own disputes, whether regularly or irregularly; they would have to submit to a power external to them, imposing itself as a judicial political power' (Foucault 2000: 42). He is undoubtedly wrong in suggesting that oath-swearing exhibited the presence of an external political power since such localized oath-swearing contests did not require monitoring from outside; instead, they could function effectively so long as neither side could take the risk of resort to open hostilities between the contesting groups. What Foucault fails to provide is any account of either how new dispute procedures less unstable than oath-swearing arose or how external political authority found the need to impose itself on local practices. Rather than pursue the conditions which led to the intervention of more centralized power Foucault turns instead to identify a new stage in which witnesses appeared. He fails to note the small shifts by which our modern concept of 'witness' came into play. Witnesses at first were usually oath-helpers in which the oath procedure depended on the number of helpers that the contestants could muster. Only very gradually did anything that approaches our modern sense of testimony emerge. Its first stage involved the presentation of persons swearing oaths on the basis of their knowledge of the status or reputation of the disputants. Only in a subsequent stage did testimony come to relate to knowledge of the circumstances of the dispute.

These procedures were not so much about testimony but contests as to the respective strength of the parties; the stronger being likely to marshal more 'witnesses'. These contests often became formalized verbal contests counterposing numbers of individual supporters or 'witnesses' and often requiring an exact recitation of a form of words. As feudal relations became consolidated, oath-swearing contests came to take the form of tests by means of bodily physical contests which we know as 'ordeals' (hot coals, and so forth). Alternatively, tests by combat became more frequent in the first instance between the disputants and where persons of rank were involved the combat took place between their appointed champions. Originally, feudal authority was only present to ensure strict compliance with procedure. Foucault does not dwell on the intricacies of these procedural changes but proceeds directly to what is evidently the major contention he wishes to advance, namely, the emergence of the 'inquiry'.

The inquiry is crucial for Foucault because it is this form which originates as a juridical procedure but subsequently widens and expands and becomes a major form of knowledge, generating procedures which come down to the present. What is perplexing about his account is that he provides little specification as to what he regards as the characteristics of an inquiry, nor does he supply any account of its stages of emergence or of its varieties. He only gives two examples of early inquiries: first, the compilation of the Domesday Book in 1086; and, secondly, visitations by bishops around their diocese. What this omits is the considerable variety of inquiries. Domesday was carried out under royal edict from William the Conqueror charging appointed officials to visit each shire to find out how much each landholder held in land and livestock and what it was worth, the main purpose being to lay the basis for levying taxes. Other visitations had more legal objectives, such as to determine the number and character of persons being held charged with offences. In England this developed into the system of Assizes (sittings) in which from the twelfth century royal judges heard the most serious cases, which were presented to them by the Quarter Sessions (local county courts held four times a year). The judges acted under commissions; the commission of oyer and terminer was a general commission to hear and decide cases, while the commission of gaol delivery required the justices to try all prisoners held in the gaols. Other commissions dealt with disputes over landed property. This became the institutional structure of English criminal process and was not finally abolished until the 1970s. Other inquiries had a more specific mandate, being charged with specific investigations into unrest, disturbances or local disputes. Ecclesiastical inquiries took the form of inspections to determine such matters as church attendance, numbers of marriages and christenings, and to establish how bishops and their appointees were conducting church business. These investigations became linked to the jurisdiction of the Church Courts which existed in parallel with the Royal Courts, the two forms competing over jurisdiction for many centuries.

Foucault is keen to make the claim that the techniques adopted in inquiries contributed significantly to the forms in which knowledge is produced within modern societies. He does not specify what it is about inquiries to which he attaches significance. One possibility is that inquiries deployed systematic written record-keeping (Clanchy 1979). Whilst this is significant in terms of swelling the volume of both economic and legal transactions it is uncertain whether it involves the production of new forms of knowledge. Similarly, the increased variety of forms of evidence was undoubtedly significant; witness testimony, written dispositions and cross examination all fuelled the resources at the disposal of both legal and other forms of economic and administrative transactions. The diverse forms invented in the growth of juridical practices certainly added to the efficiency and the rationalization of both legal and administrative practices, but how they contributed to wider knowledge processes is less clear. What was certainly of considerable significance for the subsequent development of juridical processes was the emergence of the judicial inquiry. This was to have profound significance for the legal process in France (where the judicial inquiry was to become a central feature of the judicial process) and indeed elsewhere in Europe, but played a much less significant role in England where the investigative role was kept largely separate from the judicial role.

The fourth lecture starts with a familiar treatment of the rise of the 'disciplinary society' and panopticism from the end of the eighteenth century, but then disrupts the sequential account by turning to what is perhaps the most original feature of these lectures; namely, a comparison of forms of judicial process in England and France from the seventeenth century. Before considering what he has to say it should be noted that in a manner that often typifies Foucault's lectures he provides no sources or citations. He identifies the rise of new mechanisms of control that emerged in obscure corners and outside the state-controlled judicial institutions. In the late seventeenth century, groups emerged who assigned themselves the task of maintaining order and creating new instruments for so doing. The most important of these that Foucault identified was the Society for Reformation of Manners (SRM). He characterised the SRM as a petty bourgeois movement that sought to achieve a 'self-defense against the law' (Foucault 2000: 65), as resisting centralized and oppressive political power. It so happens that I fully researched this movement in the course of preparing my book *Governing Morals: A Social History of Moral Regulation* (Hunt 1999). After the constitutional settlement of 1688 there were competing versions of the reformation project within the Church of England, positions that alternated within the church leadership. The High Church wing wanted a national church, relatively non-sectarian in its theology, which could bind together church, state and gentry. The other wing, the Low Church, had a more radical commitment to the Protestant breach with Rome and were prepared to collaborate with other, non-established, Protestant sects. Both wings made use of a more or less radical discourse condemning the immorality of the Restoration period. In this context, the slogan 'reformation of manners' had broad resonances and was invoked in many different social and religious contexts and, we may presume, reflected a widely diffused popular sentiment. In modern usage, 'manners' has narrowed to refer to the rules of civility. In the early modern period, however, it had a wider meaning; 'manners' designated not only the rules of moral conduct, but the dispositions, attitudes and practices that marked civilized conduct and theological conformity.

A key feature of the reformation of manners was an emphasis on the participatory responsibilities of the devout Christian. This view found its expression in the formation of a wide variety of specifically Christian lay associations concerned to create an expanded space, not only for evangelical commitment by believers, but for such autonomous institutions to act upon the secular world in the name, not so much of the Church, but of Christianity. The SRM was the first of these great lay associations on the margins of organized religion; other important contemporaneous associations were the Society for the Promotion of Christian Knowledge, established in 1699, and the Society for Propagation of the Gospel in Foreign Parts, founded in 1701. The expanded conception of 'reformation' involved a project akin to what Peter Burke (1978) has described as a 'reform of popular culture'. This involves a process in which a social fissure opens up between social strata whereby the stratum seeking to assert dominance first moralizes some part of the culture of the lower strata and then – and this is the significant step – acts upon it as something that can be 'reformed'. The SRM acted as agents who reinforced the separation between a respectable urban merchant class and the unruly urban populace that spanned the social distance from small traders, artisans and apprentices, to the working poor and the under-class of street prostitutes, beggars and discharged soldiers. These strata were to be 'reformed'; in the first stage aspects of their conduct and the sites where it occurred (the streets, taverns, fairs, markets and brothels of rapidly urbanizing London) were moralized under the broad heads of 'immorality' and 'vice' which was then acted upon through the prosecution of some, if not all, forms of popular immorality. The SRM project was to carry forward this reformation of manners by the systematic legal arraignment of a number of forms of public vice, using the currently available legal process of 'informing' by laying information against offenders before Justices of the Peace (JPs). These attempts to initiate prosecutions were undertaken either by lay SRM enthusiasts or by paid agents. The objective was to try to oblige the authorities to enforce the existing laws on the urban under-classes against immorality and vice (street prostitution, brothels, drunkenness, Sabbath trading and occasionally sodomy). The SRM was quite explicit; it declined to promote any new laws, it just pressed for the enforcement of the existing laws. It is clear that Foucault erred in his characterization of the SRM in that it was not a defence against central power, but rather sought to invoke that power for the project of moral regulation.

Foucault implies that other moral regulation movements were launched at the same time as the SRM. He refers, for example, to the Proclamation Society and the Society for the Suppression of Vice (often referred to as the Vice Society). But the Proclamation Society was not formed until 1789; it was an establishment project drawing on peers and high clerics. It explicitly avoided the SRM's tactics of initiating the prosecution of vice offences; rather, it concentrated on pressurizing the authorities to enforce existing laws. It ran out of steam by 1800 and was succeeded by the Society for the Suppression of Vice (SSV), formed in 1802. The membership of the SSV was composed of urban professionals and the commercial classes. Tactically, it mixed anti-vice projects with a hostility to political radicalism, targeting Sunday traders and publishers of radical political texts, and it pressed Parliament for expanded legal regulation. But it was significant through most of the nineteenth century that the political establishment was cautious about promoting moral legislation. These movements were significant interventions into the moral arena, but while they had some contemporary impact their long-term impact was rather more limited.

Foucault also identifies another distinct form of legal activism. He refers to 'self-defense groups of a paramilitary sort' that responded to popular disturbances. He named the Military Infantry of London, and the Company of Artillery. Although I have researched this topic I have found no reference to these organizations. What existed from the end of the seventeenth century through to the mid-nineteenth century were many hundreds of 'felons associations'. In contrast to the SRM and the SSV these were all local associations, both rural and urban. Their focus was on the protection of property interests: they engaged in a variety of activities that can be understood as stemming from the inadequacies of law enforcement. They organized and paid for their own watches and patrols that constituted pressure for the establishment of what were to become police forces. Members initiated and shared the costs of prosecutions of trespassers, smugglers and poachers and in general pressured local JPs to enforce property offences (Philips 1989; Shubert 1981).

The English felons associations contrasted with the complex manifestation of vigilantism in the USA. Some such as the Ku Klux Klan employed terroristic methods to intimidate African-Americans and prevent them registering or voting; but in the twentieth century they were active in using illegal tactics to support the Prohibition Amendment by firing saloons and attacking bootleggers. Typically, American vigilantism used coercive tactics where no legal institutions existed in order to intervene in socio-economic clashes, such as those between ranchers and farmers, or where one side in a hostility was powerful enough to ignore legal provisions, and to intervene in conflicts such as those between farmers and cattle rustlers.

The distinctive feature of the movements that sprang up in English civil society that acted on the periphery of the legal system was that they were neither entirely inside nor outside the juridical realm. Foucault contrasted the French experience with an account of *lettres de cachet*. These were a key instrument of absolutism. They functioned through supplication to the absolutist authorities; they were significantly mobilized by individuals seeking to elicit intervention in familial relations. Husbands outraged by the behaviour of their wives and fathers dissatisfied with their children applied for a *lettre de cachet* which, if granted, led to the imprisonment of the offending family member for an indefinite period until such time as familial authority was successfully reasserted. Rather strangely, Foucault describes this practice as an action 'from below' (Foucault 2000: 65). I suggest it is more accurate to regard *lettres de cachet* as actions 'from above', since they were overwhelmingly invoked by aristocrats and depended on their relations with ranking functionaries within the absolutist regime.

The comparison between England and France is best understood in terms of the earlier growth of civil society in England which manifested itself in the variety of forms in which civil associations both acted on their own account to pursue their own interests and acted upon the authorities, both local and national, to press for juridical action in the form of the implementation of existing laws and, occasionally, to secure new laws. While I have identified problems with Foucault's treatment, these lectures were nevertheless important in opening up the field of the juridical to which I now turn.

Juridical assemblages

Since the early phases of legal development which Foucault explored in his Rio de Janeiro lectures, there has been a continuing expansion in both the volume and the forms of law and in the aspects of social life on which law impacts. It is also evident that law has become increasingly connected with other forms of governance such as administration and regulation. It is now more important than ever finally to abandon the project pursued for so long by legal philosophy and jurisprudence, namely, the attempt to define 'What is law?' in such a way as to separate and distinguish it from all related practices and institutions and, at the same time, to constitute it as a unitary object of inquiry captured by the ubiquitous phrase 'the Law'. Today, we need to explore the ways in which law is enmeshed with other mechanisms, practices and institutions. This project is important because both politically and theoretically it seems evident that law is both part of the problem and part of the solution. This epigrammatic formulation finds its most explicit and heavily theorized expression in Jürgen Habermas's account of the way in which law is both part of 'the system' (law as medium) and also functions to protect 'the lifeworld' (law as institution) from colonization by 'the system' (Habermas 1987).

In order to inquire into the connections between law and other mechanisms of governance, this chapter takes the form of an inquiry into how we can advance an understanding of law as a 'juridical assemblage' by interrogating the concepts of 'norm', 'legal' and 'juridical' which Foucault's interventions have brought into proximity. An assemblage involves the presence of elements that do not necessarily constitute a system. It is particularly pertinent to consider the part played by norms within juridical assemblages, and it is to this which I now turn.

Norms, normal, normative

Foucault argues that 'the law operates more and more as a norm' (Foucault 1978: 144). What does he mean by this? I will suggest that there is an interesting bifurcation in Foucault's usage of the term 'norm'. The etymological root of 'norm' can be traced back to the Latin 'norma', a carpenter's set-square. This gave rise to the first extension to mean 'perpendicular'. The key developments did not occur until the nineteenth century when there was an explosion of new meanings. First came the very widely used word 'normal', meaning an 'average of observed quantities' (*Oxford English Dictionary*, 1859) and this expanded further to designate a 'usual state or condition'. At much the same time (1865) the words 'normalize' and 'normalization' came to specify the process of making something conform to the normal or average. Last to emerge was 'normative' (in 1880); and it is in this sense that the bifurcation in meaning is most evident.[1] On the one hand it remains close to its objectivist roots meaning 'involving a norm or standard' but it also departs from this descriptive lineage by designating the expansion of meaning that is involved in the transition from standard to values (as in 'social norms').

Foucault's usage of the term 'norm' is predominantly influenced by the objectivist tradition. This is especially evident in the emphasis he places upon the link between 'discipline' and 'normalization'. The class-room and the factory are involved in projects that create normal adults, normal citizens and normal workers. Thus when he uses 'norm' its meaning is nearly always close to 'normal' and thus 'normalization' specifies the processes whereby individuals are rendered 'normal'. This usage is apparent in his remark that the:

> judges of normality are present everywhere. We are in the society of the teacher-judge, the doctor-judge, the educator-judge, the social worker-judge; it is on them that the universal reign of the normative is based.
>
> (Foucault 1977: 304)

What implications do these etymological considerations have for Foucault's thesis that the 'law operates more and more as a norm'? The sense to be attributed to this formulation depends on whether his usage of 'norm' leans towards 'normal' or 'normative' in the sense of the importation of values. Foucault's emphasis on norm as the inculcation of the normal would seem to imply that he advances the contention that law articulates what has been designated as normal (normal conduct) and then seeks to fix it prescriptively by conferring normative force on it.

Yet there is an alternative interpretation of Foucault's thesis that law comes to operate as a norm if the term 'norm' is linked to the 'normative' – although, as I have suggested, this is not his immediate intent. This would imply that law comes less to be characterized by the formulation of prescriptive rules of conduct in the form 'If conduct X occurs sanctions Y shall be imposed'. There is a move away from legal rules that take the form of interdictions and prohibitions, the law which says 'No'. Rather, law becomes increasingly characterized by legal rules that take a form that enunciates norms which are matters of policy or principle. For example, when a legal rule requires parties to act in 'good faith' such a rule stipulates a normative criteria without specifying the particular conduct that would constitute a breach of the requirement. Thus the increasing importance that attaches to the legal deployment of norms is one, but only one, of the means whereby, over a protracted period, the range and reach of legal incursions expand. It should be noted that legal forms combine prescriptive rules along with general norms or principles.

Nikolas Rose and Mariana Valverde offer a somewhat different account of the link between 'norm' and 'normal'. They proceed by exploring the distinction between 'rules' and 'norms':

> A rule is external to that which is governed: it is imposed upon its subjects in relation to an extrinsic standard of authority, morality, virtue, order, duty or obedience. A norm, on the other hand, appears – or claims – to emerge out of the very nature of that which is governed. Its normativity is predicated upon and justified by its normality: the normal child, the normal family, normal conduct, normal business practice.
>
> (Rose and Valverde 1998: 572)

Not only does this formulation elide norm and normal, but it gives a strangely ethereal quality to the norm. Furthermore it seems to rely upon a strangely un-Foucaultian quest for an origin in 'the very nature' of that which is governed. My reservations can be illustrated by considering the example of the 'normal child'. Such a child is not the statistically average child, but rather a construction built upon a statistical average by the addition of normative judgments as to what the attributes the normal child *should* exhibit (age of walking, reading and so forth) and thus does not arise from 'the very nature' of the child.[2] In precisely the same way legal (and other) rules enshrine a normative judgment about the proper conduct of the class of persons to whom the rules are applied. Thus the Rose and Valverde distinction between rule and norm would seem unsatisfactory.[3]

There is a further feature of Foucault's use of the term norm to be considered. It is one that is connected with his preoccupation with the processes of normalization that play a central part in his account of disciplinary mechanisms. His deployment of the concept norm links discipline to the problematization of the role of law:

> The power of the Norm appears through the disciplines. Is this the new law of modern society? Let us say rather that, since the eighteenth century, it has joined other powers – the Law, the Word (*Parole*) and the Text, Tradition – imposing new delimitations upon them.
>
> (Foucault 1977: 184)

Foucault is at pains to distinguish between 'law' and 'discipline'. The following is probably his key formulation:

> The disciplinary mechanisms secreted a 'penality of the norm', which is irreducible in its principles and functioning to the traditional penality of the law. The minor court that seems to sit permanently in the buildings of discipline, and which sometimes assumes the theatrical form of the great legal apparatus, must not mislead us; it does not bring, except for a few formal

> remnants, the mechanisms of criminal justice to the web of everyday existence; or at least that is not its essential role; the disciplines created – drawing on a whole series of ancient procedures – a new functioning of punishment.
> (Foucault 1977: 183)

In this passage Foucault proposes a demarcation between legal and disciplinary punishment. By 'penality of the norm' Foucault seems to suggest that the disciplines work by attaching penalties for breach of 'normalized' conduct. But it is far from clear why such penalties are in some essential aspect different from legal penalties. It is undoubtedly the case that discipline operates through micro-penalties, but these are not in any sense that he discloses 'irreducible' to the forms of legal penalties in the same way that legal sanctions include a wide variety of what may likewise be termed 'micro-penalties' (tariffs of 'points' for traffic offences, cautions, conditional discharges).[4]

Having considered Foucault's contention that 'law acts as a norm', I return to the second element of his basic formulation (quoted above) that states that 'the juridical institution is increasingly incorporated into a continuum of apparatuses (medical, administrative and so on) whose functions are for the most part regulatory' (Foucault 1978: 144). He is undoubtedly correct in drawing attention to the increasing significance of dispersed forms of government, which I am calling a juridical apparatus, that make use of a wide range of both state and non-state expertise, the enhanced role of the 'medical, administrative, and so on', along with the dispersed forms of technical expertise associated with the period that has come to be characterized as the welfare state.[5] It is, however, less than self-evident that law becomes 'incorporated' along with these other forms of expertise. Rather, the relationship between legal and other forms of expertise is better grasped as one that shifts between competition and cooperation between legal and other forms of expertise in which legal professionals seek to harness external expertise to their own internal mode of thought. Law receives information from outside (for example, expert testimony from forensic scientists or psychiatrists); and this information is then evaluated not in terms of the rules of the expert disciplines, but rather according to legal canons.[6] Briefly, it is important to draw attention to the battle which legal expertise and judicial discourses wage continuously to assert their primacy. Legal expertise strives to reduce other forms of expertise, whether it be the complexities of DNA testing or the arcane knowledge of psychiatry, to the status of a servant rather than a master of the legal arena. Thus, rather than an already existent juridical apparatus, I suggest it is more useful to think in terms of less unitary juridical assemblages.

There can be little doubt that the developing and shifting role of norms provides a significant feature of the trajectory of modern law. However, we should reject any suggestion that it is evidence of the diminution of the role of law and it is certainly not confirmation that law is becoming subsumed under a generalized disciplinary regime. In particular, great caution should be exercised in assuming that there is a necessary linkage between the role of legal norms and processes of normalization. Having considered the relationship between law and norms, the relationship between the legal and the juridical can now be explored.

The juridical

It is now time to return to the central issue under debate – namely, the place of the concept of the juridical in the theorization of law (and to an assessment of Foucault's use of this concept). Unfortunately, this is by no means an easy task. I will first consider Foucault's own treatment of the concepts of the juridical and the legal. In order to gain access to his usage of the concept of the juridical it is necessary to consider his frequently used concept of the 'juridico-discursive' conception of power, for it is in this context that he provides his most explicit elaboration of the concept of the juridical. It is this concept that governs both the 'thematics of repression and the theory of the law' (Foucault 1978: 82).[7] His substantive contention is that it is necessary to free ourselves from a 'juridico-discursive representation' of power (Foucault 1978: 82). He specifies the characteristics of 'juridico-discursive' power as:

- it lays down 'rules' that take a binary form (e.g. licit/illicit, permitted/forbidden);
- it is negative, it says 'no';
- it lays down the law by means of a 'cycle of prohibition' ('Thou shall not. . . .'); and, lastly,
- it manifests itself in a discourse that 'speaks' the rule.

(Foucault 1978: 84)

From this last feature we discover how it is that the 'discursive' aspect enters the 'juridico-discursive'. In brief, the juridico-discursive is a prohibitory discourse.

Far from drawing a distinction between the juridical and the legal, Foucault's formulations suggest an identity between the juridical and an imperative conception of the legal.[8] The equation of law with prohibitory rules or commands ('Thou shall not . . .') reinforces the commonplace reduction of law to criminal law. This is the position famously espoused by the English jurist John Austin, who defined law in just this way, namely as the commands of the sovereign backed by sanctions (Austin 1955). Much of the history of legal theory, particularly in the English-speaking tradition, has been taken up with breaking free from this imperative fallacy that equates law with commands (Hart 1961; Dworkin 1977). It is not necessary to retrace that important but lengthy journey but I will, without any claim to be exhaustive, consider some of the more important discussions of the ways in which the concept of the juridical has been understood and deployed in literature engaging with Foucault.

Victor Tadros, for his part, is content to return to just such an imperative conception of the juridical, instanced above. He argues that 'law, for Foucault, is not necessarily juridical and . . . the juridical does not always find its expression in law' (Tadros 1998: 76).[9] While implying (correctly in my view) that law is not reducible to commands, he only succeeds in leaving Foucault stranded because he offers no distinctive conception of what is meant by legal. Tadros makes one further attempt to identify the juridical, by picking up on Foucault's contention that the juridical conception of power expresses itself in prohibitions of specific 'acts' that function by means of binary oppositions distinguishing between acts which are prohibited and those which are permitted.[10] From this line of thought, Tadros advances his own definition of the juridical as 'any form of power which attempts to prevent a certain type of action through the threat of legal or social sanctions' (Tadros 1998: 78). In so doing, he fails to notice that this results in a full-scale retreat to an imperative conception of law as orders/rules backed by sanctions. The only element of his definition which escapes the imperative fallacy is the apparently innocent phrase 'and social sanctions'. But the phrase is far from innocent since it expands the reach of 'the juridical' to any sanctioned conduct thereby giving the juridical an unsustainable reach. Once the concept becomes this wide it loses any analytic capacity; moreover, it returns us to the detour that impacted so heavily on the social sciences during the 1960s and 1970s when all exercise of social power became subsumed under the generic label of 'social control'. While Tadros performs the useful task of alerting us to the possibility that there might be a significant distinction to be drawn between the juridical and the legal, he fails to advance a viable distinction between the two.

François Ewald, significant because of his association as a student with Foucault, proposes a rather different distinction between the legal and the juridical. He argues that it is necessary to 'distinguish between law (and its formal expression) and the juridical' (Ewald 1990: 138).[11] He locates the juridical historically, in much the same way as does Foucault, arguing that it 'served as a "code" that enabled monarchical power to constitute itself, formalize its structures and reflect upon its own workings' (Ewald 1990: 139). The juridical in this context refers to the discourses through which monarchical power legitimized itself. Thus Ewald appears to equate the juridical with constitutional discourses. Such a move narrows the reach of the term to something like constitutionalism or constitutional discourses. It is not clear that this view of the history helps to account for the continuing waves of constitutionalization that marked the transition from monarchical regimes to representative democracies, let alone the expanded role of rights discourses into wider social fields.

Ewald's discussion becomes more significant when he links it to his own field of historical research on the emergence of industrial standards, weights and measures and, more generally, to the emergence of social insurance and workmen's compensation from the late nineteenth century (Ewald 1986a). In the era in which government became increasingly preoccupied with the socio-economic conditions of the working population, the era of 'biopower', these forms of governance typically involve an expanse of regulation. Ewald argues that 'the most typical mechanisms of juridical power can no longer be represented in legal form' (Ewald 1990: 139). It is in this context that it becomes apparent that Ewald employs a very different conception of 'norm' to that encountered thus far. Here the norm is a means of creating and disseminating common standards and these are generated not by a legislature, but by a host of specialist institutions which function to 'produc[e] ... a common standard' and to introduce 'measurement techniques and standards' (Ewald 1990: 159). Under these conditions 'Parliament no longer establishes the fundamental principles of law; it can only set forth regulations' (Ewald 1990: 155).[12] Some care is needed at this point about terminology. The standards (norms) are largely created outside legislation in the form that I would prefer to term 'regulations'. What the modern legislature does, and significantly also the courts of law, is to attempt to exercise some measure of surveillance over regulatory processes. Ewald draws the conclusion that in the era of biopower 'any reference to the juridical is illusory since the language of bio-power is purely technical and has almost nothing to do with the law as such' (Ewald 1990: 159).

While I concur with the emphasis Ewald places on the extra-parliamentary production of standards and other regulatory devices, he goes too far in claiming that these mechanisms have 'nothing to do with the law as such'. Courts seek to exercise supervisory jurisdiction; most commonly this takes the form of laying down principles (norms in the 'normative' sense) which provide the grounds for the exercise of legal jurisdiction with respect to standards and regulations. For example, the requirement that standards be 'reasonable' is frequently invoked as a ground for asserting court jurisdiction. As a consequence of this assertion of legal jurisdiction, standards and regulations are commonly promulgated in a way which takes account of these potential juridical interventions.

The interpenetration of law and regulation can perhaps best be captured by Habermas's concept of juridification, which allows one to make the point that much discipline and regulation functions 'in the shadow of law' by drawing attention to the way in which these mechanisms increasingly tend to be cast in forms that more or less mimic the juridical form (Habermas 1987). An example familiar to many readers is to be found in the disciplinary codes of universities which have been becoming increasingly legalistic. Two factors explain this development: first, what we may call the 'form of rights' has come increasingly to dominate the discursive field of discipline; and, secondly, the codes are written with a close eye, some may say an over-close eye, on avoiding litigation that might arise from carelessly drafted provisions. The alternative approach is to attend to an important feature of the interpenetration between law and regulation; namely, that rather than one form or the other becoming transcendent they are in a permanent condition of competition. Regulatory mechanisms attempt to immunize themselves from juridical scrutiny and jurisdiction while legal institutions strive to expand their surveillance over regulatory practices.

There are other positions that have employed a distinction between the legal and the juridical. Perhaps the best known is Evgeny Pashukanis's commodity theory of law (Pashukanis 1980). He argued that the juridical form arose from the commodity relations which structure the market and are expressed in the creation of individualized rights. The juridical is thus profoundly implicated in capitalist economic relations. He distinguished the juridical from legislation which characterized the growth of state economic regulation within capitalist economies from the late nineteenth century onwards. Pashukanis insisted that the growth of state regulation does not constitute an expanding role for law; on the contrary, it marks the beginning of the 'inevitable withering away of law' (Pashukanis 1980: 240). It is not my intention to debate the merits of Pashukanis's position, but merely to draw attention to the fact that his theory involves a conception of the juridical which focuses attention on contractual and other private legal relations arising from economic exchange that generate actionable private rights.[13] However, his contribution is significant for its attention to the interconnection between economic relations and their constitutive role in the emergence of distinctive juridical relations.

A more recent and contrasting attempt to articulate the distinctive features of juridical relations is advanced by Jerry Palmer and Frank Pearce. They identify the juridical relation as: 'a form of social organization whose basis is the ascription of clear rights and obligations devolving equally upon all individuals, a set of legal rules and specified penalties' (Palmer and Pearce 1983: 363).[14] This distinction between the juridical and the legal is thus one between the general (the juridical) and the particular (the legal). This approach is not without its problems. First, while universal rights are important in some fields of law such as criminal liability and citizenship rights, this is by no means typical and has no necessary general application in many fields of law. Secondly, they incorporate a reprise for Foucault's concern with 'penality'; as has already been noted this preoccupation arises from inquiries which take as their general model an imperative version of criminal law as commands backed by sanctions. In addition it is by no means self-evident that it is necessary to invoke 'legal rules' since prescriptive legal rules (generated by legislative or judicial authority) are not necessary conditions for the creation of enforceable rights as the example of the simple contract makes clear, where self-binding enforceable lawmaking is its core feature as exemplified in Pashukanis's account of juridical relations.

The alternative conception of the juridical that I now advance is intended to overcome the problems with the versions of the juridical concept discussed above. I suggest that the concept of the juridical can be most fruitfully employed to designate those social relations and practices that involve the application of rules by means of prescribed processes and procedures through which decision-making occurs that involves a determination of the rights of the participants and where this invocation of rights serves to confer legitimacy on such decisions. The juridical thus designates a process model that serves to provide a useful and fairly stable distinction from the legal. The 'legal' is characterized by its primary orientation to the making of, the content of, the interpretation and application of, and, in general, the priority accorded to, substantive rules. In contrast, the juridical is oriented towards the means (rather than the content) that are deployed in response to specific social conflicts. It follows that the juridical can be differentiated from other forms of response to conflict, such as arguing, shouting, fighting or forms of direct action. The juridical invests everyday relations with what may be termed a supplement which serves to differentiate their content from mere usage or custom.[15]

The realms of the juridical and the legal, although overlapping, are not coextensive. It should be stressed that the proposed distinction between the juridical and the legal is not a closed distinction such that any particular situation must be either one or the other. Rather, both dimensions will often be present; situations of conflict may involve both juridical and legal elements while others may partake of neither. Thus, for example, debating has a pronounced juridical form in that it requires the parties to agree to some minimal procedural requirements which confer specific rights upon participants and thereby distinguishes debating from mere arguing.[16] Negotiation is a more complex process for while it involves juridical elements relating to its processes, it also involves non-juridical elements such as threats of coercive conduct (lockouts, strikes and so forth) which can and do impinge on the juridified forms of 'normal' negotiation. Even forms of fighting can become complexly implicated in juridification. War is conducted in the shadow of rules of war, war crimes and, increasingly, human rights discourses.[17] A now defunct, but classic instance of 'juridical fighting' was the 'duel' conducted according to strict procedures whose origins lay in the practices of chivalry.

Juridical processes create roles for 'juridical agents' and it is important to stress that these are not necessarily 'legal agents' and certainly not necessarily 'professional legal agents' (judges, lawyers). Juridical agents employ a procedural orientation ('following the procedures laid down'). Important instances of 'juridical agents' are the roles of arbitrators and mediators; additionally, many non-specialized agents perform juridical functions in non-professional capacities. Thus, the officials of an association who implement stipulated procedures for the election of officers act as juridical agents; if a dispute arises over the eligibility of a candidate they engage in adjudication which evaluates the rights of the parties and thus functions juridically.

A more detailed illustration of juridical processes is provided in the important field of the interaction between law and administration that extends my earlier remarks on the competition between legal and regulatory institutions. Administrative law is intensively juridified in that the matters to which it is applied frequently concern the extent to which legal remedies are available to disturb administrative decisions. The most general principle that can be stated is that courts of law do not purport to make substantive regulatory decisions, but rather seek to regulate the processes whereby administrative decisions are reached. Thus an important arena of state activity that is a consequence of the complex network of administrative bodies which used to act subject only to political control by a centralized hierarchy (ministries, cabinets) has become increasingly juridified and epitomizes what Foucault has termed the governmentalization of the state (Foucault 1979: 21).

Another way of explicating the proposed conception of the juridical is to note that it generally exhibits a 'legal form'. A legal form identifies the way in which social relations are constructed so as to render them justiciable and thus capable of being subjected to juridical processes and determination through the application of legal rules. A crucial point is that there is no single legal form, but rather a variety of legal forms which coexist in complex combination.[18] Neither the 'penal legal form' (the legal form to which Foucault generally refers) nor Pashukanis's 'commodity legal form' exists in isolation. The distinct legal forms exhibit a periodization, but do not occur in any linear sequence. Thus, for example, in the period of the great expansion of state legal systems in the late Middle Ages there existed – in complex combination – feudal forms characterized by legal rules and processes that associated both rights and liabilities with status;[19] these became increasingly penetrated by features of private property forms. These forms gradually displaced local customary forms of law (the law of place/status) under pressure from an expansionary logic that subjected whole populations to increasingly centralized forms of criminal law. Over the subsequent centuries these legal forms were supplemented, for example, by corporate legal forms and administrative legal forms which laid the basis for forms of social law which were characteristic of the growth of welfare states.

It is not my purpose to chart all of these shifting legal forms. However, in order to avoid any linear or evolutionary model of legal forms a concept is needed which focuses attention on the key significance of the complex coexistence and interpenetration of multiple forms. This task can be performed by making use of the concept of 'juridical assemblages' which designates the coexistence of different combinations of legal, judicial and normative elements.[20] The concept of assemblage has come to attract considerable interest. Most prominently it was used by Deleuze and Guattari in *A Thousand Plateaus* (1987). In an interview Deleuze defined the concept in these terms: 'In assemblages you find states of things, bodies, various combinations, hodgepodges; but you also find utterances, modes of expression, and whole regimes of signs' (Deleuze 2007: 177). I do not wish to follow Deleuze into the realm of hodgepodges, but rather to take up the concern with heterogeneity in the sense of a group of elements or components which first of all change the specific combination of elements, but more importantly exhibit changes in the specific modes of combination. Thus, juridical assemblages exhibit different combinations of practices, discourses, expertises and institutions in which the different elements vary in their role and significance. Sometimes a juridical assemblage is very proximate to a standard conception of law such that courts, judges, rules and decisions are the most prominent features. But in other instances, as for example in mediation practices, judges and rules are much less evident, while negotiation, compromise and norms are to the fore. The key feature of the assemblage concept is that it involves a differential set of combinatory elements and that these elements play different roles in each variant assemblage.

The deployment of the concept of the assemblage makes it possible to bring together some of the disparate elements found in Foucault's engagement with the juridical field. We no longer need to castigate him for his narrow emphasis on the imperative dimensions of law. We can appreciate that his focus on the interaction between different fields of power, knowledge and governance manifested itself in his substantive preoccupation with the ways in which forms of law interact with mechanisms of discipline and with strategies and techniques of governance. This in no way impedes the interrogation of the diverse forms in which the historically changing forms of the juridical manifest themselves where disciplinary elements do not constitute the central features of juridical assemblages.

Notes

1 Georges Canguilhem offers a politicized interpretation of these etymological changes: 'Between 1759, when the word "normal" appeared, and 1834 when the word "normalized" appeared, a normative class had won the power to identify – a beautiful example of ideological illusion – the function of social norms, whose content it determined, with the use that that class made of them' (Canguilhem 1978: 151).

2 Mitchell Dean makes the important point that the 'normal man' is a fictional entity that functions as a means through which society views itself. Norms in themselves are counter-factual and self-referential; that is, they operate 'as if' such a 'normal man' existed and proceed to act as if they specify the characteristics of the aggregate population (Dean 1998).

3 Rose subsequently advances a formulation closer to the position argued in this chapter. He draws attention to the ambiguity of the dual sense of norm as average and as desirable. Once the norms of conduct are elaborated they simultaneously define the capacities of the normal individual and individualize the miscreant who deviates from them: 'From this point on, the norm would be that which is socially worthy, statistically average, scientifically healthy *and* personally desirable' (Rose 1999: 76, emphasis in original).

4 It might be worth further consideration as to whether these 'legal' micro-penalties could be considered evidence of the interpenetration of the disciplines into the corpus of law.

5 We may note in passing that Foucault sets up an interesting contrast between 'discipline' (directed towards the individual body) and 'regulation' (directed towards the population). It is this shift of focus to 'biopower' that leads on to his increasing preoccupation with government and political rationalities (Foucault 1978: 139–45).

6 This line of argument is most fully developed by the variants of autopoietic theory advanced by Luhmann (1985) and Teubner (1992).

7 The concept of the 'juridico-discursive' theory of power plays a key role in Foucault's account of the way in which sex and power are connected and, in particular, how the conventional image (which he styles the 'repressive hypothesis') that sex is something that was 'repressed' during the nineteenth century and is now in the process of being liberated, is fundamentally flawed. For detailed discussion and criticism of Foucault's treatment of the 'repressive hypothesis', see Giddens 1992; Hussain 1981; Porter 1991.

8 This imperative conception is particularly evident in one of his most characteristic descriptions of law: 'Law cannot help but be armed, and its arm, *par excellence*, is death; to those who transgress it replies, at least as a last resort, with that absolute menace. The law always refers to the sword' (Foucault 1978: 144, emphasis in original).

9 Tadros's treatment of the juridical is advanced in the context of the 'inadequacies of recent jurisprudential scholarship on Foucault' in the course of which he criticizes my 'expulsion thesis' on the grounds that it commits the error of equating 'juridical' with 'law' (Tadros 1998: 77).

10 Foucault uses the argument that law prohibits 'acts' while 'discipline' is directed at the individual. It hardly needs saying that while simple criminal prohibitions fit this vision of law, the wide-ranging arenas of private and administrative law do not. I see no value in claiming that these forms of law are directed at individuals since the distinction acts/individuals seems to offer little help in formulating a distinction between law and discipline.

11 I pass over Ewald's unexplained suggestion that there is a distinction to be drawn between 'law' and 'its formal expression'.

12 Ewald associates the creation of standards with the emergence of 'social law' (Ewald 1986b) in a line of thought which draws on an earlier tradition exemplified by Georges Gurvitch's advocacy of social law as the basis for a modern sociology of law and as a political programme (Gurvitch 2001).

13 Although very different in its substantive content, Wesley Hohfeld's (1978) discussion of juridical relations is heavily focused on private juridical relations. Hohfeld was primarily concerned with the internal classification of such relations.

14 Palmer and Pearce challenge the opposition which Foucault sets up between law and discipline. They argue that in bourgeois society they are not opposed; rather, each is the support of the other. I elaborate a position compatible with their line of argument, below.

15 There is at least one instance in which Foucault makes use of a conception of the juridical similar to that which I propose. In *The Care of the Self* he refers to the emergent principles governing marital sexual relations as laying the ground for a 'subsequent "juridification" of marital relations' (Foucault 1986: 184).

16 It may be noted that some forms of arguing may develop quasi-juridical forms. For example, academic disciplines develop protocols, not only about the forms of evidence capable of lending legitimacy to the content of communicative activity, but also about the permissible forms of rhetoric in which argumentation may be expressed.

17 It should be stressed that this does not imply that war is necessarily conducted according to these rules. Indeed there has been an interesting mutation from an emphasis on the rules about the conduct of war (Geneva Convention) to an *ex post facto* approach organized around discourses of war crimes and genocide.

18 It is particularly important to avoid any suggestion that legal forms involve any necessary historical sequence. While the forms of law have a history no assumptions should be made about its 'stages'. This point is well argued by Blankenburg (1984).

19 It should be noted that status was never fully displaced by individual or associational rights; for example, it persisted in labour law with the master–servant doctrine and in family law where status rights were attributed to husbands and fathers. More generally there has been an influential strand of argument which suggests that status has been accorded a new lease of life in association with the rise of the welfare state (Friedman 1959; Selznick 1969).

20 The concept of the 'juridical assemblage' fulfils much the same role as the concept of the 'legal complex' suggested by Rose and Valverde (1998: 571) and Bourdieu's concept 'juridical field' (Bourdieu 1987). Bourdieu draws attention to the fact that a field does not exist as an abstract social space but is the result of activity and work. Bourdieu views the juridical field as being organized around a professionally generated 'legal culture' (professional instituted assumptions, values and so forth). Struggle and competition occur with those outside the field for legitimacy and control of boundaries. This conception of the struggle between fields is similar to my discussion, above, of the competition between courts and regulatory agencies.

References

Austin, J. (1955) *The Province of Jurisprudence Determined and the Uses of the Study of Jurisprudence*, London: Weidenfeld & Nicolson

Blankenburg, E. (1984) 'The Poverty of Evolutionism: A Critique of Teubner's Case for "Reflexive Law"', *Law & Society Review*, 18: 273–90

Bourdieu, P. (1987) 'The Force of Law: Towards a Sociology of the Juridical Field', *Hastings Law Journal*, 38: 805–54

Canguilhem, G. (1978) *On the Normal and the Pathological*, trans. C. Fawcett, Dordrecht: D. Reidel

Clanchy, M. T. (1979) *From Memory to Written Records in England 1066–1307*, London: Edward Arnold

Dean, M. (1998) 'Normalising Democracy: Foucault and Habermas on Law, Liberalism and Democracy', in S. Ashenden and D. Owen (eds) *Foucault Contra Habermas: Recasting the Dialogue Between Genealogy and Critical Theory*, London: Sage

Deleuze, G. (2007) 'Eight Years Later: 1980 Interview', in G. Deleuze, *Two Regimes of Madness: Texts and Interviews 1975–1995*, New York, NY: Semiotext(e)

Deleuze, G. and Guattari, F. (1987) *A Thousand Plateaus: Capitalism and Schizophrenia*, trans. B. Massumi, Minneapolis, MN: University of Minnesota Press

Dworkin, R. (1977) 'The Model of Rules: I', in R. Dworkin, *Taking Rights Seriously*, Cambridge, MA: Harvard University Press

Ewald, F. (1986a) *L'état providence*, Paris: Grasset

___ (1986b) 'A Concept of Social Law', in G. Teubner (ed.) *Dilemmas of Law in the Welfare State*, Berlin: de Gruyter

___ (1990) 'Norms, Discipline and the Law', *Representations*, 30: 138–61

Foucault, M. (1970) *The Order of Things: An Archaeology of the Human Sciences*, New York, NY: Pantheon Books

___ (1977) *Discipline and Punish: The Birth of the Prison*, trans. A. Sheridan, New York, NY: Pantheon Books

___ (1978) *The History of Sexuality, Vol. 1: An Introduction*, trans. R. Hurley, New York, NY: Pantheon Books

___ (1979) 'Governmentality', *Ideology & Consciousness*, 6: 5–21

___ (1980) 'Two Lectures', in C. Gordon (ed.) *Power/Knowledge: Selected Interviews and Other Writings 1972–1977*, Brighton: Harvester Press

___ (1986) *The Care of the Self, Vol. 3: The History of Sexuality*, trans. R. Hurley, New York, NY: Pantheon Books

___ (2000) 'Truth and Juridical Forms', in J. D. Faubion (ed.) *Essential Works of Foucault 1954–1984 Vol. 3: Power*, New York, NY: The New Press

Friedmann, W. (1959) *Law in a Changing Society*, Harmondsworth: Penguin

Giddens, A. (1992) 'Foucault and Sexuality', in A. Giddens, *The Transformation of Intimacy: Love, Sexuality and Eroticism in Modern Societies*, Cambridge: Polity Press

Gurvitch, G. (2001) *The Sociology of Law*, New Brunswick: Transaction Books

Habermas, J. (1987) *The Theory of Communicative Action, Vol. 2: Lifeworld and System*, Boston, MA: Beacon Press

Hart, H. L. A. (1961) *The Concept of Law*, Oxford: Clarendon Press

Hohfeld, W. (1978) *Fundamental Legal Conceptions*, Westport, CT: Greenwood Press

Hunt, A. (1992) 'Foucault's Expulsion of Law: Towards a Retrieval', *Law and Social Inquiry*, 17: 1–38

___ (1999) *Governing Morals: A Social History of Moral Regulation*, Cambridge: Cambridge University Press

Hunt, A. and Wickham, G. (1994) *Foucault and Law: Towards a Sociology of Law as Governance*, London: Pluto Press

Hussain, A. (1981) 'Review of Foucault's *History of Sexuality*', *M/F*, 5: 169–91

Luhmann, N. (1985) *A Sociological Theory of Law*, London: Routledge & Kegan Paul

Palmer, J. and Pearce, F. (1983) 'Legal Discourse and State Power: Foucault and the Juridical Relation', *International Journal of the Sociology of Law*, 11: 361–83

Pashukanis, E. B. (1980) *Pashukanis: Selected Writings on Marxism and Law*, London: Academic Press

Philips, D. (1989) 'Good Men to Associate and Bad Men to Conspire: Associations for the Prosecution of Felons in England, 1760–1860', in D. Hay and F. Snyder (eds) *Policing and Prosecution in Britain 1750–1850*, Oxford: Oxford University Press

Porter, R. (1991) 'Is Foucault Useful for Understanding Eighteenth and Nineteenth Century Sexuality?', *Contention*, 1: 61–81

Rose, N. (1999) *Powers of Freedom: Reframing Political Thought*, Cambridge: Cambridge University Press

Rose, N. and Valverde, M. (1998) 'Governed by Law?', *Social & Legal Studies*, 7: 569–79

Selznick, P. (1969) *Law, Society and Industrial Justice*, New York, NY: Russell Sage Foundation

Shubert, A. (1981) 'Private Initiative in Law Enforcement: Associations for the Prosecution of Felons, 1744–1856', in V. Bailey (ed.) *Policing and Punishment in Nineteenth-Century Britain*, London: Croom Helm

Tadros, V. (1998) 'Between Governance and Discipline: The Law and Michel Foucault', *Oxford Journal of Legal Studies*, 18: 74–103

Teubner, G. (1992) *Law as an Autopoietic System*, Oxford: Basil Blackwell

Chapter 4

Law, literature, morality: Michel Foucault and the problem of judgment

Lissa Lincoln

Within literary depictions, there is a frequent and often trite conflation of law and morality, with the figure of the judge, for example, being exposed as laying claim to a transcendental authority or a priest or moral leader being revealed as imposing law-bound dogma on civil society. It would seem that literature enjoys a privileged aesthetic authority that allows it to portray and even expose the moral authority that these figures exercise. But can literature really claim to sit 'outside' of the complicity between these discourses? To what extent can the role of the author be compared to that of a moral counsellor, an arbiter or a judge? Can there be a space of artistic 'ethics' immune to the critiques that literature attempts to level at discourses of morality? 'Morality', said Sainte-Juste, 'is stronger than tyrants' (in Camus 1991: 63). The French existentialist author Albert Camus, considered by many to be a moralist writer *par excellence*, expounds upon this affirmation with fervour: 'Morality is stronger than tyrants', he agrees, because '[e]very form of disobedience to law therefore comes, not from an imperfection in the law, which is presumed to be impossible, but from a lack of virtue in the refractory citizen' (Camus 1991: 66).

However, despite his intransigent (theoretical) position regarding systems of morality, literary criticism has traditionally associated the work of Camus, whether positively or negatively, with a very specific or, more precisely, very moral conception of literature. In this way, his more 'philosophical' works (namely, his essays) are seen as demonstrations of the moral 'message' that his truly literary works strive to transmit. Generally speaking, this perspective can be divided into two categories.[1] On the one hand, we have an image of Camus the literary genius whose creative work brilliantly reflects the rigorous (moral) philosophical system laid out in his theoretical thought, the latter being expressed, for the most part, through his non-fiction writing (namely, *The Myth of Sisyphus* and *The Rebel*). This viewpoint is usually associated with the image of Camus the eminent humanist. This is apparent, for example, in the growing tendency in contemporary Camus studies to 'rescue' the author's thought from the misconceptions it has suffered, thus re-establishing him as a great thinker whose philosophical talent has gone unrecognized. On the other hand, Camus is seen as a very unoriginal or even weak thinker philosophically speaking, whose theoretical writings lack both intellectual rigour and integrity; at best a hasty and less than accurate revision of Nietzsche, and at worst a dangerous strain of the armchair humanism so often associated with the monstrosities of the Second World War. This viewpoint, while still generally according the status of brilliance to Camus's literary work, sees within it a subjacent drive to promote the philosophical ideas, or 'theses', conveyed in the author's non-literary essays. It is thus that Camus is dismissed as a moralist and his fiction, however brilliant on an artistic level, reduced, on the theoretical level, to relatively dangerous *romans à thèse*.

Perhaps one of the most lacerating critiques of his thought – apart from those made by Jean-Paul Sartre,[2] of course – can be found in a statement made by Michel Foucault, who classified Camus amongst the 'pale figures of our Culture' and considered him as an example of the 'totalizing intellectual' – the epitome of what he called 'soft humanism':

> I adopted the expression 'soft humanism' . . . but on second thought, I'd have to say that it's a purely redundant formula, and that in any case, humanism necessarily implies softness. . . . It is precisely this humanism that served in 1948 to justify Stalinism and the hegemony of Christian democracy . . . it is the very humanism that we find in Camus or in the existentialism of Sartre. At the end of the day this humanism has been the little prostitute of all thought, of all culture, of all morality and of all politics for the last 20 years.
> (Foucault 1967a: 643–4)

So what is a chapter on the quintessential humanist and moralist author Albert Camus doing in a volume on Foucault and the law? Well, this classic image of the 'engaged' humanist writer, a presupposition that informs much, if not all, critical commentary on Camus, including that of Foucault himself, becomes problematic if we take seriously Camus's explicit refusal to surrender to any form of dogma. For if the surrender to dogma constitutes for Camus the greatest threat to revolt and represents its potential capitulation into revolution and terror, then the question becomes how to reconcile the image of a twentieth-century moralist[3] with that of a writer who saw in any moral system a direct path to tyranny?[4] A facile response to this question might allow us to dismiss Camus's 'revolt' as nothing but a façade designed to conceal a profound dogmatism, a 'humanism' that he was simply not capable of thinking through thoroughly. In that case, the revolt and the absurd, commonplaces of post-war thought, simply serve as alibis for sidestepping a reflection on the relationship between literature and *engagement* (moral/political commitment) that Camus (contrary to Sartre, for example) was not capable of theorizing.

However, and perhaps paradoxically, it is Foucault who provides us with an entry into a more complex understanding of the coexistence in Camus of the refusal of totalizing systems of thought and the prescriptive transmission of ethical messages that his work is so often interpreted to exemplify. Indeed, I would like to suggest that it is precisely in this apparent contradiction that we discover an interesting, if unexpected, connection between Camus and Foucault. In examining a number of Camus's literary works through the lens of a few central Foucaultian concepts, we shall see that far from being a vehicle for traditional humanist values and universal justice, Camus's work seeks rather to destabilize these notions, specifically through a radical interrogation of the problem of judgment.

It is precisely this problem that makes Foucault so compelling in an analysis of Camus, for he allows us to apprehend the problem of judgment not only conceptually but methodologically. For the question, of course, is how to *judge* a discourse of judgment. Foucault's analytical approach itself opens up new possibilities for reading Camus (and literature more generally) thus allowing us to engage the author's work in a different way, and apart, from the conventional (mis)readings that accompany his work. In a word, Foucault allows us to think Camus *autrement.*

To *penser autrement*, this thinking the object of analysis otherwise, is of course Foucault's primary objective as a philosopher.[5] And it is an objective that demands a very particular rapport with judgment on the part of the theorist. In a 1978 interview with the Italian communist journalist Duccio Trombadori, Foucault describes his work of writing as an experience: 'experience has the function of wrenching the subject from itself, of seeing to it that the subject is no longer itself, or that it is brought to its annihilation or its dissolution. This is a project of desubjectivation' (Foucault 1994: 241). In other words, rather than approaching our object of analysis from a perspective of legitimation – or of condemnation – of what we think or of whom we are, Foucault compels us to step back from our usual way of thinking and to feel less comfortable in our usual way of being. Hence his insistence on the importance of a method which has as its goal not so much a distancing from positions of judgment (as if some such position of exteriority, outside judgment, could exist), but rather one that is interested in the *mechanics supporting a system of judgment* rather than judgment itself as a moral question.[6] This is why he insists on *la souci de la methode* (a care of method) – a method, or analytical approach, which acts as a kind of safeguard against the ever-present danger of falling into a position of legitimation or of condemnation. As we shall discuss in more detail later, this calling into question of self-legitimating discourse, or what we might call justificatory discourse, and its ubiquitous nature,[7] is also a central preoccupation for Camus, who was very suspicious of these discourses that traditionally serve to explain and to justify our existence.

What is particularly interesting in Camus is that he calls into question not only non-literary discourse, but the discourse of literature itself. As we shall see, for Camus literature is itself a discourse of justification. Yet, how to approach such a paradoxical venture? How to call into question an act of writing through an act of writing, discourse through discourse, literature through literature? Once again, how to judge a discourse of judgment without falling into judgment oneself? This is where Foucault's methodology becomes very interesting, notably in what the philosopher calls: 'The little question, What happens?' (in Dreyfus and

Rabinow 1983: 217). The radical shift of perspective implied by this 'little question' is perhaps best highlighted by opposing it to the 'big question' which informs the majority of philosophy: *qu'est-ce que c'est?* (What is it?). It implies a radical shift in perspective because it requires that the philosopher (theorist and so forth) no longer take himself for a judge (of determining what something 'is'), but rather that he place himself in the role of the clinician (describing how something functions). It is in this sense that Foucault speaks of philosophy as an 'activity of diagnostics', contrasting the '*grande époque* of philosophy, that of Sartre or Merleau-Ponty', which he sees as an enterprise of 'totalization', to an activity of diagnostics:

> [T]here was the *grande époque* where a philosophical text, a theoretical text, told you, finally, what life was, what death was, what sexuality was, whether God existed or not etc, . . . one now has the impression that this kind of philosophy can no longer take place . . . I would say that if there is perhaps now an autonomous philosophical activity, it could be described as follows: an activity of diagnostics.
>
> (Foucault 1967b: 690)

In short, Foucault's genealogical method of examination (which leads to a certain *vertige* because it is about exposing the very norms upon which we stand and assume to make our own positions and thus judgments) is one that allows for a reading of Camus 'otherwise'. This methodological approach which allows Foucault to consider his object of analysis without falling into a position of legitimation (and hence judgment) finds its literary correlate in the *oeuvre* of Camus, and this similarity presents us with another commonality between the two thinkers; that is, the critical response to their work. If we consider the majority of critical responses to Foucault's understanding of law, and those regarding Camus's understanding of justice, respectively, when read through Foucault's own methodological approach we begin to see that these reactions reflect, and in fact demonstrate, the very mechanisms of judgment that both Foucault and Camus set out to expose and interrogate.

In order to contextualize our principal discussion, I would like to begin with a brief look at these phenomena in Foucault before taking up a properly literary analysis of the same occurrence in Camus. In both cases it necessitates a displacement of the usual focus of inquiry. In Foucault, we shall take as a starting point not the question of the legitimacy of law (as do most of the critical readings of Foucault on law) but rather the discourse surrounding his reading of law. Likewise, we shall concern ourselves not with the question of justice *per se* in Camus, but rather with the question of *how it is decided* that a given discourse is 'just'. In both cases, as we shall see, it is a question of exposing the mechanisms of the system of judgment underlying *all* discourse.

Generally speaking, then, the overall reproach made against Foucault can be traced back to three fairly simple points: (a) his anti-juridical analytic, namely the absence in Foucault of law as a philosophical precondition for 'thinking' (that is, for the analysis of power within society); (b) reductionism, that is, the lack of recognition in his work of the juridical as a domain capable of an autonomous *scientific* analysis; and, finally, (c) the denial of the legal subject as a foundation for political reclamation. In short, and what all of these objections contend, Foucault 'minimizes' law.[8]

However, as we shall see, Foucault neither 'refuses to take law into account', nor refuses to think law; rather, he refuses *the manner in which law is ordinarily thought*, which means he also refuses thinking society by way of borrowing categories from law. Simply put, Foucault's theory on power seeks to destabilize the standard (that is, juridical) models through which we think the relation between man and truth. As such, he opens the possibility of thinking that relation 'otherwise'. Hence, for Foucault, what is of foremost importance is not to deliver a verdict, as it were, on the role and importance of law in the effective functioning of societies, but rather to analyse, and then rid ourselves of, a discourse that reads the composition of political society through law. Hence Foucault's assertion that the analysis of power in modern societies must break with what he refers to as juridico-discursive theory. In other words, locating the historical *function* of (meta-juridical) discourse *demands a transformation in the way in which the theorist regards his object of analysis*. This brings us back to our point of departure: the importance of method, according to Foucault, for an adequate understanding of the functioning of power in modern society.

If we consider the three central objections to Foucault's reading of law in this light, what emerges as their underlying premise is a refusal of Foucault's mandate for rupture with juridico-discursive theory. Indeed, law remains the central authority through which the composition of society is read for those positing these objections. In other words, they 'still have not cut off the head of the king' (Foucault 1978: 89). Consequently, they necessarily *cannot* apprehend law in a new way, cannot 'think it otherwise' and thus fail to see the true specificity of law in the analysis of power. Hence, it becomes possible to think, non-paradoxically, that an analysis of power which no longer takes law as its starting point – either in its categories, or in its privileged objects – not only can be accomplished, but can, in reality, offer a better understanding of law because it does not make it absolute, for motives of *legitimation* (Potte-Bonneville 2003: 9). To conclude, we might say that Foucault's method is one that 'arrests' itself when it becomes complicit with and/or begins to *replicate* the juridico-discursive power it claims to be analysing.

Like law in Foucault, justice in Camus is revealed to be a theme that is much more complex than it might appear at first glance. Instead of the simple defence of one idea (for example, justice) against another, opposite idea (for example, injustice), or an attempt to justify his convictions about what is just (and, in consequence, what is not), as the majority of literary criticism interprets Camus's work as doing, a Foucaultian reading indicates that the author's interest in this theme stems from a more nuanced objective. Indeed, it would seem that his concern lies not in transmitting (whether through promotion or denunciation) an idea or an ideal of justice but rather in questioning the very mechanics of *how we decide* what is just in a given situation or context.

Historically, the concept of justice has always been linked to both morality – a subjective, even individual, dimension – and politics – an objective, or social, dimension. Traditionally, then, justice was first and foremost a moral virtue. According to this perspective, a perfect society would be a society of just individuals. But, of course, social existence cannot depend on the virtues of the individuals who compose it: not all individuals being necessarily just, it becomes necessary to render them just by force. Hence the necessity of laws, and the reason why 'objective' justice will always consist of an 'objectivity' endorsed by force. He who does not recognize moral law from within must be constrained (to recognize it) from without:

> If justice, in its first sense, refers to an internal, subjective virtue, law appears as something objective, like a force outside of the self, thus surpassing the register of simple intersubjective relation. Hence, justice designates not only the moral virtue of humans but also the whole of social procedures by which we can constrain individuals to respect, whether they want to or not, the rules held to be just by the community. This is why the idea of justice first and foremost constitutes the privileged articulation of morality and accepted standards of behaviour, or again, an individual's own virtue and the virtue required of all in the social space.
>
> (Collin 1997: 4, author's translation)

This social space created by and for the perpetuation of accepted standards of behaviour is what Foucault refers to as the normative space. As he lays out in *Discipline and Punish*, it is precisely the coming of a normative age that characterizes modernity, an age where all values, all power, all meaning is created and can only exist within a system of perpetually redirected references. Indeed, Foucault asserts that there is something that traverses and exceeds this traditional concept of justice; namely, the norm. It is precisely this concept of the norm that provides us with a new conceptual framework for considering Camus's understanding of justice. Foucault thus provides us with an analytical tool for questioning justice that Camus did not have: the conceptual framework of mechanisms of power – a way of articulating norms that opens up an entirely new perspective on Camus's *oeuvre*.

To situate this in the juridical framework, let us remember that for Foucault one of the effects of forming a normative society is an astonishing proliferation of legislation, in other words a society that is increasingly prescriptive. But, at the same time, Foucault is careful to specify that the reference to the judicial is always essential: 'I do not mean to say that law fades into the background or that the institutions of justice tend to disappear, but rather that the law operates more and more as a norm, and that the judicial institution is increasingly incorporated into a continuum of apparatuses (medical, administrative, and so on) whose functions are for the most part regulatory' (Foucault 1978: 144). Law then cannot be reduced to the forms of its expression (constitution, codes, laws). Rather, as we know from Foucault's tracing of the evolution of law (from laws to norms) in *The Will to Knowledge*, law consists of an ensemble of procedures that prescribe behaviours through reference to norms. For Foucault, it is a question of examining the use of law as a model of analysis and in such an examination his interest is in the relationship between the juridical and the political, between law and power, as conditions of a suitable analysis of mechanisms of power. What is at work in the juridical framework then, as in the domain of knowledge, is an ensemble of conditions permitting the existence of a certain normative space.

These procedures are all based on limits and prohibitions anchored in a *devoir être*. It is thus a question not only of imposing a prescribed behaviour, but also of internalizing a norm. In the juridical field, the two procedures overlap:

> We have entered a phase of juridical regression in comparison with the pre-seventeenth-century societies we are acquainted with; we should not be deceived by all the Constitutions framed throughout the world since the French Revolution, the codes written and revised, a whole continual and clamorous legislative activity: these were the forms that made an essentially normalizing power acceptable.
>
> (Foucault 1978: 144; further see Ewald 1991)

Far from being objective references against which we can measure the justice of a given act, laws for Foucault prove to be the catalysts of a dissimulation that hides the true sources of power (norms) while at the same time facilitating, even assuring, their internalization.

Particularly interesting in Foucault's perspective for our analysis is the fact that every utterance regardless of its nature – be it knowledge, morality or law – is necessarily bound to some kind of knowledge–power relationship. As he asserts in *Discipline and Punish*:

> We should admit . . . that power produces knowledge (and not simply by encouraging it because it serves power or by applying it because it is useful); that power and knowledge directly imply one another; that there is no power relation without the correlative constitution of a field of knowledge, nor any knowledge that does not presuppose and constitute at the same time power relations.
>
> (Foucault 1977: 27)

If one takes the question of discursive power as an example, this means that literature and law must submit themselves to the entity of rules and codification of language that is rhetoric (as an instrument of power). For there is no literature, and there is no law, that is not in relation with this particular power game.

In this sense, Foucault's identification of an inevitable knowledge–power relationship in the utterances of knowledge, morality or law, finds a literary counterpart in Camus. For Camus, as for Foucault, knowledge and power are not distinct or separate entities, but rather are intertwined in an intimate and complex manner, at once constituting and constituted by one another.

It was Camus's acute awareness of this inescapable link between power and knowledge in literature itself that was at the root of his search for an alternative discourse, one that would fall between surrealism and engaged literature, the two opposite poles of literature that provided antithetical answers to the power of rhetoric in their own discourses during his epoch. Camus sought another response, a literature that would not set itself up as a discourse of justification, a creative *lieu* outside discursive systems based on power–knowledge games which always – necessarily – conceal a root of dogmatism or tyranny. Camus's objective was to find a way of living within a kind of perpetual tension, something that would demand a constant effort of challenging the dominant values imposed by the norm. In this sense the Camusian concept of the absurd can be seen as a sort of 'point zero' of thought; an attempt to found all effort and all direction of thought on the doubt of its own validity, on an awareness of the inescapable nature of its inherent *parti pris*.

Obviously, this conceptual link between Camus and Foucault, grounded in their respective understandings of the overlap between the domains of knowledge and power, is not a kind of precursor of the philosopher that we discover in the author, but rather the echo of what is probably their strongest conceptual link: Nietzsche. For Camus (as for Foucault), what is at the root of the knowledge–power relation is the acknowledgement that truth is in fact produced in discourse. This is of course an idea that we find in Nietzsche, who maintains that if truth is produced, it is because religion, the monarchy, law, reason, in short the dominant knowledge of a given epoch, will always need a justification.[9] It is precisely upon this will to justification that the thought of both Foucault and Camus is based. Foucault contends that this will to truth is a system of exclusion linked to a desire for power. In Camus, this same assertion is made through numerous literary figures through which the author interrogates the discourse of justice.

In this sense, we might see the central character of Camus's seminal work *The Outsider*, Meursault, as being the representative of a perspective that is 'other' – one that refuses this universe of the will to truth based on justificatory discourse. As such, he is impermeable to the stakes of discursive rhetoric. It is in this sense, of course, that Meursault can be considered a moral danger to the universe of traditional justice. Thus the righteous sense of justice is unmasked, revealing it to be a discourse of justification *par excellence*, a tyranny of idealistic (moral) knowledge inextricably linked to power.

While this critique is woven throughout Camus's *oeuvre*, in *The Outsider* we have a paradigmatic example of this justificatory universe with the masters of discourse in power (the judge, the prosecutor, the priest and so forth), who try at all costs and by all means to force reality (in this case represented by Meursault) to bend to their own moral precepts. The reader is particularly struck by the role, as sinister as it is subtle, played by rhetoric. Indeed, it is the rigorous logic of this discourse constructed according to rhetorical techniques that hides the monstrosity of its absurd result: a man condemned to death, not for the murder he admits to having committed, but because he did not cry at his mother's funeral.

The image of the judiciary system that Camus depicts in *The Outsider* evokes Foucault's claim that, as a result of an internalized penal system, we have today come to a system that no longer judges nor punishes the body but rather the soul of the criminal:

> The criminal's soul is not referred to in the trial merely to explain his crime and as a factor in the juridical apportioning of responsibility; if it is brought before the court, with such pomp and circumstance, such concern to understand and such 'scientific' application, it is because it too, as well as the crime itself, is to be judged and to share in the punishment.
>
> (Foucault 1977: 18)

Indeed, in the novel we are presented with a kind of theatrical staging – produced by the masters of discourse – of a monstrous and hardened soul that almost obliterates the crime for which he was originally condemned.[10] The fact that Meursault maintains his naïve stance right to the end, refusing to recognize any connection between the death of his mother and the murder of the Arab on the beach, renders him incapable of entering into the game that is being played out – this game of justificatory discourse. Here we see the Foucaultian concepts of confession and normalization come into play (the first being absolutely necessary in order to ensure the second).[11] If Meursault had been willing to 'play the game' for the sake of saving his life, what could he have resorted to but confession? For, as Foucault points out: 'Since the Middle Ages at least, Western societies have established the confession as one of the main rituals we rely on for the production of truth' (Foucault 1978: 58). 'The obligation to confess', notes Foucault, 'is now relayed through so many different points, is so deeply ingrained in us, that we no longer perceive it as the effect of a power that constrains us' (Foucault 1978: 60). Hence, believing that confession brings freedom, 'one goes about telling, with the greatest precision, whatever is most difficult to tell. . . . One confesses – or is forced to confess' (Foucault 1978: 59). For the restoration of order, at least from the perspective of justificatory discourse, Meursault would have had to recognize himself as guilty so that he too, despite his guilt, would acknowledge and perpetuate the value system set up by and for the norm, thus rendering it incontestably 'true' – beyond the reach of any challenge to its validity. Hence, there is a continuous attempt to extract this confession from Meursault. However, every attempt to force this confession out of him fails, Meursault not seeming sufficiently to recognize this universe based on justification to even feel any kind of pressure to conform to its rules. Because Meursault is unaware of not only the rules, but the very existence of the game itself (his own existence being 'outside' the justificatory universe), it is impossible for him to react in a manner that satisfies the jurists. He keeps colliding with what we have seen Foucault calls the will to truth. This will to which our society is so attached and for whom it seems so natural and necessary is, to the contrary, entirely foreign to Meursault – he is quite literally an 'outsider' to its logic. In any and all circumstances he tries, albeit unconsciously – almost intuitively – to circumvent the will to truth. His suspicion, or perhaps more precisely his incomprehension, when confronted with justificatory discourse, is evinced in his oft-repeated phrase: 'it doesn't mean anything'. The guardians of power, that is, the masters of discourse – who thus fail in their vain attempts to bend this 'other' reality (which is Meursault) to their own moral precepts – unable to absorb or assimilate it, are forced to annihilate this lack of cohesion within their system of thought in order to ensure the system's survival. Meursault unwittingly sums up his own experience with the justice system when he recounts the frustrated outburst of his lawyer at the beginning of the trial: 'Here we have the epitome of this trial. Everything is true and yet nothing is true!' (Camus 1982: 88). Thus we come back to our point of departure: truth is produced in and by discourse. One might say that Meursault's very existence seems to denounce the will to truth itself, that which Foucault would later define as a 'prodigious machinery designed to exclude' (Foucault 1981: 56).

Hence we begin to see the extent to which the notion of justice is problematized in both Camus and Foucault. Not only do their interpretations of it run contrary to traditional understandings of the term, but in both thinkers there is an attempt to express, conceptualize and identify a phenomenon, indeed even a system, which overtakes and exceeds it. In Foucault, we have seen, it appears in the form of a *dispositif* of power, based on the norm – a concept that the philosopher meticulously developed with rigorous methodology. In Camus we find the same phenomenon treated on a more intuitive plane, namely in metaphor – dissimulated and transformed by the ambiguous and abstract language of literature but nonetheless expressive from an artistic perspective of that which Foucault elaborates on the methodological plane. That which we know from Foucault as 'the norm' finds its analogue, implicitly, in Camus's interrogation of justice.

Contrary to the traditional concept of justice, Foucault and Camus thus highlight the illusory nature of law's alleged objectivity and, consequently, of all juridical systems of which it is the formal expression. Indeed, the illusory aspect of this supposed objectivity makes itself increasingly felt in all domains of knowledge today. Thus, in systems of legal thought, philosophy and literature, we observe a calling into question of these 'universal values' to the extent of doubting their very existence.

This kind of malaise with respect to universal values is, of course, an accurate description of the impasse in which philosophy finds itself today, one that would seem to hold equally true for the domains of literature and law. This miraculous position which would provide a privileged point of view external to any subjective value systems simply does not exist, for neither law, philosophy nor literature can consider itself as having access to a universal vision of things, all three of these domains having been confronted with the same conceptual dilemmas within an increasingly heterogeneous society. Indeed, 'in these conditions, there is no longer a place for a totalizing knowledge, for a totalizing philosophy, for a universal philosophy that synthesizes all particular knowledge . . . the solution is neither on the side of synthesis nor on the side of morality' (Ewald 1986: 66). The situation of all of these systems of thought is rendered even more problematic today by the realization of two things: first, the impossibility of citing universal values as the basis for the systems; and, secondly, the fact that these systems of thought cannot even hope to escape the limitations of their own value systems in order to have a more objective perspective – because there is no point of view, no external position which would allow or provide them with such an objectivity.

In this sense Foucault's project of defining philosophy as an activity of diagnostics can be compared to the model that Camus finds in Nietzsche. How to salvage the figure of the intellectual in a philosophy of the absurd? How to avoid moralism and justificatory discourse? Camus himself provides us with the response: 'But we can draw no conclusions from Nietzsche except the base and mediocre cruelty that he hated with all his strength, unless we give first place in his work – well ahead of the prophet – to the diagnostician. The provisional, methodical – in a word strategic – character of his thought cannot be doubted for a moment' (Camus 1991: 35). Camus, like Nietzsche and Foucault, was himself (and in his way) a diagnostician. He was primarily interested in describing the experience of his immediate entourage, in the framework of specific, individual cases, refusing a prescriptive thought that would impose grand universal theories for mankind in general. For Camus, all systems of thought (all thought which considers itself a 'theory' to be applied) are to be avoided because they are necessarily based on an idealist ideology. As soon as thought becomes anchored in any kind of an ideal, it necessarily becomes a thought of judgment (*pensée de jugement*), because it measures everything around it against this ideal. In this sense, we could ascribe to Camus the attitude he himself points out in Nietzsche – for whom the world, once divested of divine will (and, as a result, of cohesion and purpose), cannot be judged. Because for Camus, as for Nietzsche, 'any attempt to apply a standard of values to the world leads finally to a slander on life. Judgments are based on what is, with reference to what should be – the kingdom of heaven, eternal concepts, or moral imperatives. But what should be does not exist, and this world cannot be judged in the name of nothing' (Camus 1991: 36). By the same token, we touch here upon the foundation of Camus's critiques of the most important intellectual movements of his time, notably surrealism and existentialism; that is, the same phenomenon that Nietzsche considered the 'infirmity' inherent to all nihilism: a moral behaviour that is always firmly anchored in some sort of ideal. For morality 'wants to substitute the mere shadow of a man for a man of flesh and blood. It condemns the universe of passion and emotion in the name of an entirely imaginary world of harmony' (Camus 1991: 36). For Camus this same 'infirmity is at the root of all idealism' (Camus 1991: 37).

Hence, whether it be existentialism, surrealism, Christianity or Marxism, the infirmity and danger remain the same, because they are dangers inherent to all idealist, that is, all totalizing, thought. The only safeguard against this tendency towards idealism is, for Camus, to maintain a state of perpetual tension that would eliminate any possibility of tipping towards the comfort of absolutes or certainties, in short, of *systems* of thought. In other words, the conceptual positioning of both Camus and Foucault implies a perpetual calling into question of their own discourses. In this way, and following Nietzsche, neither one of these thinkers would envisage the question of justice or the norm (or the production of truth) from a perspective of knowing what is true or how we know that it is true. They endeavour, rather, to understand how a discourse of truth (justice, the norm) could have been brought into being, how it functions. It is a kind of inversion of the direction of analysis. One needs to take these 'mechanisms' (producers of knowledge, multipliers of discourse, generators of power and so forth) as the point of departure, and thence 'try to discover how the related facts of interdiction or concealment are distributed with respect to them. In short, we must define the strategies of power that are immanent in this will to knowledge' (Foucault 1978: 73). In other words, both Camus and Foucault understand the problem (of the will to truth, of justice, of the norm) as a question of function ('How does it work?') that implies a descriptive rather than a prescriptive approach. This comes down to saying that we are dealing with a perpetual interrogation of one's own positions with regards to a given problem. Camus and Foucault maintain that a critical perspective claiming objectivity implies the existence of an impregnable site where the question of 'the will to truth' would somehow disappear; as if, on the one hand, one could keep all discourses at a distance in order to judge them, and, on the other, one could escape the norms which traverse all discourses.

There is one work in particular that provides us with a trenchant example of Camus's approach. It has one theme – judgment – revealed as being at the crossroads of confession and guilt, one character – an ex-lawyer-come-'judge penitent' – and one voice – a rhetorical *tour de force* – which is disturbingly reminiscent of an inquisition. *The Fall*, Camus's last novel and masterpiece, is also the most controversial and least 'humanist' of his novels, one that had those who saw in him a champion of humanism reeling with shock and even indignation. Indeed, this most 'non-Camusian' of texts was perceived by many to be a dark work of cynical resentment; a bitter, disillusioned attack against his contemporaries at best, and against 'humanity' as a whole at worst.[12] But what if, far from being an exception to the author's work, we were to consider *The Fall* as a key to reading Camus 'otherwise', as a kind of unravelling of the judgments informing those very interpretations that see it as an aberration to his *oeuvre*?

In this novel we have a particularly penetrating example of the discourse of judgment in that the central character, Clamence, compels the reader (as Clamence's sole interlocutor) to participate in the problem, and ultimately entraps him/her in the snare, of judgment. As a result, the text serves not only to illustrate the problem of judgment for the reader, but in fact subjects him/her to it directly.

Seduced by the charm and rhetoric of the narrator, the reader at first allows himself to be lured into a quest for a universe beyond judgment, lulled into a sense of safety by the distance tacitly marked between him and the object of Clamence's sharp-witted (but scathing) judgments. However, as the distance between himself and the object judged progressively shrinks, he begins to experience a certain destabilization. If he does not feel in any way concerned by the judgments pronounced on the rough and taciturn manager of the Mexico City bar ('our friend the primate'), he feels more concerned by the judgments Clamence launches next, against the Parisian bourgeois society with which he risks having much more in common. Adding to this malaise is the growing awareness that the narrator's discourse is proving to be less and less reliable. Clamence systematically invites the reader to judge a given action or *milieu* from the position of an external perspective, one that would somehow legitimize the 'objective' nature of the judgment. However, no sooner does the reader think he has established himself in this position 'beyond' judgment (and from which he feels himself justified in his own judgments), than this position too becomes Clamence's target. The reader thus finds himself yet again invited to judge from another external position, bourgeois values are hence unmasked in their hypocrisy, revealing the smug condescension that they conceal:

> Yes, I have never felt comfortable except in lofty surroundings . . . I needed to feel above . . . Thus, I took pleasure in life and in my own excellence. My profession satisfied most happily that vocation for summits. It cleanses me of all bitterness towards my neighbor, whom I always obliged without ever owing him anything. It set me above the judge whom I judged in turn, above the defendant whom I forced to gratitude. Just consider this, cher monsieur, I lived with impunity. I was concerned in no judgment; I was not on the floor in the courtroom but somewhere in the flies like those gods that are brought down by machinery from time to time to transfigure the action and give it its meaning. After all, living aloft is still the only way of being seen and hailed by the largest number.
>
> (Camus 1957: 19)

Recognizing his own self-satisfied existence as the object of Clamence's judgment, the reader suddenly finds himself implicitly invited to judge it from an external position, one that can legitimately, that is, objectively, critique the weaknesses revealed. This change in terrain destabilizes the reader, particularly as it demands that he detach himself rapidly from the first position in order to immediately latch on to the second, if he wishes to remain sheltered from judgment himself. Having adhered, once again, to the new system of values presented (in this case lucid disillusionment), he can re-establish his reassuring sentiment of having attained a position from which his judgment will be morally justified. However, this new position collapses in turn, as Clamence begins to reveal his strategy:

> I have been practicing my useful profession . . . for some time. It consists to begin with, as you know from experience, in indulging in public confession

> as often as possible. I accuse myself uphill and down dale. It's not hard, for I have now acquired a memory. But let me point out that I don't accuse myself crudely, beating my breast. No, I navigate skillfully, multiplying distinctions and digressions too – in short, I adapt my words to my listener and lead him to go me one better. I mingle what concerns me and what concerns others, I choose the features we have in common, the experiences we have endured together, the failings we share – good form, the man of the moment, in fact such as reigns in me and in others. With all that I construct a portrait which is the image of all and of no one. A mask in short, rather like those carnival masks which are both lifelike and stylized so that they make people say 'why surely I've met him!' When the portrait is finished, as it is this evening, I show it with great sorrow, 'this, alas, is what I am!' The prosecutor's charge is finished. But at the same time, the portrait I hold out to my contemporaries becomes a mirror.
>
> (Camus 1957: 102)

Thus, despite a growing resistance to Clamence's discourse, the reader feels compelled to follow him, always hoping to find, at the end, the 'real' or 'true' perspective that would allow him to interpret 'objectively' everything that he is being told. However, what he discovers at the end of the story is that this perspective simply does not exist. There is no 'true' or 'false' which exists outside Clamence's discourse, and which would allow him to judge it, for it is this discourse itself which creates these impressions (of truth or of falsity) within the reader, according to the interpretation that the narrator wishes to produce. In the case of Clamence, it is a discourse with a very clear purpose: rendering the reader guilty in order to attain his own innocence. In the end, Clamence's 'solution' for escaping judgment consists of setting himself up as supreme judge, by means of the confession of his interlocutor.

In this way, Clamence's discourse continually escapes the reader's expectations of it, ceaselessly disappointing him by a series of flights, forever disappearing from one site, only to reappear in another, until the final revelation of its ultimate strategy. By the time the reader becomes aware of this objective, he has already been caught up in the snares of a system of judgment:

> Covered with ashes, tearing my hair, my face scored by clawing, but with piercing eyes, I stand before all humanity recapitulating my shames without losing sight of the effect I am producing and saying: 'I was the lowest of the low'. Then, imperceptibly I pass from the 'I' to the 'we'. When I get to 'This is what we are', the game is over and I can tell them off. I am like them, to be sure, we are in the soup together. However, I have a superiority in that I know it and this gives me the right to speak. You see the advantage, I am sure. The more I accuse myself the more I have a right to judge you. Even better, I provoke you into judging yourself, and this relieves me of that much of the burden. Ah, mon cher, we are odd, wretched creatures and, if we

> merely look back over our lives, there's no lack of occasions to amaze and scandalize ourselves. Just try. I shall listen, you may be sure, to your own confession with a great feeling of fraternity.
>
> (Camus 1957: 103)

Far from providing the reader with a means of escaping judgment through a procedure of distancing, the author brings him to recognize the impossibility of such an exercise.

We begin to see, then, how this work indicates the particularity of Camus's interest in the mechanics supporting the system of judgment, much more than judgment itself as a moral question. His technique in *The Fall* is one of inverting traditional analyses of judgment. He has no interest in convincing the reader that Clamence is right or wrong, that he is good or bad, moral or immoral, guilty or innocent. Rather, he is interested in tracing, examining and describing the functioning of different strategies inherent to all systems of judgment, and consequently of all prescriptive discourse, including literature itself.

This novel, in the form of a monologue, and in which discourse plays a supreme role, thus calls into question the role played by discourse in the fabrication of any 'reality'. Where Clamence possesses total power over his interlocutor's conception of reality, the author – any author – has this same role in relation to his readers. Likewise, on a larger scale, whoever incarnates dominant discourse (the narrator on the level of the story, the author on the level of literature, the judge on the level of law, and so forth) will always be the one who creates 'Truth', through the imposition of his interpretation of reality in order to assure the perpetuation of his own value system. Seen from this angle, a reading of *The Fall* which would look to confront Clamence's discourse with a 'true' or 'false' outside the text would prove very limited, for truth and falsehood are fabricated by the organization of the text itself. Hence, the very possibility of justifying a discourse of truth is shaken in its foundations. Once truth is revealed to be nothing but a construct that serves to perpetuate a value system, there is no longer any point in justifying it, nor, for that matter, in condemning it. Within this configuration, what becomes important is to observe *how* the system *works*. In this sense, rather than a text of cynical moralism, resentment or even self-flagellation, *The Fall* becomes a sort of instruction manual, taking as its foundation not the moral question of judgment, but rather the discursive mechanism upon which all systems of judgment depend.

Thus we see emerge a very interesting slippage from the domain of literature into the central preoccupations of Camus's era, but which are also very much in the forefront of our own world today. Through the character of the judge-penitent, Camus managed to position himself with regards to a particular cultural and political climate in a very nuanced manner, and was thus able to illustrate all of the dangers and limitations that he considered inherent to engaged literature. By means of the highly manipulative discourse of Clamence, Camus revealed the prescriptive discourses that he saw as underpinning this kind of literature, and that the intellectuals of his time used, whether consciously or otherwise, for the imposition and justification of their own value systems. He wanted to illustrate the mechanisms (that he saw as underlying the existentialist movement) of manipulation that consisted of making people think that they were responsible for everything (that is, establishing their guilt).[13] Thus we see that far from corresponding to the classic image of the engaged writer, engaged literature (one of the literary expressions of existentialism) represented a conception of literature that was the extreme opposite of that of Camus, one that touches the question of the central role of the writer in society. For Camus, engaged literature was founded on the rapport between knowledge and power. He saw the engaged writers as setting themselves up as the judges of a humanity of which they esteemed themselves to be the representatives. They felt themselves to be justified in this role not by a superiority based on morality (they were the first to accuse themselves) but, rather, a far subtler strategy, by a superiority based on knowledge. Much to the contrary of this vision of a literature having the right to accuse people on the basis of a superior knowledge of its own guilt, Camus conceives of a literature whose power is based rather on the recognition of its incapacity to 'know', a recognition which compels it to perpetually ask questions, including that of the possibility of its own justification.

Hence, the author unmasks the problems inherent in engaged literature, problems which were not recognized as such by his contemporaries. And in so doing, Camus established, on the one hand, the power of literature to speak of politics in a purely artistic discursive space, and, on the other, the capacity of literature to deal with these questions through art in a subversive manner.

To come back to our original problem – How to indicate the limitations of one kind of literature without promoting another? How to highlight the dangers of prescriptive discourse without falling into 'prescribing' oneself? How to judge a discourse of judgment? The author of *The Fall* responded to this challenge by making this story a sort of *mise en abyme* of the question of judgment. As such, the reader participates in a perpetual de/construction of each of its sites as the narrator progressively presents them to him. Duped every time anew because he believes himself to have achieved, at last, a space outside judgment (where it would be possible to put these sites at a distance in order to judge them) the reader is incited to judge each new instance only to see it dissolve again.

In this way, the reader is brought to a continuous calling into question of his own position of judgment. Wanting to bring an end to judgment we find ourselves at an impasse: either we accept to live in a state of illusion, in which case we can (at least temporarily) convince ourselves that we have escaped, or we accept it, even embrace it, either through making it weigh heavily on others directly (using guilt to extract confession), or (following Clamence's example) by first making it weigh heavily on ourselves, thus using self-confession to extract guilt from the other. The latter thus becomes an act of self-destruction which allows us to better judge others, as Clamence's discourse demonstrates, at once desperate and sincere, outraged against discourses of judgment, but himself obliged to admit that there is no way out.

In the final analysis, what is particularly interesting in Clamence's discourse is its scope. Not satisfied with imposing norms in one particular domain (as when he was a lawyer), his need to create his own reality (in order to then prescribe it to others) seeks to impose laws of behaviour in *all* domains. These laws (enforced via his very particular, inverted, use of guilt and confession) serve to reinforce his value system and to justify a world vision that he has constructed as Truth. Representative of the imperious need to prescribe behaviours which justify his vision of reality, Clamence's discourse is unable to reduce itself to one domain, be it politics, religion or law. His discourse surpasses and indeed absorbs all the others. To conclude, we might perhaps see in this discourse which transcends various forms of prescriptive discourses a sort of 'legal' discourse *par excellence*, in that its essential interest lies in the prescription of laws (what must be done, what is just) – the specific domains (religious, juridical, political and so forth) in which these laws are applied being relatively indifferent. A work like *The Fall* clearly indicates that the imposition of a value system is inseparable from an objective of judgment and thus from a will to power. Paradoxical as it may appear, it is not the value *per se* that entices the will to power; rather, it is the will to power that fixes itself within a system of values. Whether these values be religious, juridical, social, political or cultural, therefore changes nothing in the actual dynamic of judgment of the discourses.

To conclude, the Foucaultian concept of discourse (as being created by and for power) would seem to provide a key to a more nuanced understanding of Camus's perception of and interest in the crossroads of law, literature and morality. Foucault, despite his criticism of Camus, offers us a 'diagnostics' that in a sense *undoes* this very criticism, and reveals a more complex reading whereby the two thinkers are both invested in a certain vertiginous interrogation of law and justice through a radical questioning of the power/knowledge network that conditions both law and literature. Foucault allows us to see that Camus, far from incarnating the 'engaged writer' prescribing humanist values of morality and justice, actually radically destabilizes these notions, thus calling into question the 'will to truth' underlying the need for self-justification in all discourse, including that of literature itself.

Notes

1 For an overview of both these categories, see Amiot and Mattéi 1997.

2 Sartre, as is well known, penned numerous blistering public criticisms of what he saw to be Camus's lofty moralism that the latter handed down to his readers regarding social justice and Camus's refusal of any explicit political commitment. There are countless books on what is known as the Camus–Sartre debate around these issues. See, for example, Anderson 2005.

3 See, for example, Braun's comments: 'Albert Camus is usually regarded as an existential moralist because his ethics are not derived from a pre-established set of values, but are based on a special kind of experience for which he claims universal validity' (Braun 1974: 13).

4 'Conformity is one of the nihilistic temptations of rebellion which dominate a large part of our intellectual history. It demonstrates how the rebel who takes to action is tempted to succumb, if he forgets his origins, to the most absolute conformity. And so it explains the twentieth century' (Camus 1991: 47).
5 See, for example, the second volume of *The History of Sexuality*, where Foucault gives his definition of 'philosophical activity today': 'But, then, what is philosophy today – philosophical activity, I mean – if it is not the critical work that thought brings to bear on itself? In what does it consist, if not in the endeavor to know how and to what extent it might be possible to think differently, instead of legitimating what is already known?' (Foucault 1992: 9).
6 Foucault advances the possibility of a non-judgmental criticism in a 1980 interview for *Le Monde* with Christian Delacampagne: 'I can't help but dream about a kind of criticism that would not try to judge, but to bring an oeuvre, a book, a sentence, an idea to life; . . . It would multiply, not judgments, but signs of existence; it would summon them, drag them from their sleep. Perhaps it would invent them sometimes – all the better. . . . Criticism that hands down sentences sends me to sleep; I'd like a criticism of scintillating leaps of the imagination. It would not be sovereign or dressed in red. It would bear the lightning of possible storms' (Foucault 1988: 326).
7 In the same interview Foucault humorously evokes the ubiquitous nature of mankind's compulsion to judgment: 'And you know very well that the last man, when radiation has finally reduced his last enemy to ashes, will sit down behind some rickety table and begin the trial of the individual responsible' (Foucault 1988: 326).
8 For a full discussion of these points, see the outstanding analysis of Potte-Bonneville (2003), a paper given at Pierre Machery's study group, *La philosophie au sens large*.
9 'Science itself henceforth *requires* justification (which is not to say that there is any such justification). Consider on this question both the earliest and most recent philosophers: they are all oblivious of how much the will to truth itself first requires justification; here there is a lacuna in every philosophy – how did this come about? Because the ascetic ideal has hitherto *dominated* all philosophy, because truth was posited as being, as God, as the highest court of appeal – because truth was not *permitted* to be a problem at all. Is this "permitted" understood? – From the moment faith in the God of the ascetic ideal is denied, *a new problem arises:* that of the *value* of truth' (Nietzsche 1989: 152–3, emphasis in original).
10 Indeed, at one point Meursault is accused of not having a soul at all: 'I tried to listen [to the proceedings] because the prosecutor had begun talking about my soul. He said he'd peered into it and found nothing, gentlemen of the jury. He said the truth was that I didn't have one, a soul, and that I had no access to any humanity nor to any of the moral principles which protect the human heart' (Camus 1982: 98).
11 See Sjursen 1989: 95–104.
12 I am thinking here of the reponses, for example, of Émile Henriot and André Wurmser. For further discussion on the difficulty for commentators in reconciling what they saw as the grating cynicism of *The Fall* with the publicly applauded humanism of Camus's other work, see Fitch 1995: 110: '*The Fall* is particularly disconcerting for those of its readers already familiar with the rest of the author's works [. . .] in fact, *The Fall* can be seen to put seriously into question the whole of the author's previous literary output – the existentialism of *The Stranger* just as surely as the humanism of *The Plague*.'
13 In the words of Clamence: 'No excuses ever, for anyone; that's my principle at the outset. I deny the good intention, the respectable mistake, the indiscretion, the extenuating circumstance. With me there is no giving of absolution or blessing. Everything is simply totted up, and then: "It comes to so much" . . . In philosophy as in politics, I am for any theory that refuses to grant man innocence and for any practice that

treats him as guilty. You see in me, *très cher*, an enlightened advocate of slavery' (Camus 1957: 96–7).

References

(*Editor's note*: references to texts from the two-volume edition of *Dits et écrits* are cited, above, and listed chronologically in the References, below, according to their initial date of publication (and not the date of their subsequent publication in *Dits et écrits*).)

Amiot, A.-M. and Mattéi, J. F. (eds) (1997) *Albert Camus et la philosophie*, Paris: PUF

Anderson, R. (2004) *Camus & Sartre: The Story of a Friendship and the Quarrel that Ended It*, Chicago, IL: University of Chicago Press

Braun, L. (1974) *Witness of Decline: Albert Camus, Moralist of the Absurd*, Rutherford: Farleigh Dickenson University Press

Camus, A. (1957) *The Fall*, London: Penguin

___ (1982) *The Outsider*, London: Penguin

___ (1991) *The Rebel*, New York, NY: Vintage

Collin, D. (1997) *Les grandes notions philosophiques: La justice, le droit*, Paris: Seuil

Dreyfus, H. L. and Rabinow, P. (1983) *Michel Foucault: Beyond Structuralism and Hermeneutics*, 2nd edn, Chicago, IL: University of Chicago Press

Ewald, F. (1986) 'Droit: systèmes et stratégies', *Le Débat*, 41: 63–9

___ (1991) 'Norms, Discipline, and the Law', trans. M. Beale, in Robert Post (ed.) *Law and the Order of Culture*, Berkeley, CA: University of California Press

Fitch, B. (1995) *The Fall: A Matter of Guilt*, New York, NY: Twayne

Foucault, M. (1967a) 'Qui êtes-vous, professeur Foucault?', in D. Defert and F. Ewald (eds) *Dits et écrits I, 1954–1975*, Paris: Gallimard

___ (1967b) 'Foucault répond à Sartre', in D. Defert and F. Ewald (eds) *Dits et écrits I, 1954–1975*, Paris: Gallimard

___ (1977) *Discipline and Punish: The Birth of the Prison*, trans. A. Sheridan, Harmondsworth: Penguin

___ (1978) *The Will to Knowledge*, trans. R. Hurley, Harmondsworth: Penguin

___ (1981) 'The Order of Discourse', trans. Ian McLeod, in R. Young (ed.) *Untying the Text: A Poststructuralist Reader*, Boston, MA: Routledge and Kegan Paul

___ (1988) 'The Masked Philosopher', in L. Kritzman (ed.) *Politics, Philosophy, Culture: Interviews and Other Writings, 1977–1984*, Routledge: London

___ (1992) *The Use of Pleasure*, trans. R. Hurley, Harmondsworth: Penguin

___ (1994) 'Interview with Michel Foucault', in J. D. Faubion (ed.) *Essential Works of Foucault 1954–1984 Vol. 3: Power*, New York, NY: The New Press

Nietzsche, F. (1989) *On the Genealogy of Morals*, trans. W. Kaufmann and R. J. Hollingdale, New York, NY: Vintage

Potte-Bonneville, M. (2003) 'Foucault et le droit', paper presented at Pierre Machery's study group *La philosophie au sens large*, http://stl.recherche.univ-lille3.fr/seminaires/philosophie/macherey/Macherey20022003/PotteBonneville.html (accessed 12 March 2012)

Sjursen, N. (1989) 'Meursault un rescapé de la normalization', *La Revue des Lettres Modernes*, 904–910: 94–104

Part 2

Sovereignty, surveillance, biopolitics

Chapter 5

Sovereignty by acquisition at the Cape: Foucault, Hobbes and de Mist

George Pavlich

> *All the sins of the past, those of omission and those of commission, can now be wiped out as with a damp sponge, with one stroke of the pen all the old contentions can be blotted out and forgotten; and on the clean white page may be written the new Charter for the settlement, framed with wisdom, mildness and discretion, but always tempered with a proper firmness. Thus this colony may be given a new lease of life, and, by God's mercy, may become in time one of the most important possessions of the State.*
>
> (de Mist 1920: 172)

These words, written in 1802 by J. A. de Mist, form part of a report for the 'Department of Indian Affairs' of the Batavian Republic, recommending an appropriate form of administration and government for the Cape of Good Hope. Reproduced as a *Memorandum on the Cape*, penned while the Treaty of Amiens was in process, the report uniquely lays out de Mist's view of the Cape Colony in respect of such matters as: its commercial potential hampered by unfair trade and tax laws; the perpetual dissent within and between various classes of indigenous and settler inhabitants, reflecting insufficient government; the shortcoming of the Dutch East India Company's (VOC) commercially focused governance and administration for the Cape as a victual station rather than a growing colonial settlement; and a description of 'the miserable state of justice and its administration' that remained 'oppressive' and in a 'disgraceful condition . . . right up to the time of the capitulation of the Cape to the English' (de Mist 1920: 234–5).

De Mist, of course, was referring to the VOC's abrupt 1795 collapse following a brief but resolute British invasion that ended an almost 150-year rule (Anderson 2008: 55ff.; Ross 1993). Several events in Europe favoured this invasion, including: Britain's war with France; Napoleon's hand in forging the Batavian Republic from a vanquished Holland; and Prince William of Orange's exile in Britain. Within the complexities of this political climate, arguments for the Cape's strategic importance to Britain, and its geographical role in preserving lucrative trade routes to the East, won out (Du Toit and Giliomee 1983; Giliomee 1975). Yet, scarcely eight years after the Dutch capitulation, Britain signed a treaty with France that returned the Cape (in 1803) to the Batavian Republic. The Batavian interregnum, under the leadership of de Mist as Commissioner-General and his appointed Governor (J. W. Janssens), was itself to last only a few years before a second British occupation in 1806 successfully reasserted sovereignty over the Cape (Elphick and Giliomee 1989; Freund 1972). These notable sovereignty shifts were accompanied by specific political and jurisprudential philosophies, and their successive emergence in such a short space of time had significant effects on the development of Cape politics and law.

Of course, this broad history could be – and has been – analysed in various ways (Ross 2008; Giliomee and Mbenga 2007; Fine 1991). In this chapter, however, my aims are considerably narrower. I wish to focus specifically on a limited set of concepts associated with the emergence of Batavian rule at the Cape by reading de Mist's document through its attachments to Hobbes's *Leviathan*. In so doing, the chapter offers a somewhat unusual way to conceptualize the politics of colonial sovereignty embedded within the *Memorandum*. To be sure, de Mist is usually associated with shades of republicanism, or 'political pluralism', rather than the absolute sovereignty sometimes associated with Hobbes (Murray 1960). As others have noted, de Mist's *Memorandum* is noticeably influenced by versions of natural law theory, republicanism and Bodin's empirical formulations of sovereignty (Murray 1960: 29–31), but I shall argue that it is equally useful to highlight the oft overlooked – but no less profound – Hobbesian foundations that shape part of de Mist's thinking. His familiarity with Hobbes was already evident in a 1789 commentary on a friend's manuscript (Wiselius) where de Mist bluntly observed that the motives of revolutionaries rarely reflected a concern for the people's happiness. More often, they were spurred by a frenzied jostling for plum government posts:

> Thus the beautiful Revolution creates a real *Hobbesianismus – bellum omnium contra omnes*. First the one, then the other, sits on top of the wheel, while the quiet friend of men perches on the axil or hangs on to the spokes and must revolve round with them all, till first one, then the other, are ground to pieces.
> (in Murray 1960: 61, emphasis in original)

Aside from revealing his revulsion with aspects of the revolution, this quotation evokes an interesting use of Hobbes that suggests revolutionary politics evinced, rather than overcame, a version of the 'war of all against all'.

Yet de Mist was not opposed to all facets of revolution. On the contrary, as Walker points out, he may be described as a 'determined though mild revolutionary' (Walker 1935: 140), a view underscored by passages of the *Memorandum* where de Mist appeared to spurn the horror of revolutions but nevertheless saw them as invaluable for achieving needed and substantial social reforms in a short space of time:

> [N]one can have a greater horror of all so-called revolutionary measures than we, yet we feel that this is perhaps the most important, if not the happiest

> outcome of periods of anarchy or epochs of war and peace, that at such times, as if by electric shock, the whole order of things is changed, and sweeping reforms which have been needed for many years are immediately instituted.
> (de Mist 1920: 171)

He thus recognized that while wars or revolutions may produce periods of anarchic instability, the very disorder enabled 'immediately instituted' and significantly reformed socio-political orders. His view also outlines – and this is the main thrust of the *Memorandum* – how effective colonial sovereignty, framed by law, could manage the transition from disruptive disorder to the institution of a more advanced socio-legal and political order. In working through this particular matter, de Mist referenced a version of Hobbesian thought, and confronted what he took to be 'lawless' and 'debased' elements of Cape society as impediments to effective colonial governance and a new sovereign, civil order. At the same time, as Murray points out, he did not favour Hobbes's idea of a single, imposing, 'central sovereign' as 'the depository of rights and liberties' (Murray 1960: 68), opting instead for *multiple* contracts in civil society, less between individuals and more between 'corporations' as compound unions of individuals with one will. Law, for de Mist, was the glue that could hold such contracts together to yield a suitable order.

However, as might already be evident, de Mist's evocation of Hobbes is uneven. Nonetheless, he was influenced by the latter's thinking in several consequential ways. This is rendered particularly plain when one enlists Foucault's perceptive interpretation of Hobbes in the lecture course '*Society Must be Defended*' (Foucault 2003) to approach the *Memorandum* and to conceive of colonial sovereignty politics beyond the imposing force of a conquering power over a vanquished people. Drawing on a 'softer' version of Hobbes, colonial sovereignty might equally be understood less as a top-down imposition following conquest, and more as an ongoing achievement of local power relations that seek to fashion legitimate and effective legal or governmental forms. In other words, by returning to Foucault's interpretation of Hobbes, this chapter draws attention to de Mist's emphasis on the ongoing, dynamic, and always-volatile bottom-up political relations that must be harnessed for effective juridical and sovereign governance to emerge. No doubt my endeavour runs counter to Murray's more conventional view of de Mist as someone who was 'never Hobbesian' or even 'found on the road to Hobbes' (Murray 1960: 109). I want, by contrast, to argue that an alternative view of both Hobbes and de Mist is possible. Specifically, one might recover an image of sovereignty that is detectable in both writers, but which Murray attributes only to de Mist; namely, that sovereignty has its 'origins in an organic way in the community itself, in those aspects in which there is association among various peoples. It is not imposed on the people in a unilateral way' (Murray 1960: 109). If one accepts that the 'community' is never devoid of power relations any more than are historical forms of the sovereign, then one might also say that together they are constituted through the complexities of local power relations and the enveloping structures these contingently form. From this line of reasoning, one need not view Hobbes or de Mist as unqualified advocates of the view that modern sovereignty politics by definition required the imposition of an absolute, all-powerful sovereign (whether through conquest or otherwise) as a decisive force to stamp out disobedient communal forms. Drawing on Foucault, one might instead point to the way that Hobbes too emphasized the dynamic role that power relations amongst local subjects, and indeed amalgams of subjects, play in fashioning themselves and law-based sovereignties. Of course, this is not the only reading of Hobbes, but it is one that helps us to better glimpse the underlying Hobbesian context of de Mist's emphasis on shaping local Cape power dynamics and harnessing these to good law and effective colonial governance.

Will, fear and the *state* of war

Although only briefly suggested in his text, Murray's conventional reading of Hobbes is familiar. One might recast that reading as follows. The imposition of an absolute sovereign suppresses an imagined, yet brutal, 'state of nature' where there is 'warre, as is of every man, against every man' (Hobbes 1985: 185). This state is without industry, arts, letters, navigation, time, society and 'worst of all' beset by 'continuall Feare, and danger of violent death; And the life of man solitary, poore, nasty, brutish, and short' (Hobbes 1985: 186). To escape this potential condition, people need a 'common Power' that keeps them in 'awe', so that they check their unruly passions, and instead pursue passions that 'encline men to Peace' (for example, desire for 'commodious living', 'industry', and so forth – Hobbes 1985: 188). This common power is therefore premised on a continuous *fear* that propels subjects to transfer rights to a sovereign, through a special contract, compact or covenant with others (Hobbes 1985: 196). Crucially, but oft overlooked, this fear contours the obedience required for Hobbesian sovereignty. People are, to offer the point bluntly, equally able to kill one another: 'for as to the strength of the body, the weakest has strength enough to kill the strongest, either by secret machination, or by confederacy with others' (Hobbes 1985: 183). This basic equality is coupled with a free, egoistic, calculating nature, which suggests that, left to their own devices, people naturally fear the possible consequences of an anarchic 'state of nature' (Hobbes 1985: 187), and so yield rights and offer obedience in return for the protection and security of an all-powerful, absolute Leviathan.

This interpretation has recently been challenged and recast through close readings of Hobbes as a more complicated analyst of an emerging sovereignty politics (Fitzpatrick 2007; Martel 2001). Through such re-readings, Martel even argues that Hobbes may be, on one interpretation at least, cast as a radical democrat of sorts (Martel 2007). Without echoing that view, but seeking also to re-read Hobbes, I shall focus on Foucault's (2003: 89ff.) intriguing discussion of *Leviathan*, which emphasizes Hobbes's use of war analogies to understand how sovereign states form, and once formed, how the perpetual *threat* of force sustains their ensuing politics. Foucault detects two crucial questions behind Hobbes's account: the first concerns the kinds of warring relations that the sovereign is supposed to end; and the second relates to how particular forms of sovereignty emerge out of different warlike circumstances. Both questions can help us to explore facets of de Mist's *Memorandum* – the first is discussed below, while the second frames the next section. This opens the way for the third section's discussion of law, concluding with a glance in the direction of how colonial thinking recursively shaped imperial rule.

Throughout the *Memorandum*, one finds echoes of Hobbes in de Mist's description of the Cape as a disordered colony where relations between inhabitants are too often characterized by dissent, rebellion, corruption, immorality, criminality, slavery, dissatisfaction, injustice, incivility, 'barbarism', 'savagery' and political turmoil. He portrayed a basic 'corruption of moral sense' in a context responsible for the 'rebellious conduct of the last few years, and the unreasonable behaviour' of Cape inhabitants, especially in far-flung 'country districts' (such as Graaff-Reinet). Impeding cultured refinements amongst inhabitants, several conditions conspired to produce exigent social relations (de Mist 1920: 198–9): long distances between settlements, boredom, 'lack of social intercourse with civilized individuals', a diet of meat and the 'flesh of wild animals', the 'war' or rather the 'organized hunt' against indigenous people ('which taught our people to shoot down a fellow-being with as little compunction as they would a hare or a wolf'). Together with the Cape government's pursuit of policies based on 'severity rather than tolerance and persuasion', these factors 'all combined in fostering the demon of discontent', leaving a disordered and unstable social context vulnerable to malicious manipulation: 'At this juncture some malicious adventurer was easily able to abuse the opportunity of lashing these half-wild Europeans to still further displays of savagery' (de Mist 1920: 199).

Alongside such portrayals of 'half-wild Europeans', de Mist described – in a denigrating way, resonant with the times – the added influence of 'former inhabitants of this country'; namely, the 'Aborigines' and the 'neighbouring Tribes' (de Mist 1920: 253). If a Rousseau-inspired condescension of 'these poor creatures' is evident here, de Mist also criticized the 'ill-treatment meted out to them by the Company's servants from the very founding of the Colony'. Such ill-treatment reduced many indigenous people to a 'state of subjection' that forced them, 'in fear of their lives, to seek shelter in the depths of wild caves and forests, and callously allowed them to sink into a state of utter barbarism' (de Mist 1920: 254). Coupled with disordered and debased relations amongst colonists generally, such situations, for de Mist, speak directly to Hobbes's so-called war of all against all in a 'state of nature':

> These people have now become the most dangerous enemies of the Colony, and a continual guerilla warfare of defence and attack has to be waged against Bushmen-Hottentots, in which all the principles of civilization and humanity are lost sight of. The border farmers in the Graaff-Reinet district

> seem to realize in their conduct the tragic ideal of Hobbes, *Bellum omnium contra omnes.*
>
> (de Mist 1920: 254, emphasis in original)

Through this explicit reference to Hobbes, de Mist considered the border areas to have decayed to the point of embodying the wild anarchy to which Hobbes referred. Significantly, however, de Mist was careful to use the conditional words 'seem to realize', thus recognizing Hobbes's view of a state of nature as a 'tragic ideal' – one that may reference particular situations, but whose broader symbolic import is of greater consequence. Foucault (2003: 90) spins this primitive 'war of every man against every man' as a generalized abstraction, connoting a permanent, minatory possibility rather than a realized condition. Here one has to be careful, however, for while Hobbes indicates that the state of nature and its war has never been a universal condition, there are particular examples of its presence.[1] As if in an anachronistic dialogue with Foucault, Hobbes tells us that some might think:

> there was never such a time nor condition of war as this; and I believe it was never generally so, over all the world: but there are many places where they live so now. For the savage people in many places of America, except the government of Small Families, the concord whereof dependeth on Naturall lust, have no government at all, and live at this day in that brutish manner, as I said before.
>
> (Hobbes 1985: 187)

Foucault perhaps overstates his claims that the Hobbesian war in a state of nature is always an ideal, but his more encompassing argument holds: the symbolic import of such a state is general, and serves to structure subjects' perceptions as they approach political terrains. Furthermore, says Foucault, if natural (that is, irreversible) differences in the strength of certain subjects over others existed generally, and the state of nature were thus universal, then political relations would be decided by those irreversible differences. The analogy would then cease to play the role that it does for Hobbes's theory of sovereignty, as would the requisite fear that impels subjects to covenants. This is why Hobbes cannot ever admit the state of nature as a general condition, but only as a permanent possibility that is realized in limited and exemplary arenas. Moreover, Foucault observes that in Hobbes natural differences between individuals would eventually yield peace, and not a continual 'war of all against all' that leads subjects to secure sovereign protections:

> If, says Hobbes, marked natural differences did exist, there would therefore be no war because either the relationship of force would be established from the outset by an initial war that precluded the possibility of its continuation; or that relationship of force would remain virtual, precisely because the weak

> are timorous. If, then, there were differences, there would be no war. Differences lead to peace.
>
> (Foucault 2003: 91)

On this basis, Foucault argues it is precisely the equal ability to fight, to overcome 'natural differences', coupled with the permanent fear and threat of anarchy (and the fear this provokes), that provides an indeterminate foundation – the tense threat of unending local warfare – for all political formations, including state sovereignty. Thus, for Foucault, Hobbes's limited conception of a 'state of nature' should be countered with analyses of a general and virtual fear that Foucault refers to as a pervasive *state of war*. The latter, rather than the former, drives politics.

What does Foucault's Hobbesian-inspired state of war involve? To begin with, both weak and strong subjects are inevitably involved in this condition. Those who wish to avoid the warlike state of politics must nevertheless demonstrate that they are *not* willing to abandon the thought of war through their interactions with others. Here, Foucault mobilizes Hobbesian thinking in support of his relational conception of power where subjects, in specific contexts, participate in a kind of 'agonistic' play of force, of provoking and responding, in attempts to shape the actions of others. The outcome of such relations is always undecided and uncertain, but Foucault identifies three elements of such relational contests. First, subjects are required to make concrete calculations and presentations regarding the strength of others in relation to themselves. Secondly, subjects make their demands (will) clear through definite statements of what they seek, thereby affirming that they have in no way abandoned the idea of war, but only participation in tangible, directly combative relations. Thirdly, subjects employ 'intimidating tactics' to ensure that all opponents remain as afraid of a state of war as they might be, thus producing relatively ordered or stable political theatres. Foucault again emphasizes that such relations do not involve direct confrontations or clashes between 'savage forces' to directly and violently accost one another. Rather, from his vantage:

> There are no battles in Hobbes's primitive war, there is no blood and there are no corpses. There are presentations, manifestations, signs, emphatic expressions, wiles, and deceitful expressions . . . We are in a theater where presentations are exchanged, in a relationship of fear in which there are no time limits; we are not really involved in a war.
>
> (Foucault 2003: 92)

In short, for Foucault, the most consequential element of Hobbesian accounts of the state of nature is not the literal war that one may or may not find in limited examples, but, instead, a generalized 'state of war'. This *state* of war may be spurred by the fear of incarnating the brutish 'state of nature' in a specific context, but that state is less about violent battles, or even direct confrontations.

Rather, through the tensions and threats that pervade this condition, subjects provide continual signals and reminders that they do not plan to abandon the prospect of war through demands (their will); which remind others that war could be declared, as it were, at any moment. Fearing this possibility, subjects are intangibly, but generally, pushed towards ordered political horizons that 'encline men to Peace' (Hobbes 1985: 188). In other words, the abstracted state of war is characterized by a clash of presentations, representations and calculations, and this produces a condition that, in turn, enables political arrangements (such as colonial sovereignty) to emerge in history. Such a condition also requires that the will of subjects be made known in a 'system of representations and manifestations that is effective within this field of primal diplomacy', and here an 'interplay of representations' is without end (Foucault 2003: 93).

Through this interpretation, and with echoes of de Mist's previously noted assessment of revolutionary politics, Foucault argues that the emergence of sovereignty is founded upon a *state* of war rather than a means of overcoming that state by imposing an ordered resolution. As such, a *state* of war comprises the very basis of sovereignty, and indeed the multifarious, local 'interplay of representations', the many petty clashes of will, ultimately condition and give birth to – in specific historical contexts – sovereignty politics. To repeat, Foucault calls on Hobbes to help define politics as an 'unending diplomacy' between 'rivals who are naturally equal' that amounts to not a war, but a 'state of war' (Foucault 2003: 92). That primordial condition is never abandoned, even with the appearance of a sovereign state; on the contrary, this condition provides a 'sort of permanent backdrop' to all forms of politics, including seemingly consensual popular sovereignty by 'the people'.

Returning to de Mist's *Memorandum*, one can detect echoes of Foucault's Hobbes in the refusal to approach governance at the Cape as a simple matter of conquest and forceful political resolution. At the opening of his text, de Mist certainly described the Cape's occupying past, but he did not then champion an account of how to impose a conqueror's order by simply unleashing coercive forces over vanquished subjects. Instead, de Mist's report offers readers a nuanced analysis of how the complex 'interplay of representations', in which the diverse demands of subjects (or associations of subjects) located at different socio-economic and legal parts of the Cape, needed to be shaped and then harnessed to effective governance. His emphasis on 'settlers', and the decided marginalization of indigenous people and people of bondage, certainly betrayed the Eurocentric context of de Mist's biases, but in so doing it also referenced his underlying Hobbesian quest to enunciate a 'civil' commonwealth. In that quest, he acknowledged a generalized condition contoured by the perpetual *threat* of war, rather than the direct war of conquest itself; and this provided a way to conceptualize the background for the sweeping governmental reforms de Mist's *Memorandum* proposed.

Phrased thus, one may say that de Mist outlined how the complex 'state of war' at the frontiers and at Cape Town itself had generated a dissatisfied population whose diverse aspirations could no longer be contained within the previous, commercially driven, VOC institutions that were initially designed to support a refreshment station. With a stagnating economy, a tainted tax system, a harsh and arbitrary judicial system, a backward and depraved cultural milieu, a *maladroit* political environment ill-equipped for dealing with contending interests, the Cape – according to de Mist – was ripe for significant change. The surprising fact of the Cape at that time was not the fact of dissent, but why dissension was not even more pervasive. However, in his view, '[t]he oppressiveness of the present system of Government and the ill-feeling which its administration engenders is chiefly responsible for the persistent discontent, murmuring and rebellion of the settlers' (de Mist 1920: 183). Therefore, de Mist underlined the necessity of reformulating the 'present system of Government', and he aimed to do so by taking account of the local conditions in which such discontent had surfaced. And vital to these local conditions were the relationships through which contested presentations of will were coupled with an underlying refusal of governance structures and attendant calls for new political orderings. On the basis of this 'state of war', the multiple 'presentations' and 'representations' of local subjects, de Mist advocated a 'just and humane Government' to 'introduce . . . revised methods of administration and commerce at the Cape, such as will remove the causes for the present unrest by providing for the happiness of the settlers' (de Mist 1920: 183). His conceptions of revised governance structures considered legitimate by said 'settlers' required their integral attachments to local power relations. The happiness of subjects had to be secured by shaping local power relations and aligning them with appropriate governance structures. The ensuing 'popular' sovereignty politics, contoured by cultural and associational institutions that together with a legitimate force of law, could then further entice local subjects to pursue 'ordered' political relations. In time, these emerging relations would, he believed, yield political structures that would encompass the aspirations of thriving, obedient settlers and the demands of effective colonial governance. Such governance could, in light of Foucault's Hobbes, be seen to emerge out of a war-like condition contoured by local presentations by subjects, minor clashes of will, dissenting and assenting tactics as well as an overarching fear of force. Clearly, at stake here is much more than a simple proclamation of political order imposed by a conquering sovereign over a vanquished people. And this is precisely why de Mist's *Memorandum* offered so much detail on the views of, and relations between, subjects at the Cape in his explicit attempt to outline the nature of good governance in context.

The Batavian Cape Colony: sovereignty by acquisition

With the previous section in mind, one might say that contexts and structures create particular sorts of sovereignty, but they do so in rather unique ways. As noted, Hobbes's well-known version of 'sovereignty by institution' has an all-powerful Leviathan, a common power, absorbing vast rights yielded by a covenant between subjects and wielding formidable power over them. However, Hobbes also detailed a less well-known, different kind of sovereignty to which Foucault

(2003: 95ff.) usefully attends – 'sovereignty by acquisition' (see Hobbes 1985: 251–61). With this form of sovereignty, subjects do not necessarily enable a sovereign to represent them out of fear of one another; rather, they agree to obey out of direct fear of the conquering force itself. Anticipating precisely such situations, Hobbes nicely distinguished between two kinds of sovereignty by acquisition – by 'generation' and by 'conquest'. Intriguingly, the former refers to parental domination over a child who must submit to the sovereignty of a parent, while the latter involves the conquest of war as in the spoils that accrue to a victor.

The Batavian Republic's impending takeover of the Cape worked out in a treaty provided an example of sovereignty by acquisition through an indirect conquest of sorts. In this instance, a real war, a tangible array of battles through which Napoleon's forces defeated the States of Holland, prefaced the treaty that assigned the Cape to the Batavian Republic (Schama 1975). After all the bloodshed, violence and pain, including the harsh terms of the Treaty of the Hague (1795), a satellite state called the Batavian Republic was created. Some eight years later, another treaty (of Amiens) saw the British cede the Cape Colony to that Republic and hence de Mist's *Memorandum* on how best to govern the colony. Under these circumstances, inhabitants of the Cape found themselves threatened by a stark command of this sort: you are released from your sworn oaths of allegiance to the British, but now you must obey your new Batavian governors, and benefit from their offers of justice, trade, etc., or face the forceful consequences of disobedience. Through such injunctions, inhabitants were abandoned to confront the demands of Batavian rulers directly. As was the case some eight years previously, with the first British occupation, short of taking up arms against the incoming powers, inhabitants faced the bald choice of having their lives and/or livelihoods spared in return for cooperation with, and obedience to, the new Batavian rulers. That is, at the very moment of takeover, inhabitants were required to cooperate or face banishment, ruin, punishment or even death if they willed (newly defined) treasonous pursuits.

De Mist phrased this opening moment of sovereignty by acquisition in rather incongruous terms as a 'reciprocal contract' between inhabitants of the colony and the imperial Batavian Republic which had asserted (acquired) sovereignty over the Cape:

> In order to introduce a better regime into the Colony with the least display of compulsion, the Cape should be primarily considered as a distant portion of the Batavian Republic . . . [I]t cannot participate in the decisions and deliberations of the State Parliament. It must be regarded as having made a reciprocal contract with the rest of the citizens of the Netherlands, which, on the part of the Colony is embodied in the condition *do ut facias*, and on the part of the Motherland *facio ut des*, that is to say, *we will protect and help you if you will bring your produce to our market and provide our ships with whatever they need.*
>
> (de Mist 1920: 186, emphasis in original)

There, in a nutshell, a basic 'contract' between conqueror and vanquished sets out a distinctive demand. The latter is rendered even more crisply in literal translations of the quoted Latin phrases: the first is 'I give that you may do', and the second 'I do that you may give'.[2] Failing to obey or accede to these demands risked direct confrontation and descent into open battle. However, and this is an important point, as soon as colonial subjects agreed to obey, the new political ordering would emerge from the same fearful conditions (state of war) that propelled sovereignty by institution into being.

On this point, Foucault usefully argued that while Hobbes's sovereignty by acquisition has a trajectory different from sovereignty by institution, both end up with sovereignty-based political structures contoured by clashes of will in a 'state of war' and a pervasive fear:

> It is fear, the renunciation of fear, and the renunciation of the risk of death. It is this that introduces us into the order of sovereignty and into a juridical regime . . . The will to prefer life to death: that is what founds sovereignty, and it is as juridical and legitimate as the sovereignty that was established through the mode of institution and mutual agreement.
>
> (Foucault 2003: 95)

Consequently, reflecting across these forms of sovereignty, Foucault detected in Hobbes a sense that both forms involve a 'radical will' to live and an associated fear of death. In other words:

> sovereignty is always shaped from below, and by those who are afraid . . . no matter whether we are talking about a covenant, a battle, or relations between parents and children, we always find the same series: Will, fear, and sovereignty.
>
> (Foucault 2003: 96)

On this basis, for Foucault, Hobbes does not simply offer a 'might makes right', or conquest-based, theory of state sovereignty that proceeds from the top-down. Instead, there is a pervasive 'popular' element, fashioned through local power relations, that always grounds sovereignty politics. To be sure, this popular dimension is less about the voluntary choices of the 'people' and more about the outcome of multifarious and local clashes of will that surround attempts to secure the consent of subjects and to afford legitimacy to sovereign political structures. Foucault's Hobbes becomes the resigned author of this basic understanding of juridical sovereignty politics:

> [W]ar or no war, defeat or no defeat, Conquest or covenant, it all comes down to the same thing: 'It's what you wanted, it is you, the subjects, who constituted the sovereignty that represents you.'
>
> (Foucault 2003: 98)

Without claiming that de Mist echoed this understanding in so many words, he was nevertheless acutely aware that effective Batavian sovereignty in the colony could only ever emerge through the active approval of Cape inhabitants. Consequently, he described how to secure the (economic, cultural, political, legal) well-being of subjects as a way to reconcile colonists with collective Batavian colonial governance. In addition, he emphatically insisted on keeping the report secret, betraying his recognition that 'political' forms of government – as opposed to the 'commercial' governance of the VOC – had always to enlist, secure and manage the active consent of its subjects for political outcomes. With this important point in mind, he offered the following advice:

> It is impossible to emphasize too strongly the necessity for keeping this report secret, since the premature publication of the projected changes sometimes gives rise to erroneous impressions, which, passed from one to another by word of mouth, gradually become distorted, and reported by letter to the Cape in a new form, rousing the minds of the people against every innovation, and thus rendering the introduction of reforms a most difficult task.
>
> (de Mist 1920: 189)

As noted, the sovereign's legitimacy rests on having a keen sense of – and indeed a strategic hand in creating – the 'pulse' of the people, and the 'play of representations' at hand. On this point, de Mist argued that it was essential to harness the opinions of the most 'capable, experienced, and intelligent colonists' (de Mist 1920: 190); at the same time he advocated for the education, religious well-being and civilization of all subjects in ways that complement the interests of the sovereign. His report thus championed the political utility of restricting government intervention in certain instances: '*[T]he inhabitants at the Cape, under reasonable conditions should be allowed the unrestricted exercise of their trades and occupations, in so far as these can be reconciled with the interests of the mother country*' (de Mist 1920: 190, emphasis in original). His emphasis on associations, and contracts between these, is clear. Such a fundamental reconciliation is, for de Mist, mediated through the language of law, and one might add – with Comaroff (1998) – that this is the argot by which various forms of sovereignty appear at the Cape Colony (Pavlich 2011). If sovereignty develops through the unending action of local power relations, involving prior political actions that create obedient associating subjects, the role of law in such political formations assumes some urgency in de Mist's text. His high regard for law's pivotal role in bridging social and political realms is highlighted throughout the text and is clear from this open declaration: 'I am the slave of the law we have given ourselves' (de Mist in Murray 1960: 7).

Law and sovereignty at the Cape

Consistent with the approach taken so far, one might return to Foucault's engagement with Hobbes to explore the question of law's place in sovereignty-based colonial governance. To be sure, Hobbes's approach to law is far from unambiguous (Finkelstein 2005), even if he is sometimes cast as an uncomplicated command theorist. After all, he does assert:

> And first it is manifest, that Law in generall, is not Counsell, but Command; nor a command of any man to any man; but only of him, whose Command is addressed to one formally obliged to obey him.
>
> (Hobbes 1985: 312)

Taken in isolation, Hobbes might be seen here to advocate that law is no more than the will of a sovereign, expressed as a written command that subjects of a commonwealth are obliged to obey. De Mist's emphasis on a relatively independent law would surely run counter to this approach. However, Hobbes at the same time embraces a natural law approach, consistent with the *Memorandum*, that extends beyond simple command theories. For instance, he tells us that the laws of nature are not 'properly' civil laws because they refer to 'qualities that dispose men to peace, and to obedience' (Hobbes 1985: 314). Civil law is then the written command of sovereign made possible because the unwritten 'right of nature' impels subjects to accept and obey civil law (Hobbes 1985: 215). As a result, the two forms of law are mutually sustaining in the sense that '[t]he Law of Nature therefore is a part of the Civill Law in all Common-wealths of the world. Reciprocally also, the Civill Law is part of the Dictates of Nature' (Hobbes 1985: 314). Stated differently, he tells us that '[t]he law of Nature, and the Civill Law, contain each other, and are of equal extent' (Hobbes 1985: 314).

De Mist implicitly echoed this view of the links between 'the law we have given ourselves' and the underlying 'laws of nature and humanity' which appear to us through 'conscience', and paid considerable attention to the precise form of justice he envisaged for the Cape. In his understanding of a 'reciprocal contract' between empire and colony previously described (recall the Latin: 'I give that you may do' and 'I do that you may give'), de Mist also appears to echo Hobbes's analysis of law's mandate in the specific context of sovereignty by acquisition. For Hobbes:

> If the Soveraign of one Common-wealth, subdue a People that have lived under the written Lawes, and afterward govern them by the same Lawes, by which they were governed before; yet those Lawes are the Civill Lawes of the Victor, and not of the Vanquished Common-wealth. For the Legislator is he, not by whose authority the Lawes were first made, but by whose authority they now continue to be Lawes.
>
> (Hobbes 1985: 315)

With Hobbes in mind, we can perhaps understand de Mist's document as an earnest attempt to authorize laws and particular kinds of juridical processes as the basis of good government, and a fitting type of acquired sovereignty. Several aspects of this specific authorization are worth noting.

First, despite Hobbes's claim that natural law 'disposes' people to obey the sovereign's law, *Leviathan* also articulates the need for the threat and actual force of the sword of Damocles when obedience is not forthcoming. The argot and force of law becomes crucial to definitions of sovereignty in a colonial context where the authority of local governance is contested. Echoing this logic, de Mist pointed out that maintaining a garrison of 5,000–6,000 men might ordinarily be superfluous, but in the Cape context of the time it would be strategically important to maintain such a force. This would avoid appearing 'inferior to the English' (who maintained such numbers), and ensure at least 'one battalion of experienced militia' from the 'Motherland' thereby providing assurance that any newly established – and necessarily multinational – Cape colonial forces could be kept in check. In addition, however, such a garrison would be important

> [s]o that the new Governor and Commissioners may be provided with a proper show of power and authority when they introduce the numerous improvements and retrenchments contemplated; and that rebellious persons may be intimidated.
>
> (de Mist 1920: 264)

He considered this 'show of force' especially important 'in a land where a spirit of restlessness and attempts at rebellion and revolution are only too common' (de Mist 1920: 265). However, one should read de Mist carefully here, because the 'proper show of force' – not the force alone – is emphasized to preserve the legitimacy of law, and so to nurture an appropriate kind of sovereignty. No doubt this reading recalls Foucault's emphasis on this *threat* of force as the primary vehicle for Hobbes's sovereign to maintain authority. The mere deployment of force was not the decisive factor for instituting Cape juridical sovereignty; rather, the permanent and visible threat of its credible deployment was key to authorizing the argot of colonial law (Pavlich 2011).

Secondly, Hobbes's point that the dictates of nature, as reflected in 'natural law', dispose people to obedience, suggests that nature is the ultimate foundation of sovereign law. On this point, however, Foucault (2003: 111) challenged Hobbes's return to a seemingly absolute human nature as an attempt to expiate versions of a 'political historicism' that had surfaced amongst notable political commentators of his day. But if we accept that power relations always play themselves out in indeterminate and contingent ways, acknowledging that all sovereign juridical structures remain products of historical conditions, then Hobbesian versions of sovereignty as absolute, natural and necessary become problematic. To avoid eviscerating the indeterminacy of power relations, Foucault argued thus:

> Once we begin to talk about power relations, we are not talking about right, and we are not talking about sovereignty; we are talking about domination, about an infinitely dense and multiple domination that never comes to an

> end. There is no escape from domination, and there is therefore no escape from history. Hobbes's philosophical juridical discourse was a way of blocking this political historicism, which was the discourse and the knowledge that was actually active in the political struggles of the seventeenth century . . . Hobbes's operation consisted in exploiting every possibility . . . to silence the discourse of political historicism.
>
> (Foucault 2003: 111)

By trying to silence his contemporaries who understood emerging political configurations in historical terms, Hobbes had – for Foucault – evoked judicial reasoning as a fixed mainstay, which contradicted his 'command theory' comments. Out of this tangle, Foucault argues that a historicized account of local power relations should form the basis of any strategic envelopes (for example, sovereignty), and these point to the necessary indeterminacy implied if new forms of sovereignty are to emerge. Such indeterminacy is also required for legal rule that must change and respond to a particular context if it is to be regarded by historically situated subjects as legitimate. For Foucault, then, any semblance of popular juridical sovereignty, of harnessing the consent of those who are governed, is purely a historical matter that is neither necessary, nor does it emerge from a nature or form an all powerful Leviathan.

Instead, we are told, '[s]overeignty is always shaped from below, and by those who are afraid' (Foucault 2003: 96). Thus, before juridical sovereignty can surface, the obedience of those subjects to whom it will be addressed must be forged, shaped and secured. As a historical achievement, therefore, any 'law and sovereign' exercise of power requires local level work that may – depending on contingent circumstances – give rise to wider political or legal structures. If the latter position appears to be somewhat at odds with Hobbes, we could note a tension where he regarded education as important for shaping obedient subjects:

> The People are to be taught, First, that they ought not to be in love with any forme of Government they see in their neighbour Nations, more than with their own, nor . . . to desire change . . . takeaway in any kind of State, the obedience, (and consequently the Concord of the People,) and they shall not only not flourish, but in short time be dissolved.
>
> (Hobbes 1985: 379–80)

Without overstating the case, one might say that law plays a part in educating and shaping subjects by translating and rendering ideas public; it also punishes transgressions in efforts to secure the ongoing obedience of the sovereign's subjects. It is, in short, a key mechanism for nurturing the consent of subjects.

From such tension, we might return to de Mist who explicitly argued that good governance is entirely dependent upon procuring consent and obedience from subjects – hence the emphasis he places on shaping subjects ('civilizing the colonists') and providing them with 'good' government that they deem legitimate. The following conveys the importance of this point for de Mist:

> [T]he work of civilizing the colonists and rousing their moral sense, based on sane and simple laws, and encouraged by a beneficent religion, seems of such importance to us that unless it is achieved, all other political innovations and reforms must be considered valueless. The settlement must stand or fall by it.
>
> (de Mist 1920: 200)

For that reason, effective governance and the language of law must rest upon prior subject intervention designed to shape the *obedience* of colonial subjects:

> [I]n a word, their happiness should be the first consideration of the Government, for in that case they will not wish to leave the Colony, nor will they then, as a nation, with wise leaders, become as thoroughly discontented and rebellious, as they are at present.
>
> (de Mist 1920: 188)

A key way to achieve such happiness is to develop and let subjects be 'governed by lenient but well-defined laws' because:

> A whole community is never discontented unless there is some cause for it. First restore the happiness of the community by establishing just laws and institutions, and then punish the transgressors.
>
> (de Mist 1920: 178)

Again, the emerging language of law provides a foundation for shifting images of colonial sovereignty in context. For de Mist, prior to enforcing any sovereign decree, it is essential to work with subjects to secure their obedience through diverse means – law, education, religion, the arts, a printing press, and even the attractions of a military band! As well, he emphasizes the 'incalculable benefit' that would flow from establishing a Cape newspaper ('edited by a loyal and efficient individual' (de Mist 1920: 203)). De Mist assumed the value of these indirect forms of governance in arguing for an appropriately 'lenient' justice to redress the 'miserable state' and 'defective administration' that for too long has oppressed subjects and solicited their legitimate complaints. If this view appears to reach beyond Hobbes, it does concur with the notion that it is important to work with the 'laws of nature' to teach, secure and develop the obedience of subjects so that the laws and legal procedures that they find fitting, just and legitimate may be developed to the benefit of a commonwealth. Moreover, Murray usefully describes de Mist's plural approach to power as having 'made law the authority, and the state derived its functions from legal grounds' (Murray 1960: 126). One might question, however, whether law for de Mist is founded on some mystical customary basis (cf. Murray 1960: 99ff.), or whether it too has a historically fashioned dimension that emerges out of local political struggles and representations.

Thirdly, de Mist implicitly confronts the extent to which a bald law and sovereignty theory can sufficiently address colonial power relations. Foucault's well-known critique of Hobbes made the point by arguing that a 'theory of sovereignty' may have captured the 'general mechanics of power' in 'feudal-type societies', but modern societies introduced a 'new mechanism of power' – discipline – that appears to be 'absolutely incompatible' with relations of sovereignty, and could even be an 'exact, point-for-point opposite of the mechanics of power that the theory of sovereignty described or tried to transcribe' (Foucault 2003: 35–6), making it necessary to 'abandon the juridical model of sovereignty' (Foucault 2003: 265) and to approach things quite differently: 'We have to study power outside the model of the *Leviathan*, outside the field delineated by juridical sovereignty and the institution of the state' (Foucault 2003: 34). The thrust of his critique centres on the requirement to analyse power at local extremities, at the points where 'its exercise [becomes] less and less juridical' (Foucault 2003: 28), and this led him to his well-known analyses of such 'political technologies' as discipline, biopower and govermentality.

Hobbes did not in fact entirely overlook power outside sovereignty; after all, he recognized that an almighty and fearsome sovereign is also one that permits degrees of subject discretion within its rule, as well as 'other' liberties beyond its reach:

> As for other Lyberties, they depend on the silence of the Law. In cases where the Soveraign has prescribed no rule, there the Subject hath the liberty to do, or forebear, according to his own discretion.
>
> (Hobbes 1985: 271)

However, Hobbes adds quickly that the sovereign determines such discretion. Intriguingly, too, he tells us subjects have the right to bring suits against the sovereign (Hobbes 1985: 272), and may in certain extreme cases be 'absolved of their obedience to their Soveraign' (Hobbes 1985: 272) – captivity, banishment or where a sovereign abdicates. Of course, it is doubtful that this thinking opens sufficient theoretical space to accommodate Foucault's more encompassing call to view power outside of sovereign structures, but we should also note that Foucault's ambivalent and indeed disparate comments on juridical sovereignty may be used to consider law and sovereigns in ways that de Mist's *Memorandum* anticipates. Foucault contradicts his own strident reproach of Hobbes elsewhere, especially when adopting a rather more irresolute sense of law (see Golder and Fitzpatrick 2009: 53–97). There is an intriguing sense that Foucault's 'other view of law' may address a contradictory finite judgment and open responsiveness within law, and the sorts of sovereignty that such contradictions imply.

Without here reflecting the nuances of the important debates Golder and Fitzpatrick raise, one might at least focus on Foucault's call for local, historical analyses of power relations as the basis of politics, including juridical sovereignty politics. This view allows one to approach de Mist's call for disciplinary (moral correction, religious instruction, civilizing techniques, education and so forth) and biopolitical (massively increasing the population of the Colony – de Mist 1920: 193 ff.) mechanisms as relevant political innovations for seeking out appropriate, effective and just, juridical structures. He understood that, 'The author of quarrels lies not with the wrath of an act in itself but he that gives the cause of wrath with them.'[3] In other words, the disgruntlement with authority in the Cape, and the rebellious climate, rests not so much with law as such, but with bad law that has engendered hostility towards the sovereign. De Mist here recognized that the legitimacy of colonial law – the basis of the modern sovereign – rests on a vast and changing warp and weft of underlying power relations whose weave contours the changing social fabrics of history. And here he insisted on attending to the happiness of the community and eradicating the source of wrath: discipline coupled with a reformed legal administration.

Conclusion

Foucault's intriguing interpretation of Hobbes's *Leviathan* offers a rather different way to understand the latter's political philosophy, and in turn to approach de Mist's *Memorandum* and his vision of the most appropriate kinds of colonial sovereignty for the Cape. As seen, Foucault traces a line of thought in Hobbes that challenges a common view of the sovereign as deployed from the top-down, over subjects. This interpretation of Hobbes allows one to understand and approach de Mist's attention to local struggles. De Mist's discussion appears to echo Foucault by recognizing that an all-powerful imperial Leviathan cannot simply except itself from law and thus yield absolute power over obedient colonial subjects who have ceded rights through a mutual compact. Rather, it is possible to recover a different horizon of meaning in which sovereignty emerges as a historical achievement, an outcome, of complex local power relations contoured by fear, petty calculation, diverse 'plays of representation' and a pervasive threat of descent into a warlike state. Such elements in concert form a complex condition that in modern colonial contexts produced idiomatic political forms, including the significance attached to colonial law and sovereign models of power. Therefore, paying attention to local power relations enables de Mist's discussion of juridical sovereignty to go beyond the narrow confines of formal enunciations of imperial and colonial government, or conquest. It also allows one to understand why de Mist's *Memorandum* pays so much attention to diverse micro processes and political techniques designed to secure popular consent, shape obedient but economically resourceful subjects, and institute juridical forms that key subjects deem legitimate and just – thus curbing widespread dissent and rebellion.

Moreover, by attending closely to Hobbes's discussions of two different kinds of sovereignty, as does Foucault, one is able to highlight an 'acquisitive' form as somewhat more complex than sovereignty by institution, and as the sort more commonly associated with colonial conquest. In turn, this approach allows one to read de Mist as not simply an advocate of conquest as the central, or dominant, element in generating colonial sovereignty. Rather one can identify the *Memorandum* as articulating the implicit demands underlying sovereignty by acquisition through conquest, but then immediately attending to the more general political problem of instituting sovereignty politics within conditions propelled by locally inflected fear, contested wills and battles of representation. Finally, the language of colonial law, supported and bolstered by extra-juridical power relations that define appropriate juridical subjects, provides one of the key vehicles for defining the colonial sovereign on an ongoing basis.

Far from that sovereign being the one who is excepted from law, this approach shows that the law – and the underlying political infrastructure required to sustain juridical forms – actually provides the language by which the colonial sovereign most commonly appears at specific historical moments. Such definitional capacity provides a foundation of sorts, and one that resounds through modern sovereignty politics – colonial or otherwise. Indeed, much was learned from discourses of colonial governance, and lest that analytical and historical matter be forgotten, one might end this discussion by recalling one of Foucault's keen insights:

> It should never be forgotten that while colonization, with its techniques and its political and juridical weapons, obviously transported European models to other continents, it also had a considerable boomerang effect on the mechanisms of power in the West, and on apparatuses, institutions, and techniques of power. A whole series of colonial models was brought back to the West, and the result was that the West could practice something resembling colonization, or an internal colonialism, on itself.
>
> (Foucault 2003: 103)

De Mist's careful attention to indirect governance and, associational representations, as well as to the basic role played by law in generating, sustaining and shaping sovereignty politics, incarnates precisely the reversed illumination of a legacy that continues to shape emerging sovereignty politics.

Acknowledgements

This chapter was generously supported by a research grant from the Social Sciences and Research Council of Canada. I wish also to acknowledge Peter Fitzpatrick and Ben Golder for their astute engagements with, and comments on, a previous version of this chapter.

Notes

1 I wish to thank Peter Fitzpatrick for bringing the complexity of this issue to my attention.
2 See http://blackslawdictionary.org (accessed 31 October 2011).
3 De Mist uses the Latin phrase '*Rixarum author non est, gui ira aliquid facit sed qui irce causum dat*' (de Mist 1920: 178) – modified Google translation (accessed 15 March 2011).

References

Anderson, M. R. D. (2008) *Blue Berg: Britain Takes the Cape*, Cape Town: Mark Robert Dunbar Anderson

Comaroff, J. (1998) 'Reflections on the Colonial State in South Africa and Elsewhere: Fragments, Factions, Facts and Fictions', *Social Identities*, 4: 321–61

de Mist, J. A. (1920) *The Memorandum of Commissary J. A. de Mist Containing Recommendations for the Form and Administration of Government at the Cape of Good Hope, 1802*, Cape Town: van Riebeck Society

Du Toit, A. and Giliomee, H. B. (1983) *Afrikaner Political Thought: Analysis and Documents*, Berkeley, CA: University of California Press

Elphick, R. and Giliomee, H. (1989) *The Shaping of South African Society, 1652–1840*, 2nd edn, Middletown: Wesleyan University Press

Fine, H. (1991) 'The Administration of Criminal Justice at the Cape of Good Hope, 1795–1828', unpublished PhD thesis, University of Cape Town

Finkelstein, C. (ed.) (2005) *Hobbes on Law*, Aldershot: Ashgate

Fitzpatrick, P. (2007) '"What are the Gods to us Now?": Secular Theology and the Modernity of Law', *Theoretical Inquiries in Law*, 8: 161–79

Foucault, M. (2003) *'Society Must be Defended': Lectures at the Collège de France, 1975–76*, trans. D. Macey, London: Allen Lane

Freund, W. M. (1972) 'The Eastern Frontier of the Cape Colony during the Batavian Period (1803–1806)', *Journal of African History*, 13: 631–45

Giliomee, H. (1975) *Die Kaap Tydens die Eerste Britse Bewind, 1795–1803*, Cape Town: Hollandsch Afrikaansche Uitgevers

Giliomee, H. and Mbenga, B. (eds) (2007) *New History of South Africa*, Cape Town: Tafelberg

Golder, B. and Fitzpatrick, P. (2009) *Foucault's Law*, London: Routledge

Hobbes, T. (1985) *Leviathan*, London: Penguin

Martel, J. R. (2001) *Love is a Sweet Chain: Desire, Autonomy and Friendship in Liberal Political Theory*, New York, NY: Routledge

—— (2007) *Subverting the Leviathan: Reading Thomas Hobbes as a Radical Democrat*, New York, NY: Columbia University Press

Murray, A. H. (1960) *The Political Philosophy of J. A. De Mist, Commissioner-General at the Cape 1803–1805: A Study in Political Pluralism*, Cape Town: HAUM.

Pavlich, G. (2011) 'Sustaining Sovereignty through Law at the Cape Colony: 1795–1803', *Journal of Forensic Psychology Practice*, 11: 1–19

Ross, R. (1993) *Beyond the Pale: Essays on the History of Colonial South Africa*, London: Wesleyan University Press

—— (2008) *A Concise History of South Africa*, 2nd edn, New York, NY: Cambridge University Press

Schama, S. (1975) 'The Exigencies of War and the Politics of Treaties in the Netherlands, 1795–1810', in J. M. Winter (ed.) *War and Economic Development*, Cambridge: Cambridge University Press

Walker, E. A. (1935) *A History of South Africa*, London: Longmans, Green and Co.

Chapter 6

The status of the gaze in surveillance societies

Véronique Voruz

Introduction

This chapter is a reflection on the status of the gaze in our societies, often called control (Deleuze 1992) or surveillance societies (Lyon 2002).[1] Though I will be looking for indications in Foucault's work, my orientation is distinct from frequent attempts in surveillance studies and criminology either to apply panopticism 'as an analytical ideal type' procuring 'an adequate understanding of society' (Boyne 2000: 285, 302) or to adapt the panoptic framework[2] to conceptualize or formalize contemporary practices in fields said to be predominantly biopolitical (criminal justice, public hygiene, medicine). The prolific morphing of the term itself – Synopticon (Mathiesen 1997), Oligopticon (Latour 1998), Panoptic sort (Gandy 1993), Polyopticon (Allen 1994) – indicates well enough the unsuitability of what Foucault termed panopticism as a grid of intelligibility for the present. And I would argue that holding on to the term itself, albeit in its mutant manifestations, is making us blind to the heterotopic[3] nature of our present.

I will distance my approach from such renderings of the social for two additional reasons. For a methodological reason first: to use Foucault's concepts in the manner of universals (see Deleuze 2007: 343) with which to apprehend given dimensions of the human experience goes against the grain of his own insistence on using concepts as *a posteriori* 'principles of intelligibility' rather than as *a priori* universals, even when they are historicized to fit current practices (Foucault 2008: 2–3). The latter approaches amount to a reduction of genealogy to sociological methods (see Harcourt 2008; Voruz 2011). By contrast, a principle of intelligibility is produced through an analytical description of a chosen aspect of the human experience, naming a hitherto invisible solidarity between heterogeneous practices.[4] To invert the genealogical process makes us blind to the discontinuities wherein the possibility of becoming other than who we are lies. And secondly, for a strategic reason, because my purpose here is to question the status of the gaze in the twenty-first century rather than to engage in yet another denunciation of surveillance and control. We must resist the temptation to give in to paranoid[5] interpretations of the present, not because they are not 'true', but because such interpretations consolidate objectivities that function as hegemonic truths rather than opening other modalities of the relation of self to self wherein the only possibility of resistance lies.[6] To quote Deleuze, 'reason may cause the greatest problem because processes of rationalization can operate on segments or regions of all the lines' (Deleuze 2007: 342–3) that make up the apparatuses delineated by Foucault.

In my endeavour to circumscribe something of the eye, and of the gaze, today, I will engage with Foucault as someone who dedicated a considerable amount of time and energy to mapping the articulation of the visible with statements as the two halves of truth[7] in knowledge, most explicitly in *The Birth of the Clinic* (Foucault 2003b). Foucault also supplemented his analysis of forms of knowledge by mapping the instrumentality of the gaze in power-diagrams, in *Discipline and Punish* (Foucault 1991a) of course, but also in shorter interventions such as 'Truth and Juridical Forms' (Foucault 2000e) and 'The Eye of Power' (Foucault 1980a). These texts contain the successive scansions Foucault makes on the operation of the gaze in 'epistemological power' (Foucault 2000e: 83). A close scrutiny of the gaze, and of what the gaze is made to perform in Foucault's own work, may help us fruitfully to elucidate whether it is truly the *visual* which is at stake in our closed-circuit television (CCTV) culture, but also in multi-factorial risk registers, DNA databases and the current tendency to introduce practices bypassing subjective responsibility in criminal justice via neuro-scientific visibilization of the operation of the brain in the emergent field of neuro-law (Greene and Cohen 2004). My working hypothesis is that what is at stake in surveillance today is rather the *mode of being* of language: if the successive modes of being of language, identified by Foucault in *The Order of Things* as resemblance, representation and history (see Gutting 2005: 16–17), name the way in which we combine the visible and the articulable in distinct epistemic eras, have we not now moved to *virtualization*[8] as a way of incorporating the material world into symbolic reality?

Leaving this hypothesis aside for now, this chapter will seek to map what Foucault says of the gaze at different times. His engagement with the gaze is far more subtle than most commentators give him credit for[9] – or perhaps it is far less clear-cut, more ambivalent. For, indeed, what is the gaze for Foucault? Is the visible identical to the visual? How does the visible correlate to statements, to the 'articulable' (Deleuze 1988: 47–69)? Is the visible coextensive with the gaze? Or does the gaze extend beyond the visible as a *metaphor* for the will to knowledge, as *The Birth of the Clinic* seems to conclude? Is it the eye, a corporeal *object* separated from the body and harnessed to circuits of visibility in order to reinforce an intrinsically weak power, as would appear from Foucault's discussion of panopticism in *Discipline and Punish*? Is the instrumentalization of the gaze in judicial procedures a condition of possibility of the human sciences, as 'Truth and Juridical Forms' and *Discipline and Punish* suggest? Does the eye function as a *symbol* of something beyond itself, as Foucault points out in 'The Eye of Power' in his passing reference to the French Revolution (see, also, Stolleis 2009)? And what is the nature of the relationship between *opacity* and *transparency* (Starobinski 1998)? Is the invisible not visible because it is hidden, repressed, concealed? Or is it invisible because the light of language does not shine upon it? I am not sure that we will be able to extract a coherent theory of the gaze from Foucault's work, but it seems to me that his various propositions are crucial to the diagnostic approach implicit in the strategies we name, after Foucault, histories of the present.

We are effects of multi-linear apparatuses

Foucault's paramount concern was with knowing *who we are* in order to then be otherwise. When he started his intellectual life in post-war Paris, the terms of the philosophical debate were entrenched, framed by Marxism, existential phenomenology and an emergent structuralism (Dreyfus and Rabinow 1983).[10] To further his own personal inquiry, Foucault engaged in a complete epistemological overhaul of the foundations of contemporary thought. Displacing both existing forms of thought and attendant political agendas, Foucault premised the structural absence of absolute, transcendental or permanent characteristics of the human, but also of objects classically considered as 'natural' (see, also, Veyne 1997). There is no such thing as human essence: 'all my analyses are against the idea of universal necessities in human existence' (Foucault 1988: 1598). Things themselves 'have no essence, or . . . their essence was fabricated in a piecemeal fashion from alien forms' (Foucault 2000b: 371). Even the body is 'moulded by a great many distinct regimes; it is broken down by rhythms of work, rest and holidays; it is poisoned by food or values, through eating habits or moral laws; it constructs resistances' (Foucault 2000b: 380). '[E]verything is already interpretation' (Foucault 2000a: 275), objectivities are effects of regimes of truth, and subjects are the effects of modes of subjectivation (Foucault 2000d). Language itself has modes of being (Foucault 1994).

Implicit in Foucault's epistemological *tabula rasa* is the recognition that subjects, a word he rarely uses (for good reason), are not essential, transcendental entities but historically contingent, always fluctuating *effects*. What are we, human beings, individuals, subjects of rights, populations, bodies, today's networked subjectivities and human fluxes, the effects of? Are we merely effects of the signifier, of the statements that configure the field of human experience at a given time? No, not merely. We are the effects of matrices, formalized by Gilles Deleuze in *What is a Dispositif?* (his reflection on Foucault) under the name of *dispositifs* or apparatuses. For Deleuze, an apparatus is:

> a multilinear whole. It is composed of lines of different natures . . . visible objects, articulable utterances, forces in use, subjects in position are like vectors or tensors. Thus the three main instances Foucault successively distinguishes – Knowledge, Power and Subjectivity – . . . are chains of variables that are torn from each other.
>
> (Deleuze 2007: 338)

The two dimensions of Foucault's work – concisely presented as the *archival* and the *diagnostic* by Deleuze in the same piece – are logically correlated to his concern with who we are. The archival dimension seeks to know how we became who or what we are (see, on this point, Foucault 1991b); the diagnostic dimension aims to intervene strategically in the present in order to become other than who we are. As Deleuze observes: 'In every apparatus we must untangle the lines of the recent past from the lines of the near future: the archive from the current, the part of history and the part of becoming, *the part of analysis and the part of diagnosis*' (Deleuze 2007: 346, emphasis in original). These two dimensions combine to form histories of the present as *strategies*.[11]

What, more precisely, are *dispositifs*? Rendering them visible, untangling their constituent lines, lines which are in constant motion, is the work of the cartographer (Deleuze 1988: 21–38). Deleuze lists the series of lines successively identified by Foucault: '[T]he first two dimensions of an apparatus or the ones that Foucault first extracted are the curves of visibility and the curves of utterances.' These are the constituent lines of knowledge: 'It is not an exaggeration to say that every mechanism [*dispositif*] is a mushy mixture of the visible and the articulable' (Deleuze 1988: 38). Curves of utterances because apparatuses make one talk, they define the regimes of enunciation, the subjective positions within the apparatus; curves of visibility because apparatuses make one see: '[E]ach apparatus has its regimen of light, the way it falls, softens and spreads, distributing the visible and the invisible, generating or eliminating an object, which cannot exist without it' (Deleuze 2007: 339). There are, additionally, spatial, architectural arrangements that configure regimes of light: places of visibility. Thus the asylum is a place of visibility for madness (Foucault 2001; Deleuze 1988: 47); the hospital is a place of visibility for illness (Foucault 2003b); the prison a place of visibility for criminality (Foucault 1991a).

The third dimension of an apparatus is lines of force, or power relations. Power forms diagrams which 'affect visible matter in general . . . but also in general pass through every articulable function' (Deleuze 1988: 34). Hence the power/knowledge binary: power does not *determine* knowledge but it affects the visible and the articulable in *determining* yet *non-determinable* ways. The final dimension is made up of lines of subjectivation and refers to the ways in which we individuate ourselves in processes of play with the other lines that configure our reality. Deleuze summarizes what an apparatus is in the following terms:

> Apparatuses are therefore composed of lines of visibility, utterances, lines of force, lines of subjectivation, lines of cracking, breaking and ruptures that all intertwine and mix together . . . all of the lines are lines of variation that do not even have constant coordinates.
>
> (Deleuze 2007: 342–3)

Leaving aside the multiplicity and indeterminacy of the lines at play in all apparatuses for now, I will begin my discussion of Foucault's gaze by engaging with his analysis of the constitution of modern medical knowledge in *The Birth of the Clinic*. In this study of the medical gaze, Foucault isolates the first two series of lines constituent of knowledge: 'Knowledge is a practical assemblage, a "mechanism" [*dispositif*] of statements and visibilities' (Deleuze 1988: 51). Despite the importance accorded to visibility in this book, Foucault also acknowledges the primacy of the statement over the visible,[12] but a visible that cannot be reduced to, or fully determined by, the statement. How do curves of utterances 'relate to' curves of visibility? What is Foucault's achievement in this book? A superficial reading shows Foucault demonstrating that language structures perception, that there is no such thing as a neutral gaze, and that the gaze has little to do with sight. Reading the text more closely, however, we also see Foucault identifying a profound shift in the relation between the visible and the articulable. This shift is correlated to the constitution of finite man, of 'the Man-form' (Deleuze 1998: 124–32) apprehended in its physical individuality as a knowing subject, duplicated in an object to be known, through the gaze of modernity.

The two halves of truth

The best companion piece to *The Birth of the Clinic* on the question of the articulation between lines of visibility and curves of utterances is undoubtedly the third chapter of Deleuze's *Foucault*, entitled 'Strata or Historical Formations: The Visible and the Articulable (Knowledge)' (Deleuze 1988: 41–58), and I will be drawing from it in my exposition of the argument in *The Birth of the Clinic*. This section will start by mapping the inversion of the classic account of the emergence of modern medicine which Foucault performs in that text. I will then try to outline the theory of the gaze underpinning this work. Finally, I will tentatively address the question of the relation between the instrumentality of the gaze in the human sciences and the drive to mastery implicit in the will to knowledge in its modernity-specific form.

The dominant hypothesis refuted – that myth gave way to neutral, scientific observation

The event analysed in *The Birth of the Clinic*, an 'ineradicable chronological threshold' (Foucault 2003b: 241), is the sudden, radical restructuring of French medicine at the time of the Revolution. Faithful to his method, Foucault first identifies an event,[13] an epistemic break, and then the dominant interpretation to be displaced. Classically, the rupture in medical knowledge was interpreted as a foregoing of the dimension of dreams and myths in favour of an objective truth on the body and illness, obtained through a truly scientific gaze: 'From the modern perspective of careful perception and neutral description, the older medical accounts seem not only false but literally incomprehensible' (Dreyfus and Rabinow 1983: 12–3). Or, in Foucault's words, 'doctors, free at last of theories and chimeras, agreed to approach the object of their experience with the purity of an unprejudiced gaze' (Foucault 2003b: 241). Far from rallying behind this hypothesis, Foucault instead re-centres the analysis on the status of visibility in the formation of knowledge:

> But the analysis must be turned around: it is the forms of visibility that have changed; the new medical spirit to which Bichat is no doubt the first to bear witness in an absolutely coherent way cannot be ascribed to an act of psychological and epistemological purification; it is nothing more than a syntactical reorganization of disease in which the limits of the visible and invisible follow a new pattern; the abyss beneath illness, which was the illness itself, has emerged into the light of language – the same light, no doubt, that illuminates the *120 Journées de Sodome*, *Juliette*, and Goya's *Désastres*.
>
> (Foucault 2003b: 241–2, translation modified[14])

This quotation, drawn from the conclusion to *The Birth of the Clinic*, encapsulates the two dimensions of Foucault's gaze at this stage of his reflection. On the one hand, we find the idea of the gaze as a metaphor for the light of language: there is a being-light of language. On the other hand, the idea that the will to mastery, the sadistic drive – evoked here with the passing reference to Sade's writings and Goya's engravings – is at the heart of the will to knowledge, and is linked to the *scopic* drive:

> To know life is given only to that derisory, reductive and already infernal knowledge that only wishes it dead. The Gaze that envelops, caresses, details, atomizes the most individual flesh and enumerates its secret bites is that fixed, attentive, rather dilated gaze which, from the height of death, has already condemned life.
>
> (Foucault 2003b: 210)

The correlation between the will to knowledge and the destruction of the human is also evoked by Foucault at the end of 'Nietzsche, Genealogy, History' (Foucault 2000b: 387–8) and in the recently published *Leçons sur la volonté de savoir* (Foucault 2011). Let us retrace how Foucault reaches these conclusions in *The Birth of the Clinic*.

Using the method Foucault scholars are now familiar with, the book proceeds to undermine the dominant interpretation of a given event by identifying the conditions of possibility of that event. The first condition of possibility of the 'radical restructuring' of medicine is the creation of the general hospital, which produces a new visibility of the bodies caught within that space. For modern medicine to become possible, 'the patient has to be enveloped in a collective, homogeneous space' (Foucault 2003b: 242):

> The figures of pain are not conjured away by means of a body of neutralized knowledge; they have been redistributed in the space in which bodies and eyes meet. What has changed is the silent configuration in which language

> finds support: the relation of situation and attitude to what is speaking and what is spoken about.
>
> (Foucault 2003b: xi)

The new architectural figure of the hospital implies a redistribution of the subject-positions within the field of medicine. Doctors, those who speak (or *are spoken* by the apparatus), access a new visibility of the objects to be spoken about: the body, diseases, death. The hospital, the product of a new diagram of power, is the first comprehensive place of visibility of the sick body. Places of visibility are the condition of possibility of statements that can only be uttered from such places, and from the subject-positions within. For '[t]he subject who sees is himself a place within visibility, a function derived from visibility' (Deleuze 1988: 57). They are new ways of making one see, and statements are new ways of speaking.

We can illustrate the concept of a place of visibility with a more contemporary example, which I draw from the empirical research carried out by Francis (2011) on the CCTV network of the Belgian railways – one of the most extensive such networks currently in operation in Europe. The images, captured by the networked cameras covering the 51 largest train stations and platforms, are sent to a CCTV control centre where they are visualized in real time by CCTV operators. The operators' task is to direct ground interventions in order to ensure the smooth running of the train services, and to encode all incidents according to a very precise taxonomy in a feedback process relayed to the system designers. Francis's hypothesis is that the CCTV control centre is a place of visibility that 'visibilizes' hitherto invisible – *but not hitherto inexistent* – objects for the gaze of the observers: fluxes of passengers, suicide attempts, clusters of stagnant populations such as homeless people or groups of teenagers, but also the deviant behaviour of the railway staff. A place of visibility does not create new objects for knowledge, it is not even created to make the objects it visibilizes visible. There is no relationship of *determination* between the place of visibility and the visibilities it produces: the visibilities are *determined* but not *determinable*. For instance, Francis shows that staff deviance, which was visibilized by the apparatus, was an unexpected visibility which, once seen, had to be addressed. A place of visibility makes existent 'objects' visible, they acquire a being-light which, in turn, gives rise to new curves of utterances pronounced from within that place: the statements of the operators, of the system designers, of the police officers that rely on it as a source of evidence, but also of the academic researcher and in turn, the academic community.

The second condition of possibility of today's medical gaze is the generalization of autopsy in anatomical pathology. The practice of dissection was not new, but autopsy is correlated to the coming of the Enlightenment. As Alibert, a doctor quoted by Foucault, put it in 1817: 'When philosophy brought its torch into the midst of civilized peoples, it was at last permitted to cast one's searching gaze upon the inanimate remains of the human body, and these fragments, once the vile prey of worms, became the fruitful source of the most useful truths' (in

Foucault 2003b: 153). What differentiates autopsy from dissection, and makes it a condition of possibility of modern medicine, is the instrumentality of the gaze. For Wajcman, a psychoanalyst and art critic, with the Enlightenment the world is no longer 'a book to be deciphered but a visible reality that can be observed' (Wajcman 2010: 239). To illustrate his thesis, Wajcman contrasts early dissection practices with anatomical pathology. In the first case, the master explained bodily functions to students from his chair, reading from the anatomy treatises of Galen and Aristotle while barbers carved out the corpse, while in the second illustration, the Renaissance doctor Vesalius performed the autopsies himself, proving or disproving the written text with visual evidence.

Autopsy is a process characterized by 'the thought that the real is visible' (Wajcman 2010: 239): in Foucault's words, 'the corpse became the brightest moment in the figures of truth' (Foucault 2003b: 153), or again '[t]he living night is dissipated in the brightness of death' (Foucault 2003b: 180). With the autopsy, 'the emergence of the gaze as a new instrument of knowledge' (Wajcman 2010: 240) is averred. It is this emergence which Foucault identifies, not only as condition of possibility of modern medicine, but more generally of all contemporary knowledge. A really interesting point here is the shifting status of the visible: because the corpse offers its solid materiality to the gaze, the autopsy is no longer about unveiling or uncovering a hidden signification. The play between the visible and the hidden gives way to that between the visible and the invisible, an invisible buried in the materiality of bodies and things, it gives way to the idea that truth is inscribed in the real. This is what Foucault says of death at the end of his chapter on the visible invisible, for example: 'Death left its old tragic heaven and became the lyrical core of man: his invisible truth, his visible secret' (Foucault 2003b: 211). An invisible truth because the living individuality is not hidden but only revealed post-mortem, a visible secret because the incommunicability of death is exposed through autopsy: the autopsied corpse is 'the interior revealed' (Foucault 2003b: 242). The anatomo-clinical method is henceforth a 'structure, in which space, language and death are articulated' (Foucault 2003b: 242–3).

Making the conditions of possibility of modern medicine *visible* allows Foucault not only to displace the classic thesis of the emergence of a pure, scientific, neutral and unprejudiced gaze, but also to hypothesize a shift in 'the constitution of the sciences of man . . . [whereby t]he possibility for the individual of being both subject and object of his own knowledge implies an inversion in the structure of finitude' (Foucault 2003b: 244). Why is medicine a privileged discipline for the finitude of man to be so readily accepted? Because 'medicine offers modern man the obstinate, yet reassuring face of his finitude; in it, death is endlessly repeated, but it is also exorcized; and although it ceaselessly reminds man of the limit that he bears within him, it also speaks to him of that technical world that is the armed, positive, full form of his finitude' (Foucault 2003b: 244–5).

How can we understand this somewhat sibylline expression, 'an inversion in the structure of finitude'? Beyond the field of medicine, it is the sciences of man which Foucault targets: knowledge is henceforth no longer the finite knowledge of an infinite being, but an infinite knowledge of finite man. Deleuze elucidates this inversion further in the fourth chapter of his *Foucault* and again in the Appendix, entitled 'On the Death of Man and Superman' (perhaps not the best translation for Nietzsche's *Übermensch*). Deleuze posits that 'Foucault's general principle is that every form is a compound of relations between forces' (Deleuze 1988: 124). Man, having no essence, is therefore a compound of relations between forces: the forces within man enter into a relation with forces that first come *as if* from the outside and are then appropriated. Through a close reading of *The Order of Things*, Deleuze demonstrates that the figure of man, or the Man-form, superseded the God-form. In the classical age the God-form emerged as an effect of the *unfolding* of infinite series in a 'continual development towards infinity, formations of continuums, and unveiling of scenes: the continual need to unfold and "explain". For what is God, if not the universal explanation and supreme unveiling?' (Deleuze 1988: 126). By the nineteenth century, the God-form had given way to the Man-form, which emerged as a two-stage *fold* correlated to the forces that the forces of man interact with. These forces are 'Life, Labour and Language – the triple root of finitude, which will give birth to biology, political economy and linguistics' (Deleuze 1988: 127). The two-stage fold involves, first, 'the force within man . . . confronting and seizing hold of the forces of finitude as if they were forces from the outside . . . [and t]hen and only [then] . . . does it create from this its own finitude, where its knowledge of finitude necessarily brings it to its own finitude' (Deleuze 1988: 127). Or again '*These dark forces of finitude are not initially human* but enter into a relation with the forces of man in order to bring him down to his own finitude, and communicate to him a history which he then proceeds to make his own' (Deleuze 1988: 88, emphasis in original). This is also why Foucault identifies history or historicity as the privileged mode of being of language in modernity. And when Foucault evoked the possible death of man,[15] an often misunderstood proposition, it was the death of this figure of finitude.

The status of the gaze in The Birth of the Clinic

With the argument of *The Birth of the Clinic* now in mind, let us see what more we can draw from the text with regards to the gaze. What Foucault demonstrates most clearly in this book is that the gaze is not the eye, the organ of sight, and that visibilities are nowhere near equivalent to the visual. The gaze is not a sensory organ, a medium of perception amenable to a neutral deciphering of the world, nor is it an unprejudiced mode of relation between a knowing subject and an object to be known. The gaze is not about *what one sees* but rather *how one looks*.[16] How does Foucault construct his position?

The gaze of modernity, argues Foucault, developed in two successive stages: first in the clinical experience; and then subsequently in anatomical pathology. We can map its emergence according to the two-stage fold constituting the Man-form: first the forces within man enter into a relation with the forces of finitude as if they came from the outside, then there is an appropriation of these forces in the form of history (clinical history in the case of medicine). The clinical experience initially 'rests on a formidable postulate: that all that is *visible* is *expressible*, and that it is *wholly visible* because it is *wholly expressible*' (Foucault 2003b: 142, emphasis in original). What we have in this first moment is a fantasy of reversibility between the visible and the articulable, a point by point correlation between the two halves of truth. At this stage, the gaze is a surface gaze: everything that can be said can be seen, and everything that can be seen can be said in a 'perpetual and objectively based correlation of the visible and the expressible' (Foucault 2003b: 242):

> Over all these endeavours on the part of clinical thought to define its methods and scientific norms hovers the great myth of a pure Gaze that would be pure Language: a speaking eye . . . [that] would be the servant of things and the master of truth.
>
> (Foucault 2003b: 141)

There is a direct correlation between 'the *spatialization* and *verbalization* of the pathological' (Foucault 2003b: xii, emphasis in original). The visible, equated with the visual, is privileged in the establishment of the truth-value of knowledge. The gaze mistakes itself for the eye, believes itself to be able to bring truth to light, a truth freed from the veils of fantasies, myths, dreams and theories. The *gaze* of medical knowledge takes itself for scientific *sight* as it receives the visibilities brought to light by the hospital.

In anatomical pathology, the second moment of the emergence of modern medicine, the non-reversibility of statements and visibilities, is actualised. The gaze then draws the invisible to the surface in a 'spatial assignation of the invisible' (Foucault 2003b: 202). The gaze becomes a metaphoric gaze, drawing definitive truth from the autopsy. It initially rests on the senses, on hearing, sight and touch, 'until such time as death brings to truth the luminous presence of the visible' (Foucault 2003b: 203). Here Foucault talks about a duplication of the gaze, the redoubling of the first fold:

> [T]he medical gaze is duplicated: there is a local, circumscribed gaze, the borderline gaze of touch and hearing, . . . which operates on little more than the visible surfaces. But there is also an absolute, absolutely integrating gaze that dominates and founds all perceptual experiences. It is this gaze that structures into a sovereign unity that which belongs to the lower level of the eye, the ear, and the sense of touch. When the doctor observes, with all his senses open, another eye is directed upon the fundamental visibility of things, and, through the transparent datum of life with which the particular senses are forced to work, he addresses himself fairly and squarely to the bright solidity of death.
>
> (Foucault 2003b: 203–4)

The gaze which Foucault discusses from that point on has little to do with the visual: it is the 'absolute eye of knowledge' which is at stake, which organizes all other perceptions through a 'suzerainty of the visible' (Foucault 2003b: 204). We note here that Foucault chooses the term 'suzerainty' over that of 'sovereignty' of the visible. His precise choice of words underlines the primacy of the statement over the visible, although the visible is irreducible to the statement. Deleuze elucidates the relation between the visible and the articulable in the following terms: 'The statement has primacy by virtue of the spontaneity of its conditions (language) which gives it a determining form, while the visible element, by virtue of the receptivity of its conditions (light), merely has the form of the determinable. Therefore, we can assume that determination always comes from the statement, although the two forms differ in nature' (Deleuze 1988: 67). Statements determine visibilities, but visibilities are not determinable by statements. And for Foucault, it is power-diagrams, strategies of power, which produce the various combinations between the two strata of knowledge: regimes of visibility and regimes of enunciation.

The gaze is not the light which reveals hidden things, 'visibilities are not forms of objects, nor even forms that would show up under light, but rather forms of luminosity which are created by the light itself' (Deleuze 1988: 52) – the being-light of language. To put it in plainer terms, we do not see things but visibilities. For example, when the twenty-first century neuroscientist looks at a brain, he sees neural pathways, when our probation officers look at re-offending probabilities they see risk factors, when cognitive behavioural therapists look at symptoms they see cognitive dysfunctions and when CCTV operators look at fluxes they see the possibility of obstruction. Further, visibilities organize the play of light and opacity, as for example the panoptic tower does: the central tower is opaque, the 'peripheral cells' are bathed in light (Deleuze 1988: 58). Not only do visibilities create forms of luminosity, they also create zones of opacity. Thus, paradoxically, as Miller points out (Miller 1987: 4), in the panoptic tower it is the eye which is bathed in opacity. And opacity itself has a function: it orchestrates the visible. The gaze itself is *invisible*, and subsumes all other senses in its operation.

So what is Foucault's visibility? Quite plainly, it is not the visual but a 'virtual visibility' which dominates all sensory experiences, including sight. Visibility, then, is thought itself: 'Thought is what sees and can be described visibly' (Deleuze 1988: 59). Seeing and speaking are the 'two halves of truth',[17] and their mode of 'relation' is a non-relation: they 'spill over into one another, as in a battle' (Deleuze 1988: 66), in procedures for truth. And the visible is part of language; it is the being-light of language, what makes us see. It follows that, given the drive to mastery over the material world that impels modernity, in order to see as much as possible, we need to introduce as much language as possible on singularity, to circumscribe the invisible as closely as possible with the *light of language*. It is the work of language that exposes the singularity of the living, and produces knowledge on the individual. There needs to be language, taxonomies and codes, in order to translate images into significations. We can illustrate this point with the invention of Bertillonnage, beautifully documented in *L'image accusatrice*. Bertillonnage is a 'global system for the identification of suspects associating . . . anthropometrical measurements, photographic portraits and rigorous methods for the description of the individual' (Phéline 1985: 11). The point of Bertillonnage is to establish a person's identity without fail through measurements that would remain constant throughout a lifetime.

Finally, the gaze, as distinct from perception, has implications for the status of the secret. 'Each historical formation sees and reveals all it can within the conditions laid down for visibility, just as it says all it can within the conditions relating to statements. Nothing is ever secret, even though nothing is ever immediately visible or directly readable' (Deleuze 1988: 59). In the end, it is knowledge of the individual which is produced by 'the absolute eye of [medical] knowledge' (Foucault 2003b: 204): introducing language 'where the gaze is bereft of words' (Foucault 2003b: 208). And it is the violence of language which Foucault expresses distaste for.

Will to knowledge

This section of my chapter is speculative. It seems to me that some of Foucault's works, in particular *The Birth of the Clinic* (Foucault 2003b) and *Discipline and Punish* (Foucault 1991a), but also *Psychiatric Power* (Foucault 2006), *Abnormal* (Foucault 2003a) and the first volume of *The History of Sexuality* (Foucault 1980b), are documentations of the violence inflicted by language[18] on individuals in the name of knowledge. Sadism is inherent to the diagrams of power of the disciplinary era, a sadism relayed by the scopic drive. For what does Foucault document but the intrusiveness of the gaze, searching the bodies and souls of men? What, indeed, does he document in *The Birth of the Clinic*, if not the destruction of the image of man, his body, so as to extract and render visible its secrets? Whether it be the gaze of doctors, psychiatrists and all manners of educators, Foucault's distaste for the surveillance practices of power is evident, as is apparent from his tone in *Discipline and Punish*, when for example he refers to 'the minor civil servants of moral orthopaedics' (Foucault 1991a: 10). But, and this is where this chapter becomes more tentative – is the sadism inherent to the operation of the gaze in modernity a constant effect of power-relations, or is it correlated with the advent of the Man-form? And, more importantly, is it possible to dissociate the gaze from the will to mastery? Foucault is ambivalent on this point, as emerges from his discussions of Nietzsche's will to knowledge. Two texts are key here. The first of them is the French edition of Foucault's first lecture series at the *Collège de France*, entitled *Leçons sur la volonté de savoir*, which includes a lecture on Nietzsche that Foucault gave at McGill in April 1971. The second important text, contemporary with this lecture, is the text entitled 'Nietzsche, Genealogy, History' (Foucault 2000b). Similar themes are also rehearsed in the first of the five lectures that Foucault delivered in Brazil in 1973, published under the title of 'Truth and Juridical Forms' (Foucault 2000e).

First, we note that Foucault translates Nietzsche's *Wissentrieb* – we recognize here the German *Trieb*, the Freudian term for the drive – as *volonté de savoir*: not only will *to know*, but also will *to knowledge*. Indeed the French term *savoir* is both 'knowledge' and the verb 'to know'. This is important in that for Foucault what is at stake is not a simple, 'natural' wanting to know but the will to a particular form of knowledge, relying on the 'knowing subject-object to be known' dichotomy: a form of knowledge he argues, after Nietzsche, which is neither natural nor eternal but historically specified (Foucault 2011).

In his McGill lecture Foucault develops Nietzsche's hypothesis that knowledge (*connaissance*) is an invention.[19] What does it mean to say that knowledge is an invention? First, it means that knowledge is not man's oldest instinct, 'inscribed in human nature'. But also, and more importantly, that 'its possibility is not defined by its form. The possibility of knowledge is not a formal law' (Foucault 2011: 195–6). These propositions indicate that knowledge does not unfold according to reason but rather according to forces at play within man, such as doubt, negation, instincts and so forth. Knowledge is not about the deciphering, perception or representation of objects lying there, waiting to be seen and known through empirical means. On the contrary, what lies behind knowledge, says Foucault, is what is 'completely other to it, foreign, opaque, irreducible' (Foucault 2011: 196). Knowledge does not precede itself; it does not advance fully formed towards the objects of the world. Behind knowledge lies the wall of non-knowledge. It follows that knowledge is 'the result of a complex operation' (Foucault 2011: 196), a play of forces which Foucault refers to as the 'deathly malice of knowledge' (Foucault 2011: 198). The 'malice' of knowledge leads one to seek mastery over the thing, to destroy its appearance, to extract its secrets from it. But what impels us to know, if it is not a natural wish to perceive and see the world? For Nietzsche, what prevents us from knowing, the opaque, the obstacle, is the very root, impetus and dynamism of knowledge: its *force*, and not its *form*. Knowledge, although it is not an instinct (Foucault 2000e: 8), is thus the 'outcome of the interplay, the encounter, the junction, the struggle, and the compromise between instincts' (Foucault 2000e: 8). And in the age of the Man-form, what is the obstacle to knowledge if not man himself? '[Man] himself is in the way,' writes Foucault, quoting Nietzsche, 'he conceals things' (in Foucault 2011: 199). So man becomes the obstacle to knowledge, and arouses its 'lethal fierceness' (Foucault 2011: 198). And the relation between knowing subject and object to be known, instead of being knowledge's foundation, is in fact *produced by* knowledge, the form of knowledge modernity favours since Descartes split the mind from the body.

Is it possible to know otherwise? If knowledge is not defined by its form, then it should follow that it is the case. In the essay 'Nietzsche, Genealogy, History', Foucault opposes *connaissance* and *savoir*, two words rendered by knowledge in English. *Connaissance*, he argues, has to do with suppressing one's individuality, one's singularity, from the knowledge one produces. *Connaissance* is thence produced as neutral, objective and objectively true. This truth is however of the order of the error – '[t]ruth is undoubtedly the sort of error that cannot be refuted'

(Foucault 2000b: 372) – of the lie (Foucault 2011: 204). Foucault looks to Nietzsche for another form of knowing, namely what he calls *savoir*, borrowing from Nietzsche's account of effective history. Nietzsche's effective history reintroduces the body, blood, contingency, filiation, passions, instincts, events, struggles and battles to destroy reality, identity and truth, to destroy recognition, continuities and *connaissance*: 'History becomes "effective" to the degree that it introduces discontinuity into our very being – as it divides our emotions, dramatizes our instincts, multiplies our body and sets it against itself' (Foucault 2000b: 380). No longer the neutral gaze of the impartial observer, the gaze of genealogy refuses identity, it dismisses the 'consoling play of recognitions [*connaissances*] – because "knowledge is not made for understanding; it is made for cutting"' (2000b: 380). This gaze 'refuses the certainty of absolutes':

> It corresponds to the acuity of a gaze that distinguishes, separates, and disperses; that is capable of liberating divergence and marginal elements – the kind of dissociating view that is capable of decomposing itself, capable of shattering the unity of man's being through which it was thought that he could extend his sovereignty to the events of his past.
>
> (2000b: 379, translation modified)

The gaze of the genealogist is 'a gaze that knows where it is looking from as well as what it is looking at' (Foucault 2000b: 382, translation modified).[20] We can illustrate this point by recalling the opening pages of *Discipline and Punish*. The original French edition, as pointed out by Boullant, opened with two series. First, a series of *images* designed to render disciplinary power visible before the argument was made – 'the images evidenced the invisible solidarity of disciplines before offering it up to our thought' (Boullant 2003: 33) – and then, secondly, a series of *statements* – the description of Damiens's punishment (Foucault 1991a: 3–6), starkly contrasted with an enumeration of the rules for 'the House of young prisoners in Paris' (Foucault 1991a: 6–7), the 'public execution and a timetable' (Foucault 1991a: 7). The gaze of the genealogist knows what it is looking at: the *visibilities* and *statements* that intertwine in disciplinary power, substituting itself for the panoptic gaze that orchestrates the play of utterances and visibilities whilst remaining comfortably shrouded in opacity. By contrast, not only does the gaze of the genealogist agree to make itself visible, to include itself in what it describes – 'it knows where it is looking from' – but also, in doing so, it brings the invisible gaze of power-knowledge to the light of language.

So it is pretty clear that at this stage in his work Foucault is opposing *savoir* to *connaissance*, and the will to knowledge to *volonté de connaissance*, which he argues, after Nietzsche, became historically associated with the will to truth (see Foucault 2011). Are these however Foucault's last words on the subject? The last pages of 'Nietzsche, Genealogy, History' are far from being wholeheartedly sold to the will to knowledge. There Foucault mentions that the sacrifice of the subject of knowledge [*connaissance*], the:

> rancorous will to knowledge . . . does not achieve a universal truth; man is not given an exact and serene mastery of nature. On the contrary, it ceaselessly multiplies the risks, creates dangers in every area; breaks down illusory defences; it dissolves the unity of the subject; it releases those elements of itself that are devoted to its subversion and destruction.
>
> (Foucault 2000b: 387)

What the will to knowledge achieves is, in the last analysis, 'the destruction of the man who maintains knowledge [*connaissance*] by the injustice proper to the will to knowledge [*savoir*]' (Foucault 2000b: 389). So the gaze of the genealogist as a form of resistance to *connaissance* is also pregnant with danger and destruction. Is this not why, at the end of his work, Foucault rehabilitates *a form of truth*[21] – which he terms auto-veridiction as opposed to hetero-veridiction – as distinct both from *connaissance* and *savoir*? The *courage of truth* (Foucault 2010), the Greek *parrhesia*, is developed by Foucault as an alternative to all normative uses of language, since normativity is the very essence of language. Fundamentally, what we need to resist in order to be as free as humanly possible is *language*, even those uses of language designed to resist the present. Thus, in *The Government of Self and Others* (2010), Foucault reflects on the position of enunciation of the philosopher in terms of the effect he comes to believe is the only legitimate 'mission' of the philosopher: to participate in the substitution of *autonomy* for *heteronomy* for those that listen to him, bearing in mind that this substitution has to be accomplished individually through what Foucault terms practices of the self as 'a practice of freedom' (on this, see Foucault 1997). And indeed, when we see the way in which Foucault's work is re-appropriated in so many disciplines in order to consolidate and entrench the counter-truths he had hoped would undermine and displace, *not hegemonic truths but the hegemony of truth*, we can but welcome his 'ethical turn'.

Surveillance and the gaze

Panopticism is one of the most commented upon aspects of Foucault's work, so I shall not engage in an exhaustive rendering of it here. Instead, I shall merely extract a few elements which I consider to be indicative of a shift in his theory of the gaze.

The appropriation of the gaze by disciplinary societies

In the mid-1970s, notably in 'Truth and Juridical Forms' and *Discipline and Punish*, Foucault discusses the gaze in terms of its *appropriation by surveillance*, the model of knowledge-power central to disciplinary practices. 'Truth and Juridical Forms' proposes a genealogy of the historical mutation of the status of the gaze through a reading of a series of judicial procedures. Thus, in the second lecture, Foucault illustrates a first shift by contrasting the resolution of a conflict between two Greek warriors, a story narrated in Homer's *Iliad*, with the search for truth in

Sophocles' play, *Oedipus the King*. The resolution of the conflict between Menelaus and Antilochus takes the form of a challenge [*épreuve*], with Menelaus challenging Antilochus to take an oath: 'Swear by Zeus that you didn't commit any foul' (Foucault 2000e: 18). No eye-witness is summoned to testify whether Antilochus did or did not cheat in the race. But in *Oedipus the King* 'the gaze of the witness' (Foucault 2000e: 23) appears for the first time in the recorded history of judicial procedures. The effect is to shift the 'enunciation of the truth' from prophecy (the oracular statements of the seers) to the evidence provided by eye-witnesses (Foucault 2000e: 23). Here Foucault presents the gaze as a democratic force. The gaze of the humble shepherd is opposed to the gaze of Oedipus the tyrant, 'the man of seeing, the man of the gaze . . . the man who, all by himself . . . wishes to see with his own eyes' (Foucault 2000e: 29). That is, a 'powerless truth' is set against 'a truthless power' (2000e: 33).

Why this interest in ancient judicial procedures? The overarching argument of the lecture series is that judicial models of decision-making are also models for knowledge (Foucault 2000e: 50–1). Thus, at the time of the test (*épreuve*), such as the one imposed by Menelaus, the model for knowledge was the struggle between two forces. Foucault illustrates his point with alchemy – where knowledge is produced in a struggle between 'the alchemist, who wanted to know, and . . . nature, which guarded its secrets' (Foucault 2000e: 50) – and the academic practice of *disputatio*, where the winning party was the one who had the most supporters rather than the one who established the truth of his argument (Foucault 2000e: 51). By contrast, when judicial truth is obtained via the *inquiry*, the model for knowledge becomes that of the establishment of truth through testimonies and observations, and this is also the case for the contemporary sciences of botany, medicine and zoology (Foucault 2000e: 50). These models are *forms* of knowledge, of knowledge-power (Foucault 2000e: 52); the content is secondary to the form.

The third form of knowledge-power is correlated with disciplinary societies, 'the age of social orthopaedics' (Foucault 2000e: 57). The model for judicial truth becomes the examination, or surveillance, which is distinct from inquiry in that it seeks to correct 'potentialities' rather than punish crimes (Foucault 2000e: 57). In the inquiry model, testimonies and observations seek to reactualize a past; whereas the examination model requires constant and total surveillance (Foucault 2000e: 59). Examination as a form of knowledge-power gives rise to the sciences of man, psychiatry, psychology and sociology (Foucault 2000e: 59). These disciplinary practices are required by new demographic factors (Foucault 2000e: 62) – 'the problem of the accumulation of men' (Foucault 1980a: 151) – and emergent capitalism, with its 'new material form of wealth' (Foucault 1980a: 168) necessitating storage and accumulation of goods, and thus protection from theft. A new problem arose, an architectural problem: what technology of power would enable a shift from civilizations of the *spectacle*, in which as many people as possible could see the acts of a few, to civilizations of *surveillance*, where one person could see as many as possible. Bentham's solution was the Panopticon, a re-organization of *space* in order to maximize the visibility of the many by the few.

Foucault developed the concept of panopticism to include the self-surveillance produced by the institution of the soul, an *event* which can be referred to as an *internalization of a scopic division* within individuals themselves (see, for example, Foucault 1980a: 155).

In 'Truth and Juridical Forms', Foucault ascribes three functions to panopticism, to the gaze in disciplinary societies: control, surveillance and correction (2000e: 70). The 'society of generalised orthopaedics' (Foucault 2000e: 58) appropriates the gaze. At this stage in his reflection, Foucault argues that panopticism is 'a utopia that was actually realised' (Foucault 2000e: 58), that 'today we live in a society programmed basically by Bentham, a panoptic society, a society where panopticism reigns' (Foucault 2000e: 70). Panopticism implies permanent, continuous and absolute surveillance; it requires the transparency of man whose opacity as object must give way to the empire of the gaze, itself shrouded in the opacity of the tower. We recognize a similar structure to that exposed in *The Birth of the Clinic*, with the 'absolute eye of knowledge' now presented in terms of the constitution of docile bodies, and the institution of the prosecutor recast as the model for the absolute eye of power:

> The prosecutor is, above all, a gaze, an eye constantly trained on the population. The eye of the prosecutor must transmit information to the eye of the attorney general, who in turn transmits it to the great eye of surveillance, which at the time was the minister of police. The latter transmits information to the eye of the one who is at the highest point of society, the emperor – who, as it happens, then used the symbol of an eye. The emperor is the universal eye observing the entire expanse of society, an eye assisted by a series of gazes, arrayed in the form of a pyramid starting from the imperial eye, and watching over the whole of society . . . [for the jurists of the empire], this great pyramid of gazes constituted the new form of judicial process.
>
> (Foucault 2000e: 73)

By the mid-1970s Foucault's gaze is therefore the key technology for the subjectification of individual existence through a pyramidal structure[22] of constant observation. The objective of surveillance, beyond the control of time and bodies, is also cast in terms of the creation of a 'polymorphous, polyvalent power' (Foucault 2000e: 82–3). This power is economic (in that it makes people work), it is political (in that it gives orders, makes decisions and so forth), it is judicial (in that it punishes and rewards), and, most importantly, it is epistemological. On this latter score, it extracts knowledge *from* individuals by appropriating their know-how in the workplace. It also extracts knowledge *about* individuals through observation and classification, with the groups produced by observation giving rise to the disciplines of criminology, pedagogy, psychiatry and psychology for purposes of social control. Finally, these disciplines, modelled on surveillance, caused 'man as an object of science to appear . . . as the fundamental, privileged object of [a] type of knowledge' (Foucault 2000e: 87, translation modified).

This is the version of panopticism most often used to account for the omnipresent gaze of surveillance in our societies. Yet Foucault himself rapidly relented on his oppressive account of surveillance and as early as 1977, in an interview with J.-P. Barou and Michelle Perrot published as a preface to the French edition of Bentham's *Panopticon*, he put panopticism in perspective.

Scopic fantasies

This 1977 interview, entitled 'The Eye of Power', is the final text I shall consider in this chapter. Here Foucault acknowledges that the gaze is only one among many other technologies of power. As he puts it, 'the procedures of power that are at work in modern societies are much more numerous, diverse and rich. It would be wrong to say that the principle of visibility governs all technologies of power used since the nineteenth century' (Foucault 1980a: 148). Or again, '[the gaze] is far from being the only or even the principal system employed' (Foucault 1980a: 155). He also accepts that the emergence of surveillance practices during the French Revolution was correlated to the depersonalization of power (see, also, Stolleis 2009; Starobinski 1998). The politics of the gaze participated in the protection of citizens against inequality, social dangers and the return of absolutism and, since with the Panopticon power is an effect of 'a machinery that no one owns' (Foucault 1980a: 156), it also prevented individual identifications with power. Foucault also gives a place to people's resistance, their 'revolts against the gaze' (Foucault 1980a: 162) which occurred very rapidly in workshops and factories, actualizing the failure of the politics of the gaze and precipitating its replacement with *actual* machines.[23]

What is really striking in this text, by contrast to the writings preceding it by a few years, is that Foucault is presenting Bentham's Panopticon as the utopian fantasy of its author. This fact is further reinforced by Foucault adding that Bentham 'was the complement of Rousseau' (Foucault 1988: 152). Rousseau's dream was of a 'transparent society . . . [,] the dream of there no longer existing any zones of darkness . . . [and] it was the dream that each individual . . . might be able to see the whole of society, that men's hearts should communicate, their vision be unobstructed by obstacles' (Foucault 1980a: 152). Interestingly, Foucault's reference here is to Jean Starobinski's reflection on Rousseau, *La transparence et l'obstacle*. In this remarkable book Starobinski, who initially trained as a medical doctor and worked in psychiatry, demonstrates how Rousseau's obsession with transparency was a personal symptom raised to the dignity of a principle of political organization. Thus Rousseau and Bentham complement each other in that they share a fantasy: the fantasy that there would be nothing left over (on this point, see Miller 1987), left out, unaccounted for, hidden, unseen, opaque. For Bentham, the fantasy is that mastery over the world of men and things would obtain through the gaze. For Rousseau, it is with everyone watching everyone else that equality would obtain, as an effect of the democratic gaze relayed by public opinion. And here, in this text, Foucault recognizes this dream for what it is: the highly obsessive fantasy of men – 'Rousseau's lyricism and Bentham's obsession' (Foucault 1980a: 152) – for whom the world may have been so dark that they felt the need for light, men who were fearful of the shadow – men who wanted to eliminate arbitrariness, to calculate the effects of all causes, to suppress causes with unpredictable effects. The gaze, in these fantasies, is an instrument in the eradication of the causal gap, the very one which Foucault is so at pains to preserve as the (however slim) condition of possibility of freedom.

I would therefore venture to interpret this text as Foucault's own separation from a similar investment in the scopic drive, a separation actualized in his subsequent pluralization of technologies of power.

Conclusion

In the texts reviewed here, Foucault makes different effects of the gaze visible. To borrow Lacanian terms, we could say that Foucault shows that the gaze is an object-cause: it is a cause insofar as it causes regimes of visibilities and utterances to emerge in places of visibility, and it causes our investment in the material world. But it is also an object, albeit in the psychoanalytic sense: the objects of psychoanalysis are objects which cannot be seen, and yet are more present than visual objects. The gaze, as object-cause, is caught up within different regimes of power-knowledge, traversed by different lines of subjectivation. Ultimately, there is nothing natural about seeing, showing, observing, watching. Foucault shows us that what and how we see, what and how we look, is an effect of the apparatuses within which we see and look. This is what is really interesting about his work on the gaze. And panopticism is a mere avatar of his reflection, an avatar strictly correlated to disciplinary societies, not *the* grid of intelligibility for the present.

To conclude on my exposition of the gaze in Foucault's work, I would like to formulate a couple of hypotheses that seem worth exploring:

1 It seems clear that the mode of being of language is in the process of changing from *historicity* to *virtualization*. At stake here is the relation between the *image* and the *written*; or, rather, the *appearance* and the *code*. This is apparent in scientific attempts to 'break' the human code (DNA, the human genome, attempts in artificial intelligence and neuroscience at replicating the functioning of the brain), but also in the redoubling of the physical body with a digital body (Bogard 1996) consisting of all the data pertaining to the same individual. The human gaze, a central technology of power of the disciplinary era, is also being superseded by algorithmic surveillance (Norris *et al.* 1998): 'intelligent' cameras have replaced the scrutinizing gaze of the sciences of Man.
2 Deleuze argues that the Man-form is giving way to 'man-machine' systems: 'Is it not commonplace nowadays to say that the forces of man have already entered into a relation with the forces of information technology and their third-generation machines which together create something other than man,

indivisible "man-machine" systems?' (Deleuze 1988: 89). Deleuze develops his analysis of this third form in the Appendix to his *Foucault*: 'What would be the forces in play, with which the forces within man would then enter into a relation? It would no longer involve raising to infinity or finitude but an unlimited finity, thereby evoking every situation of force in which a finite number of components yields a practically unlimited diversity of combinations' (Deleuze 1988: 131).

To these two elements, we can also add the observation made by Wajcman (2010) that today's eye is but a technological, dead, blind metonymy of the living gaze, whether that gaze was real or fantasized (as was the case with the Panopticon). From webcams to social networking, CCTVs and Magnetic Resonance Imaging, we are all so busy *seeing* and *being seen* that nobody bothers *watching*. We are all exhibitionists in search of an audience.

Notes

1 As argued by Lyon in his editorial for the first issue of *Surveillance & Society*: 'Surveillance of all became routine during the twentieth century. Visibility became a social and a political issue in a new way' (Lyon 2002: 2).
2 For critical engagements with applications or adaptations of panopticism to apprehend contemporary practices of surveillance see Wood 2007; Yar 2002.
3 In the sense Foucault gives to this term in the Preface to *The Order of Things*, namely as a place for which the principle of intelligibility cannot be found (Foucault 1994: xv–xxiv).
4 As is the case for discipline in *Discipline and Punish*. This is also how Foucault chooses to apprehend the state in *The Birth of Biopolitics*, namely as a principle of intelligibility.
5 I am using the term 'paranoid' in the psychiatric sense: a paranoid symptom is a way of giving consistency to an inconsistent world by ascribing a malevolent intentionality to otherwise discrete practices. This intentionality is localized in the gaze or the voice of an Other. We recall that for Lacan the structure of personality is paranoiac for all subjects (Lacan 2006).
6 As Foucault argues in *The Hermeneutics of the Subject*: 'it is true after all that there is no first or final point of resistance to political power other than in the relationship one has to oneself' (Foucault 2005: 252).
7 The expression is Deleuze's (1988: 64) but we can find a discussion of the 'rule of halves' in the establishment of truth in Foucault's reading of Oedipus as a story on the judicial search for truth in 'Truth and Juridical Forms' (Foucault 2000e: 19).
8 In other words, the reduction of every sensory experience – sound, image, bodily phenomena – to the number, to statistical data, and in the last analysis to the binary codes of digitization.
9 Yar, for example, in a reductive rendering of Foucault's gaze, equates it with the visual, and the visual in turn with domination. He concludes his paper by saying: 'The fundamental thrust of the argument has been directed at the way in which Foucault's conception of visuality-as-domination might fail to take proper cognisance of the polyvalent and complex character of visual experience' (Yar 2002: 267). We might retort that most sociological accounts of Foucault's work fail to take proper account of the layered sophistication of his thought, as I hope to demonstrate with regards to the gaze in this chapter.

10 See also Foucault's own accounts in 'Structuralism and Post-structuralism' (Foucault 2000c) and the interview 'Méthodologie pour la connaissance du monde: comment se débarasser du marxisme' (Foucault 1978).

11 On Foucault's constant concern with strategies see for example Arnold Davidson's introduction to the English edition of *'Society Must be Defended'* (Foucault 2003c). See also in a 1984 interview with C. Baker: 'Situations can always give rise to strategies. I do not believe we are trapped in history, on the contrary all my work consists in showing that history is traversed by strategic relations which are therefore mobile and can be changed. On condition, of course, that the agents of these processes have the political courage of changing things' (Foucault 1984: 1510).

12 The first edition of the book was subtitled 'An Archaeology of the Gaze', a subtitle Foucault later disavowed because it did not sufficiently emphasize the primacy of the statement over the visible (see Deleuze 1988: 49).

13 'An event . . . is not a decision, a treaty, a reign, or a battle, but the reversal of a relationship of forces, the usurpation of power, the appropriation of a vocabulary turned against those who had once used it, a domination that grows feeble, poisons itself, grows slack, the entry of a masked "other"' (Foucault 2000b: 380–1).

14 The last reference is not to a work by Sade but to a series of engravings by Goya entitled *Désastres de la guerra* (1810–15).

15 Thus the oft-quoted concluding lines of *The Order of Things*: 'If those arrangements were to disappear as they appeared, if some event of which we can do no more than sense the possibility – without knowing either what its form will be or what it promises – were to cause them to crumble, as the ground of Classical thought did, at the end of the eighteenth century, then one can certainly wager that man would be erased, like a face drawn in sand at the edge of the sea' (Foucault 1994: 387).

16 The schism between the eye and the gaze is also developed by Lacan in his *Seminar XI* (Lacan 1978). He also supplemented Foucault's reading of *Las Meninas* in *Seminar XIII* (Lacan 1965), in a lecture which Foucault attended. The disagreement between Lacan and Foucault on the gaze is something I hope to engage with in a further paper, but here I have simply wanted to do justice to Foucault's own rendering of the gaze.

17 The two halves of truth as the visible and the articulable are also at play in Foucault's reading of *Oedipus Rex* in *Le savoir d'Œdipe* (see Foucault 2011), in which he shows that Oedipus reconstructs his truth from a combination of eye witnesses and oracular statements.

18 In his presentation of Sacher-Masoch's *Venus in Furs*, and in a masterful rehabilitation of what we are accustomed to see as perversions since Krafft-Ebbing's *Psychopathia Sexualis*, Deleuze indicates that sadism and masochism are non-symmetrical subjective positions that testify to a revolt against the violence of language (Deleuze and Sacher-Masoch 1991). Foucault's own preferences being well known, we may venture to see his work as such a revolt of his being against the violence language exerts on living bodies.

19 Foucault, quoting Nietzsche, writes: 'In some remote corner of the universe, bathed in the fires of innumerable solar systems, there once was a planet where clever animals invented knowledge. That was the grandest and most mendacious minute of "universal history"' (in Foucault 2000e: 6; and see Foucault 2011: 195).

20 The English translation, for some reason, reads: 'it gives equal weight to its own sight and to its objects'.

21 Surprisingly, since most of Foucault's early work can be envisaged as an attempt to 'destroy the will to truth', a proposition he agrees with during the roundtable – untranslated in the English edition – that followed the 'Truth and Juridical Forms' lecture series (Foucault 1974: 1502).

22 See also Stolleis (2009) for an analysis of the symbolism of the eye during the French revolutionary period, including the empire.
23 Michelle Perrot, a historian of industrial relations, gives an example of how the counter-power exercised by skilled workers as part of these 'revolts against the gaze' was dealt with. As soon as they could, factory managers replaced workers with machines: 'in the rolling-mills the chief of a shop had the capacity to resist a boss up until the time when semi-automatic machines were installed. In a flash the thermal control mechanism replaced the expert mill-hand, able to judge – at a glance, once again – the instant the material was ready. Reading a thermometer was sufficient' (in Foucault 1980a: 163).

References

(*Editor's note*: references to texts from the two-volume edition of *Dits et écrits* are cited, above, and listed chronologically in the References, below, according to their initial date of publication (and not the date of their subsequent publication in *Dits et écrits*).)

Allen, M. (1994) 'See You in the City! Perth's Citiplace and the Space of Surveillance', in K. Gibson and S. Watson (eds) *Metropolis Now: Planning and the Urban in Contemporary Australia*, Sydney: Pluto Press

Bogard, W. (1996) *The Simulation of Surveillance in Telematic Society: Social Control in the 1990s*, Cambridge: Cambridge University Press

Boullant, F. (2003) *Michel Foucault et les prisons*, Paris: Presses Universitaires de France

Boyne, R. (2000) 'Post-Panopticism', *Economy and Society*, 29: 285–307

Deleuze, G. (1988) *Foucault*, trans. S. Hand, London: Athlone

___ (1992) 'Postscript on the Societies of Control', *October*, 59: 3–7

___ (2007) *Two Regimes of Madness: Texts and Interviews 1975–1995*, New York, NY: Semiotext(e)

Deleuze, G. and Sacher-Masoch, L. von (1991) *Masochism: Coldness and Cruelty & Venus in Furs*, New York, NY: Zone Books

Dreyfus, P. H. and Rabinow, P. (1983) *Michel Foucault: Beyond Structuralism and Hermeneutics*, 2nd edn, Chicago, IL: University of Chicago Press

Foucault, M. (1974) 'La vérité et les formes juridiques', in D. Defert and F. Ewald (eds) *Dits et écrits I, 1954–1975*, Paris: Gallimard

___ (1978) 'Méthodologie pour la connaissance du monde: comment se débarasser du marxisme', in D. Defert and F. Ewald (eds) *Dits et écrits II, 1976–1988*, Paris: Gallimard

___ (1980a) 'The Eye of Power', in C. Gordon (ed.) *Power/Knowledge: Selected Interviews and Other Writings 1972–1977*, Brighton: Harvester Press

___ (1980b) *The History of Sexuality, Vol. 1*, trans. R. Hurley, New York, NY: Vintage

___ (1984) 'Interview de Michel Foucault', in D. Defert and F. Ewald (eds) *Dits et écrits II, 1976–1988*, Paris: Gallimard

___ (1988) 'Vérité, pouvoir et soi', in D. Defert and F. Ewald (eds) *Dits et écrits II, 1976–1988*, Paris: Gallimard

___ (1991a) *Discipline and Punish: The Birth of the Prison*, trans. A. Sheridan, Harmondsworth: Penguin

___ (1991b) 'Politics and the Study of Discourse', trans. C. Gordon, in G. Burchell, C. Gordon and P. Miller (eds) *The Foucault Effect: Studies in Governmentality*, Chicago, IL: University of Chicago Press

___ (1994) *The Order of Things: An Archaeology of the Human Sciences*, trans. A. Sheridan, New York, NY: Vintage Books
___ (1997) 'The Ethics of the Concern for Self as a Practice of Freedom', in P. Rabinow (ed.) *Essential Works of Foucault 1954–1984 Vol. 1: Ethics*, London: Penguin
___ (2000a) 'Nietzsche, Freud, Marx', in J. D. Faubion (ed.) *Essential Works of Foucault 1954–1984 Vol. 2: Aesthetics*, Harmondsworth: Penguin
___ (2000b) 'Nietzsche, Genealogy, History' in J. D. Faubion (ed.) *Essential Works of Foucault 1954–1984 Vol. 2: Aesthetics*, Harmondsworth: Penguin
___ (2000c) 'Structuralism and Post-structuralism', in J. D. Faubion (ed.) *Essential Works of Foucault 1954–1984 Vol. 2: Aesthetics*, Harmondsworth: Penguin
___ (2000d) 'The Subject and Power', in J. D. Faubion (ed.) *Essential Works of Foucault 1954–1984 Vol. 3: Power*, New York, NY: The New Press
___ (2000e) 'Truth and Juridical Forms', in J. D. Faubion (ed.) *Essential Works of Foucault 1954–1984 Vol. 3: Power*, New York, NY: The New Press
___ (2001) *Madness and Civilization*, trans. R. Howard, Abingdon: Routledge
___ (2003a) *Abnormal: Lectures at the Collège de France 1974–75*, trans. G. Burchell, New York, NY: Picador
___ (2003b) *The Birth of the Clinic: An Archaeology of Medical Perception*, trans. A. M. Sheridan, Abingdon: Routledge
___ (2003c) *'Society Must be Defended': Lectures at the Collège de France, 1975–76*, trans. D. Macey, London: Allen Lane
___ (2005) *The Hermeneutics of the Subject: Lectures at the Collège de France, 1981–82*, trans. G. Burchell, New York, NY: Palgrave Macmillan
___ (2006) *Psychiatric Power: Lectures at the Collège de France, 1973–74*, trans. G. Burchell, New York, NY: Palgrave Macmillan
___ (2008) *The Birth of Biopolitics: Lectures at the Collège de France, 1978–79*, trans. G. Burchell, New York, NY: Palgrave Macmillan
___ (2010) *The Government of Self and Others: Lectures at the Collège de France 1982–83*, trans. G. Burchell, Houndmills: Palgrave Macmillan
___ (2011) *Leçons sur la volonté de savoir: Cours au Collège de France (1970–1971) suivi de Le savoir d'Oedipe*, Paris: Gallimard/Seuil
Francis, V. (2011) 'Ecran total. Une observation directe du PC-vidéo de la Société Nationale des Chemins de fer Belges', *Revue Internationale de Criminologie et de Police Technique et Scientifique*, 64: 187–212
Gandy, O. H. (1993) *The Panoptic Sort: A Political Economy of Personal Information*, Boulder, CO: Westview
Greene, J. and Cohen, J. (2004) 'For the Law, Neuroscience Changes Nothing and Everything', *Philosophical Transactions of the Royal Society B: Biological Sciences*, 359(1451): 1775–85
Gutting, G. (2005) 'Michel Foucault: A User's Manual', in Gary Gutting (ed.) *The Cambridge Companion to Foucault*, 2nd edn, Cambridge: Cambridge University Press
Harcourt, B. E. (2008) '*Supposons que la discipline et la sécurité n'existent pas:* Rereading Foucault's Collége de France Lectures (with Paul Veyne)', paper presented at *Le Carcéral, Sécurité*, and Beyond: Rethinking Michel Foucault's 1978–1979 Collège de France Lectures Bilingual and Interdisciplinary Colloquium at the University of Chicago Paris Center, June 2008
Lacan, J. (1965) 'Le seminaire Livre XIII: L'objet de la psychanalyse', unpublished typescript
___ (1978) *Seminar XI. The Four Fundamental Concepts of Psychoanalysis*, trans. A. Sheridan, New York, NY: WW Norton & Company

___ (2006) *Écrits: The First Complete Edition in English*, trans. B. Fink, New York, NY: WW Norton & Company

Latour, B. (1998) 'Virtual Society: The Social Science of Electronic Technologies', paper presented at the CRICT 10th Anniversary Conference, Brunel University

Lyon, D. (2002) 'Surveillance Studies: Understanding Visibility, Mobility and the Phenetic Fix', *Surveillance & Society*, 1: 1–7

Mathiesen, T. (1997) 'The Viewer Society: Michel Foucault's "Panopticon" Revisited', *Theoretical Criminology*, 1: 215–35

Miller, J. A. (1987) 'Jeremy Bentham's Panoptic Device', trans. R. Miller, *October*, 41: 3–29

Norris, C., Moran, J. and Armstrong, G. (1998) 'Algorithmic Surveillance: The Future of Automated Visual Surveillance', in C. Norris, J. Moran and G. Armstrong (eds) *Surveillance, Closed Circuit Television, and Social Control*, Aldershot: Ashgate

Phéline, C. (1985) *L'image accusatrice*, Laplume: Association de Critique Contemporaine en photographie

Starobinski, J. (1998) *La transparence et l'obstacle*, Paris: Editions Flammarion

Stolleis, M. (2009) *The Eye of the Law: Two Essays on Legal History*, Abingdon: Birbeck Law Press

Veyne, P. (1997) 'Foucault Revolutionizes History', trans. C. Porter, in A. I. Davidson (ed.) *Foucault and his Interlocutors*, Chicago, IL: University of Chicago Press

Voruz, V. (2011) 'Politics in Foucault's Later Work: A Philosophy of Truth; Or Reformism in Question', *Theoretical Criminology*, 15: 47–65

Wajcman, G. (2010) *L'oeil absolu*, Paris: Denoël

Wood, D. M. (2007) 'Beyond the Panopticon? Foucault and Surveillance Studies', in S. Elden and J. W. Crampton (eds) *Space, Knowledge and Power: Foucault and Geography*, Aldershot: Ashgate

Yar, M. (2002) 'Panoptic Power and the Pathologisation of Vision: Critical Reflections on the Foucauldian Thesis', *Surveillance & Society*, 1: 254–71

Chapter 7

The birth of biopolitical justice

Pat O'Malley

There is a holy trinity integral to *Discipline and Punish*, in which Jeremy Bentham, the Panopticon, and discipline, are wrought together in such a way that each in some degree invokes the whole. In this trinity, Bentham receives, understandably, least attention. After all, he is merely the specific 'inventor' of an institutional formation that is itself only the epitome of a broader technology of power. Arguably, a focus on Bentham can be counterproductive, as when scholarship has sought to centre his allegedly baser motives in proposing a penal regime that would profit him directly as the contractor appointed to operate the penal Panopticon (Himmelfarb 1968). But there are sound reasons why some more attention to Bentham may be productive for a Foucaultian analysis of penality. As a key organic intellectual of the liberal bourgeoisie, Bentham assembled a rationale and apparatus for the classical liberal way of punishment, in which the liberal and bourgeois ideologies of industry and diligence were promulgated and enforced, and in which the panoptic prisons and workhouses would create 'docile bodies' out of the mass of the dangerous classes.

With some key refinements to be raised later, this is a viable view, but it confronts difficulties if 'classical liberalism' is read as a unity. Bentham's political biography is worthy of attention precisely because of his own political migration from a conservative toryism in which the criminal classes were to be retributively punished, through to a more Radical stance in which the Panopticon project emerged as still punitive but reformist (O'Malley 2010b). Of course, this was not a complete rupture in his political life or in liberal penology. Often passed over in the more modernist accounts of the Panopticon is the fact that Bentham himself insisted that the disciplinary prison be a source of pain and punishment rather than simply a schoolroom with bars. But Bentham did not die in the 1790s, when the Panopticon was the centrepiece of his penal vision. If Bentham to that point had brought together technologies of discipline and sovereignty, in his later years the third element of Foucault's famous triangle, 'government', made a decisive appearance as that 'very complex power that has the population as its target, political economy as its knowledge, and apparatuses of security as its essential technical instrument' (Foucault 2007: 108).

In his 'Principles of Penal Law', Bentham (1962a: 468–70) embarks on a discussion of 'pecuniary forfeitures' in which he maps out the various virtues of fines and damages – a distinction in turn that he regards as merely procedural. All money sanctions, he urges, conform to the aim of all punishment, for they inflict the pain of privation. They also have an array of characteristics necessary to his penological vision, notably that they are infinitely gradable and may thus be matched to the gravity of the offence, while the equality of their impact on the various social orders may be assured by tailoring the quantum of fines to the total sum of the offenders' wealth. As well, delivering their pain indirectly through denial of the pleasures or expectations of consumption, fines escape the 'infamy' that attaches to corporal punishments. However, a series of 'striking advantages' associated with pecuniary sanctions were to move him toward regarding money as the *optimal* punishment. Pecuniary sanctions exceed all others with respect to 'popularity', as they were the only sanction against which popular objection had not been raised. They were 'in an eminent degree advantageous' because they were perfectly remissible in the event of a miscarriage of justice being proved. And while penal servitude – and here he clearly refers to the Panopticon project – could also be turned to profit, money sanctions were unique because 'the quantity of profit is not limited in this case as in that'. In part this follows because money sanctions are cheaper to administer than panoptical reform. Money sanctions make value available to those, including the state, harmed by crime and wrongdoing. This is the pecuniary sanction's 'peculiar excellence; and this it is that adapts it particularly to the purpose of compensation' (Bentham 1962a: 468). This purpose follows from his acute observation that unlike other penalties, money sanctions do not involve simple negation – say, of liberty, or of the body. The 'pleasure resulting from the use of that money (i.e. extracted from the wrongdoer) is neither diminished nor increased by the operation: it only changes hands' (Bentham 1962a: 469). That the 'peculiar excellence' of monetary punishment eventually came to be crucial to Bentham is made clear in the closing passages of the *Principles*, where he concludes that 'by good laws almost all crimes may be reduced to acts which may be repaired by a simple pecuniary compensation; and that when this is the case, the evil arising from crimes may be made almost entirely to cease' (Bentham 1982: 580). In effect:

> Everything that can be repaired is nothing. Everything which may be compensated by a pecuniary forfeiture is almost as non-existent as if it had never existed; for if the injured individual always receives an equivalent compensation, the alarm caused by the crime ceases entirely, or is reduced to its lowest term. The desirable object is, that the funds for compensation should be drawn from the mass of delinquents themselves . . . If this were the case, security would be the inseparable companion of innocence, and sorrow and anguish would only be the portion of the disturbers of the social order. Such is the point of perfection which should be aimed at though there be no hope of attaining it but by degrees.
>
> (Bentham 1982: 579)

There is much to be gained by an analysis of this turn in Bentham's thought, although by no means did it represent a rejection of the Panopticon. However, if effected, it would make concern with stamping out crime more or less superfluous, because crime's impact would be neutralized. As he makes clear, perfect monetary compensation to victims of crime was an ideal, something to be worked toward in the long term not least because in his lifetime the poor – who made up the majority of criminals – had no money to provide adequate compensation. As will be argued later in this chapter, money sanctions and compensation are envisaged as the penal regime appropriate to a society in which the liberal project has succeeded in creating a society of 'abundance'. The Panopticon retains its place as a necessary evil required as part of the apparatus to transform the 'barbarous' masses into liberal subjects. For this to occur, the masses must become docile bodies; specifically, diligent and prudent labourers. But through this transformation, in the fullness of time and given the proper exercise of law and policy, the masses would become wealthy. In this process, and in a way that is not at all lost on Bentham, the subject of law – or at least the recipient of punishment – changes its character from that of a producer to a consumer. In the disciplinary institution the subject learns to labour. In the process of pecuniary punishment, the transfer of money inflicts a pain of privation on offenders and delivers solace to victims in both cases precisely through the capacity of money to purchase pleasure.[1] And the specific identity of offender and victim are obliterated, for each is merely a *Homo economicus*, crime becomes an illegal action, and civil offences become wrongs that do harm but are capable of money compensation.

This is exactly how the neoliberals, epitomised by Gary Becker, envision crime and penology. While Foucault recognizes this (Foucault 2008: 253), and argues that in the neoliberal way 'punishment is the means employed to limit the negative externalities of certain acts', the nexus is far closer than he imagines because of what Bentham had to say about fines as compensation.[2]

The law thereby becomes a market in harms, and good justice ensures the circulation of money is effected to maximize security. If this is not immediately obvious, some further clues are more or less plainly visible. To begin with, the focus in Bentham's discussion of pecuniary sanctions focuses on harm minimization, on restoration for the harmed rather than on the punishment of the offender. The latter is not unimportant for pain is thereby delivered, but delivered to any rational choice actor rather than to a criminal type. But Bentham goes on to suggest that given the generally impecunious state of offenders an insurance scheme could be established to which they can at least contribute, and in any case argues that the state should pick up the shortfall because it has failed to deliver the security that is part of the implied social contract with liberal subjects (Bentham 1982: 579).

Over and above this, money sanctions differ from disciplinary sanctions because they do not take hold of the offenders and seek to transform them. At best there is a deterrent effect, but this cannot be thought of as individuating. Other characteristics of money sanctions, that will come into their own in subsequent argument, make this all the clearer, for money is an anonymous sanction. Money is the only sanction that need not be delivered upon the wrongdoer *per se* – others may pay and law cares not one jot. This is the case whether the wrongs considered are civil and subject to damages, or criminal and subject to fines. Again, Bentham was aware of this, but noted calmly that in their proximate suffering and deprivation the legal sanction still had its effect by working on the social environment of the wrongdoer.[3] In short, this law is concerned with the wrongs rather than the wrongdoers, who become merely one of the vectors through which the law may have its effects, the nature of which is to work upon distributions – on rates and volumes of unwanted behaviour and on minimizing their impact. As others have noted (Rusche and Kirchheimer 1939; Coffee 1981), money sanctions are not applied where the law's intention is to eradicate behaviours. Rather, money sanctions seek to contain such actions and harms within 'acceptable' limits – they are a sanction singularly apposite to a cost-benefit mentality of the sort neoliberals were to become associated with in the late twentieth century.

This focus on the money sanction brings to the fore certain issues that have been more or less completely disregarded in Foucaultian scholarship – not least being the emergence of biopolitical sanctions in the early nineteenth century and their ascendancy (to be seen shortly) in the twentieth century to the status of the default sanction of modern law. Fines and (increasingly) fees are the predominant sanction with respect to those 'traditional' offences that make up the bulk of everyday criminal justice – across the board about 70 per cent of sentences are fines in countries such as England, Germany, Canada and Australia (O'Malley 2009a, 2009b). Money damages are the remedy as of right in civil law. And dwarfing both damages and fines in 'traditional' criminal justice, fines are of course the primary sanction for all manner of regulatory offences and infringements – most notably traffic offences that make up 90 per cent of what we call 'justice' (Fox 1995, 1996). The prison, panoptical or not, has become a side show, albeit of enormous political prominence.

From classical to neoliberal justice?

In *The Birth of Biopolitics*, Foucault (2008: 248–9) recognizes that Bentham and other classical criminologists used a grid of economic intelligibility in their analysis of criminality and penal justice – something shared with modern neoliberals. This 'economic form' adopted at the end of the eighteenth century appears as the search for 'the least costly and most effective form for obtaining punishment and the elimination of conducts deemed harmful to society' (Foucault 2008: 248). This emerged in a formula relied upon by Beccaria and Bentham, in which crime is defined as a breach of the law, fixed penalties are made available for such breaches, and these are graduated according to the seriousness of the crime. In this way, Foucault argues that *Homo penalis* – the man who can be punished by law – was rendered into *Homo economicus*, namely an actor who responds rationally to changes in the environment (Foucault 2008: 269). For Bentham, the criminal actor is reduced to a universal rational choice offender who can, of course, be anyone. Performing the felicity calculus, the non-criminal actor will be that subject who makes the decision not to offend under the conditions mapped out in the formula – where the benefits of the offence will be cancelled by the (graduated) punishment. Given perfect enforcement, the *Homo economicus* would refuse crime. However, the nineteenth century produced an unanticipated change, arising out of what Foucault refers to as an 'ambiguity'. Since acts themselves cannot be punished, the focus on the subject was central and there emerged 'a tendency towards an increasingly individualizing modulation of the application of law and, as a consequence of this, a reciprocally psychological, sociological and anthropological problematization of the person on whom the law is applied' (Foucault 2008: 269–70). In other words, *Homo penalis* drifted away from *Homo economicus* toward *Homo criminalis*. The course of this transformation, involving the individualization of justice and corrections, Foucault (1977) had effectively mapped out in *Discipline and Punish*.

This genealogy of the departure from a penology based on *Homo economicus* provided Foucault with a foil against which the neoliberals could be contrasted. But interestingly Foucault does not pursue this genealogy – which was certainly more complex than intimated. Instead, he turns his attention to the way in which the penal disciplinary project was linked to another assumption said to be at the heart of Benthamite penality, namely: that 'the whole penal mechanism of Bentham's dreams had to be such that, at the end of the day, there would be no crime, even if this could not happen in reality' (Foucault 2008: 255). Such a 'nullification of crime' Foucault saw as 'the organizing principle of penal calculation in the reforming mind of the eighteenth century' (Foucault 2008: 256). Foucault here links together three things: the Panopticon, Bentham and the eradication of crime. The question of *Homo criminalis* seemingly has been forgotten or passed over. We are left with a question: What is the critical issue to be – the abandonment of *Homo economicus* in favour of *Homo criminalis* or the adoption of a programme of eradication of crime?

Foucault suggests that there is no problem here. Put simply, he argues that the questions are inseparable for the disciplinary Panopticon is the technology to eradicate crime. If we move away from the goal of eradication, then the need for the Panopticon disappears: in this event, 'society does not need to conform to an exhaustive disciplinary system' (Foucault 2008: 256). It is at this point that Foucault turns in a serious fashion to outlining the neoliberal position of Gary Becker and his colleagues Stigler, Ehrlich, Eatherly and Moore. In their framework, 'penal policy has absolutely renounced the objective of the complete suppression and exhaustive nullification of crime' (Foucault 2008: 256). Instead, crime is dealt with in terms of a cost-benefit analysis: the question is no longer how can we eliminate crime, but how can we bring crime down to a level that is tolerable and achievable at a cost that is tolerable? For Becker, Foucault notes, this boils down to the questions of how many offences should be permitted, and how many offenders should go unpunished – but always within the framework of what it costs to society to achieve such levels. Foucault concludes the lecture of 21 March 1979 with the following passage:

> You can see that what appears on the horizon of this kind of analysis is not at all the ideal or project of an exhaustively disciplinary society in which the legal network hemming in the individuals is taken over and extended internally by, let's say, normative mechanisms. Nor is it a society in which a mechanism of general normalization is needed. On the horizon of this analysis we see instead the image, idea or theme-program of a society in which there is an optimization of systems of difference, in which the field is left open to fluctuating processes in which minority individuals and practices are tolerated, in which action is brought to bear on the rules of the game rather than on the players, and finally in which there is an environmental type of intervention instead of the internal subjugation of individuals.
>
> (Foucault 2008: 259–60)

All of this, of course, may be seen as Foucault's continuation of his discussion in *Security, Territory, Population* (Foucault 2007), of the so-called mechanisms of security, the assemblages for governing populations rather than individuals, in which environmental modification displaces in degree the disciplinary enclosures. It is also the foundation on which Deleuze (1995) based his brief commentary on control society, to which this discussion will later return in more depth. It is in short an analysis of a society in which biopolitical governance – and more specifically here, biopolitical penality – becomes ascendant.

At the same time, from a penological viewpoint, Foucault's analysis is frustrating precisely because it is *not* about the 'birth' of biopolitical justice. Rather, it takes the form of a condensed genealogy borrowed from *Discipline and Punish* to demonstrate how it came to be that penality gravitated toward a particular intensification of disciplinary penology, and in which a focus on the offender conceived as an abstract, universal, rationally choosing *Homo economicus* was displaced by an anthropology of offenders. The neoliberal penology is introduced almost as a sharp break with this, as though such a 'biopolitical penology' (as opposed to just the deployment of the *Homo economicus*) were the intellectual invention of these 1970s neoliberals. A genealogy of the birth of biopolitical punishment needs to start exactly where Foucault set its starting point – with the penology of Bentham. But instead of tracing the line of flight into individualization opened up by the panoptic enterprise, I suggest it needs to examine the fate of those 'pecuniary' sanctions that Bentham had turned to in his later years. But first, it is important to elaborate briefly the nexus between Bentham and the neoliberals beyond the rather cursory remarks offered by Foucault.

Bentham and the neoliberals

Monetary sanctions, as mentioned, are completely ignored by Foucault's analysis in *The Birth of Biopolitics*, even though they were central both to the later Bentham's, and to Becker's, thinking on crime and law. Bentham's immersion in what Foucault saw as an economic framework of penology extended beyond imagining the rational choice offender, or even of regarding a key aim of punishment as the minimization of the costs of crime. By envisaging a system of fines that would contribute to victim compensation, Bentham set up two possible trajectories for justice, neither of which involved a disciplinary logic, both of which were shaped by certain properties of money as the universal unit of exchange.

First, as noted, fines would operate to punish in an economic fashion; that is, in the sense of a graduated array of sanctions that would punish and deter. But their character *qua* money sanctions meant that they *could not* launch or sustain a disciplinary project. As Rusche and Kirchheimer (1939) observed, fines do not operate by seizing and working upon individuals with the intention of changing them. Fines merely extract a price for unwanted behaviour. Nor, they stressed, do fines operate in a way that is premised on the intent to extirpate a given behaviour, something that intersects directly with Foucault's argument above. As Bentham famously remarked, fines are a licence paid in arrears. Instead of extirpation, Ruche and Kirchheimer argued – and it follows from what has just been said that Bentham was perfectly aware of this – fines (licences) are set in place where the state seeks only to contain an unwanted action, to keep it at a level that is tolerable rather than to stamp it out. Fines, in short, 'work' in a fashion that conforms exactly with the neoliberal imaginary of a market for crime, where the costs of prevention and punishment or compensation are 'set' by a cost-benefit formula in which the other side of the equation is the cost of crime itself. Further, Bentham's point that fines as compensation would make things *as though* crime had not occurred performs precisely that quintessentially 'neoliberal' exercise of pricing everything, of assuming that whatever harm victims (or the state on their behalf) suffered law could put an economic value on it.

From this point of view, neoliberals merely reproduced and refined the Benthamite imaginary, as Becker (1974: 30–4) himself makes clear. But what Becker also makes clear, and Foucault does not, is how central to this imaginary was the money form of the fine itself. For Becker the fine was the criminal sanction *par excellence* for all the reasons Bentham had outlined, and this made it more explicit that penality would be a *pricing* mechanism. Like Bentham, the neoliberals realized that this was a literal rather than figurative manoeuvre. It was not that penalties would be 'like' a pricing mechanism – pecuniary sanctions are literally the currency of justice, in terms of which harms and compensations can be expressed and exchanged exactly, in monetary terms.

Here we come to the second of the Benthamite trajectories. In *An Introduction to the Principles of Morals and Legislation*, Bentham (1982: 579) is found arguing for an insurance scheme to which offenders would contribute. He was perfectly aware that the full cost of compensation could not be met by offenders. In this model, thus, while he suggests that ideally fines would punish, his emphasis clearly has shifted away from offenders and toward the social and individual costs of crime. The end point of such thinking is extrapolated by Becker (1974: 33) in such a way that, he recognizes, would 'significantly modify' the traditional approach to criminal law:

> First and foremost, the primary aim of all legal proceedings would become the same: not punishment or deterrence, but simply the assessment of the 'harm' done by defendants. Much of the traditional criminal law would become a branch of the law of torts, say 'social torts' in which the public would sue for 'public' harm. A 'criminal' action would be 'criminal' precisely because it results in uncompensated 'harm' to others. Criminal law would cover all such actions while tort law would cover all other (civil) actions.
>
> (Becker 1974: 33)

It should be stressed that the later, 'Radical', Bentham would have been rather unconcerned with this statement simply because in Bentham's view damages and fines were both 'punishments' – all that differed were niceties of procedure and the identity of the party (the state or private individuals) to whom the money was eventually paid. From the penal point of view, the pain suffered by the offender was the same. Indeed, this was not a view peculiar to Bentham, for even long after Bentham's time the object of damages was not primarily compensation but punishment (White 1995). Despite this identity of fines and damages in Bentham's thought, it is worth examining the development of money damages and money fines distinctly, as two related forms of biopolitical sanction that became predominant in the twentieth century.

A very brief genealogy of biopolitical compensation

The punitive or disciplinary role of nineteenth-century civil law emerged primarily in relation to the effort to create liberal subjects who were prudent – in the sense of thinking ahead to take account of the consequences of their actions for themselves and others. In this sense, civil law damages worked in parallel with the Panopticon, focusing on individuals and their normalization. Of course, compensation to the person harmed was the formal means through which this was effected, but that the main emphasis was on the punitive side of things is suggested by the fact that with respect to torts, for example, it is not until 1880 that compensation is defined clearly and unambiguously.[4] More clearly, as Horwitz (1977) has pointed out, the nineteenth century witnessed a series of developments that *progressively restricted* access to compensation by making it conditional on questions of prudence. The introduction of a requirement that access to compensation required proof of negligence by the tortfeasor, and the corresponding rule barring compensation where the injured parties negligently contributed to their own harm, were interpreted by Horwitz as a manoeuvre to minimize the costs to capital in an era of industrialization. While this undoubtedly was an effect of the change, we need not speculate here about concealed capitalist interests, for the courts themselves made clear that the restrictions on recovery were in accord with a rationale requiring liberal subjects to exercise 'reasonable foresight'. Damages would flow, or not, according to the failure of one or other party to exercise this capacity. The same standard applied with respect to such other restrictions on recovery as *volenti*. Here the evident assumption was that where a worker was harmed in a dangerous occupation, he or she should already have exercised reasonable foresight and insisted on danger money before voluntarily assuming the risk. Having accepted higher wages to compensate for the risk, there could be no right to further compensation if injury eventuated. Likewise, where injury was caused by the negligence of a fellow worker, recovery should be sought from that party rather than the employer. The reasoning here was that it was not the employer's negligence that caused the injury, while the fellow worker should be held responsible as the person on hand able to prevent harm – even though in practice fellow workers were too poor to pay meaningful compensation (O'Malley 2000).

While this array of developments meant that very many injured workers went uncompensated, it is most likely that Bentham would have approved of them as 'just' and as creating responsible subjects through exemplary means. Transformation of this state of affairs came about in multiple ways around the turn of the twentieth century. With respect to workers' injuries, the rise of the labour movement created significant pressures on a body of law seen as creating multiple injustices. Of particular importance was the accumulation of statistical evidence that dangerous and non-dangerous industries retained constant and distinctive rates of accident and injury from year to year. Injury was thus made to appear not as a matter of individual foresight but as an effect of factors operating at the level of 'industries'. On this basis, an apparatus of individual discipline was thus extensively transformed into a biopolitical apparatus of security, one that worked at the aggregate level, directed at creating environmental conditions conducive to harm minimization. In part, this meant increased regulation of industries to increase safety, but of more relevance to this analysis, reliance on tort law was extensively displaced by the assemblage of workers' compensation insurance. Echoing Bentham's economistic discourse, it came to appear that the harm suffered by individuals would be compensated by money, and in key respects at least (such as loss of income) it would be as if the harm had never existed (O'Malley 2009a).

Commentators at the time (Quick 1915) were clear that this arrangement was closely connected to the rise of a consumer society – Bentham's society of 'abundance'. As manufacturers would build the cost of workers' compensation insurance into the price of their goods, so in effect worker-consumers insured themselves as workers whenever they purchased a commodity. An almost invisible 'private' but 'social' insurance apparatus emerged that worked through the circuits of consumption. Parallel developments were to emerge during the twentieth century with respect to harms delivered to consumers. In the USA, where this developed farthest and fastest, it was again observed that harms to consumers occurred systematically – that is in a regular and patterned way – and frequently where negligence was not at issue. To begin with, certain 'inherently dangerous' commodities – including automobiles – were made to appear in much the same light as dangerous industries as intrinsic producers of harms, so that victims could be compensated regardless of the duty of care exercised by the manufacturer. Over the course of the twentieth century, this reasoning was generalized to almost all commodities in what came to be known as 'enterprise liability' (O'Malley 2009a). The punitive deployment of damages for negligent harms to consumers thus gave way to another biopolitical apparatus of security. Manufacturers and retailers were forced – sometimes by the risk of legal liability and sometimes by legislative fiat – to take out liability insurance, and most responded by building the premiums for this insurance into the pricing of their commodities. Thus a second 'private' social insurance apparatus emerged in which, effectively, worker-consumers insured themselves *qua* consumers through the purchase of goods and services. Indeed, Priest (1990) has argued that the emergence of enterprise liability in the USA was the result of a judicial strategy to create an alternate social insurance that would make up for the inadequately developed welfare state.

By the last quarter of the twentieth century, therefore, changes in and around the law of torts effectively created a biopolitical form of justice that functioned through circuits of money. Money damages, various forms of compensatory insurance and commodity pricing mechanisms were assembled together into an apparatus of security that largely displaced disciplinary regimes of negligence, in which the societal management of distributions of harm and risk were of far more central concern than questions of fault.

A very brief genealogy of biopolitical punishment

While the market vision of penality as crimes compensation was explicit in Bentham's later writings, the Panopticon is still given a place precisely because Bentham recognized that the social conditions for the compensatory scheme were not yet in place. Why, then, does the Panopticon retain its place? Is it merely a stopgap until such time as the altogether better pecuniary arrangement could be installed? In order to answer this question, a genealogy of biopolitical punishment needs to examine issues other than the unforeseen individualization of justice that emerged from the panoptic project. Foucault's question merely explains how a trajectory evolved that took penality away from the *Homo economicus* model, and leaves us with a historical void rather than a genealogy linking Bentham's and Becker's closely aligned visions.

At the time Bentham wrote, the fine was alive and well and arguably the dominant sanction, certainly for routine offences such as assault, public disorder and the like (King 1996; Sharpe 1990). Bentham's observation that fines were as yet an ideal sanction only thus did not relate to fines *per se*. Rather, it related to money sanctions substantial enough to operate as meaningful compensation, for on average fines in his time were very small amounts – a few pence or shillings, even though these had a significant punitive effect on poor people. Rusche and Kirchheimer's (1939) well-known thesis that fines could not be a dominant sanction until the late nineteenth century, that is until the masses had sufficient income to pay them, was thus incorrect. Fines did not come into being in the late 1800s; they were, rather, revived and restored as the predominant sanction. Fines had slipped from their former position of predominance to the status of only a marginal sanction more or less at the time Bentham was writing. Ironically, this was precisely because of the increasing belief that disciplinary prisons would reform offenders rather than merely punish. Fines were thus denigrated as merely negative punishment. In an irony of history, Bentham's panoptic child, the offspring of his middle years, sidelined the fines project that he came to favour in later life. It is therefore not altogether surprising that the re-emergence of fines as a common sanction was directly associated with recognition that the disciplinary penal project had its limits. From the 1870s on, reformers and criminologists observed repeatedly that prisons could have no reforming impact on prisoners incarcerated for only a few weeks or months, and such sentences likely had a deleterious influence by exposing minor offenders to major criminals.

Significantly, then, the fine made its reappearance precisely at the limits of discipline, as a punishment familiar from the past – rather than a new invention – and seemingly appropriate to take up its old role sanctioning minor offenders. As such, fines took on a new character that differentiated them from 'early' fines. The reborn fine was set against or to one side of discipline, as governing where discipline could not. Rather than simply being one punishment among many, it was now that which governed beyond discipline. Its attraction as a low cost sanction was not lost on governments and doubtless this contributed to its rapid rise to become the most frequently used sentence by the early years of the twentieth century. If there was a distinctly economic 'logic' in this shift, this is also expressed in the fact that the subject of the sanction was once again *Homo economicus*, the universal abstract subject who would comply with law to avoid the pain of deprivation. The matching abstract universal nature of the fine sanction *qua* money – the universal unit of exchange – made delving into the unique biography of the offender pointless in determining the sanction.

Hence, by the early twentieth century an economic register had in fact displaced the disciplinary or anthropological for the bulk of crime! *Homo economicus* was restored as the predominant subject of penology in practice if not in ideology and politics. Gary Becker's argument for the fine as the predominant punishment was not in advance of its time, for the fine already occupied that status and had done so for more than half a century when Becker wrote. The neoliberal case appeared radical because of Becker's avocation that other sanctions should largely disappear and that fines would appear as compensation, even though he regarded this as an ideal and unlikely to be realized – but again, Bentham had already made this case.[5]

As noted, Rusche and Kirchheimer were wrong about why the fine made its reappearance in Europe and elsewhere. It was not a simple economic effect of increasing real incomes but a shift in penal imaginaries that was critical. The poor still could not pay the new fines – as evidenced by the flurry of innovations such as 'time to pay', 'payment by instalment' and 'taking the means of the offender into account' that accompanied the reintroduction. Yet their 1939 observations on the importance of the improved material condition of the mass of the population were to be of extreme significance if longer-term developments after the Second World War are considered. The rise of a consumer society during the twentieth century was to create new problems of legal governance that could not conceivably be managed by a disciplinary apparatus. At the forefront of these was the rise of the automobile and its development from a toy of the wealthy to a mass commodity – which occurred in the USA in the inter-war years, and in Europe largely after the Second World War. The sheer volume of motoring offences and infractions stimulated two linked innovations: the enormous expansion in the use of fines increasingly divorced from the threat of imprisonment even in default of payment – what Bottoms (1983) refers to as the 'modern fine'; and a progressive stripping away of the procedures of justice in ways that owed much to the political meanings associated with money sanctions.

Because money sanctions do not generate the same liberal political shibboleths associated with loss of liberty, the re-emergence of the fine around the turn of the twentieth century had allowed the streamlining of court procedure – notably forms of summary justice – resulting in substantial increases in court throughputs (Garton 1982). Even before the Second World War this 'solution' was applied extensively to the new problem of traffic, although in effect there was still a formality of individual justice. Beginning in the 1960s, however, the geometrically increasing volume of traffic and traffic offences made further streamlining of justice essential. The solution, rapidly adopted around the globe, was the 'on the spot' fine or 'penalty notice'. While in itself a humble administrative technique, it became the launching point for the ascendancy of biopolitical justice. Fines were set exactly by tariff, so that by and large individualized sentences were abandoned in favour of a fixed pricing schedule matched to specific offences. In a sense, the action rather than the actor now became the object of the sanction. If under individual justice fines were set by courts, taking into account individual circumstance and condition, now they were set strictly by the nature of the offence: so much for running a red light; so much for speeding x or y kilometres per hour over the speed limit; so much for failing to wear a seat belt, and so on. At first, offenders were given an opting-out clause with incentives in terms of reduced fines if they paid the fine without going to court. As this proved only marginally effective in reducing volumes of court business, a *de facto* reverse onus provision was introduced linked to an opting-in format. Henceforward, vehicle owners were presumed guilty of the offence concerned unless they chose to challenge this either by establishing that another driver was in control of the vehicle, or by opting to challenge the charge in court. Considerable disincentives were put in the way of opting-in. Fines are discounted by up to two thirds if paid without challenge, the trouble and cost of court appearance is avoided, and frequently no conviction is recorded. All of these inducements are lost if the recipient opts-in and is convicted, and as well he or she is likely to be inflicted with court costs. *Homo economicus* was being used to transform justice.

For all practical purposes, individual justice has been removed in favour of a pricing system in which consumers pay a set price for performing unwanted actions. To the extent that the action and not the individual is thereby the focus – even more so than with traditional punitive fines – then Rusche and Kirchheimer's point, that fines are put in place where the intention is to work on rates of offending rather than on the extinguishment of offending, becomes all the more accurate. As well, it must be recognized that courts are unable to determine precisely who pays a fine. In Simmel's (1990) term money is 'undifferentiated' – we cannot tell whose money is being paid over. Courts thus have rarely even considered the question of the identity of the payee, and will fine in the full knowledge that a parent, spouse or employer will pay.[6] As with damages, who pays is far less important than the fact that *someone* pays – and in this way, this form of justice appears even more precisely as a market in harms and wrongs: a price is set, payable by anyone, with the aim of driving down or containing rates of unwanted action. This biopolitical justice is a model that in recent years in England, Scotland and Australia has been progressively extended to a wide variety of regulatory offences and most recently to minor offences such as cannabis possession, vandalism, petty theft and shoplifting, affray, public drunkenness, malicious mischief and public order offences.[7]

Consumption, control and biopolitics

Deleuze's (1995) outline of control societies in many ways prefigured the course that has been taken by subsequent developments in biopolitical justice. As governance moved beyond the disciplinary enclosures and became more and more embedded in the regulated environment, immanent modulation of what Foucault (2008: 18) referred to as 'good' and 'bad' circulations has permeated contemporary societies. Individuals are displaced by 'dividuals', the binary coded entities that are the objects of control, uniquely identifiable by their codes yet fragments of being that only *correspond* to liberal subjects. This is epitomized by traffic regulation, the circulation *par excellence* of the twenty-first century, as increasingly traffic codes (licence plates, transponders, bar-coded licences, etc.) are registered by remote electronics, offences are recorded and tallied against a price tariff, and fines are issued electronically and paid by the same means (credit card, electronic funds transfer, bar-coded cheque). Codes and their monitoring have extensively displaced individual enforcers and enforced, with pricing becoming perhaps the principal means whereby modulation is effected (O'Malley 2010a). It is a biopolitical mode of governance that works through, and relies upon, the commodification of existence in consumer societies. The effect of such governance, as Foucault suggests, is to maximize 'good' circulations, for in effect good circulations are uninterrupted by touchless contact. The swiping of access cards, of credit cards and passports, the registering of transponders and the gate-keeping carried out via electronic protocols, these now normal and everyday procedures sort out for closer attention only those that register as problematic. Only then may they be translated from dividuals to individuals.

Not only does much of this control occur through commodified conduits, but the statuses regulated are themselves often commodities: purchased *privileges* – from credit cards and passports, to drivers' licences, access and membership cards. In their turn, these generate further layers of modulation. Licences and memberships can be revoked or suspended remotely and electronically when dividuals become too risky – as when, for example, traffic demerit points pass a certain threshold and re-register the driver as a high risk particle of bad circulation. Even here, the individual is not brought into being. The driver with the suspended licence is merely a dividual – still a code, and only the risky dividuality has been cancelled. Governance will remain at the level of the code unless or until the risky drivers prove themselves too risky for such governance by continuing to drive. Until that day – when they are called into being and hailed as individuals – only their purchased privilege in the form of the licence has been stripped: the politically cumbersome and expensive assemblage of individual liberal rights is scarcely touched.

In this way, *Homo economicus* appears in a new light. For Foucault in *The Birth of Biopolitics*, the re-emergence of this entity is reconfigured in neoliberalism to become an entrepreneur of the self. But this is not the only neoliberal reconstitution, for *Homo economicus* equally appears as the sovereign consumer: the rational choice actor who expends money to produce its own satisfaction through the purchase of commodities (Rose 1999). If we take seriously the fact that the vast bulk of 'justice' is made up of the routine and everyday array of traffic infringements and offences, this is the new *Homo economicus* of justice, and it brings us back to Bentham.

In his analysis of the objects of law, Bentham (1962b: 300–2) ranked security as principal, for only security 'necessarily embraces the future'.[8] The point of security is to guarantee the future safety of the subject and his property in such ways and degrees that a general plan of conduct may be formed. This 'disposition to look forward' was fundamental in Bentham's imaginary because it underlay the capacity of liberal subjects to govern themselves: it was the rationality underlying accumulation and independence. It allowed the prudent subject to recognize and avoid risks and to minimize harms, and it enabled the entrepreneur to calculate opportunities for gain. This subject is the *Homo economicus* that Foucault pinpoints in *The Birth of Biopolitics*, who responds rationally to events in the environment. But it is crucial to see that Bentham did not imagine this as naturally emerging or as given in human nature. The contrast he drew between the barbarous hordes of American natives whose lives were nasty, brutish and short, and the orderly and prosperous white settlers, pivoted around security and 'the yoke of foresight'.

It was the function of the disciplinary apparatuses to teach subjects to take on this yoke – not simply to become the 'docile subjects', creatures of habit that emerge in certain readings of *Discipline and Punish*. Bentham's improved subjects were planful, imagining futures and bringing them into being, and prospering as a result. There was no difference in this abstract subject between the entrepreneur and labourer.

Of course, Bentham had no illusions that all his nineteenth-century subjects could become entrepreneurs, and in this much Foucault is right to see the universalization of entrepreneurial subjectivities as characteristic of the neoliberal imaginary. For the mass of Bentham's subjects, the yoke of foresight condemned them to lives of self-denial, prudence, industry and thrift. But this was a 'realist' reading of his present. In the longer term, government through lawful security would eventually produce 'abundance' – for the long-term benefits of diligence, thrift and saving by the poor and speculative enterprise by the wealthy would render all deserving subjects prosperous. This was the imagined future in which Bentham's dream of the fines and damages compensating all those through no fault of their own harmed by crimes and civil wrongs, would be realized. It is the world imagined too in Becker's treatise – with imprisonment reserved only for those who could not pay fines or damages, or whose riskiness to others was too great to allow them to be free. It is a world of *Homo economicus*, simultaneously the entrepreneur of the self and the 'consumer of satisfaction'. As Jonathan Simon (1987) long ago perceived, the relationship between discipline and biopower is not simply that of two axes of power, as mapped out by Foucault; it is also a relationship in which the conditions of existence of generalized biopower and biopolitical justice are established through the disciplinary apparatuses. Only once the dangerous classes had been pacified through discipline could biopower assume ascendancy – but not simply by inuring them to drudgery. Through the production of abundance, the dangerous classes would re-emerge as the consuming classes. As Foucault observes in the passage quoted earlier, biopower emerges as a tolerant power that does not – because it need not – rely upon normalization and constraint. Indeed, a world of enterprise and consumption is scarcely consistent with the moral straitjacket of normalization. Biopower operates a domain of governance policed primarily at the margins by risk, within which there is a 'floating' of the moral order, in which the market and money optimize all circulations, good and bad.

Notes

1 'The pain then, that is peculiar to this species of punishment, is neither more nor less than the pain of disappointment produced by the destruction of those expectations which the parties in question has been accustomed to entertain of continuing to participate in the fortune of their principal' (Bentham 1962a: 469).

2 In the neoliberal imaginary '[t]he criminal, any person, is treated as anyone whosoever who invests in an action, expects a profit from it and who accepts the risk of a loss . . . The penal system itself will not have to deal with criminals but with those people who

produce a certain kind of action. In other words it will have to react to the supply of crime. What will punishment be under these conditions? Well, punishment is the means employed to limit the negative externalities of certain acts. Here again, you can see that we are very close to Beccaria and Bentham' (Foucault 2008: 253).

3 'Along with the delinquent, other parties are innocent are exposed to suffer; to wit, whatever persons were comprised within the circle of his dependents. This suffering is not the mere pain of sympathy . . . It is an original pain produced by a consciousness of the loss which they themselves are likely to incur by the impoverishment of their principal' (Bentham 1962a: 469).

4 The key cases are *Robinson v. Harman* (1848) 1 Ex 850 in contract law, and in tort law *Livingstone v. Raywards Coal Co.* (1880) 5 App Cas 2. In the latter case, compensation was defined at p. 39 as 'that sum of money which will put the party who has been injured in the same position as he would have been if he had not sustained the wrong for which he is now getting his compensation or reparation'. It will be noted that the harmful action is still defined as a 'wrong'.

5 There is a profound irony in all this. Outside the USA, fines became the principal sanction for minor criminal convictions in common law countries and much of Western Europe as early as the 1930s (Ruche and Kirchheimer 1939; Bottoms 1983). But for reasons as yet unclear, this development did not occur in the USA, and it is still the case that American courts at both federal and state levels use fines as a primary sanction less than a quarter as often as their European and Australasian counterparts (Hillsman 1990; O'Malley 2009b). By implication, it could be assumed that the arguments of Becker and his colleagues have fallen on deaf ears in their own country. However, matters are more complex than this suggests. As Harris and his colleagues discuss (Harris *et al.* 2010; Beckett and Harris 2011), in recent years in the United States fines and fees have been increasingly levied as punishments loaded on top of primary sentences of imprisonment. More precisely, it is not so much that fines have been increasing in number in this respect, so much as that fees are being charged for many penal 'services' including imprisonment itself (O'Malley 2011). That is, the arguments of the law and economics advocates have been picked up in a way that has in theory allowed the advocates of imprisonment to reduce the costs of the sanction in a way Bentham would have approved of heartily. However, it should be stressed that successful collection of fines and fees, often for considerable sums of money and levied against impoverished ex-prisoners, are very low. Consequently, the actual impact of this move is likely more symbolic than economically rational (Harris *et al.* 2010).

6 In a rare exception, the English *Road Traffic Law Review Report* (Home Office 1988: 133) considered the question of whether to prohibit payment of fines for traffic infringements by a third party. The report expressed regret at this practice, especially with respect to situations where corporations paid such fines on behalf of their employees. However, it could find no practicable means of enforcing such a rule.

7 For a recent document illustrating such shifts and their underlying logic, see the NSW Law Reform Commission's consultation paper on *Penalty Notices* (NSW Law Reform Commission 2010: 141–57). Significantly, one of the principal grounds put forward for the extension of 'criminal infringement notices' was their cost effectiveness.

8 The four objects of law were listed as: Subsistence, Abundance, Equality and Security. Of these, security – the protection of person and property – was ranked foremost because Bentham argued security would guarantee to them 'the fruits of industry'. In this way, subsistence and abundance would follow without much legal intervention: 'command production – command cultivation; you will have done nothing: but secure to the cultivator the fruits of his labour, and you have most probably done enough' (Bentham 1962b: 303). Nature has created motives to provide for subsistence, and self-interest will provide for abundance, while legislating to produce equality will reduce the

good to society by removing the motive to labour and accumulate: 'If the condition of the industrious were not better than the condition of the idle, there would be no reason for being industrious' (Bentham 1962b: 303).

References

Becker, G. (1974) 'Crime and Punishment: An Economic Approach', in G. Becker and W. Landes (eds) *Essays in the Economics of Crime and Punishment*, New York, NY: Columbia University Press

Beckett, K. and Harris, A. (2011) 'On Case and Conviction: Monetary Sanctions as Misguided Policy', *Criminology and Public Policy*, 10: 509–37

Bentham, J. (1962a) 'Principles of Penal Law', in J. Bowring (ed.) *The Works of Jeremy Bentham, Vol. 1*, New York, NY: Russell and Russell

___ (1962b) 'Principles of the Civil Code', in J. Bowring (ed.) *The Works of Jeremy Bentham, Vol. 1*, New York, NY: Russell and Russell

___ (1982) ed. J. Burns and H. L. A. Hart, *An Introduction to the Principles of Morals and Legislation*, London: Methuen

Bottoms, A. (1983) 'Some Neglected Features of Contemporary Penal Systems', in D. Garland and P. Young (eds) *The Power to Punish*, London: Heinemann

Coffee, J. (1981) '"No Soul to Damn: No Body to Kick": An Unscandalized Inquiry into the Problem of Corporate Punishment', *Michigan Law Review*, 79: 386–99

Deleuze, G. (1995) *Negotiations 1972–1990*, New York, NY: Columbia University Press

Departmental Committee (1934) *Imprisonment by Courts of Summary Jurisdiction in Default of Payment of Fines and other Sums of Money*, London: His Majesty's Stationery Office

Foucault, M. (1977) *Discipline and Punish*, trans. A. Sheridan, London: Peregrine Books

___ (1984) *The History of Sexuality, Vol. 1*, trans. R. Hurley, London: Peregrine Books

___ (2007) *Security, Territory, Population: Lectures at the Collège de France, 1977–78*, trans. G. Burchell, New York, NY: Palgrave Macmillan

___ (2008) *The Birth of Biopolitics: Lectures at the Collège de France, 1978–79*, trans. G. Burchell, New York, NY: Palgrave Macmillan

Fox, R. (1995) *On the Spot Fines in Victoria*, Melbourne: Faculty of Law, Monash University

___ (1996) *Criminal Justice on the Spot. Infringement Penalties in Victoria*, Canberra: Australian Institute of Criminology

Garton, S. (1982) 'Bad or Mad? Developments in Incarceration in NSW 1880–1920', in Sydney Labour History Group (ed.) *What Rough Beast? The State and Social Order in Australian History*, Sydney: Allen and Unwin

Harris, A., Evans, H. and Beckett, K. (2010) 'Drawing Blood from Stones: Legal Debt and Social Inequality in the Contemporary US', *American Journal of Sociology*, 115: 1755–99

Hillsman, S. (1990) 'Fines and Day Fines', *Crime and Justice: A Review of Research*, 12: 50–98

Himmelfarb, G. (1968) *Victorian Minds*, New York, NY: Alfred Knopf

Home Office (1988) *Road Traffic Law Review Report*, London: Home Office

Horwitz, M. (1977) *The Transformation of American Law*, Cambridge, MA: Harvard University Press

King, P. (1996) 'Punishing Assault: The Transformation of Attitudes in the English Courts', *Journal of Interdisciplinary History*, 27: 43–74

NSW Law Reform Commission (2010) *Penalty Notices*, Sydney: NSW Law Reform Commission

O'Malley, P. (2000) 'Uncertain Subjects: Risk, Liberalism and Contract', *Economy and Society*, 29: 460–84

___ (2009a) *The Currency of Justice: Fines and Damages in Consumer Society*, London: Routledge/Cavendish

___ (2009b) 'Theorizing Fines', *Punishment and Society*, 11: 67–83

___ (2010a) 'Simulated Justice: Risk, Money and Telemetric Policing', *British Journal of Criminology*, 50: 795–807

___ (2010b) 'Jeremy Bentham', in S. Maruna, J. Mooney and K. Hayward (eds) *Fifty Key Criminological Thinkers*, London: Routledge

___ (2011) 'Politicizing the Case for Fines', *Crime and Public Policy*, 10: 547–53

Priest, G. (1990) 'The New Legal Structure of Risk Control', *Daedalus*, 119: 207–20

Quick, J. (1915) *The Annotated Workers Compensation Act 1914*, Melbourne: Maxwell

Rose, N. (1999) *Governing the Soul: The Shaping of the Private Self*, 2nd edn, London: Free Association Book

Rusche, G. and Kirchheimer, O. (1939) *Punishment and Social Structure*, New York, NY: Columbia University Press

Sharpe, J. (1990) *Judicial Punishment in England*, London: Faber and Faber

Simmel, G. (1990) *The Philosophy of Money*, enl. edn, New York, NY: Routledge

Simon, J. (1987) 'The Emergence of a Risk Society: Insurance, Law, and the State', *Socialist Review*, 95: 61–89

White, G. (2003) *Tort Law in America: An Intellectual History*, exp. edn, Oxford: Oxford University Press

References to primary sources of law

Robinson v. Harman (1848) 1 Ex 850

Livingstone v. Raywards Coal Co. (1880) 5 App Cas 2

Part 3

Rights, counter-conduct, revolution?

Chapter 8

Michel Foucault and the question of right

Philippe Chevallier

Is law the poor relation among the topics of Foucault's work? There has been widespread complaint to this effect,[1] often with the suggestion that the philosopher remained limited here to a narrow, statist view of law and right, a viewpoint largely guided by the Napoleonic codes, which fails to take account of contemporary developments which multiply the possibilities for individuals of legal recourse, including against the state. Foucault, it is claimed, neglected the virtues of political justice, which he discounted as an abstract, transcendental doctrine of traditional political thought, ill-suited for grasping the real functioning of modern power in its two principal forms, 'disciplinary power' and 'biopower'. For this French philosopher, starting with the early modern 'classical age', political power over the bodies of individuals operated principally through a *physis*, as a science of the growth and multiplication of beings, relegating juridical fictions to the prop room.

This is a severe judgment, and one which seems in contradiction with Foucault's own practice, where he can be seen in his own militant interventions constantly invoking individual rights and respect for laws in opposition to state violence. There is a paradox here which seemed to amuse Foucault himself in his televised debate with Noam Chomsky in 1971, where concern to distance himself from Chomsky's political utopias drove him to refuse any definition of the terms 'just' and 'legal'. On being told at the end of the debate that he has only two minutes more speaking time, Foucault retorts with a laugh 'well, I say that is unjust!'. 'Yes, absolutely!', Chomsky backs him up (Foucault 1974a: 1374).

To try to clarify this apparent paradox, I will focus here on the series of *Collège de France* lecture courses, from 1973–4 (*Psychiatric Power*) to 1978–9 (*The Birth of Biopolitics*), collating them with texts of contestation written by Foucault during this same period.

Is right a good description of power?

When Foucault addresses the question of right, he does so through the prism of a certain political philosophy which he terms, in the lecture of 14 January 1976, the 'theory of sovereignty' (Foucault 1997: 31–6). He is here targeting not so much the actual functioning of law as the theoretical presuppositions of thinkers such as Hobbes and Rousseau: where there rules a law reasonably constituted by the people or by particular wills, there is both a unity of power, and limits set to its scope. In the juridical conception of politics developed in France and Britain during the seventeenth and eighteenth centuries, these presuppositions become an unshakable confidence in law as the sufficient qualification (*marquage*) of power. Foucault's concern is to question the pertinence of this model for analysing the mutations of power in post-revolutionary societies, with the emergence of the 'bio' and 'disciplinary' powers.

'Sovereignty' is understood here by Foucault not as referring to the exercise of a massive and repressive power, but as a power conceived first of all as grounded on the economic model of exchange, even of contract. It is about constituting the right of public power on the basis of the sacred and natural rights of subjects. Individuals are the original bearers of rights, ontologically primary in relation to every juridical system, which they will cede or delegate to found the action of the public power which will watch over them. It is a 'cycle from subject to subject' (Foucault 1997: 37), from natural subject to political subject. The primary object of the interventions of this sovereign power is the land and its produce, by exercising its levy on the goods and revenues of individuals.[2] The juridical edifice serves to codify these state interventions as legitimate or illegitimate, as the exercise of right or the abuse of power. In the thinking of the seventeenth- and eighteenth-century jurists, reacting against the excesses of monarchy, law is the limit of the sovereign's power.

We need to specify these terms of 'right' and 'law' further. Within the French juridical edifice that emerged from the Revolution, it is customary to distinguish between:

1. The supraconstitutional principles of *natural rights*. As formulated in the Declaration of 26 August 1789, these fix the 'inalienable and sacred natural rights of man'.
2. The *constitution*. Posterior in fact (dating from 1791) and in right to natural rights, the constitution is subject to ratification by the people or its proxy. Its first role is to define the role of the public power, and the extent and the limit of its powers.
3. The *laws*. These are subject to the deliberation of Parliament and to the test of compliance with the provisions of the constitution.

When Foucault speaks of 'law' and 'right' as a model which impedes the analysis of power, he has in mind the union of the above three levels.[3] This explains why, until 1979, he abstains from any other analysis of law, such as an approach which would side-step its founding ideals and idealities, to locate it first in a concrete historical setting of non-violent political and economic conflicts.[4] Foucault continues to characterise right as the constitutional assignment of the scope of public power, founded *a priori* on the inalienable rights of contracting subjects, and applied *a posteriori* through different juridical codes. The Napoleonic codes are referred to in the lecture of 14 January 1976 as direct products of the theory of sovereignty.

Foucault does indeed exclude the use of this model for the analysis of power. He does so in the first place for methodological reasons: power must be analysed first of all in its concrete exercise, where it is first of all a relation.[5] It is not an asset which some individuals possess, while others have ceded or lost it. It is an interaction between individuals, and it is this interaction which will qualify the respective position of the participants (as governing and governed), independently of the roles set for them by law. The condition of possibility of a power-relation is the sustained openness, from end to end of the relation, of a field of action, which makes the respective position of the players interchangeable and keeps the balance of forces unstable. This relation does not necessarily give rise to confrontation or oppression, it can equally well mark out a certain government of liberties which allows a space of possibilities without inflicting violence on it. This supple and polymorphous vision of power – which is at work from Foucault's earliest courses at the *Collège de France* – is being developed contemporaneously with new approaches in the sociology of organizations, which discard the hierarchical model as their main schema of intelligibility, opting instead to treat each individual, regardless of their job title or function, as an actor in a play of relations (Crozier and Friedberg 1977).

Foucault at this point also excludes the use of the sovereignty model for historical reasons, namely the nineteenth-century generalization and developing state-control of a disciplinary power which is no longer exclusively conceived in the form of law. Over the years, nevertheless, the interpretation in the *Collège de France* lectures of the relations between law and discipline evolves: in 1973, Foucault makes the disciplined individual the historical condition of emergence of the juridical individual (Foucault 2003: 56–7). In his analysis, the sites of education and training (schools, workshops, barracks) introduce to the political scene the body of the individual, with its movements, positions, displacements and temporality, as an object of knowledge and surveillance, in the name of science and economics. Power needed to concern itself with inquiry as well as control, applied not only to a territory but also to the 'somatic singularities' (Foucault 2003: 56–7) which inhabit it, in order for the individual thereby to become a juridical subject, accoutred with new rights which serve to dissimulate the prior mastering of the subject's mobility. Revolutionary right had done no more than inscribe in the marble of its codes the product of disciplinary technique: the 'individual', the result, effective from the classical age, of the capture of political power over bodies. In 1976, by now more sensitive to the heterogeneity of strategies, and abandoning the hypothesis of an essentially hidden power, Foucault stresses the open confrontation, from the nineteenth century, between two incompatible yet often complicit discourses: the discourse of discipline and the discourse of law (Foucault 1997: 34). This inflection seems to me to offer a much richer framework of interpretation, as we can shortly verify in the case of penal justice.

Let us sum up the two main derogations of disciplinary power relative to the juridical model as set out above:

1 Its object is not the possessions but the bodies of its subjects, whose development, health, sexuality and productivity it will supervise and correct.
2 This power is constantly applied and supported by a form of knowledge. If the places of discipline (schools, prisons, hospitals) are created by public initiative, they deploy methods of surveillance and 'veridiction' which no longer belong to the field of law. The knowledge which the psychiatrist produces and uses to care and correct is not the result of a constitution of his particular sovereignty, it is not coded by the distinction between legitimate and illegitimate, but by the distinction between true and false.

From the apparatus of sovereignty to the apparatuses of discipline, the nineteenth century thus slips from law to norm, from a juridical rule to a natural rule, along with a new way of conceptualizing and grasping subjects. Where law seeks to exclude certain individuals to protect society, the norm seeks to include the maximum number of individuals in a single field of knowledge. The law makes qualitative distinctions, it marks an inside and an outside. The norm is on the contrary the possibility of an infinitesimal gradation from normal to abnormal. This gradation homogenizes the social body by measuring the deviations of each of its members in terms of non-pathological micro-anomalies – such as those which appear from 1850 in the domain of infantile sexuality. Hence, in Foucault's neat formula, 'the great ogre of the end of History becomes Tom Thumb' (Foucault 1999: 151).

Should we conclude from this that law is unmade, rendered futile or ineffective by this new power? No. What Foucault signals is the heterogeneous but mutually non-exclusive character of the two *dispositifs*. The force of his analyses consists always in advancing through differentiation, distinguishing here two quite different regimes of power, against the image of a univocal, massive entity with the state as its head and the functionaries of medicine and the prison as its inferior members. But if there is no exclusion, that means that the two apparatuses constantly overlap, either to support or extend, or on the contrary to oppose one another. Revolutionary political theory and disciplinary power simultaneously make visible the figure of the individual, whereas feudal power passed either over or beneath it.[6] But they respectively give it two radically different meanings: on one side 'the juridical individual . . . as abstract subject, defined by individual rights which no power can limit, unless the individual consents by contract', and, on the other, 'the individual as a historical reality, as a unit of productive force, a unit also of political force . . . held within a system of supervision and subjected to procedures of normalization' (Foucault 2003: 59).

These two individuals will become one and the same, once late eighteenth-century jurists call on a disciplinary instrument (the prison) to take charge of individuals in order to reinstate them as subjects of right. They become one and the same, when punishment by the law takes the form of amendment or retraining in which psychiatry will actively collaborate for its own advantage. But they will be differentiated once again when lawyers complain of being unable to assist their client in the face of an expert psychiatric opinion which is often crucial;[7] or when the French appeal court reaffirms that juridical authority is not bound by the findings of that expertise (Cass. Crim., 11 March 1958).

This encounter, variously one of fusion or conflict, between these two modes of being of the individual, is illustrated by Article 64 of the Penal Code of 1810 (122-1 in the new code) which stipulates that there is no crime if the individual is in a state of dementia at the moment of the act. As a result the law became accustomed[8] to call on the psychiatrist to evaluate the capacity of the accused, without itself being able to recode his opinion in juridical terms. When the law provides itself with its own apparatus for the production of truth, provided by experts who have their own rule for the validation of statements, it runs the risk of being constantly outreached and dominated by an instance which is supposed only to inform its judgment. This self-dispossession of the law is in conformity with the theory of sovereignty based on the implicit union of reasonable wills: the demented individual is not in a position to understand the anti-social character of his or her act, and is thus not accessible to penal sanction. But at the same time, it is law itself which here asks something other than law – namely medicine – to rule on its own competence. In 1958, there are thus defined three questions which the judge is required to put to the psychiatrist: is the individual: (a) dangerous; (b) amenable to penal sanction; and (c) curable or readaptable? (Circular of the Garde des Sceaux, and Article C345 of the *Instruction générale pour l'application du Code de procédure pénale*). Three notions which, Foucault remarks, are neither psychiatric nor juridical, but an effect of this curious coupling of law and truth (Foucault 1974b: 1536). This is the result of the intersection of two heterogeneous regimes of discourse.

Alongside this disciplinary power, what Foucault calls 'biopower' is the other example, emerging in the eighteenth century, of a proliferating, polymorphous power which does not issue from any form of juridical process. As the concrete application of statistical knowledge, rather than of political sovereignty, biopower is exercised not over subjects of right but over that new and impersonal entity, the life of a population. It has to do with the development of mechanisms of security and regulation designed to manage 'the perpetual interactions of a geographic, climatic and physical environment with the human species' (Foucault 2004b: 24).

As a power exercised not over the individual body, but over birth, death and disease, grasped as global phenomena whose regularities are determined by science, biopower is harder than disciplinary power to articulate with right. This is simply because it loses contact with what constituted the interface between law and discipline: the individual. But biopower only gets a grip on the vast domain of the living to the extent that it connects with finer-grained forms of control: such is the example cited by Foucault of the nineteenth-century workers' housing estates, as a site of intersection of mechanisms of security (hygiene regulations, an assurance system) and disciplinary mechanisms (family housing controls, police supervision) (Foucault 1997: 223–4). The framework of analysis of power as a linkage of heterogeneous systems is again pertinent here. Instead of investigating connected elements to find the inner reason for their connections, Foucault instead invites us to discern the hybrid effects and unprecedented mixes which are produced today by the fortuitous encounters of right, norm and security.

Is right a good obstruction to power?

It remains to discuss the question of political action. Right can been considered up to now as standing on the side of institutions which represent or utilize it; but is it not equally on the side of the oppressed, against the abuses of these same institutions? Must law itself not be answerable to law? Such was indeed the purpose of the sixteenth-century jurists who distinguished the state from the person of the king. The conclusion of Foucault's lecture of 14 January 1976 addresses this question directly, no longer as a matter of purely historical description:

> Against the usurpations of the disciplinary mechanism . . . we find ourselves currently in a situation such that the only existing and apparently solid recourse which we have is precisely the recourse or return to a right organized around sovereignty. [But] it is not by resorting to sovereignty that one can limit the effects which are proper to disciplinary power . . . what we need to aim towards . . . would rather be the direction of a new kind of right, an anti-disciplinary right.
>
> (Foucault 1997: 35)

Why is the theory of sovereignty, that is to say the reference to the inalienable rights of the individual, unable effectively to obstruct these disciplinary techniques? The problem, according to Foucault, is the close ties which history has woven between sovereign right and discipline, through the intermediary agency of new sciences. Disciplining individuals who are recognized as bearers of absolute rights cannot be done without the justification of a knowledge permitting reasonable intervention in the name of a norm deemed 'natural'. The human sciences thus enabled the nineteenth century to establish a mirror-relationship between man as object of respect and man as object of discipline. For the monster or madman who departs from the natural norm is none other finally than one who breaks the social contract, who 'drops out of the pact and disqualifies himself as citizen' (Foucault 1975: 120). We observe this today with the political usage of the notion of the 'dangerous' individual, the object in France of a special law which bypasses traditional legality by basing itself on a purportedly medical form of expertise.[9] Inversely, to evade this civic disqualification, each embodied individual has to be made to give an account of their history and psyche; each body has to be made into a *subject*. The individual body thus finds itself qualified, administratively and juridically, by these psychological, biological and sexual indicators.[10]

Willingly or unwillingly, the struggle against domination in the name of individual rights comes to carry 'a whole set of psychological references borrowed from the human sciences, that is, from the discourses and practices of the disciplinary domain' (Foucault 1997: 36).[11] Foucault detects, in a form of humanist thought which invokes the value of the individual and its deep subjectivity, notions in themselves absolutely worthy of respect, the hidden traces of this disciplining discourse which makes a soul from a body. The mitigating legal defence, pleaded by Robert Badinter in 1977 to spare Patrick Henry from the death penalty, is a good example: the young lawyer reproached the jury with not sufficiently *knowing* the accused subject. But, Foucault immediately remarks, such a reproach accords perfectly with the new logic of penal justice which, since the nineteenth century, seeks less to punish an act on the basis of a code, than to correct an individual in terms of their personality (Foucault 1977a: 287). In this disquieting slippage, the condemned person is placed, along with their affects, desires, and instincts, under a medico-legal surveillance which is tending to acquire an unlimited scope.[12]

Nothing nevertheless prevents Foucault, while fully conscious of the anthropological presuppositions of existing conceptions of rights, from making circumstantial uses of them, still designed to detach them from their primary function. For Foucault, to demand rights today is not to reactivate an old doctrine of sovereignty, but to recognize that the guarantees offered by law are always produced within a historical and strategic setting. It is always possible to act from within this strategic setting, rather than try to invent a new, absolutely transparent coding of right. Many rights inscribed in law only become effective for an individual to the extent that they are concretely seeking to defend themselves and engage their existence in that effort. It is this act of assuming one's rights, in the widest sense, which gives right its amplitude and effective universality. In an unsigned text of 1980, Foucault develops this pragmatic, but none the less exacting conception of the proper use of laws:

> It is not because there are laws, and not because I have rights, that I am entitled to defend myself; it is because I defend myself that my rights exist and the law respects me. It is thus first of all the dynamic of defence which is able to give law and rights the value which is indispensable for us. A right is nothing unless it comes to life in the defence which occasions its invocation.[13]
>
> (Foucault 1980)

Effective liberty and positive right never coincide immediately for everyone. They develop along separate lines, whose possible meetings need to be watched for. At this point of meeting, right becomes an instrument seized upon to attain a result which the legislator may not have necessarily envisaged at the outset. The strictly juridical argumentation which Foucault uses in 1977 to oppose the extradition to West Germany of the Red Army Faction lawyer Klaus Croissant might serve as a good example: the legal rights of political refugees, in particular their protection against extradition enacted in the European Convention of 1957, were developed for tactical considerations related to the Cold War; but this particular political context does not prevent claiming this right 'for all', for Klaus Croissant as for Eastern dissidents: 'liberties and their safeguards . . . are not always conquered in a grand struggle, a triumphant morning. They are made often out of occasion, surprise or detour. It is then that they must be seized and made valid *for all*' (Foucault 1977c: 364, emphasis added).

This strategic usage is not, however, Foucault's last word on juridical matters. In bringing together a certain number of articles and lectures from 1977 to 1982, it is equally possible to find premises for a more positive and non-disciplinary approach to right.

Outline of a solution: the liberal approach to right

The theory of sovereignty postulates three core unities which Foucault expounds at the start of the lecture of 21 January 1976, and for which he shows the greatest suspicion: (a) the unity of law (behind particular laws, a fundamental legitimacy); (b) the unity of power (the state); and (c) the unity of the subject (qualified as 'the individual endowed, naturally (or by nature) with rights, capacities, etc' (Foucault 1997: 37)). What then would be meant by a 'new anti-disciplinary right', and can one find signs of such a thing in Foucault's thought? The presentation of the theory of sovereignty offers, in negative, the specification of what this new right would have to be: it would need to be developed without postulating a unity of the subject, power or law. How, based on this specification, can governmental practice be limited without once more inscribing the imprescriptible, qualified as anthropology, in the marble of laws?

Let us consider the lectures on *The Birth of Biopolitics* from 1978 to 1979. In the lecture of 17 January 1979, Foucault contrasts a juridico-deductive (or French, via reference to Rousseau) approach to an inductive or utilitarian (or British, via reference to Bentham) approach. The first approach starts from natural rights belonging to each individual, whose partial transfer constitutes a legitimate government, which is always however externally limited by these natural rights. The second approach starts from governmental practice itself, in order to limit it from within, not by appeal to criteria of legitimacy, but by criteria of utility. Its basic rule is not an original right, but a political economy conceived as a calculation of the cost and efficacy of governmental action. This rational auto-limitation must indeed come to juridical expression, but this expression has as its first function to enunciate and subsequently to verify the principle of least government. What remains problematic is the possible place within this order of a basic right such as the right to subsistence or to work.[14]

This second way is the way of liberalism, conceived first of all as a technology of government, an art of governing well by governing economically. Foucault describes its distinctive rationality, from the Physiocrats of the eighteenth century to the German and American neoliberal schools of the twentieth century. But if this approach is so clearly contrasted with that other one, so much criticized by Foucault, based on sovereignty, are we to see it as a possible alternative? The publication in 2004 of the course on *The Birth of Biopolitics* startled a part of

Foucault's traditional audience, and certain Jacobins for whom 'liberalism' is a term always deserving of unqualified scorn. The article cited above from 1977 could however justify this hypothesis: in November of that year, on the occasion of the request for the extradition of the lawyer Klaus Croissant, Foucault signed a column in the *Nouvel Observateur* where he invoked the 'right of the governed', a right which is 'more precise, more historically determined that the rights of man' (Foucault 1977c: 362). Hardly more than a year later, at the *Collège de France*, in characterizing the new conception of liberty which emerges in liberal governmentality and which contrasts point by point with the revolutionary philosophy of the rights of man, Foucault uses a noticeably similar syntagm: that of the 'independence of the governed' (Foucault 2004a: 43). Can we therefore place in series the appeal in 1976 for a 'new anti-disciplinary right', the militant reference in 1977 to a 'right of the governed', and the liberal notion of the 'independence of the governed' expounded in 1979?

We need to tread carefully. In the first place, if one follows the lectures of 14 and 21 March 1979 devoted to the Chicago school, it can be recognized that the type of governmentality advocated by liberal post-war economists such as Theodore Schultz (1902–98) or Gary Becker (1930–) fulfils in part the requirement of a non-disciplinary form of right:

1 There is no longer a unity of law, because there is no postulate of a founding legitimation of the legislative or constitutional edifice; this legitimation is constantly produced by the sole exercise of the freedom of economic agents,[15] and is constantly subject to discussion in all its fields of application, including the domain of inter-state relations. When Foucault appeals in 1981 to the right of the governed to invite themselves into the discussion of questions of international politics previously reserved to states, he inscribes himself clearly within this lineage (Foucault 1984a: 1527).
2 There is no longer a unity of power, for its exercise is devolved as far as possible to local instances, at once collective (associations, enterprises, neighbourhood committees) and individual (the individual as 'entrepreneur of oneself', as an active agent in governmental regulation when consuming, choosing products, taking care of assets, and so forth). Between these autonomous entities, which are no longer mere ramifications of the states, there is a process of perpetual transaction. Hence the displacement of law into jurisprudence, to arbitrate differences between partners in the economic game. One may hence not be astonished that in the article of 1977 Foucault posits as an 'essential' right of the governed the right to legal defence in judicial procedure (Foucault 1977c: 365).
3 There is no longer a unity of the subject, since the object of liberal governmentality is not the individual, but only the individual's environment. Crime and health are reconceived as global phenomena whose statistical laws indicate their sufficient level of management. In this way of thinking, the criminal is no longer characterized in anthropological terms but instead

> becomes an economic subject like any other, who 'seeks in all situations to maximize his profit and optimize the relation of gains and losses' (Foucault 2004a: 264).[16] Public power must simply calculate accurately the efficacy of its intervention on this economic subject, considering the damage it may cause to the free play of interests, without resorting to an expensive disciplinary apparatus. Which means that law can tolerate without difficulty a certain level of illegality within the social body.

The result consists in this formula: less state and more government at a distance. The state is now only a partner in a perpetual negotiation between those who govern and those who are governed. It is constantly advancing or receding, ceding motorways to local authorities but taking on the struggle against cancer, and so forth. It is within this new liberal framework that one can try to give content to the notion of 'rights of the governed', the need for whose theory Foucault announces in 1977 (Foucault 1977c: 362).

The use of the participle 'governed' to qualify the new subject of rights signifies that there is no longer a reference to an abstract point of origin, but a situation of fact and a concrete individual: the human being in question is conceived as always already caught in a relation of power. As Foucault explains, the freedom which I exercise when I invoke these rights 'is never anything more than an actual, present relation between those who govern and the governed, a relation where the measure of the "too little" freedom that exists is given by the "yet more" freedom which is demanded' (Foucault 2004a: 64). This requisition escapes from the circuit of fundamental rights, a circuit which proceeds from legitimate demands to the legitimation of power and in which the basic right upon which one relies to limit the excess of power is at the same time that which founds its essential exercise. The 'right of the governed', on the contrary, cedes nothing and founds nothing, since it is a quantitative and situated protest at a simple 'too much' of governing, which does not carry a signification that the state has been diverted from its essence or its founding legitimacy. Nothing is more alien to it than natural right, in the senses that Grotius and the natural law tradition have given to this term: at once the description of a natural state anterior to the civil state, and prescription of a rule of conduct dictated by right reason. Neither prescriptive nor descriptive, the 'right of the governed', as the simple possibility of saying 'I will no longer obey',[17] is first of all an objective fact, attested by our recent history: 1971 in France (the revolt in the prisons), 1978 in Iran, 1982 in Poland. Foucault reflects on it as a historian of the present, not as a philosopher of the subject.[18]

Because it is historically encountered and not juridically constructed, this right escapes the vice-like grip in which modern legislative texts tend to confine the right of resistance. Whether it be in the Declaration of the Rights of Man and Citizen of 1789 or the Convention for the Protection of Human Rights and Fundamental Freedoms in 1950, resistance to oppression always comes up against positive law which at once grounds and limits it, in a double, unbreakable constraint. Prior to its exercise, resistance might first justify itself by reason of the violation of recognized elementary rights, in order then to be faced with the legitimate interference of the democratic state in the exercise of certain of these rights.[19] At the opposite pole, the 'right of the governed' exists through its own affirmation, without presage of its limit or foundation. But no government can long pretend to ignore it, above all when contemporary life continues to give it consistence and visibility.

Foucault nevertheless suggests the possibility of giving this right an explicit juridical form: as in the case of the right to be defended in judicial procedure by a lawyer, which he mentions in the Croissant case (Foucault 1977c: 365). But it is interesting to note that this single example concerns precisely a situation of contention – in the largest sense of this term – between the governed and the public power. The juridical form which is envisaged here would not serve to qualify the individual by acknowledging certain inherent capacities or natural dignities, but instead guarantee and optimize their possibilities of negotiation with the powers exercised over them.

Limits of the liberal approach to right

In certain of its aspects, the inductive and utilitarian approach of a certain liberal tradition accords well with the non-anthropologically founded form of right which is called for in '*Society Must be Defended*'. This approach makes it possible to envisage a perpetual adjustment of the law, without ultimate end-point or destination, in response to individual demands and interests, as in the mechanisms of the competitive market. But it is not certain that the notion of 'independence of the governed' is entirely sufficient to fulfil the demands for the 'right of the governed' set out in the *Nouvel Observateur* article of 1977. We need to note what the second expression adds to, or corrects, in the first, demarcating it from what is provided by the liberal dispensation alone.

Let us first of all recall Foucault's great vigilance towards this new dispensation, especially in its present mutations such as neoliberalism. The classical doctrine of liberalism, as represented in Immanuel Kant or Adam Smith, is akin to a naturalism. In it, right is born through exchanges between individuals and groups, through an inner necessity. To the spontaneous mechanism of the economy there correspond in Kant the spontaneous mechanisms of jurisdiction which are nature's design: thus there successively emerge individual rights within small groups, then states, international and commercial law, and so forth.[20] In the twentieth century the Freiburg school, followed by the Chicago school, opposes to the '*laissez-faire*' of classical liberals an imperative of permanent intervention. One needs not just to ensure that nothing impairs the market, but also or instead to actively and ceaselessly create this market. And this at two levels: government must intervene not only on the functional conditions of the market (stable prices, control of inflation), but also on its structural conditions (the social 'frame'[21] of the market, including education, health, the distribution of the population over the territory and so forth), so that aleatory factors do not perturb the free play of interests. These are interventions based on considerations of security, which constitute 'the obverse as well as the precondition of liberalism' (Foucault 2004a: 67). Their field of action is by definition indefinite, since they can be equally concerned with the air we breathe, the security of neighbourhoods, the mental stability of young children and so forth. They thus belong to the direct continuation of the biopower which we discussed above. Hence the paradox of liberal governmentality which Foucault underlines: 'freedom in the regime of liberalism is not a given, freedom is not a ready-made which is merely to be respected . . . Freedom is something which is created at each moment' (Foucault 2004a: 66).

In these conditions, whatever fails to react in a predictable way to modifications in its environment, or to obey the rationality of *Homo economicus*, defined as the man who seeks to fructify his human, social and cultural capital, threatens the security measures which are intrinsic to liberal policy. One of the founders of the first Chicago school, Frank H. Knight, had on this point carefully distinguished between 'risk' – which was mathematically measurable and hence manageable – and 'uncertainty', which defeats any form of probabilist modelling (Knight 1921). So it is not inappropriate that it is a question relating to terrorism which prompts Foucault in 1977 to denounce the runaway growth of measures and mechanisms of response to what the state defines as a 'dangerous accident' (Foucault 1977b: 386). The effort of some contemporary economists to integrate the suicide bomber into the theory of rational choice guided by self-interest clearly indicates their disarray in dealing with forms of conduct which no longer obey the rationality of exchange (Harrison 2003: 11–13). If terrorism is the public enemy of liberalism, this is not essentially because it represents an absolute evil – to say that would be to re-qualify ontologically the status of crime and criminal – but because it is the most manifest form of what, escaping the laws of economy, imposes the aleatory character of the event:

> The state which guarantees security is a state obliged to intervene in all cases where the fabric of daily life is broken by a singular, exceptional event. At a stroke, the law is no longer equipped to respond; at a stroke, there are needed these forms of intervention whose exceptional, extra-legal character must not at all be seen as a sign of arbitrary or excessive power, but rather as a sign of solicitude . . . This aspect of omnipresent solicitude is the way in which the state presents itself.
>
> (Foucault 1977b: 385)[22]

Liberalism does not reduce the role of the state, it redistributes its roles: it asks it to accept an ever greater pluralism of behaviours within society (for example, the consumption of drugs), while at the same time keeping uncertainty at bay. Hence the open and negotiated character of the management of risk does not preclude exceptional measures which circumvent legal limitations to annihilate an unquantifiable hazard.

Faced with this exorbitant price of security, if the independence of the governed now produces only isolated protests, limited to the pure subjective sense of the intolerable, it will be unable to effectively challenge the new pact of tranquillity between the liberal state and its citizens. The expression 'independence of the governed' is indeed highly ambiguous, for it can equally signify the autonomy of each governed individual (subjective genitive) and the *mutual* independence of the governed (objective genitive) within a society which is no more than an arbitrage between individual egoistic interests. Individual protest will always falter in the face of exceptional measures grounded on the state's calculation of the relativity of collective interest and individual interest.

My hypothesis would thus be as follows. The notion of the 'right of the governed' as Foucault employs it in his texts of combat, from the Klaus Croissant affair in 1977 to the *Solidarnosc* episode in 1982,[23] is the injection into the sphere of the independence of the governed of a collective dimension. 'We are all governed and, as such, bound by solidarity' (Foucault 1984a: 1526), Foucault declares in 1981, at a time when this proposition is by no means self-evident. But if this solidarity is not natural, it is not unthinkable. For all subjective protest has meaning only if it can connect with a concrete 'we', whatever the form that this may take. A 'we' however which does not pre-exist the act of protest from all eternity, which is inscribed in no particular version of human nature, no pre-existing contract or understanding between the governed, but one which causes Foucault to take an interest in Klaus Croissant in 1977, in the Iranians in 1978, and in the entry of non-governmental organisations[24] on to the international scene: 'We are all here as private persons whose only entitlement to speak, and to speak collectively, is a certain difficulty in bearing what is taking place' (Foucault 1984a: 1526).[25] This 'we', never definitively achieved or instituted, which can comprise at the outset a group, a minority or a whole people, undoes the state management of the relation between individual and collective interest, for it is never wholly either individual or collective.

What then is the condition under which a solitary protest can be assumed by a collectivity? Reading the articles of 1978–9 devoted to the events in Iran, one seems to see an idea emerging that the human being who stands up and says 'no', over and above a simple epidermic and circumstantial reaction, must manifest at the same time a reflected form of subjectivity, that is to say of relation to self. This involves not only the vision of a more just city which brings together the governed in a single protest, but also, and perhaps above all, a certain way of engaging in history, at the crossing-point of a transformation of the world and a transformation of self.[26]

Translated by Colin Gordon*

Notes

* *Translation*: unless otherwise indicated, '*droit*' and '*droits*' are always translated here as 'right' and 'rights', and '*loi*' as 'law'. '*Droits de l'homme*' is translated, except in the context of 1789, as 'human rights'.

1 See Renaut and Sosoe 1991: 54–5; Zarka 2002: 266. Commentary on the question in the Anglophone world has been more nuanced – see for example Patton 2004. (*Editor's note*: the chapter by Patton in the present collection (Chapter 9) develops some of the themes discussed in this 2004 conference paper.)

2 Thus the entitlement to participate in political life following the French Revolution (and the right to vote, in the constitution of 1791) depended on income and property-owning status.

3 On a single occasion, in the lecture of 14 January 1976, Foucault uses the term 'right' in an enlarged sense including a concrete application extending as far as the smallest institutional regulation. This enlarged sense clearly extends beyond the limits of sovereignty: 'when I say right, I mean not simply the law but the whole sets of apparatuses, institutions, regulations, which apply the law' (Foucault 1997: 24).

4 With the exception of the thought of Emmanuel Joseph Sieyès, upon which Foucault touches in 1976. Sieyès, according to Foucault, identifies, as the substrate of the juridico-formal conditions of nationhood, its historico-functional conditions: law is required not to guarantee ideal rights, but to enable works (agriculture, crafts, industry) and assure pre-existing functions (army, justice, church, administration) (Foucault 1997: 195–200).

5 The following is based on the great methodological article of 1982, 'Le sujet et le pouvoir' (The Subject and Power) (Foucault 1982a).

6 Individuals only occasionally came into contact with feudal power, in their status as a user (passing a toll, using a road), as a member of a family, as an inhabitant of a city, and so forth (Foucault 2003: 45–6).

7 'We attack the role of expertise, because we are completely deprived of the means to challenge it,' according to a lawyer speaking in a round-table discussion involving Michel Foucault (Foucault 1974b).

8 Expert psychiatric testimony was not an obligation in the Criminal Code of 1810. The 1958 Code of Penal Procedure requires only an investigation of 'personality'. It is usage, not the codes, which has imposed recourse to psychiatric expertise in order to determine the capacity of the accused.

9 The Law of 25 February 2008 on secure detention. For a precise analysis of this law and a history of the concept of dangerousness, drawing on Foucault's work, see Chevallier and Greacen 2009.

10 One of these markers is the person's sex, which the law cannot allow to be ambivalent. In 1981 Foucault published a preface to the American edition of *Herculine Barbin, dite Alexina B.*, the memoir of a nineteenth-century hermaphrodite originally published in the *Annales d'Hygiène Publique*. In his preface, Foucault writes: 'Beginning in the 18th century, biological theories of sexuality, the juridical status of the individual and the forms of administrative control in modern states gradually led to the refusal of the idea of a mixture of the two sexes, and a consequent restriction of the free choice of uncertain individuals. From then on, for each individual, there was to be one, and only one sex' (Foucault 1980: 935–6).

11 This is the continuation of a theme developed in Foucault 2003: 59.

12 Among recent legal measures in France: the socio-judicial injunction with or without care (Law of 17 June 1998); the creation of the computerized legal register of sexual offences (Law of 9 March 2004); mobile electronic surveillance (tagging) (Law of 12 December 2005); preventative detention (Law of 25 February 2008).

13 See Defert and Ewald 2001: 79–80 (*Translation note*: there is a translation of this text forthcoming in Falzon, O'Leary and Sawicki 2012). Foucault drafted this unsigned text at the request of the lawyer Christian Revon, in preparation for a public hearing, 'Pour la défense libre' at La Sainte-Baume (Foucault 1980). Christian Revon informed me that this movement had little success after this meeting, deep divergences becoming apparent between the participants (interview with C. Revon, May 2006).

14 These rights to subsistence or work can exist in the utilitarian perspective, but they are negotiated according to circumstance, instead of applying immediately and all at the same time.
15 This is already the idea, for the German economics minister and later Federal Chancellor, Ludwig Erhard (1897–1977), of a 'permanent genesis and genealogy of the state deriving from the institution of the economy' (Foucault 2004a: 86). This could also be the project of a European constitution, something conceived at the outset as the simple, utilitarian regulation of an already existing governmental practice. Against this, the No campaign in the referendum opposed the sovereign will of citizens: see Donzelot 2005.
16 A presentation of this liberal approach to crime through the British example can be found in Garland 1998.
17 In an article on Iran in 1979, Foucault posits as 'irreducible' the movement by which a single person, a group, a minority or a whole people says: 'I will no longer obey', and confronts a power which they judge unjust with the readiness to risk their own life (Foucault 1979a).
18 About this new 'right of the governed', Foucault adds, 'our recent history has made it a reality which is still fragile, but precious' (Foucault 1977c: 362). We should consider the new calls for the respect of human rights as a new historical phenomenon, not as the reactivation of a traditional model of right (Foucault 2004a: 43).
19 Certainly the Declaration of the Rights of Man and Citizen of 1789 cites 'resistance to oppression' among the natural and imprescriptible rights (Article II). But Article VII immediately locates, in the face of resistance, the notions of Law and Society: 'every citizen summoned or invested by virtue of the law must obey instantly: he renders himself guilty by resistance'. There is a presupposition of legitimacy in what concerns the law, as the 'expression of the general will' (Article VI) which forbids 'actions harmful to society' (Article V). This delicate confrontation reappears in the Convention for the Protection of Human Rights and Fundamental Freedoms of 1950, which recognizes the legitimate restriction of certain rights. Thus, the interference of public authority in the exercise of rights relating to private and family life is possible 'except such as is in accordance with the law and is necessary in a democratic society in the interests of national security, public safety or the economic well-being of the country, for the prevention of disorder or crime, for the protection of health or morals, or for the protection of the rights and freedoms of others' (Article VIII).
20 As dealt with in *Idea of a Universal History from a Cosmopolitan Point of View* (1784) and *Project of Perpetual Peace* (1795).
21 This notion of a 'framework' is fundamental with the German Ordoliberals (Foucault 2004a: 145).
22 This article by Foucault clearly deals with the security state, not the liberal state – the former is of course not reducible to the latter. Let us recall, however, that France in 1977 is under the presidency of Valéry Giscard d'Estaing, a political context which marks for Foucault the introduction of neoliberalism in France (Foucault 2004a: 199–213).
23 While, on his return from Poland in 1982, Foucault does not employ the expression 'right of the governed', it is clearly in this sense that he proposes to interpret the notion of human rights: 'But human rights mean above all what one opposes to governments. They are the limits set to all possible governments' (Foucault 1982b: 1168).
24 *L'Île-de-lumière* in 1979, *Médecins du monde* in 1980, the International Committee against Piracy in 1981.
25 In a 1984 interview with Paul Rabinow, Foucault returns to this 'we' which is constituted only 'based on the work that is done', and hopes to form 'a community of action' (Foucault 1984b).

26 On revolt as an imperative to change one's self, see Foucault 1979b: 749. See, also, Foucault 1979a: 793: it is through revolt 'that subjectivity (not that of great men, but that of whomever), enters into history'. (*Translation note*: in *The Hermeneutics of the Subject*, Foucault later comments that an 'ethic of the self' may be 'an urgent, fundamental and politically indispensable task, if it is true that there is after all no first or final point of resistance to political power other than in the relationship one has to oneself' (Foucault 2005: 252).)

References

(*Editor's note*: references to texts from the two-volume edition of *Dits et écrits* are cited, above, and listed chronologically in the References, below, according to their initial date of publication (and not the date of their subsequent publication in *Dits et écrits*).)

Chevallier, P. and Greacen, T. (eds) (2009) *Folie et justice: relire Foucault*, Toulouse: Erès

Crozier, M. and Friedberg, E. (1977) *L'acteur et le système*, Paris: Seuil

Donzelot, J. (2005) 'Michel Foucault et l'intelligence du libéralisme', *Esprit*, November: 60–81

Falzon, C., O'Leary, T. and Sawicki, J. (2012 forthcoming) *A Companion to Foucault*, Oxford: Blackwell

Foucault, M. (1974a) 'De la nature humaine: justice contre pouvoir', in D. Defert and F. Ewald (eds) *Dits et écrits I, 1954–1975*, Paris: Gallimard

___ (1974b) 'Table ronde sur l'expertise psychiatrique', in D. Defert and F. Ewald (eds) *Dits et écrits I, 1954–1975*, Paris: Gallimard

___ (1975) *Surveiller et punir*, Paris: Gallimard

___ (1977a) 'L'angoisse de juger', in D. Defert and F. Ewald (eds) *Dits et écrits II, 1976–1988*, Paris: Gallimard

___ (1977b) 'Michel Foucault: la sécurité et l'état', in D. Defert and F. Ewald (eds) *Dits et écrits II, 1976–1988*, Paris: Gallimard

___ (1977c) 'Va-t-on extruder Klaus Croissant?', in D. Defert and F. Ewald (eds) *Dits et écrits II, 1976–1988*, Paris: Gallimard

___ (1979a) 'Inutile de se soulever?', in D. Defert and F. Ewald (eds) *Dits et écrits II, 1976–1988*, Paris: Gallimard

___ (1979b) 'L'esprit d'un monde sans esprit', in D. Defert and F. Ewald (eds) *Dits et écrits II, 1976–1988*, Paris: Gallimard

___ (1980) 'Le vrai sexe', in D. Defert and F. Ewald (eds) *Dits et écrits II, 1976–1988*, Paris: Gallimard

___ (1982a) 'Le sujet et le pouvoir', in D. Defert and F. Ewald (eds) *Dits et écrits II, 1976–1988*, Paris: Gallimard

___ (1982b) 'L'expérience morale et sociale des Polonais ne peut plus être effacée', in D. Defert and F. Ewald (eds) *Dits et écrits II, 1976–1988*, Paris: Gallimard

___ (1984a) 'Face aux gouvernements, les droits de l'homme?', in D. Defert and F. Ewald (eds) *Dits et écrits II, 1976–1988*, Paris: Gallimard

___ (1984b) 'Polémique, politique et problématisations', in D. Defert and F. Ewald (eds) *Dits et écrits II, 1976–1988*, Paris: Gallimard

___ (1997) *'Il faut défendre la société': Cours au Collège de France, 1975–76*, Paris: Seuil/Gallimard

___ (1999) *Les anormaux: Cours au Collège de France, 1974–75*, Paris: Seuil/Gallimard

___ (2003) *Le pouvoir psychiatrique: Cours au Collège de France, 1973–74*, Paris: Seuil/Gallimard

___ (2004a) *Naissance de la biopolitique: Cours au Collège de France, 1978–79*, Paris: Gallimard
___ (2004b) *Sécurité, territoire, population: Cours au Collège de France, 1977–78*, Paris: Seuil/Gallimard
___ (2005) *The Hermeneutics of the Subject: Lectures at the Collège de France 1981–82*, trans. G. Burchell, New York, NY: Palgrave Macmillan
Garland, D. (1998) 'Les contradictions de la "société punitive": le cas britannique', *Actes de la Recherche en Sciences Sociales* 124: 49–67
Harrison, M. (2003) 'The Logic of Suicide Terrorism', *Royal United Services Institute Monitor*, 2: 11–13
Knight, F. H. (1921) *Risk, Uncertainty and Profit*, Boston, MA: Hart, Schaffner & Marx, Houghton Mifflin Co.
Patton, P. (2004) 'Governmentality, Power and Right', paper presented at the Michel Foucault (1926–1984): Other Questions, New Paths conference at the London School of Economics, September 2004
Renaut, A. and Sosoe, L. K. (1991) *Philosophie du droit*, Paris: Presses Universitaires de France
Zarka, Y. C. (2002) 'Foucault et l'idée d'une histoire de la subjectivité: Le moment moderne', *Archives de Philosophie*, 65: 255–67

References to primary sources of law

Cass. Crim., 11 March 1958
Circular of the Garde des sceaux
Instruction générale pour l'application du Code de procédure pénale
Law of 17 June 1998 (the socio-judicial injunction with or without care)
Law of 9 March 2004 (the creation of the computerized legal register of sexual offences)
Law of 12 December 2005 (on mobile electronic surveillance)
Law of 25 February 2008 (on secure detention)

Chapter 9

Historical normativity and the basis of rights

Paul Patton

Introduction

Rights, in our modern democratic societies, are increasingly enshrined in law. Their ultimate basis is therefore to be found in the political norms or principles of right that underpin our systems of law and government. Traditionally, these norms or principles were grounded in some transcendent or transcendental conception of nature. Some contemporary theorists continue to ground rights in particular rights-bearing features of human nature.[1] This implies an a-historical conception of rights according to which it makes no sense to say that new rights have come into existence or that old ones have disappeared: if a particular right exists for a given class of rights bearers then it has always existed.[2] Changes may occur in the beliefs of people about rights and rights bearers but there is no possibility of change in what rights there are. Others argue that this appeal to nature is no longer possible for us and that nature has given way to society as the only plausible basis of right (Ewald 1988: 37, 44).[3] The recent history of particular rights supports the idea that rights are inescapably social in character and a product of the relations of power, beliefs, attitudes and practices, including the legal practices, of the relevant communities in which they exist (Ivison 2008: 17–36). This calls for a naturalistic and historical conception of rights that grounds them in existing forms of political normativity and legal practice. By a naturalistic conception of rights, I mean one that does not depend on any transcendent conception of the moral basis of rights, or of the human nature in which they are grounded, and in which rights are an important part of the social world in which we live. On this view, what rights there are changes over time: old rights disappear and new ones come into existence.

In order to outline the features of such a historical conception of rights, I draw upon an unlikely assemblage of philosophical resources that includes John Rawls's political liberalism and Michel Foucault's studies of forms of European governmentality.[4] Despite their differences, both philosophers approach the bases of political and jurisprudential normativity from the perspective of actually existing practices of government and discursive reflection on these practices. In the case of Rawls, the point of departure for his later political philosophy is the question of stability for modern pluralistic liberal societies: how is it possible to sustain 'a just and stable society of free and equal citizens, who remain profoundly divided by reasonable religious, philosophical and moral doctrines'? (Rawls 2005: 4). His answer to this question makes it clear that the basis of a just, stable and democratic political society must be found in the 'considered convictions' that are expressed in the public political culture of those societies that aspire to be democratic (Rawls 2005: 8). His conception of justice as fairness is put forward as a political conception that draws upon the ideas embodied in the institutions of constitutional democracy and the public traditions of their interpretation: 'Justice as fairness is a political conception in part because it starts from within a certain political tradition' (Rawls 1985: 390). Rawls's political liberal conception of the basis of rights parallels François Ewald's interpretation of the jurisprudence of general principles implicit in constitutions and bodies of law as this developed in the aftermath of the Second World War. Recourse to general principles, he suggests, provided a degree of stability and continuity to systems of law while at the same time allowing for modification. As such, this practice of legal interpretation expressed 'a kind of will on the part of society to bind itself to itself by way of its history, its heritage and its juridical and constitutional patrimony' (Ewald 1986a: 792).

Foucault does not provide a general theory of right or law but his sketches toward a history of governmentality show how different conceptions of the purposes, methods and objects of government have succeeded one another in the European political tradition, the same tradition that produced the kind of liberal democracy the normative structure of which Rawls seeks to systematize. Over time, these 'governmental' discourses with their associated conceptions of the nature, purposes and methods of government have come to inform public political culture and to provide elements of public reason within contemporary liberal democracies (Patton 2010). As a result, these conceptions have determined the kinds of rights that have been recognized under particular regimes of government and expressed in laws and public policies. For the most part, Foucault's ambition is more modest than that of Rawls, in that he is only concerned to identify the different ways in which the exercise of sovereign power has been theorized rather than to spell out currently acceptable philosophical grounds that legitimate the exercise of such power. At the same time, his descriptive project is intended to serve a critical function. In a 1978 lecture in Japan, he provides an explicit statement of the idea that criticism must proceed on the basis of actually existing principles, when he suggests that philosophy can play a role in support of forms of resistance or counter-power only on the condition that it 'stops posing the question of power in terms of good and evil, but poses it in terms of existence' (Foucault 1978: 540). In the final section, below, I discuss some of the ways in which Foucault relies on this principle of existence, both in historical remarks about the bases of criticism and resistance to power and in his own efforts as an engaged citizen to develop arguments for new or emerging rights. Before turning to Foucault, however, I will explore further what it might mean to discuss rights in terms of existence.

Externalist conceptions of rights

So-called externalist conceptions of rights are promising contributors to a naturalistic and historical approach.[5] Whereas a-historical approaches treat rights as inherent properties of individuals or groups which then set limits to the power of others, externalists treat rights as a consequence of the social relations that obtain between individual and collective agents. Externalist approaches hold that whether or not individuals or groups possess rights depends on facts about how they are able to act and how they are treated within a given social milieu (Darby 2001: 387). Different externalist theorists offer different formulations with regard to precisely which social facts are relevant for the existence of rights. Rex Martin characterizes rights as 'established ways of acting *or* established ways of being acted toward, ways of being treated' (Martin 1993: 41, emphasis in original). The fact that the social practices relevant to the existence of rights are explained by reference to legal rights does not exclude the possibility that rights might exist in some societies by virtue of less formal institutional practices. Different expressions of rights are consistent with this general conception of rights in terms of the established behaviours open to individuals and groups. Derrick Darby specifies the meaning of 'established' in suggesting that what is required for the behaviours in question to be considered rights is 'institutional respect', where this implies some institutional mechanism for recognizing a given behaviour as a matter of right and enforcing or protecting that right (Darby 2003: 65–6; 2009: 85–90). For Darby, too, it is an advantage of this definition that it does not differentiate between political, legal or customary rights.[6]

For externalists, rights are essentially defined as positive rights, in the sense that they only exist when relevant institutional or other means of enforcement or protection of behaviours are present. Where these are lacking, the rights in question will not exist or will be purely nominal. The suggestion that rights may nominally exist points to another important dimension of externalist conceptions of rights, namely that a necessary condition for an established way of acting or being acted upon to constitute a right is that it be justified. This condition is necessary but not sufficient: where there is a justification but no established practice or means of redress, the right in question only nominally exists. The converse situation in which there is an established law or practice but no credible justification is also not sufficient for the existence of a right. This occurs, for example, when archaic laws remain in place long after they have ceased to have any socially acceptable justification. It follows that both conditions – established ways of acting or being acted upon and available justification – are separately necessary and jointly sufficient for the existence of rights.

The consensus among externalist theorists is that there must be moral justification in order for there to be a right. Some theorists specify what kind of moral justification is required for the existence of rights: Sumner takes this to mean a consequentialist argument (Sumner 1987). Others, notably Darby, present it as a virtue that their conception leaves open the question of what kind of moral theory might provide an acceptable justification, either because this unties the question of what rights there are from the larger question of identifying the true moral theory, or because it allows for the possibility of moral pluralism. In this manner, Darby limits his definition of rights to socially recognized ways of acting or being acted upon that are justified in terms of some substantive moral theory or other, while recognizing that this calls for further specification of what might constitute an adequate moral theory (Darby 2001: 407; 2003: 68; 2009: 90).

However, in all cases, these externalist theorists suppose that the rights with which they are concerned are moral rights. This is a difficulty for externalist conceptions of rights, insofar as they are supposed to apply to the conditions of modern liberal democratic societies. For, as Rawls has shown, such societies are characterized by a plurality of comprehensive moral views, not only in fact but also in principle. The free exercise of human reason and the burdens of judgment imply that a liberal society will inevitably lead to a plurality of moral, philosophical and religious points of view. Since the differences between these comprehensive moral views may be profound, even incommensurable, a stable political order cannot rely on conceptions of right that are justified by reference to particular comprehensive moral views. To do so would be to fail to meet the standard of reasonableness that, for Rawls, is a necessary condition of justice and stability in a genuinely liberal political community. Instead, conceptions of right and justice must be supported by public reasons that meet the required standards of reciprocity and reasonableness: the basic rights of citizens must be supported by reasons that citizens can offer to one another in the reasonable belief that these will be acceptable to others who might not share their own comprehensive views. I discuss Rawls's concept of public reason further, below. I invoke it here only to suggest that the appropriate form of justification for rights should be political rather than moral.

Political liberalism and the historicity of rights

Rawls's political liberalism seems a promising candidate for the justificatory dimension of a naturalistic conception of rights, for a number of reasons. First, the rights and duties of citizens are not moral but political rights. They are the product of an agreement or an overlapping consensus. As such, the basic civil and political rights of citizens belong to a freestanding political conception that is neither derived from nor dependent upon any of the comprehensive religious, philosophical or moral views represented in the community. The political conception of justice must be defensible from within the relevant comprehensive moral views, but this defence is limited to overtly political values, rights and duties. Overlapping consensus on political values, rights and duties does not require agreement on basic questions of religion, moral or political philosophy. It follows that there can be agreement on rights despite deep differences between the comprehensive views in question.

Secondly, the rights associated with a political conception of justice may subsequently be extended or supplemented. In the first instance, they are expressed in a conception of justice that attracts consensus among the comprehensive moral views present, but this conception is then supposed to be reflected in a constitution and to form the basis of further rights under laws decided by appropriate authorities, such as Parliament or the courts, which are governed by the constitution. This hierarchy of political, constitutional and legal rights creates opportunities for different historically sensitive rights at different levels of the political structure. This feature of rights as they are understood within political liberalism has particular application and appeal in the case of societies established by colonization (Patton 2009). Additional rights determined by judges or enacted in legislation must be based upon the publicly accepted principles of justice and further principles acceptable to reasonable citizens in the light of the history, institutions and culture of the society in question, including its political culture and conceptions of the nature, purposes and methods of government.

Thirdly, the political character of such rights makes it easier to defend their historical character than would be the case if they were considered moral rights. In that case, arguing for their historicity would involve argument over the truth or falsity of moral realism and moral relativism. Political liberalism finds the ground of principles of justice in an overlapping consensus among parties beholden to different, conflicting comprehensive moral, religious and philosophical views. As such, it explicitly avoids taking any position on the truth or falsity of claims made within such comprehensive views and insists only that, given the unavoidable plurality of such views, it is unreasonable to use public political power to enforce any particular view (Rawls 2005: 138).[7] Rawls's 'strategy of avoidance' means that rights accorded under a given conception or family of conceptions of justice may be historical without further implications for the truth or falsity of particular comprehensive views.

To appreciate the historical character of rights, as these are understood within political liberalism, consider the overlapping consensus among reasonable members of a society that is the basis of such rights. The possibility of such a consensus implies the achievement of a 'reflective equilibrium' between the principles of justice on which there is consensus and the 'settled' or 'considered' convictions of the society (Rawls 2005: 8; 2001: 29–32). These considered convictions are not just matters of opinion but embedded in the public political culture of the society, its laws and institutions, along with the traditional ways in which these are interpreted. In his early presentation of justice as fairness as a political conception in 'Justice as Fairness: Political not Metaphysical', Rawls makes it clear that this conception of justice is worked out for a specific kind of society, namely a modern constitutional democracy in which there is a 'plurality of conflicting, and indeed incommensurable, conceptions of the good' (Rawls 1985: 390). Under these conditions, where there are deep disagreements within the tradition of democratic thought, the most that can be hoped for is an overlapping consensus on the principles that should govern the basic structure of society. While the starting point for any such consensus can only be the 'settled convictions' of members of the society about what is just, Rawls acknowledged that 'even firmly held convictions gradually change' (Rawls 1985: 393). As examples of such change, he pointed to the widespread acceptance of religious tolerance and of the inherent injustice of slavery: no one any longer openly advocates the persecution of heretics or the reinstatement of slavery, 'however much the aftermath of slavery may persist in social practices and unavowed attitudes' (Rawls 1985: 393). The method of political liberalism is to:

> collect such settled convictions as the belief in religious toleration and the rejection of slavery and try to organize the basic ideas and principles implicit in these convictions into a coherent political conception of justice. We can regard these convictions as provisional fixed points which any conception of justice must account for *if it is to be reasonable for us* . . .
>
> (Rawls 1985: 393, emphasis added)[8]

These settled convictions are 'provisional' for at least two reasons. First, because the procedure to be followed in achieving reflective equilibrium implies that adjustments and revisions may occur on the side of our considered convictions as well as on the side of the proposed principles of justice. Secondly, because even the most firmly held moral convictions of a people may change over time. It follows that the principles of justice that can be the object of consensus are not laid down once and for all but remain subject to change over time as the settled convictions of citizens change.

In addition to simple changes in moral belief, change in the conception of justice may come about because of our unavoidable reliance upon current knowledge in working out the principles of justice. Rawls conceded in *A Theory of Justice* that there was no reasonable alternative to reliance upon 'current knowledge as recognized by common sense and the existing scientific consensus' and that 'as established beliefs change, it is possible that the principles of justice which it seems rational to acknowledge may likewise change' (Rawls 1999: 480).[9] This vector of change is especially relevant to colonial societies in which the refusal to allow aboriginal people to maintain their culture and way of life was made possible by assumptions about the superiority of European cultural ways that have now been discredited. Such beliefs contributed to the refusal to recognize distinctive ways of being as no less legitimate and entitled to appropriate constitutional and legal protection.

The recognition that changes in such beliefs may lead to modifications in the political conception of justice is also implicit in Rawls's suggestion that the conception of justice that rational and reasonable parties would adopt 'identifies the conception of justice that we regard – here and now – as fair and supported by the best reasons' (Rawls 1985: 402; 2005: 26). He refers here to the basic idea of his political philosophy that principles of justice are fair when they would be chosen under the conditions of a hypothetical original position, in which representatives of the society are supposed to sit behind a 'veil of ignorance' that limits their knowledge of facts about themselves and their society (Rawls 2005: 22–8; 2001: 14–18). This rules out the possibility that they might choose principles that favour a particular group, caste or class. The phrase 'here and now' in the passage quoted above points to the fact that the conception of justice adopted under the restrictions imposed by the veil of ignorance expresses the considered opinions of a historically specific form of society. It follows that a political conception of justice for a given society will be unavoidably historical: as settled opinions change, so will the details of the conception of justice.

In his 'Reply to Habermas', Rawls adds a further clarification of method that is especially relevant to the circumstances of liberal democratic societies with a colonial or slave-owning past, namely that the principles of justice remain open to being checked against the considered judgments or settled convictions of the people at any time (Rawls 2005: 402). At any given time, these principles must be ones that all reasonable citizens might *now* be expected to endorse. This rules out the kind of defence of unjust institutions that appeals to the inadequate knowledge or limited moral perspective of the founding fathers, who often acted without consultation or consideration of the interests of indigenous people or slaves. In other words, it prevents the acceptance of ongoing injustice on the grounds that it is the fault of previous generations rather than the responsibility of present citizens. Rawls notes that all societies are more or less unjust and that the idea of a just society has the status of an ideal: it is something to be worked towards. In this sense, he agrees with Habermas, Kant and others that a just regime 'is a project to be carried out' (Rawls 2005: 399). It follows that the political conception of justice embodied in the institutions and procedures of a given society, including its constitution, will be subject to modification in response to change in the considered opinions of citizens, not only on matters of justice but on the range of matters relevant to the circumstances of justice in the society concerned.

Public reason and the justification of rights

Rawls is widely read as offering a form of *priori* reasoning, on the basis of a limited set of premises, for substantive political conclusions, namely the two principles of justice as fairness. These are, first, the principle that everyone is entitled to the same set of basic civil and political liberties and to the same fair value of the political liberties (Rawls 2005: 5; 2001: 42). The last phrase is important as it makes it clear that a just society in accordance with this principle will not allow inequalities of wealth and power that give greater value to political liberties for some over others. The second principle states that social and political inequalities are acceptable only when they are attached to positions and offices open to all under conditions of fair equality of opportunity, and when they are to the greatest benefit of the least advantaged members of the society (Rawls 2005: 6; 2001: 42). These two principles are supposed to govern the basic structure of a well-ordered society, which means its political, legal, economic and social institutions, along with the public policies that inform the operation of those institutions. There are many questions raised about precisely what constitutes the basic structure of a society and how the principles of justice are supposed to apply to its different elements. I leave these issues aside in order to focus on the nature of the principles themselves.

Anthony Laden points out that a focus for this interpretation of Rawls's work is the argument from the original position. Thus understood, Rawls's argument proceeds from a thin theory of human nature that refers only to certain basic capacities of citizens, such as a capacity for a sense of justice, a capacity for a conception of the good, rationality and reasonableness, to the conclusion that the two principles of justice as fairness would be chosen (Laden 2003: 373). Of course, the argument relies on a number of other assumptions about the circumstances of justice and the appropriate constraints on the choice of principles in the original position that make up the veil of ignorance. Given these assumptions, the argument proceeds from an appropriately ideal conception of political society and its citizens to the conclusion that only the two principles of justice as fairness, or something like them, can serve as the basis for a just and stable liberal democratic regime. This 'standard blueprint' for reading Rawls leads to the view expressed by Habermas that whatever the deficiencies of the late Rawlsian conception of justice he has not become a contextualist (Habermas 1995: 120). In this sense, the historical circumstances of a particular community are strictly irrelevant to the principles of justice. Justice and the rights associated with it are independent of the particular beliefs, values and opinions of a given community.

In the preceding section I have tried to show some of the ways in which this universalist and anti-contextualist reading of Rawls is inconsistent with other things that he says. In this section I pursue the case for a historical conception of rights by reference to a quite different understanding of Rawls that has been persuasively argued for by Laden, particularly but not only with reference to the later writings associated with political liberalism. Laden sees Rawls's project in *Political Liberalism* as primarily defensive or 'apologetic' in the Kantian sense of that term and concerned to demonstrate the possibility of a just and stable liberal democracy in which there are fundamental disagreements about philosophical, moral and religious issues:

> we can understand Rawls as trying to show that despite appearances, the thought and practice of democratic societies are not necessarily incoherent. In particular, he argues that despite the fact that citizens in a democratic society will never come to agreement about fundamental philosophical, moral and religious matters (the fact of reasonable pluralism), they can nevertheless agree on a framework of fundamental political matters and, thus, regulate their collective lives according to principles that are supported by reasons

> each citizen can accept. Democratic legitimacy under conditions of reasonable pluralism is not incoherent.
>
> (Laden 2003: 383)

According to Laden, Rawls is less concerned to elaborate a philosophical theory of justice to be handed down to citizens as a template against which to judge existing institutions and policies than to outline the kinds of reasons in support of his conception of justice as fairness that might be offered to 'fellow reasonable citizens, taken not as stripped-down rational choosers but in all their diversity and complexity' (Laden 2003: 386). It follows that the real centrepiece of Rawls's work is not the argument from the original position but the idea and the ideal of public reason. This idea of public reason, Rawls suggests, 'specifies at the deepest level the basic moral and political values that are to determine a constitutional democratic government's relation to its citizens and their relation to one another. In short, it concerns how the political relation is to be understood' (Rawls 2005: 441–2). The idea of public reason specifies the manner in which citizens should defend their political views on constitutional matters and in addressing fundamental questions of justice such as those involving the basic structure of society. In their public deliberation, citizens in a well-ordered and pluralist society must respect a duty of civility and offer reasons to one another in terms that all can reasonably be expected to endorse. This implies relatively stringent restrictions on the kinds of reasons that citizens can put forward in arguing their case, namely reasons couched in terms of one or other of the available political conceptions of justice. The ideal of public reason is satisfied:

> whenever judges, legislators, chief executives, and other government officials, as well as candidates for public office, act from and follow the idea of public reason and explain to other citizens their reasons for supporting fundamental political positions in terms of the political conception of justice they regard as the most reasonable. In this way, they fulfil what I shall call their duty of civility to one another and to other citizens
>
> (Rawls 2005: 444)[10]

In his last writings, Rawls explicitly acknowledges that public reason is a historical phenomenon. He points out that the content of public reason will be given by a family of political conceptions of justice. He notes that political conceptions of justice may be revised as a result of their interactions with one another and as a result of the emergence of new groups and different political problems, and that new variations may be proposed from time to time just as older ones may no longer be represented: 'It is important that this be so, otherwise the claims of groups or interests arising from social change might be repressed and fail to gain their appropriate political voice' (Rawls 2005: 452). It follows that, as he points out, Waldron's criticism of political liberalism as not allowing new and changing conceptions of political justice is 'incorrect' (Rawls 2005: 452, n. 30).

These points are reiterated in the Introduction to the paperback edition of *Political Liberalism*, where he notes that the principles, ideals and standards of argument that make up the content of public reason are those of 'a family of reasonable political conceptions of justice *and this family changes over time*' (Rawls 2005: li, emphasis added). Changes may result from the debates between different reasonable conceptions of justice but also from social changes and the emergence of views raising new questions about issues such as ethnicity, gender and race. In short, as Rawls says here, '[t]he content of public reason is not fixed, any more than it is defined by any one reasonable political conception' (Rawls 2005: li).

The content of public reason is given by the publicly acceptable conceptions of justice that can be objects of overlapping consensus in a given society at a given time. This content will reflect the settled convictions of members of the society as well as the background culture that sustains efforts to systematize and theorize such judgments and that provides conceptions of the nature and business of government. It provides the discursive frameworks within which citizens and public officials can argue in ways that are not beholden to their particular moral, philosophical or religious views and that each can reasonably expect that others could endorse. At any given moment, what can properly be said within the sphere of public reason will be constrained by the norms of the prevailing family of reasonable conceptions of justice. The historical character of public reason implies that the ways of acting or being treated that can be justified in a given society will vary according to its content at a given time. It follows that it is a historical matter what rights there can be in a given society at a given time.

New ways of being treated might be justified by reference to the considered or settled convictions within the public political culture of a given society at a given time, along with existing public conceptions of the nature and functions of government. So, for example, acceptance of the idea that self-respect is an important component of individual well-being, a primary good in Rawls's sense of the term, coupled with the idea that government has a responsibility to provide for such well-being, might enable a compelling justification of the right to employment on the part of disabled people in societies such as our own. A further condition of such a justification might include the idea that paid work is an important means to maintain self-respect (Kavka 1992: 270–3). There is no reason to suppose that such justifications would always be convincing. However, when they are, we can say that particular rights should exist and that the appropriate institutional mechanisms should be put in place. An advantage of understanding the concept of a right in this way is that we can preserve the critical function of appeals to rights, without supposing that they are universal and have always existed.

Justification and the principle of existence

A naturalistic conception of rights, I suggested at the outset, views them as established and justified ways of acting and being treated. Rawls provides a political conception of the justification of particular ways of acting that is compatible with the plurality of comprehensive moral views in modern liberal societies. However, the conception of justification remains open to interpretation in ways that readily lead back towards an a-historical conception of rights. For example, the justification of particular ways of acting in accordance with public reason might be understood as the offering of reasons that ought to be compelling to reasonable citizens because they accord with a reasonable conception of justice. This way of understanding justification assimilates it to proof based on reasonable premises, regardless of whether or not the premises in question are available to the parties to the dispute.

This is not how Rawls understands justification. Already in *A Theory of Justice*, he distinguished between the proof of a proposition and its justification, where the latter is understood as a mode of argument 'addressed to those who disagree with us, or to ourselves when we are of two minds' (Rawls 1999: 508). In other words, justification presupposes a difference of views and seeks to convince the parties by proceeding from premises that both sides accept. It follows that the justification of particular rights claims implies the presence of a common discursive framework and the availability of the relevant discursive elements to the parties concerned.

Martin offers an account of justification that points to the historical conditions under which behaviours can be established. He argues that the normative force of rights claims means that they involve some direction of behaviour, for example that others must provide or at least not impede our access to the good in relation to which we have a right. The normative direction of individuals' behaviour is taken to mean that they can experience the requirement to act or to refrain from acting in certain ways as a duty. He relies on a principle derived from Kant, to the effect that people cannot be supposed to have duties of which they cannot be aware, to argue that the relevant ways of acting or refraining from action only become rights when people can effectively become aware of the justification, given the moral views and other beliefs they have (Martin 1993: 79). For this to be the case, however, it is not sufficient that there be some form of moral justification for the right. Rather, the justification must also be accessible to agents on the basis of their actual moral and other beliefs:

> For obligations or duties that cannot be acknowledged in a given society, or that cannot be shown to follow, discursively, from accredited principles of conduct which are at least reflectively available to persons in that society, cannot be regarded as proper duties which could normatively bind conduct in that society.
>
> (Martin 1993: 78)

On this view, if the acknowledgement of something as a duty is blocked by beliefs about the incapacity or unworthiness of those to whom the duty would be owed, then there is no duty. This is arguably what occurred in relation to colonized peoples and slaves. If there is now widespread agreement that such people are entitled to the same rights as others, or that they are, in Rawls's phrase, 'self-authenticating sources of valid claims', this is because the beliefs that underpinned their former exclusion no longer hold sway (Rawls 2005: 32). Consider the now widely accepted rights of indigenous peoples to their traditional lands and ways of life.[11] Given what we know about the theories of civilization, property entitlement and racial hierarchy that were common in Europe between the sixteenth and nineteenth centuries, and given what we know now about the levels of ignorance with regard to indigenous culture that prevailed throughout the period of European colonization, it is implausible to suggest that these rights always existed and that people were simply ignorant or unaware of their existence. Private opinion and public political reason alike were supported by pseudo-scientific theories about the supposed cultural inferiority of indigenous peoples and ill-informed beliefs about the absence of political organization or property in land that characterized their societies. Such beliefs were relied upon to deny any entitlement on the part of indigenous peoples to their lands or ways of life. No doubt there were dissenting views within the culture of the colonizing peoples, but these were in a minority. However, in recent years, such prejudicial beliefs have become more difficult to sustain. The commitment to equality has become stronger and more extensive. In this sense, there has been real epistemic and moral change, the effects of which are manifest in law and public policy. Adequate understanding of this process requires an explicitly historical concept of rights and the forms of their legal and institutional expression. This implies abandonment of the widespread conception of rights as a-historical features of certain kinds of beings in favour of the idea that there is real change in public political morality and a genuine historical dimension to the existence of rights.

Foucault on political normativity and rights

Although he does not directly address the conditions under which individuals come to experience particular ways of acting as duties, Foucault's principle of existence serves a parallel function to that of Martin's accessibility condition. Thus, in his lectures on governmentality, he implicitly relies on the principle that criticism of the exercise of power, often in the name of particular rights, invariably draws upon rationalities of government that are available in the prevailing political culture. This principle is evident in his analysis of the forms of 'counter-conduct' that flourished alongside the institutions and practices of pastoral power in medieval and early modern Europe. He argues that the precise mechanisms through which it sought to direct the conduct of individuals provided the basis for forms of counter-conduct through which some dissident subjects sought to conduct themselves differently: these included asceticism, different forms of community, mysticism, eschatology and disputes over the proper interpretation of the Scripture (Foucault 2007: 194–216). Similarly, in relation to the *raison d'état* conception of government that developed from the eighteenth century onwards, the different forms of counter-conduct that emerged were based upon elements of this governmentality and in some cases took the form of claims founded on fundamental rights: to the primacy of civil society over the state, to economic truth as opposed to error, and to an 'absolute' right to revolt or to revolution (Foucault 2007: 356).[12] The general principle behind these analyses is that resistance on the part of citizens to the ways in which they are governed draws upon the very conceptions of government that inform those practices.

A further illustration of the way that elements of modern political reason have sustained the critique of state power can be found in Foucault's brief sketch of the forms of legitimation and limitation of liberal government. In the second lecture of his 1978–9 course, he outlines the principal modern forms of justifying the basis and limits of government. One approach sought the limits to the legitimate functions of government on the basis of a theory of the natural rights of individuals. This was the path followed by the American Declaration of Independence, Rousseau and the French revolutionaries. It drew upon the tradition of social contract theories of the nature and limits of sovereign power, which began with a conception of the natural or original rights of the individual and proceeded to define the circumstances in which, and the reasons for which, individuals would consent to cede some of those powers to a sovereign.[13] Foucault summarizes this approach as 'starting from the rights of man in order to arrive at the limitation of governmentality by way of the constitution of the sovereign' (Foucault 2008: 39). A second approach was developed by English radicalism at the end of the eighteenth and beginning of the nineteenth century. It began not with the inalienable rights of man but with the question of utility: what it was useful or futile for government to undertake given its objectives, its objects and resources. In practice, answers to this question relied upon a calculus of interests, since it was the concept of interest that linked the liberal concern with the self-regulation of markets and the utility of public policy. Government now aimed at increasing both the forces of the state and the well-being of its citizens, and at achieving this through the free operation of the market, thereby ensuring that individuals are governed as little as possible. The justification and the limits of government were to be understood in terms of a complex interplay of individual and collective interests: 'Governmental reason in its modern form, in the forms established at the beginning of the eighteenth century with the fundamental characteristic of a search for the principle of its self-limitation, is a reason that functions in terms of interests' (Foucault 2008: 44).

This brief sketch of the two forms of limitation of the powers of governments effectively identifies the two poles of one of the central concepts within modern political normativity. Foucault distinguishes between a juridical concept of freedom based on the imprescriptible rights of individuals and a utilitarian concept of freedom as simply 'the independence of the governed with regard to government' (Foucault 2008: 42). His characterization of the utilitarian conception of freedom corresponds in many respects to the freedom of the moderns that Benjamin Constant sought to contrast with the freedom of the ancients. Whereas the latter consisted in active participation in the collective power of the people concerned, the former consisted above all in the independence of the citizen in the pursuit of his private life, an independence made all the more necessary and valuable by the development of commerce (Constant 1988). Foucault points out that both the revolutionary theory of human rights and the radical theory of human interests remain active and available forms of limitation and legitimation of government throughout the modern period. He suggests that the fact that both the discourse of natural rights and that of human interests remain present in modern public political culture explains why the contemporary problem of human rights can take either the juridical form of basic rights or the utilitarian form of affirming or demanding independence on the part of the governed (Foucault 2008: 42).

Foucault's comments on the different forms of limitation of state power associated with modern conceptions of government point to the role of these conceptions in the public political culture of liberal democracies. They provide a historical perspective on the 'common languages' that enable the citizens of a modern democratic polity to justify particular rights to one another. They also provide a historical perspective on some of the elements, tensions and developments within the kind of normative structure that Rawls and other theorists of liberal democracy seek to defend (Patton 2010). In these terms, for example, we can appreciate how the predominance of the utilitarian conception of freedom ensures the possibility of arguing for more comprehensive conceptions of individual interests. The underlying principle of a transaction between individual and governmental interests allows for the extension of the freedom of individuals to take into account a broader range of individual interests, including the kinds of primary social good addressed in the second principle of Rawls's conception of justice. The Rawlsian citizen is ultimately a subject of interest endowed with a capacity to form a conception of the good and a life plan 'designed to permit the harmonious satisfaction of his interests' (Rawls 1999: 80). Rawls's difference principle transforms into a political right the idea that all citizens have an interest in maximizing their access to primary social goods, in so far as this is consistent with preservation of the scheme of fundamental juridical and political rights.

Foucault's comments in 1981 in support of a humanitarian intervention to assist Vietnamese refugees show how existing rationalities of government can be mobilized to argue for the existence of new rights (Foucault 2000; Patton 2005). Here, he appeals to particular, historically determined elements of modern political rationality, and corresponding forms of right, in order to justify an emerging right. He appeals to particular elements of historically available and effective forms of governmental reason – in this case, the independence of the governed and the implicit pact which grounds the legitimacy of government in its concern for the welfare and security of its citizens – in arguing for the right of private individuals to intervene in support of stateless refugees. He argues that the right of private individuals 'to effectively intervene in the sphere of international policy and strategy' is a new right that has emerged within the power relations between governments and governed (Foucault 2000: 475). He points to the role of new non-governmental organizations such as Amnesty International, *Terre des Hommes* and *Médécins du Monde* in the emergence of this right. These self-appointed organizations are relatively independent of all governments and it is this independence that 'constitutes' the right of these private international citizens to speak and to act (Foucault 2000: 474).

He also points to the role of widely accepted beliefs about the role and purpose of government in providing normative leverage. It is the fact that 'we are all members of the community of the governed', he argues, that makes us all parties to an international citizenship and that obliges us 'to always bring the testimony of people's suffering to the eyes and ears of governments' (Foucault 2000: 474). This new right arises partly because governments of all persuasions believe and would have others believe that they are concerned for the welfare and security of their citizens. It is because the governed accept that their security falls within the sphere of governmental power that governments have a right to act in this regard.[14] Conversely, to the extent that governments rely on this shared belief to justify their actions, they make themselves accountable for their action or inaction in relation to the security of individuals. This mutually accepted relationship between governors and governed is one of the conditions that enable governments to be held responsible for the suffering of people even outside their borders. The fact that it is widely accepted by the governed allows them to experience a duty to speak out against abuses or derelictions of power.

Rawls's historical conception of the conditions under which particular ways of behaving or being treated may be justified shows us how rights can be historical, and therefore particular rather than universal, while preserving normative force. Unlike Rawls, Foucault is not interested in formulating a systematic theory of the basis of rights in modern liberal and democratic societies. However, this does not mean that he discounts the importance of liberal rights or their potential for resisting abuses of power. For example, in a short text published in 1977 in response to the extradition of the German lawyer for the Red Army Faction, Klaus Croissant, he referred to the 'rights of the governed that were slowly and by tortuous paths in the process of being recognized' (Foucault 1977b: 365). These rights of the governed, he suggested, were 'more precise and more historically determined than the rights of man' (Foucault 1977b: 362). Among these rights was one that had been abused by the French government in its handling of the Croissant case, namely the right of every person to legal representation. Foucault's characterization of this right goes well beyond a mere formal or procedural right to be represented in court. It includes, he argues, the right to a legal representative who speaks with and for the accused, enabling them to be heard and seeking to protect their life, their identity and the force of their refusal (Foucault 1977b: 365). In contrast to Rawls, his historical and critical approach combines a sensibility to the emergence of new rights with a willingness to argue for the limitation or the extension of existing rights by reference to existing legal and political norms. In this sense, as Ewald suggests, he offers a novel form of non-transcendent, immanent critique of existing forms of right (Ewald 1986b).

Acknowledgements

Earlier versions of this chapter were presented at the Australasian Association of Philosophy Conference in Dunedin, July 2011; at the American Political Science Association Conference in Seattle, September 2011; at the Political Theory Colloquium, Institute for Political Science, Technische Universität Darmstadt, October 2011; and at the Being In-Human: The Critical Theory and Law of Human Rights Conference at the Birkbeck Institute of the Humanities, November 2011. I am grateful to many participants on those occasions for their helpful comments and questions, but especially to Moira Gatens, Matheson Russell, David Owen, Peter Niesen and Ben Golder.

Notes

1 Examples of this approach include Alan Gewirth, who suggests that all humans have a right to freedom and well-being since these are necessary conditions of agency, and Joseph Raz who argues that individuals or groups have rights when some aspect of their well-being is a ground for holding others to be under a duty (Gewirth 1984; Raz 1986).

2 Gewirth provides an extreme statement of the a-historical view in speaking about human rights in the following terms:

> The existence of human rights depends on the existence of certain moral justificatory reasons; but these reasons may exist even if they are not explicitly ascertained. Because of this, it is correct to say that all persons had human rights even in ancient Greece, whose leading philosophers did not develop the relevant reasons. Thus, the existence of moral reasons is in important respects something that is discovered rather than invented.
>
> (Gewirth 1984: 4)

3 Elsewhere, Ewald argues that from the end of the nineteenth century and the concomitant rejection of natural law, 'law can no longer find its legitimacy anywhere but in the fact of its being social, in other words in being the adequate expression of "social norms," as evolutive and changeable as society' (Ewald 1986a: 790).

4 For political liberalism, see Rawls 1985, 1993, 2001 and 2005. For governmentality, see Foucault 2007, 2008.

5 See Sumner 1987; Martin 1993; Darby 1991, 2001, 2003, 2004 and 2009.

6 Nietzsche's genealogical account of the origin of rights and duties anticipates these contemporary externalist conceptions. On the basis of a broad view of power as the capacity of individual or collective agents to act in certain ways, he advances the hypothesis that rights originate as 'recognised and guaranteed degrees of power'. My rights, he argues in *Daybreak*, paragraph 112, 'are that part of my power which others have not merely conceded me, but which they wish me to preserve'. I discuss Nietzsche's analysis of the origin of rights and duties in more detail in Patton 2004 and 2008.

7 See, also, *Political Liberalism*, Chapter 4, ξ4, where he defends the idea that, within political liberalism, we try 'so far as we can, neither to assert nor to deny any particular

comprehensive religious, philosophical or moral view, or its associated theory of truth and the status of values' (Rawls 2005: 150).

8 Although this passage appears almost identically in *Political Liberalism*, only the earlier version is explicit that the settled convictions are 'the provisional fixed points which any conception of justice must account for if it is to be reasonable for us' (Rawls 2005: 8).

9 Richard Rorty relied upon this concession to describe Rawls's conception of justice as fairness as 'thoroughly historicist and antiuniversalist' (Rorty 1991: 180).

10 In a quite different context, Foucault invokes a similar principle of civility in explaining why he does not engage in polemical discussion. He contrasts an ethic implicit in the relationship of parties engaged in a serious dialogue, 'in which each of the two partners takes pains to use only the rights given him by the other and by the accepted form of the dialogue', with the relationship towards others implicit in polemics, heresiology, judicial inquisition or party political combat (Foucault 1997: 112). In each of the latter cases, the other is treated as an enemy to be defeated, a heretic to be convicted of deviation from established dogma, or an accused whose guilt or innocence must be proved, but never as an equal with reciprocal and equal rights. Rawls's egalitarian and reciprocal principle of civility defines the fundamental political relation between citizens of a democratic society. Foucault may well have been prepared to endorse such a conception of the political relation in which each citizen 'takes pains to use only the rights given to him by the other' (Foucault 1997: 112). (I am indebted to Ben Golder for drawing my attention to these remarks and their resonance with Rawls's duty of civility.)

11 I am thinking particularly of the acceptance of indigenous rights in common law countries such as Australia, Canada and New Zealand.

12 Against the principle of *raison d'état* that insisted on the obedience of individuals to the state, Foucault suggests, there emerged a form of counter-conduct the meaning of which was: 'There must be a moment when, breaking all the bonds of obedience, the population will really have the right, not in juridical terms, but in terms of essential and fundamental rights, to break any bonds of obedience it has with the state . . .' (Foucault 2007: 356).

13 Similarly, in 'What is Critique?', he points to the historical importance of appeals to natural law as one of the ways in which limits were set to the right to govern (Foucault 1996).

14 In an interview in 1977 around the time of the Croissant affair, Foucault suggested that the contemporary relationship of a state to its people took the form of a 'security pact' that he glosses in the following terms:

> Formerly, the state could say: 'I will give you a territory' or 'I guarantee that you will be able to live in peace inside your frontiers.' This was a territorial pact and the protection of the frontiers was the primary function of the state.
>
> Today the frontier problem hardly ever arises. The pact that the state proposes to its population is: 'You will be guaranteed.' Guaranteed against every form of uncertainty, accident, damage, risk. Are you ill? You will have Social Security! You have no job? You will have unemployment benefits . . .
>
> (Foucault 1977a: 385)

References

Constant, B. (1988) 'The Liberty of the Ancients Compared with that of the Moderns', trans. B. Fontana, in B. Fontana (ed.) *Political Writings*, Cambridge: Cambridge University Press

Darby, D. (1999) 'Are Worlds without Natural Rights Morally Impoverished?', *Southern Journal of Philosophy*, 37: 397–417
___ (2001) 'Two Conceptions of Rights Possession', *Social Theory and Practice*, 27: 387–417
___ (2003) 'Unnatural Rights', *Canadian Journal of Philosophy*, 33: 49–82
___ (2004) 'Rights Externalism', *Philosophy and Phenomenological Research*, 68: 620–34
___ (2009) *Rights, Race and Recognition*, Cambridge: Cambridge University Press
Ewald, F. (1986a) 'Une expérience foucaldienne: les principes généraux du droit', *Critique*, 471–472 (August–September): 788–93
___ (1986b) 'Pour un positivisme critique: Michel Foucault et la philosophie du droit', *Droits: Revue Française de Théorie Juridique*, 3: 137–42
___ (1988) 'The Law of Law', in G. Teubner (ed.) *Autopoietic Law: A New Approach to Law and Society*, Berlin and New York, NY: Walter de Gruyter
Foucault, M. (1977a) 'Michel Foucault: la sécurité et l'état', in D. Defert and F. Ewald (eds) *Dits et écrits II, 1976–1988*, Paris: Gallimard
___ (1977b) 'Va-t-on extruder Klaus Croisant?', in D. Defert and F. Ewald (eds) *Dits et écrits II, 1976–1988*, Paris: Gallimard
___ (1978) 'La philosophie analytique de la politique', in D. Defert and F. Ewald (eds) *Dits et écrits II, 1976–1988*, Paris: Gallimard
___ (1996) 'What is Critique?', in J. Schmidt (ed.) *What is Enlightenment?*, Berkeley and Los Angeles, CA: University of California Press
___ (1997) 'Polemics, Politics and Problematizations: An Interview with Michel Foucault', in P. Rabinow (ed.) *Essential Works of Foucault Vol. 1: Ethics*, New York, NY: The New Press
___ (2000) 'Confronting Governments: Human Rights', in J. D. Faubion (ed.) *Essential Works of Foucault 1954–1984 Vol. 3: Power*, New York, NY: The New Press
___ (2007) *Security, Territory, Population: Lectures at the Collège de France, 1977–78*, trans. G. Burchell, New York, NY: Palgrave Macmillan
___ (2008) *The Birth of Biopolitics: Lectures at the Collège de France, 1978–79*, trans. G. Burchell, New York, NY: Palgrave Macmillan
Gewirth, A. (1984) 'The Epistemology of Human Rights', *Social Philosophy and Policy*, 1: 1–24; reprinted in E. Paul, F. Miller and J. Paul (eds) (1984) *Human Rights*, Oxford: Blackwell
Habermas, J. (1995) 'Reconciliation through the Public Use of Reason: Remarks on John Rawls's *Political Liberalism*', *Journal of Philosophy*, 92: 109–31
Ivison, D. (2008) *Rights*, Stocksfield: Acumen
Kavka, G. S. (1992) 'Disability and the Right to Work', *Social Philosophy and Policy*, 9: 262–90
Laden, A. (2003) 'The House that Jack Built: Thirty Years of Reading Rawls', *Ethics*, 113: 367–90
Martin, R. (1993) *A System of Rights*, Oxford: Clarendon Press
Patton, P. (2004) 'Power and Right in Nietzsche and Foucault', *International Studies in Philosophy*, 36: 43–61
___ (2005) 'Foucault, Critique and Rights', *Critical Horizons*, 6: 267–87
___ (2008) 'Nietzsche on Rights, Power and the Feeling of Power', in H. W. Siemens and V. Roodt (eds) *Nietzsche, Power, and Politics: Rethinking Nietzsche's Legacy for Political Thought*, Berlin: Walter de Gruyter
___ (2009) 'Rawls and the Legitimacy of Australian Government', *Australian Indigenous Law Review*, 13: 59–69

___ (2010) 'Foucault and Normative Political Philosophy', in T. O'Leary and C. Falzon (eds) *Foucault and Philosophy*, Oxford: Wiley-Blackwell
Rawls, J. (1985) 'Justice as Fairness: Political not Metaphysical', in S. Freeman (ed.) *John Rawls: Collected Papers*, Cambridge, MA: Harvard University Press
___ (1993) *Political Liberalism*, New York, NY: Columbia University Press
___ (1999) *A Theory of Justice*, rev. edn, Cambridge, MA: Harvard University Press
___ (2001) *Justice as Fairness: A Restatement*, Cambridge, MA: Harvard University Press
___ (2005) *Political Liberalism: Expanded Edition*, New York, NY: Columbia University Press
Raz, J. (1986) *The Morality of Freedom*, Oxford: Clarendon Press
Rorty, R. (1991) *Objectivity, Relativism, Truth: Philosophical Papers, Vol. 1*, Cambridge: Cambridge University Press
Sumner, L. W. (1987) *The Moral Foundation of Rights*, Oxford: Clarendon Press

Chapter 10

Is revolution desirable?: Michel Foucault on revolution, neoliberalism and rights

Jessica Whyte

> *You know full well that the problem today is whether revolution is desirable.*
>
> (Foucault in Lévy 1995: 370)

In *The Hermeneutics of the Subject*, in the midst of a discussion of Platonic and Christian forms of conversion, Foucault makes an intriguing suggestion: one day, he writes, 'the history of what could be called revolutionary subjectivity should be written' (Foucault 2005: 208). Posing a hypothesis that the idea of 'converting to the revolution' emerged only in the wake of the French Revolution, and indeed precisely as a response to that founding event, he posits that we cannot understand either revolutionary practice throughout the nineteenth century or the revolutionary individual without taking into account the schema of conversion to the revolution (Foucault 2005: 208). While he does not dwell on this, except to suggest that belonging to the revolution through conversion was ultimately replaced by belonging through the party, he makes a remark that helps to illuminate both the context in which he was working and his own attitude to it: these days, he notes, in the 'somewhat bland experience of our immediate contemporaries – we only convert to renunciation of revolution' (Foucault 2005: 209). Implicitly addressing those former Maoists with whom he was closely aligned at the time, Foucault suggests that the 'great converts today are those who no longer believe in the revolution' (Foucault 2005: 209). Indeed, the 1970s was a decade in which the publication of Solzhenitsyn's *The Gulag Archipelago* caused tumult in France, undermining support for revolutionary Marxism, and in which François Furet's *Penser la révolution française* turned the criticisms of Bolshevism against France's own revolution in an attempt to abolish what the historian referred to as the 'exorbitant privilege assigned to the idea of revolution' in French thought (in Khilani 1993: 157). As Foucault notes elsewhere, the idea that had once seemed so self-evident to those on the Left, namely 'that history is dominated by revolution', had by then crumbled under the weight of Khrushchev's speech, the Soviet suppression of the Hungarian uprising and de-Stalinization (Foucault 1997: 445). What, then, were the consequences of this climate for Foucault's political thought? How is the trajectory of his late thought bound up with this inverted conversion, this renunciation of the revolutionary idea? And, more importantly, can his thought shed light on the consequences of this renunciation for politics itself?

We find a possible answer to the last of these questions in an interview with one of those people Foucault may well have had in mind in speaking of 'the somewhat bland experience' of his contemporaries: Bernard-Henri Lévy. Along with the other self-styled *Nouveaux Philosophes*, Lévy is a former Maoist who played an important role in the 1970s in discrediting revolutionary Marxism, which he framed as a 'barbarism with a human face' (Lévy 1979). In this interview – the title of which, 'What if the Revolutionary Dream was an Intrinsically Barbaric One?', reflects Lévy's line of questioning – Foucault remarks that '[p]olitics has existed since the nineteenth century because of revolution' (in Lévy 1995: 370). As he depicts it here, revolution is not simply a particular form or area of politics. Rather, it provides the terms in which all politics has to be defined. When pushed about whether he actually *wants* a revolution, Foucault responds that he has no answer. Instead, he proposes that the question of the desirability of revolution should remain a question – and indeed, one which anyone wishing to 'engage in politics in such a way as to avoid mere politicking' must attempt to answer as honestly as possible (in Lévy 1995: 370). Against the model of the Greek sage, the Jewish prophet and the Roman legislator, he tells Lévy that he longs for a form of intellectual who, wherever he found himself, would 'pose the question as to whether revolution is worth the trouble, and if so which revolution and what trouble' (in Lévy 1995: 373).

It would be tempting to view the trouble that followed Foucault's enthusiastic endorsement of the 1979 Iranian revolution in light of this new role he ascribes to the intellectual.[1] Instead, here I wish to pursue his indication that the very nature of politics hangs on the answer provided to this question. When asked whether politics could remain as he has described it if he were to answer in the negative, Foucault's answer is instructive: 'No I don't think so,' he replies. 'One would have to invent another form or a substitute for it' (in Lévy 1995: 373). Not only can we not assume that politics would remain the same, but Foucault suggests that the demise of revolution may well result in its disappearance. 'Because if it's true revolution opened up the whole field of politics and if revolution can no longer be discussed in these terms', he explains, 'then there is a risk that politics will disappear' (in Lévy 1995: 371). It is my contention that this insight can help us to reflect on a related area of Foucault's trajectory that has been the source of both controversy and perplexity. In the past decade, prompted in large part by the publication of his late lectures at the *Collège de France*, a growing body of literature has sought to understand his shift from the strident criticisms of rights and juridical discourses more broadly that typify his middle works to his later strategic uses of the language of rights. Critics have debated how best to understand how the thinker who had proclaimed that 'in the West, right is the right of royal command' (Foucault 2003: 25) could go on to affirm that '[a]gainst power one must always set inviolable laws and unrestricted rights' (Foucault 2000e: 453). This 'rights talk', as Duncan Ivison has noted, seems incongruous in relation to his work as a whole, given Foucault's reputation as a radical critic of liberalism and rights (Ivison 1997: 41). For some thinkers, this incongruity is evidence of Foucault's late embrace of the very ideas of humanism, the founding subject and human rights that he had previously rejected (Paras 2006: 4; Wolin 2010: 343). For others, such 'narratives of return, revelation and recantation' (Golder 2010: 373) obscure the novelty of the new account of rights that appears in his late work by simply assimilating it to the juridical discourses he had previously problematized (Golder 2010; Patton 2005).

My wager here is that Foucault's turn to the language of rights can best be understood by situating it in relation to his changing responses to a question previously posed by Max Horkheimer: 'But is this revolution really such a desirable thing?' (Foucault 2000e: 450). This chapter traces the way that this question, and its various answers, shaped his later thinking on rights. In doing so, it aims both to situate his contribution to the formulation of a new politics of rights, exercised by those he termed 'the governed', and to explore some of the tensions generated by its birth, in the midst of an assault on the 'revolutionary privilege'. It thus examines the relation between Foucault's contribution to the development of a new form of right that would not be reducible to the old sovereign right, and the new interventionist politics of human rights that emerged in the 1970s, and suggests that his thought not only was influenced by this new politics but also influenced its development in turn. Further, it situates this shift away from revolution in light of the genealogy of governmental rationalities that Foucault undertook between 1977 and 1979, in his lecture courses *Security, Territory, Population* and *The Birth of Biopolitics* (Foucault 2007, 2008). A key claim of these lectures is that specific governmental rationalities were accompanied by equally specific forms of resistance, or 'counter-conducts', which made use of the same elements in order to open up spaces of freedom for the governed: 'the art, project, and institutions for conducting men', as he put it, 'and the counter-conducts that were opposed to this, developed in correlation with each other' (Foucault 2007: 355). With extraordinary prescience, Foucault's 1978–9 course, *The Birth of Biopolitics*, examines the emerging neoliberalism of the Freiburg and Chicago schools (Foucault 2008), yet without considering the forms of counter-conduct appropri ate to this new governmental rationality.

In what follows, I explore the hypothesis that the new interventionist politics of rights that emerged in the 1970s is the correlate of the neoliberal governmental rationality that came to prominence at the same time. In the wake of the decline of revolutionary Marxism and the defeat of development programmes in the Third World, the implementation of neoliberal economic policies resulted in global economic restructuring, the slashing of welfare states and social spending, and the removal of price controls. Far from providing a bulwark against this attack, the new politics of human rights helped to facilitate state interventions aimed at re-making societies on the model of the market. The new politics of rights shared key elements of the neoliberal consensus, not least a belief that the organization of life through the market was the best insurance against totalitarianism. In order to explore this contention, this chapter examines Foucault's contribution to the development of a new politics of rights, exercised by what he termed 'the community of the governed' (Foucault 2000a: 474). It situates his new account of rights in relation to the rise of a new interventionist politics of human rights, epitomized by *Médecins sans Frontières* (*MSF*), and it traces the relation between this new politics of rights and the emerging neoliberalism, which Foucault maps in *The Birth of Biopolitics* (Foucault 2008). In doing so, it aims both to shed light on Foucault's account of rights, and to chart the transformations in the idea of politics brought about by the demise of revolution, in order to open the space for thinking a new form of politics in the present.

A substitute utopia: Foucault and the new politics of rights

In 1977, as Foucault was pondering the future of politics in the absence of revolution, a new form of politics had already swept from the margins to the centre of international consciousness. Beginning with US President Carter's January inauguration speech, in which he proclaimed '[o]ur commitment to human rights must be absolute', 1977 ended with the award of the Nobel Peace Prize to Amnesty International (AI) (Moyn 2010: 154). In this 'year of shocking and altogether unexpected prominence of human rights' (Moyn 2010: 121), the language of rights was taken up by diverse movements, from Latin American oppositionists to Soviet dissidents, and formed the central plank of a newly moralized US foreign policy. For many, this new attention to rights seemed to offer a substitute utopia that could replace the now much-damaged utopianism of revolutionary Marxism (Moyn 2010). For others, the uptake of the language of rights was a worrying trend: Noam Chomsky, for instance, argued at the time that 'the human rights campaign is a device to be manipulated' by those who wish to gain popular support for 'counter-revolutionary interventions' (in Moyn 2010: 157). Whatever the differences between the two thinkers over humanism and political transformation, revealed so starkly in their televised debate (Chomsky and Foucault 1997), Chomsky's point would seem to resonate with Foucault's previous account of rights as both permanent agents and masks of relations of domination (Foucault 2003). And yet, as early as his 1975–6 course, '*Society Must be Defended*', in which he provides a powerful indictment of the complicity of the discourse of right with disciplinary power, Foucault had already noted that the struggle against the disciplines required not a return to the old right of sovereignty, but 'a new form of right' which must break both with the disciplines and with sovereign power (Foucault 2003: 40). As Paul Patton has suggested, Foucault's claim was both normative and descriptive – at once directing us towards already existing forms of right in the present, and suggesting that these provide a normative basis for challenging disciplinary power (Patton 2005: 283).

In 1981, Foucault delivered the statement 'Confronting Governments: Human Rights' at the UN in Geneva, to mark the establishment of a committee against piracy, under the leadership of Bernard Kouchner of *Médecins du Monde* (*MDM*), which sought to protect Vietnamese asylum seekers from pirates who were viciously attacking boats in the South China Sea. By this time, Foucault seems to have identified the possibility of a new form of right in the practices of a new generation of activist human rights and humanitarian non-governmental organizations (NGOs).[2] 'The suffering of men', he argued, 'must never be a silent residue of policy. It grounds an absolute right to stand up and speak to those who hold power' (Foucault 2000a: 475). The argument that suffering generates such a right had already appeared repeatedly in his political interventions in the late 1970s and early 1980s, in response to attacks on Vietnamese asylum seekers, the suppression of Poland's *Solidarnosc* movement, and the repression that followed the 1979 Iranian revolution, for instance (Foucault 2000a, 2000c; Macey 1993). In his Geneva address, Foucault credited AI, *Terre des Hommes* and *MDM* with creating this new right of 'private individuals' to effectively intervene in the sphere of international policy and strategy (Foucault 2000a: 475). In language that resonated with that of the new NGOs, he evoked a global community of the governed, with a duty to intervene wherever rights were abused. Since then, this idea has dramatically transformed international relations and re-oriented the normative basis of sovereignty, not least due to the efforts of Kouchner, with whom Foucault worked closely on a number of campaigns in the 1970s, while the former was the President of *MSF* and then *MDM*.[3] At the time, however, Foucault heralded this new right precisely because it broke with the sovereign monopolization of the power to intervene on the international stage. By refusing to be bound by borders, this new activist humanitarianism seemed to challenge the prerogatives of sovereignty and bring into being a new form of global community – the community of the governed.

To understand the novelty of the concern with human rights that emerged in the 1970s, it is worth examining its genesis in the organizations to which Foucault credits its creation. Doing so reveals a real tension that marked this new politics of rights: while AI arose, according to its founder Peter Benenson, as a 'non-political, non-sectarial international movement', which sought to provide an alternative idealism to those who had become disenchanted with emancipatory politics in the Cold War period (Moyn 2010: 130), *MDM* was a split from *MSF*, which was itself born of dissatisfaction with the neutral, non-political humanitarianism of the Red Cross, and pioneered a new, explicitly political, form of interventionist humanitarianism (Rieff 2002). While the shift away from humanitarian impartiality prompted a new concern with the *politics* of humanitarian action, this politics was premised on replacing all-encompassing and global theories, such as Marxism, with more local and discontinuous forms of resistance, and on the replacement of grand political visions with a morality focused on alleviating suffering (Moyn 2010: 165). The new NGOs provide us with one attempt to answer the question of what becomes of politics after the collapse of revolution. Indeed, answering this question was part of their *raison d'être*. According to Benenson, AI, for instance, was designed to absorb the enthusiasm of 'idealists who have, since the eclipse of Socialism, become increasingly frustrated' (in Moyn 210: 130). Given AI's origin in Christian responses to the Cold War, it is unsurprising that its new ideal broke sharply with the vision of revolutionary social transformation. Indeed, it sought to break with politics *per se*, which it believed could be replaced with a morality focused, in the words of an early member, Columbia philosopher Arthur Danto, on 'saving the world one individual at a time' (in Moyn 2010: 132). AI's success, as Jan Eckel has noted, depended on its ability to jettison the most optimistic hopes of revolutionary idealism, while providing a substitute utopia that would be both minimalist and pragmatic (in Moyn 2010: 147).[4]

The origins of *MDM* were quite different, and stemmed not from a desire to replace politics with an impartial moralism but from a dissatisfaction with the neutrality of the Red Cross and a desire for an explicitly political humanitarianism capable of taking sides in conflicts. *MDM* emerged as a split from *MSF*, led by that organization's founder, Kouchner. The origins of this new humanitarianism can be traced back to 1968, when Kouchner was a young doctor who left the barricades of Paris to volunteer as a medic with the Red Cross in Nigeria, where the Ibo Christian minority had declared an Independent Republic of Biafra. Upon returning to Paris, Kouchner left the Red Cross, which he believed took neutrality to the point of complicity, and pioneered a new politics of humanitarianism that aimed to overcome the old divisions of the Cold War, and transcend the border between left and right. In the background of this decision to speak out was the memory of the Red Cross's failure to do so when it learned of the Nazi gas chambers in 1942 (Rieff 2002: 76). 'By keeping silent', Kouchner reflected afterwards, 'we doctors were accomplices in the systematic massacre of a population' (in Rieff 2002: 83). In breaking the Red Cross vow and founding *MSF*, Kouchner hoped that never again would the prerogatives of sovereignty provide justifications for states to dispose of their populations as they saw fit.

Whatever their differences, the organizations Foucault credits with pioneering a new form of right both emerged as responses to the decline of revolutionary politics. Since then, these NGOs have been enormously successful both in undermining the Westphalian principles of sovereignty and in hegemonizing the terrain of 'idealism' once occupied by revolutionary Marxism. In the process, however, the politics of intervention has been transformed in a crucial sense. Foucault celebrated these NGOs for wresting from states the monopolization of the power to act in international relations. Today, however, the subjects of such interventions are often powerful states and transnational bodies like the UN and NATO. Central to this transformation was Kouchner, who was, until recently, Foreign Secretary in France's Sarkozy government. When Kouchner left *MSF* to found *MDM*, he represented the split as a legacy of the Cold War, arguing that *MSF* was unprepared to challenge seriously human rights abuses by a communist regime – Vietnam. For those who stayed behind, the origins of the split were not about communism but about an orientation to the state. The key question, as they saw it, was whether humanitarianism would remain independent or align itself with state power (Rieff 2002). Today, the battle for an independent humanitarianism has been all but lost (Rieff 2002), and the right to intervene is a key legitimating discourse of state militarism. It is thus imperative that we subject its relation to sovereignty and discipline to closer scrutiny. Is it still possible to see this new right to intervene of the activist humanitarian NGOs as a right that is non-disciplinary and 'liberated from the principle of sovereignty' (Foucault 2003: 31)? To answer this, it is worth turning to Foucault's account of the Westphalian sovereign state system, and examining the extent to which the idea of human rights intervention marks a break with the Westphalian paradigm.

The demise of the fragile eschatology of peace and the rise of an 'intervening liberalism'

In his *Security, Territory, Population* lecture course, Foucault introduces an idea that will be the focus of all his future research: 'governmentality' – that is, a form of power whose target is the population, whose major form of knowledge is political economy and whose essential technical instrument is the apparatus of security (Foucault 2007: 108). Foucault traces the emergence of a community of the governed to the practices of the Christian pastorate, which sought to guide its members towards salvation. In identifying the pastorate as a 'highly specific form of power with the object of conducting men' he asks whether it is possible to identify 'equally specific movements of resistance and insubordination' that arose in correlation with it (Foucault 2007: 194). What Foucault terms 'the art of not being governed so much' always exists in relation to a specific art of government, and shares its elements.[5] Thus, the counter-conducts that emerged on the borders of the pastorate, he argues, relied on the same elements as Christianity itself – on eschatological expectations, the formation of communities, and a return to Scripture to challenge the power of the Church (Foucault 2007: 354). In the late seventeenth and early eighteenth centuries, these conflicts of conduct, Foucault argues, move from the religious sphere to the borders of the political. Counter-conducts, as Louisa Cadman notes, were not simply reactions to the new modes of governing, but were constitutive of these new forms of governmentality (Cadman 2010: 540). If we accept Foucault's argument that counter-conducts share a set of elements with the governmental rationality they oppose, it will therefore be necessary to examine the decline of revolution and rise of the new politics of human rights in the context of the governmental rationalities that they appeared to challenge. To what extent did the new politics of rights that emerged in the 1970s help to constitute the neoliberal governmental rationality that emerged at the same time?

It is a commonplace today that the Westphalian conception of sovereignty is being undermined by a new global commitment to human rights that refuses to be contained within national borders. Between 1977 and 1979, Foucault devoted his lecture courses at the *Collège de France* to a genealogy of Western political rationalities, reaching back to the emergence of a specific *raison d'état* of what came to be called the 'police state' in the late sixteenth century. In this context, he provides a remarkable account of the Peace of Westphalia and the emergence of a new conception of peace that was premised not on the unification of states in a single empire but on their coexistence and competition. Following the end of the Thirty Years War, the Peace of Westphalia of 1648 enshrined a model of sovereignty that broke sharply with the imperial models of Rome and the Catholic Church. In Foucault's terms, it replaced 'the absolute eschatology that posits an empire, a universal monarchy as the culminating point of history' with 'a precarious and fragile eschatology' of peace (Foucault 2007: 300). The significance of the treaty in putting an end to the hope for a united Christendom is aptly reflected in Pope Innocent X's characterization of it as 'null, void, invalid, iniquitous, unjust, damnable, reprobate, inane, and devoid of meaning for all time' (in Davis 1996: 568). By institutionalizing the disappearance of the previous forms of political and ecclesiastical universalism, the treaty led to the emergence of European states that would be 'absolute units', exercising not a claim to empire but a *de facto* domination over their own territories (Foucault 2007: 293). This new eschatology of peace would be premised not on right but on a balance of forces that would prevent any state from dominating others and ensure 'the impossibility of the strongest state laying down the law to any other state' (Foucault 2007: 299). Thus, the flip-side of the precarious peace secured by European equilibrium was the absolute power of sovereigns within their own borders: the 'object of police', Foucault writes, 'is almost infinite' (Foucault 2008: 7).

Reflecting in 1948 on the newly adopted Charter of the UN, Leo Gross noted that it 'would seem to have left essentially unchanged the framework of the state system and of international law resulting from the Peace of Westphalia' (Gross 1948: 21). Indeed, like Westphalia, the UN system combined a formal commitment to sovereign equality with mechanisms aimed at balancing the major powers. As a 2009 'concept note' issued by the Office of the President of the General Assembly noted, 'the existence of the veto . . . strengthen[s] the Westphalia paradigm as against the individual rights centered paradigm' (Office of the President of the General Assembly 2009: 3). In 1944, as plans for what would become the UN were formulated at Dumbarton Oaks, the great powers were concerned to ensure that the new organization would not – in the words of John Foster Dulles, speaking on behalf of the sponsoring states – 'go behind the governments to intervene directly' (in Mazower 2004: 393). The higher human rights moved up the agenda, the greater became the pressure to limit the new organization's power to intervene in domestic affairs (Mazower 2004). To this end, the USA, wary of intervention into its own racial relations, proposed a formulation that began: 'The International Organization should refrain from intervention in the internal affairs of any state . . .' (in Mazower 2004: 392). Since then, the Westphalian trade-off, according to which peace between nations is secured on the proviso that what happens within a territory is an internal affair, has been challenged, not least by those NGOs to which Foucault attributes the responsibility for creating a new right of the governed that would break with the principle of sovereignty.

This new sense of global responsibility and government is reflected in a question asked by the former Secretary-General of the UN, Kofi Annan: 'Why was the UN established . . .' he asked, 'if not to act as a benign policeman or doctor?' (in Rieff 2002: 217). Annan's rather misleading question is indicative of the post-1948 displacement of the question of sovereignty by disciplinary and biopolitical concerns. If the Westphalian paradigm is being eroded, what implications does this hold for politics, and for the idea of revolution? The period following the Thirty Years War, Foucault argues, gave rise to a specific art of government, a new way of thinking, reasoning and calculating, a new governmental rationality. 'This', Foucault writes, 'is what was called politics at the time, and it should never be forgotten that this was initially seen and recognized, and immediately disturbed its contemporaries as, something heterodox' (Foucault 2007: 286). Politics, in this conception, is not an a-historical universal but a new way of thinking about power and governing that arose in the sixteenth century, for which the state provided the principle of intelligibility. The state, Foucault argues, 'is essentially and above all the regulative idea of that form of thought, that form of reflection, of that form of calculation, and that form of intervention called politics' (Foucault 2007: 287). Not only was politics tied inextricably to this *raison d'état*, according to this account, but also the latter is essentially bound to revolution – indeed, it finds its *raison d'être* in the attempt to ward off revolution. In this context, however, revolution refers to a 'quasi-natural, half-natural and half-historical phenomenon' that saw states cycle from plenitude to death – a cycle epitomized by the fate of Rome. It was such a fate that threatened the new states, and what the theorists of *raison d'état* understood it to mean, Foucault suggests, 'is essentially preserving states against these revolutions' (Foucault 2007: 289) by intervening everywhere to strengthen the state's power. In his great study devoted to this new state rationality, Friedrich Meinecke notes that for the *raison d'état* tradition, the increase of the state's power is an indispensable means for securing its well-being, a means that is unqualified, 'in so far as it must even be procured if necessary at the expense of a complete disregard for moral and positive law' (Meinecke 1998: 3). At the same time, however, Foucault traces the emergence of counter-conducts that relied on juridical thought to limit this internally unlimited art of government from without. Contract theory and natural law, he suggests, are 'the other side and consequence, and the reaction against, this new way of governing on the basis of *raison d'état*' (Foucault 2008: 9). This reaction consisted in attempting to secure a line over which the sovereign could not cross, a limit provided by nature that must not be over-stepped, and that marked out a realm of natural freedom.

In the eighteenth century, in contrast, Foucault traces the rise of a new principle of governmental limitation, which was no longer external but internal to the very objectives of government. It was the *Economistes*, he suggests, who mounted a critique of this *raison d'état* and thus gestured toward the emergence of a new art of government. Nonetheless, he makes clear that the new economic reason that emerged at the beginning of the eighteenth century did not replace *raison d'état* but gave it a new content and thus transformed the rationality of the state. This new governmental rationality was liberalism, which, as Foucault understands it, is essentially a principle of internal limitation of government on the basis of the freedom of the market. This new art of government of the *Economistes*, he notes, introduces us to 'some of the fundamental lines of modern and contemporary governmentality' (Foucault 2007: 348). Notably, this transformation brings about a reversal of the relation between internal and external power enshrined at Westphalia: the liberal self-limitation of government is accompanied by the revival of the imperial problem of unlimited global objectives. 'Liberal reason', Foucault suggests, 'is correlative with activation of the imperial principle', not, this time, in the form of the old empires, but as imperialism, which he situates in relation to free competition between individuals and enterprises (Foucault 2008: 21).[6]

Amongst the central innovations of the new liberal art of government was a shift from the idea of the state as artificial to the discovery of a new naturalness of society, economy and population. From this point on, Foucault suggests, what the state must manage was a civil society composed of *Homo economicus* rather than a collection of subjects of right. Furthermore, this new conception of the naturalness of the objects of government brought with it the belief that these natural processes should be left alone by a state which always risks governing too much. This internal limitation of power was therefore no longer a juridical limitation but a *de facto* one, and the government that ignores this limit was not an illegitimate one but a clumsy one that does not do things properly.[7] The fundamental question of the new liberal rationality, Foucault suggests, is not that of the legitimacy of the sovereign's actions, but that of the *usefulness* of government. It therefore introduces a new, non-juridical, principle of limitation of governmental action: utility. Nonetheless, it did not abandon the juridical problematic, but posed the problem of the adequate juridical form for the *de facto* limitation of governmental action. We find the attempt to translate a utilitarian limitation of government into juridical terms exemplified by J. S. Mill, whose defence of liberty foregoes the 'idea of abstract right as a thing independent of utility' (Mill 1991: 15). For Mill, there is no social contract and, like Bentham before him, he regards any talk of natural rights as 'nonsense upon stilts' (Bentham 2002: 317). Nonetheless, he posits that if humans are to live together, certain of their interests must be legally recognized and protected and should therefore be considered as rights. The question of rights, and, indeed that of justice, for Mill, was entirely derived from that of utility. 'To have a right, then,' he writes, 'is, I conceive, to have something which society ought to defend me in the possession of. If the objector goes on to ask why it ought, I can give him no other reason than general utility' (Mill 1991: 189).

Clearly, such an approach differs starkly from the old natural law approach, which attempted to limit *raison d'état* by establishing external limits to the sovereign's power, granted by God or nature. And yet, Foucault suggests this older approach does not disappear as it is taken up by the revolutionaries of the eighteenth century. There is 'a continuity', he writes, 'between the seventeenth century theorists of natural law and the jurists and legislators of the French Revolution' (Foucault 2008: 40). From the middle of the eighteenth century, he notes, 'a whole series of counter-conducts have developed whose essential objective is precisely the rejection of *raison d'état*' (Foucault 2007: 355). What he describes as the 'revolutionary response' is therefore premised on the same attempt to limit governmentality by establishing a sphere of natural rights that characterized those counter-conducts that opposed *raison d'état*. It is for this reason, he suggests, that this revolutionary approach is 'retroactive, or retroactionary' (Foucault 2008: 40): it ultimately relies on those elements that were developed to limit the power of the sovereign under a previous governmental rationality. In contrast, the utilitarian approach – on which Foucault draws in formulating his own account of rights, and which conceives the limit of government in terms of a transaction that marks out a sphere of independence for the governed – is, Foucault suggests, 'structured around the new economy of government' (Foucault 2008: 41). This explains why, of these two heterogeneous forms of right, it is the utilitarian approach, which relies on the same elements as the new governmental rationality, that 'has been strong and has held fast' (Foucault 2008: 42). Nonetheless, in regard to contemporary human rights claims, he notes 'we would only need to look at where, in what countries, how, and in what form these rights are claimed' to see that sometimes what is at stake is a juridical assertion of natural rights derived from Rousseau and at others an assertion of the independence of the governed (Foucault 2008: 42). Examining Foucault's own rights declarations of the 1970s from this perspective, it is clear that while they drew on the more amorphous climate of the new politics of human rights, represented by groups like *MSF* and AI, they eschewed all reference to natural rights and were oriented to opening up spheres of independence for the governed.

Despite the introduction of the Universal Declaration of Human Rights in 1948, it was not until the 1970s that the idea of human rights inspired both a widespread global movement and a re-orientation of international law.[8] And then, Foucault played an important role in challenging the view that a sovereign is the emperor of his own domain. As he wrote in a letter addressed to the Iranian Prime Minister, Mehdi Bazargan, in the wake of the Iranian revolution, when someone on the other side of the world speaks out against the torture or condemnation of another person it 'does not constitute an interference with a state's internal affairs' (Foucault 2000c: 441). It is clear that Foucault identified the new right to intervene developed by the humanitarian NGOs, which challenged both Westphalian territorial jurisdiction and the state's monopolization of the power of international action, as 'liberated from the principle of sovereignty' (Foucault 2003: 31). Given the tight bond between the forms of right developed by utilitarianism and the disciplines, starkly expressed in Bentham's contention that 'the panopticon is the very formula of liberal government'

(Foucault 2008: 67), it is less clear that this new form of right would also be anti-disciplinary. In his consideration of this problematic, Patton has suggested that in order to counter the techniques of the disciplines, it may be necessary to make use of concepts derived not from classical liberalism, but from neoliberalism (Patton 2005: 283).[9] While, in my view, Patton is correct to identify a relation between the new form of right to which Foucault gestured and the emerging neoliberalism, the latter has itself proved to be an intensively disciplinary regime, in which 'market discipline' (Evans 2005: 1062) is enforced through norms, economic sanctions and, where necessary, direct military interventions. The acceptance by human rights NGOs of a neoliberal governmental rationality, I suggest below, has left their new right at best unable to adequately challenge, and at worst complicit in, interventions that aim to bolster free markets at the expense of social justice, self-determination and equality.[10]

Neoliberalism on the 'road to Damascus'

In his 1978–9 course, *The Birth of Biopolitics*, Foucault remarks: 'It seems to me that we are seeing the birth, maybe for a short period or maybe for a longer period, of a new art of government' (Foucault 2008: 176). With remarkable prescience, he traces the rise of both the *Ordoliberalism* of the Freiburg school and the anarcho-liberalism of the Chicago school. The central problem of this new *ordo-liberalism*, which he suggests is of greater import for the problem of governmentality, was no longer the classical liberal problem of limiting an existing state in order to secure the freedom of the market. Rather, it was a distinctive problem that arose in Germany in the wake of the Second World War: how would it be possible to found the legitimacy of a state that did not yet exist on the basis of the freedom of the market? This implied a relation between state and market quite different to that posited by classical liberal thinkers. Neoliberalism, Foucault stresses, is an 'intervening liberalism', which dispenses with the classical liberal account of the market as a natural entity and advocates 'social interventionism that is at the same time active, multiple, vigilant, and omnipresent' (Foucault 2008: 160). Thus, the role of the state would be to intervene in 'society as such, in its fabric and depth' (Foucault 2008: 143), in order to create the conditions of possibility of a market economy (Foucault 2008: 160). As well as breaking with the 'naïve naturalism' and the correlative *laissez-faire* approach of classical liberalism, Foucault sees neoliberalism as inaugurating a shift away from a formal commitment to equality, secured by the equivalence of exchange, and towards an entrepreneurial model of competition between necessarily unequal parties: 'inequality', as Wilhelm Röpke polemically stated, 'is the same for all' (in Foucault 2008: 143). This means that while the state's role would no longer be a *laissez-faire* one, which allowed the natural processes of the market to work, neither would it intervene in order to restrain the market, or redistribute wealth. Instead, its interventions would aim to restructure the whole of society along the lines of the market.

What is the relation between this new interventionist neoliberal governmentality and the new interventionist politics of human rights that came to prominence in the same period, in the context of a crisis of revolutionary Marxism? In *The Birth of Biopolitics*, Foucault cites Friedrich Hayek's remark that liberalism has been content to leave the creation of utopias to the socialists, and socialism owes much of its historical dynamism to this utopianism. 'Well,' Foucault continues, loosely paraphrasing Hayek, 'liberalism also needs a utopia. It is up to us to create liberal utopias, to think in a liberal mode, rather than presenting liberalism as a technical alternative for government' (Foucault 2008: 219). 'To each time its own utopia,' David Rieff writes in his incisive critique of the post-Cold War militarism of humanitarianism. The 'humanitarian utopia', he argues, 'was one that did not seriously challenge the reigning preconceptions of the Reagan-Thatcher era' (Rieff 2002: 108). The new politics of human rights arose as 'a minimalist and hardy utopia', premised on the abandonment of communism and prepared to weather the hard economic times (Moyn 2010: 121). It came to prominence on the back of the demise of revolutionary politics, and, as Samuel Moyn points out, was inevitably called upon to carry some of its energy. Does it answer Hayek's appeal for a liberal utopia that would be correlative to the new neoliberal governmental rationality, which had replaced the idea of equality with that of competition and stipulated that '[s]ocial policy cannot have equality as its objective' (Foucault 2008: 143)?

The new politics of human rights coincided, as Rieff notes, with the abandonment of hopes of development (and thus global equalization of living standards) in the Third World and with the beginning of the privatization of development aid (Rieff 2002). As Naomi Klein points out in *The Shock Doctrine*, this 'abandonment' was not simply a response to the failures of development, but a consequence of what she terms a 'war on developmentalism', which resulted notably in Pinochet's Chile and Suharto's Indonesia (Klein 2007: 75–128). It was in this context that organizations like AI came to prominence, and it was largely for their work in documenting abuses in Chile and Argentina that they were awarded their 1977 Nobel Peace Prize, only a year after Milton Friedman was awarded the Nobel Prize for Economics. From afar, Klein notes, it was as if the two prizes amounted to a single verdict: the torture chamber must be condemned and the economic shock treatment applauded but the two are, as President Salvador Allende's Washington Ambassador Orlando Letelier put it, with bitter irony, just before his murder, 'entirely unrelated' (in Klein 2007: 110). The Southern Cone was an experimental laboratory not just for neoliberal economic policies, but also for the new grassroots politics of rights. And, as Klein suggests, while the new human rights organizations undoubtedly curbed some of the worst of the torture, extrajudicial killing and other abuses, their determination to record human rights abuses without considering the ends for which they were carried out tended to foreclose discussion of the deeply unpopular economic regime that was being brutally imposed on these countries. AI's 1976 report on Argentina, for instance, 'offered no comment on the deepening poverty or the dramatic reversal of programs to redistribute wealth, though these were the policy centerpieces of junta rule' (Klein 2007: 119). The dramatic repression in the countries of the Southern Cone, as Moyn notes, led many on the left to draw the lesson, for initially strategic reasons, that an 'alteration of plausible hopes' must occur (Moyn 2010: 140). In a similar vein, Klein argues that the fear of becoming the next victims of the regime prompted leftists in Chile to abandon the language of right and left, North and South, rich and poor, and replace it with the legalistic language of universal human rights: 'they learned', she writes, in a stark juxtaposition of political stances, 'that their imprisoned *compañeros* were actually prisoners of conscience whose right to freedom of thought and speech, protected under articles 18 and 19 of the Universal Declaration of Human Rights had been violated' (Klein 2007: 121).

The abandonment of horizons of radical political and economic transformation created a context in which neoliberal capitalism became the sole horizon of possibilities for NGOs and humanitarian organizations. Even those voices within the human rights movement that remain oppositional often accept that global capitalism 'may indeed share the logics and the language of human rights discourses' (Baxi 2007: 165), leading to severely constrained political proposals. Furthermore, the privatization of development aid has dramatically transformed those organizations that Foucault saw as heralding a new right of the governed. Transnational NGOs like AI now command more resources than the least developed countries, and are themselves forced to compete on the 'human rights market' for finite capital (Baxi 2007: 46). In *The Birth of Biopolitics*, Foucault notes that a key goal of the neoliberals was to make the market economy the model for both state and society (Foucault 2008: 117), and to make the enterprise the key unit of economic and political rationalization. Increasingly, as Baxi has noted, the need to compete for limited resources sees 'human rights movements organize themselves in the image of markets', complete with the commodification of human suffering (Baxi 2007: 121). Human rights movements, he points out, are capital intensive, and require the 'marshalling of high entrepreneurial talent' (Baxi 2007: 125). The adoption by NGOs of a market cost-benefit rationality tends to preclude certain political tactics, such as direct action (Baxi 2007: 128). Futher, this rationality precludes imagining political horizons that are not already predetermined by the logic of the market, or that break, in any substantial way, with the dictates of neoliberal capitalism.

If the new humanitarian organizations were simply modelled on the market and thus unable to challenge it adequately, the problem would not be so dire. More dangerous, however, is the extent to which these organizations are drawn into bolstering this neoliberal order and foreclosing other political possibilities. The neoliberal abandonment of *laissez-faire*, Foucault notes, brings with it an intense concentration on questions of legal frameworks and 'governmental style' (Foucault 2008: 133). The liberal regime, as the neoliberals see it, is a result of a legal order, and not just an economic order, and thus there is a need to intervene not in the market itself but in order to create the conditions of possibility for a market competition that is conceived as both artificial and fragile. Today, Baxi argues, it is axiomatic that 'practices of global governance may legitimate themselves best by recourse to human rights languages' (Baxi 2007: 9). Simultaneously, the shift away from conceiving of rights as a realm of freedom granted by nature, which echoes the neoliberal critique of the 'naïve naturalism' of classical liberalism, has led to a greater concern amongst human rights organizations with the governance structures necessary to secure such rights, and thus to their incorporation into processes of institutional decision-making. Among the costs of this incorporation, as Baxi suggests, has been the 'displacement of the agenda of equitable re-distribution towards an agenda of global governance' (Baxi 2007: 63). More worryingly, the concerns of human rights have served to enable interventions that range from the imposition of structural adjustment programmes, which forbid 'competition distorting' food subsidies and social welfare programmes, to direct military occupation.

The 'road to Damascus' of this new neoliberalism, Foucault writes, was Nazism. Central to the neoliberal innovation was the argument that National Socialism was not a response to economic crisis but the necessary result of protectionism, economic planning and Keynesian interventions. 'English labour party socialism', he summarizes dramatically, 'will lead you to German style Nazism' (Foucault 2008: 110). With such an assumption, it became possible for the neoliberals to identify what they saw as an 'anti-liberal invariant' common to Nazism, Soviet socialism, parliamentary England and the America of the New Deal (Foucault 2008: 111). In a similar vein, Nazism provides the foundation story for the new interventionist politics of rights. Human rights, Ignatieff argues, arose in the wake of the Nazi genocide as a response to 'the discovery of the abomination that could occur when the Westphalian state was accorded unlimited sovereignty' (Ignatieff 2001: 4). As Samuel Moyn has noted, however, this familiar picture of human rights as a response to the Holocaust belies the fact that 'across weeks of debate around the Universal Declaration in the UN General Assembly, the genocide of the Jews went unmentioned', despite numerous invocations of other forms of Nazi barbarism (Moyn 2010: 82). It is true, Moyn argues, that the memory of the Holocaust was central to the crystallization of a global commitment to human rights, but this only occurred decades later. By the 1970s, the new interventionist human rights would frame itself precisely as a response to the horrors of Nazism. 'Interventionism can be summed up quite simply', Kouchner writes, '. . . Auschwitz never again, Pol Pot never again, Kosovo and Rwanda atrocities never more' (in Rieff 2002: 216). Like the neoliberals, those who advocated this new politics of rights in the 1970s displayed a marked tendency to conflate various different political regimes in a single critique of totalitarianism, prompting one of the founding members of *MSF*, Rony Brauman, to remark, apropos the *Nouveaux Philosophes*: 'We have to take into account that it is a very easy argument to say "Nazi" and "genocide" – then the curtain falls, you have to act, there is no time to reflect, and all thought is discredited' (in Seymour 2009: 232).

Foucault situates the rise of neoliberalism in relation to what he terms a 'state phobia', which was sustained not only by the German experience of Nazism, but also by the Soviet experience and English post-war planning (Foucault 2008: 76). This state phobia, he notes, has had many agents and promoters, amongst whom he singles out Austrian neoliberals like Hayek, along with Russian dissidents.[11] 'I think twentieth century political exile, or political dissidence, has also been a significant agent of the spread of what could be called anti-statism or state phobia,' he writes (Foucault 2008: 76). Earlier in the same lecture course, he had noted, in the form of an unresolved question, the proximity between the new neoliberal economic policies and the political thought of the dissidents. Asking after the relation between contemporary liberal politics and questions of rights, he asks: what is going on 'in today's debate in which Helmut Schmidt's economic principles bizarrely echo the voice of dissidents in the East' (Foucault 2008: 22)? Schmidt was a deputy of the German Social Democratic Party (SPD) and became Chancellor in 1974: 'to enter into the political game of the new Germany', Foucault writes, 'the SPD really had to convert to these neoliberal theses' (Foucault 2008: 90). In language that resonates with his later account of converting against the revolution, he remarks that from a Marxist perspective, the SPD's shift away from its commitment to the socialization of the economy could only be viewed as a 'series of renunciations, desertions, heresies, betrayals' (Foucault 2008: 89).

The rise of the dissidents was central to the wave of counter-revolutionary conversions that Foucault remarks on in *The Hermeneutics of the Subject*. As Lévy puts it, '[a]ll Solzhenitsyn had to do was to speak and we awoke from a dogmatic sleep' (Lévy 1979: 155). Solzhenitsyn's key innovation, according to Lévy, was to trace the crimes of the Stalinist state to 'the one he dares to denounce for the first time – the founding father in person, Karl Kapital and his holy scriptures' (Lévy 1979: 155). This assault on Marxism had a profound impact within France, especially amongst those former Maoists who would go on to call themselves the *Nouveaux Philosophes*. Along with Lévy, Andre Glucksmann was drawn to Solzhenitsyn (Moyn 2010), and by 1982, their conspirator Alain Finkielkraut observed that the word 'dissident' had become 'as popular today as militant and guerrilla were in the past' (in Horvath 2007: 903). Furthermore, the dissidents exercised a key influence on the organizations Foucault credits with creating a new right of the governed. Rieff notes that 'MSF comes to prominence at almost the exact moment that Solzhenitsyn's *The Gulag Archipelago* transforms the political debate in France' (Rieff 2002: 106). Far from a simple coincidence, Solzhenitsyn's 'ringing claim that there were no longer internal affairs in the world' (Moyn 2010: 152) was taken up as a mantra by the new interventionist politics of rights. Furthermore, the influence of the Soviet dissidents in propagating the conviction that 'a concern with individual people could permanently replace "abstract visions"' (Moyn 2010) is clear in the emergence of AI, which was responsible for translating early dissident texts. The dissidents, as Robert Horvarth notes, engendered a 'new kind of radical human rights advocacy, spearheaded by a group of

French anti-totalitarian militants, "the Children of Solzhenitsyn", who played a crucial role in the development of the theory and practice of humanitarian intervention' (Horvath 2007: 880). By discrediting revolutionary Marxism, they removed a key barrier to the widespread acceptance of human rights as a radical cause (Horvath 2007).

In *Security, Territory, Population*, Foucault asks an important question: 'How can we designate the type of revolts, or rather the sort of specific web of resistance to forms of power that do not exercise sovereignty and do not exploit but conduct?' (Foucault 2007: 200). Dismissing the term 'revolt' as too strong and 'disobedience' as too weak and ill-suited to capture the *productive* aspect of these forms of resistance, he remarks that a word comes to mind, but continues, dramatically: 'I would rather cut out my tongue than use it' (Foucault 2007: 200). The word was 'dissidence', which he notes is derived from the Russian *inakomysliachtichie* ('those who think differently') (Foucault 2007: 221, n. 27). Why does Foucault reject using this word, despite acknowledging that 'maybe the word dissidence is exactly suited for these forms of resistance that concern, set their sights on, and have as their objective and adversary a power that assumes the task of conducting men in their life and daily existence' (Foucault 2007: 200)? It was certainly not because he was unsympathetic to the dissidents' challenge to the Soviet regimes. That same year he had joined with Glucksmann to host a reception for Russian dissidents at the *Théâtre Récamier* to coincide with Brezhnev's official visit (Horvarth 2007: 903). Before dismissing the word 'dissidence', Foucault provides two historical reasons that justify its use: first, he notes that it has often been used to designate precisely those religious movements that resisted pastoral power on which his analysis is based; and, secondly, because 'what we [call] "dissidence" in the East and the Soviet Union, really does designate a complex form of resistance and refusal, which involves a political refusal' but also challenges the Soviet state's conduct of individuals (Foucault 2007: 201).

And yet, he notes, it is precisely because the word 'dissidence' is so localized, and so over-determined by the specific situation of the Soviet Union, that it cannot be used without drawbacks. 'After all', he asks, 'who does not have his theory of dissidence today?' (Foucault 2007: 201). As he spoke these words, Julia Kristeva, writing in *Tel Quel*, had just designated 'the dissident' as a 'new type of intellectual' (Moyn 2010: n. 94) and 'the persona of "the dissident"' had 'supplanted the revolutionary, the guerrilla and the terrorist as an ideal advocate of human liberation in the imaginations of a coterie of anti-totalitarian thinkers' (Horvarth 2007: 882). It is precisely in order to avoid these forms of substantivization and sanctification that Foucault rejects using the word 'dissident'. Such substantivization is dangerous, he remarks, because it unacceptably narrows the criteria for revolts of conduct and leads to a focus on specific individuals rather than broader practices of resistance: after all, he remarks, 'there is not much sense in saying, for instance, that a mad person or a delinquent is a dissident' (Foucault 2007: 201). Thus, Foucault rejects the word, and opts instead for 'counter-conducts'. Beyond the name, however, the counter-conducts of the late 1970s, in which he played an important role, were indelibly marked by the influence of the Soviet dissidents. And their answer to the question of the desirability of revolution was clear. In the absence of revolution, the new 'dissident' politics of human rights provided a substitute utopia, or a substitute *for* utopia, which largely accepted the rules of the neoliberal game.

Conclusion

Reflecting on the new anti-Marxist consensus in 1982, Lévy remarked: '"We have won": the human rights slogans that had once been uttered in the wilderness were now the common property of left and right, "the new 'Open Sesame' to the doors of the planet"' (in Horvath 2007: 901). Lévy's words are fitting. Indeed, since then, 'human rights' has provided a language that has enabled Western powers to step through many of the planet's doors, ostensibly to secure human rights. Most recently, Lévy travelled to Benghazi, negotiated France's recognition of the Libyan rebels, and persuaded President Sarkozy to intervene militarily in support of their attempt to overthrow Muammar Gaddafi. As he tells the story, he called the President, and told him, 'the people on the National Transition Council are good guys' (in Cockburn 2011). One glance at the composition of the rebels' National Transitional Council at the time of writing makes clear the imbrication of human rights and neoliberalism that is at stake in this intervention. Led by Gaddafi's former Justice Minister Mustafa Abdul Jalil, its Prime Minister Mahmoud Jibril served in Gaddafi's regime as the head of Nedb (National Economic Development Board) where he promoted neoliberal privatization policies, and its foreign affairs representative Ali El Eisawi has a PhD in privatization, was Minister of Economy, Trade and Investment under Gaddafi, and was appointed Director General for the Ownership Expansion Programme (privatization fund) in 2005. To assist the new counter-government, the UK has sent a fittingly-named 'stabilization team' composed of economic and juridical advisers, to help fill what they describe as the 'inevitable power vacuum' likely to result from Gaddafi's demise. Is the consolidation of a neoliberal order the only horizon for politics, even revolutionary politics, today? Does supporting human rights imply supporting Western wars, which aim to 'stabilize' the globe in order to forcibly impose such a horizon?

In 1983, Foucault was approached by Glucksmann and Kouchner, with whom he was then working closely on a number of political issues, and asked to sign a petition calling for France to take action against Colonel Gaddafi of Libya. He refused to sign on the basis that he did not wish to appear to be calling for war (Eribon 1991: 267) Today, as the right to intervene completes its metamorphosis into a legitimating doctrine for wars which often have more to do with the imposition of neoliberalism than with human rights, let alone social justice, it is worth rethinking the question: 'Is revolution desirable?' To engage in such a task cannot be simply to assume that the modern revolutionary project can be taken up again unchanged in a neoliberal governmental climate. And yet, if counter-conducts always engage in a game, attempting to open up new spaces of freedom, it is worth asking after the possibilities that exist in the present to refuse to play within the predetermined rules of that game, and to open up a new crisis of governmentality that could subvert and re-orient those rules. By speaking of a 'game', Foucault has stressed, he refers not to an amusement but to a set of procedures that lead to a certain result that can be viewed as winning or losing (Foucault 1997: 297). 'I can well imagine societies', he notes, 'in which the control of conduct is so well regulated in advance that, in a sense, the game is already over' (Foucault 1997: 300). In imagining such societies, Foucault gestures to an anthropology of which he professes ignorance, distinguishing these hypothetical societies from the numerous games he sees as characterizing societies like our own. When asked about whether these concerns could be at the heart of a new way of thinking about politics, he expresses his desire to come back to contemporary problems, but declines to answer in detail: 'I don't like to reply to questions I haven't studied,' he responds (Foucault 1997: 294). Today, at the point at which the combination of neoliberal governmental rationality and the politics of human rights has hegemonized the terrain of action, propagating the belief, to use Margaret Thatcher's infamous phrase, that 'there is no alternative', it is necessary to open up the game, to engage in counter-conducts that seek both to critique the dominant governmentalities and to open up spaces of freedom that do not presuppose the eternity of neoliberal capitalism. To do so would be to re-invent the possibility of politics, not as the exclusive prerogative of the state, but as, in Foucault's words, 'no more or less that that which is born with resistance to governmentality, the first uprising, the first confrontation' (Foucault 2007: 390).

Acknowledgements

This chapter benefited greatly from incisive editorial feedback from Ben Golder, and from conversations about Foucault, rights and neoliberalism with Mark Kelly and Paul Patton. I am grateful to them both for their generosity.

Notes

1 See, for instance, Afary and Anderson 2005.
2 I discuss this statement and its influence on the development of the 'right to intervene' in detail in Whyte 2011. See also Patton 2005, Golder 2010.
3 I discuss Foucault's relation to Kouchner in detail in Whyte 2011.
4 Amnesty's retreat from politics was demonstrated most controversially in its early decision to exclude Nelson Mandela from its list of prisoners of conscience, after he responded to charges of 'sabotage and conspiracy to overthrow the government by revolution' with a conditional defence of political violence against the apartheid regime (Williams 2010: 5).
5 For an insightful discussion of the reliance of counter-conducts on historically available discourses, see Patton 2005.
6 Foucault did not read this section of his notes.

7 For an important new account of the way this utilitarian conception of the state became central to rationalizing the practices of international executive action undertaken by the UN, see Orford 2011.
8 While the 1948 Declaration was initially supposed to be immediately followed by a binding protocol, it became clear that consensus on legal enforcement would not be achieved in the bi-polar world, and so the question of legal mechanisms was 'saved for later' and not ultimately resolved until 1976, with the adoption of the International Covenant on Civil and Political Rights and the International Covenant on Economic, Social and Cultural Rights (Moyn 2010: 63).
9 Patton 2005 refers to Foucault's own reliance on such concepts in Foucault 2000d.
10 Giorgio Agamben has described what he sees as the complicity of human rights NGOs with state power, arguing that both of them reduce their subjects to the status of what he terms 'bare life'. I discuss this critique in detail in Whyte 2009 and 2012.
11 Hayek's state phobia seems not to have extended to the Latin American dictatorships. Hayek visited Pinochet's Chile several times to examine the 'Chilean laboratory' and in 1981 selected the city where the coup against Allende had been plotted, Viña del Mar, as the venue for the regional meeting of the neoliberal Mont Pelerin Society (Klein 2007: 85).

References

Afary, J. and Anderson, K. B. (2005) *Foucault and the Iranian Revolution: Gender and the Seductions of Islamism*, Chicago, IL: University of Chicago Press

Baxi, U. (2007) *The Future of Human Rights*, Oxford: Oxford University Press

Bentham, J. (2002) 'Nonsense upon Stilts, or Pandora's Box Opened', in P. Schofield, C. Pease-Watkin and C. Blamires (eds) *The Collected Works of Jeremy Bentham: Rights, Representation and Reform*, Oxford: Oxford University Press

Cadman, L. (2010) 'How (Not) to be Governed: Foucault, Critique and the Political', *Environment and Planning D: Society and Space*, 28: 539–56

Chomsky, N. and Foucault, M. (1997) 'Human Nature: Justice versus Power', in A. I. Davidson (ed.) *Foucault and his Interlocutors*, Chicago, IL: University of Chicago Press

Cockburn, A. (2011) 'Oh, What a Stupid War', *ArcaMax*, 25 March 2011, http://www.arcamax.com/politics/alexandercockburn/s-857754 (accessed 12 March 2012)

Davis, N. (1996) *Europe: A History*, Oxford: Oxford University Press

Eribon, D. (1991) *Michel Foucault*, trans. B. Wing, Cambridge, MA: Harvard University Press

Evans, T. (2005) 'International Human Rights Law as Power/Knowledge', *Human Rights Quarterly*, 27: 1046–68

Foucault, M. (1997) 'The Ethics of the Concern for Self as a Practice of Freedom', in P. Rabinow (ed.) *Essential Works of Foucault 1954–1984 Vol. 1: Ethics*, London: Penguin

___ (2000a) 'Confronting Governments: Human Rights', in J. D. Faubion (ed.) *Essential Works of Foucault 1954–1984 Vol. 3: Power*, New York, NY: The New Press

___ (2000b) 'For an Ethic of Discomfort', in J. D. Faubion (ed.) *Essential Works of Foucault 1954–1984 Vol. 3: Power*, New York, NY: The New Press

___ (2000c) 'Open Letter to Mehdi Bazargan', in J. D. Faubion (ed.) *Essential Works of Foucault 1954–1984 Vol. 3: Power*, New York, NY: The New Press

___ (2000d) 'The Risks of Security', in J. D. Faubion (ed.) *Essential Works of Foucault 1954–1984 Vol. 3: Power*, New York, NY: The New Press

___ (2000e) 'Useless to Revolt?', in J. D. Faubion (ed.) *Essential Works of Foucault 1954–1984 Vol. 3: Power*, New York, NY: The New Press

___ (2003) *'Society Must be Defended': Lectures at the Collège de France, 1975–76*, trans. D. Macey, London: Allen Lane
___ (2005) *The Hermeneutics of the Subject: Lectures at the Collège de France, 1981–82*, trans. G. Burchell, New York, NY: Palgrave Macmillan
___ (2007) *Security, Territory, Population: Lectures at the Collège de France, 1977–78*, trans. G. Burchell, New York, NY: Palgrave Macmillan
___ (2008) *The Birth of Biopolitics: Lectures at the Collège de France, 1978–79*, trans. G. Burchell, New York, NY: Palgrave Macmillan
Golder, B. (2010) 'Foucault and the Unfinished Human of Rights', *Law, Culture and the Humanities*, 6: 354–74
Gross, L. (1948) 'The Peace of Westphalia: 1648–1948', *American Journal of International Law*, 42: 20–41
Horvath, R. (2007) '"The Solzhenitsyn Effect": East European Dissidents and the Demise of the Revolutionary Privilege', *Human Rights Quarterly* 29: 879–907
Ignatieff, M. (2001) *Human Rights as Politics and Idolatry*, Princeton, NJ: Princeton University Press
Ivison, D. (1997) *The Self at Liberty: Political Argument and the Arts of Government*, Ithaca, NY and London: Cornell University Press
Khilani, S. (1993) *Arguing Revolution: The Intellectual Left in Postwar France*, New Haven, CT and London: Yale University Press
Klein, N. (2007) *The Shock Doctrine: The Rise of Disaster Capitalism*, London: Allen Lane
Lévy, B.-H. (1979) *Barbarism with a Human Face*, trans. G. Holoch, New York, NY: Harper and Row
___ (1995) 'What if the Revolutionary Dream was an Intrinsically Barbaric One?', trans. R. Veasey, in *Adventures on the Freedom Road: The French Intellectuals in the Twentieth Century*, London: The Harvill Press
Macey, D. (1993) *The Lives of Michel Foucault*, London: Random House
Mazower, M. (2004) 'The Strange Triumph of Human Rights, 1933–1950', *Historical Journal*, 47: 379–98
Meinecke, F. (1998) *Machiavellism: The Doctrine of Raison d'État and its Place in Modern History*, trans. D. Scott, Piscataway, NJ: Transaction Publishers
Mill, J. S. (1991) *On Liberty and Other Essays*, Oxford: Oxford University Press
Moyn, S. (2010) *The Last Utopia: Human Rights in History*, Cambridge, MA: Harvard University Press
Office of the President of the General Assembly (2009) 'Concept note on responsibility to protect populations from genocide, war crimes, ethnic cleansing and crimes against humanity', www.un.org/ga/president/63/interactive/protect/conceptnote.pdf (accessed 12 March 2012)
Orford, A. (2011) *International Authority and the Responsibility to Protect*, Cambridge: Cambridge University Press
Paras, E. (2006) *Foucault 2.0: Beyond Power and Knowledge*, New York, NY: Other Press
Patton, P. (2005) 'Foucault, Critique and Rights', *Critical Horizons*, 6: 267–87
Rieff, D. (2002) *A Bed for the Night: Humanitarianism in Crisis*, New York, NY: Simon and Schuster
Seymour, R. (2009) *The Liberal Defence of Murder*, London: Verso
Whyte, J. (2009) 'Particular Rights and Absolute Wrongs: Giorgio Agamben on Life and Politics', *Law and Critique*, 20: 147–61

___ (2011) 'Human Rights: Confronting Goverments? Michel Foucault and the Right to Intervene', in M. Stone, I. Wall and C. Douzinas (eds) *New Critical Legal Thinking*, Routledge: London

___ (2012) 'The Work of Men is not Durable: Haiti, History and the Rights of Man', in S. Bignall and M. Svirsky (eds) *Agamben and Colonialism*, Edinburgh: Edinburgh University Press

Williams, R. (2010) *The Divided World: Human Rights and its Violence*, University of Minnesota Press, MN: Minneapolis

Wolin, R. (2010) *The Wind from the East*, Princeton, NJ and Oxford: Princeton University Press

Chapter 11

Human rights as technologies of the self: creating the European governmentable subject of rights

Bal Sokhi-Bulley

Introduction

Recent events have shown tensions between the European Union (EU) and international law as the EU has sought to protect its own identity as a 'virtuous international actor' (de Búrca 2010) on the basis of its commitment to human rights, and refused to uphold UN measures for the prevention of international terrorism in the case of *Kadi*.[1] A popular motto of the EU, as it becomes an ever more prominent actor on the international stage, is 'governance *without government*' (New Modes of Governance Project, emphasis added).[2] In this vein, the Commission of the EU talks of how 'we need to govern *ourselves* better, together' (COM(2002)275: 2, emphasis added). I explore in this chapter how the EU uses governance talk to speak about rights and how this, on a critical reading, reveals a new form of government – that is, a *governmentality* – of rights, where individuals govern themselves through rights.[3]

'Governance' in the EU context is intended to signify a deliberate move away from 'government' – that is, a departure from traditional, hierarchical forms of governing reliant on key, central institutions, towards more flexible and informal modes, focused on power sharing, multi-level integration, decentralization, deliberation, participation, flexibility, experimentation and knowledge-creation (Scott and Trubek 2002). Referred to also as 'new governance', or 'new modes of governance', these new assemblages depart from and offer alternatives to the classic 'Community Method' (CCM) which, according to the Commission's White Paper on European Governance, is 'premised on the Commission's exclusive right of legislative initiative and the legislative powers of the Council of Ministers and the European Parliament' – that is, mechanisms designed to produce law at the EU level (com (2001) 428 final). Essential elements of this procedure are qualified majority voting in the Council and respect for the rule of law as guaranteed by the European Court of Justice (ECJ). Against this traditional model, the new governance trend can be explained in a number of ways, including: as a means of dealing with the increased complexity and uncertainty of problems on the EU's agenda (for example, the emergence of the comitology system to deal with the complexities involved in re-regulation under the Single Market); as a reflection of developments in the fields of public administration and the law that have recognized the limits of traditional top-down regulatory approaches and encouraged in their place forms of power-sharing and experimentation; and, finally, as arising from the issue of 'competence creep' which has meant that new approaches have had to be adopted to deal with areas in which the EU has traditionally had limited or no competence, such as in the field of human rights. A good example of an alternative to the CCM is the open method of coordination (OMC), which is currently being used in areas of social exclusion and pension reform. The OMC 'aims to coordinate the actions of the several Member States in a given policy domain and to create conditions for mutual learning that hopefully will induce some degree of voluntary policy convergence' (Scott and Trubek 2002: 4–5). Member States therefore agree on a set of policy initiatives but are then free to pursue these objectives in ways that reflect their national contexts and within their own timescales. The Commission's White Paper on European Governance (com (2001) 428 final), which provides 'the most explicit use of governance in the European context' (Möllers 2006: 324), outlines how 'better governance' might be achieved by suggesting a number of reform proposals including 'better application of rules' through regulatory *agencies*. The EU's new Fundamental Rights Agency (FRA) is one such agency and it is the focus of this chapter.

The FRA is a less traditional manifestation of the incitement to rights discourse in the EU than case law and treaty amendments.[4] Established on 1 March 2007,[5] the FRA is a new institution for human rights protection that exhibits features of the new governance model I have just been describing. It was set up in order to provide 'assistance and expertise' (Council Regulation (EC) 168/2007, art. 6) to the EU institutions and its Member States and this advisory role defines the Agency as a governance structure: it is responsible for 'collective learning and guidance' (de Schutter 2007: 27), which are more flexible and informal modes of governing rights discourse, reliant on power sharing. Moreover, in order to carry out this advisory function, the FRA relies on its networks of *experts* – which provide and circulate expert knowledge on rights. It relies also upon *statistics*, which are the form of making information and data on rights intelligible. The expert networks of the Agency and the use of statistics in the collection of data and information on rights are features of the new governance model; they resemble multi-level and decentralized forms of governing the rights discourse of the EU. This chapter argues, however, that rather than simply being described as governance, the dynamics of the rights regime embodied by the FRA is best captured as a form of *governmentality*. I take governmentality to refer to disciplinary and governing practices that regulate both rights discourse and the identities of the subjects of rights. Within the FRA, there is no sovereign entity that governs, only the FRA's networks of 'experts', which 'make' the rights discourse of the FRA through statistics. The presence of a network of experts and the use of statistics are not only features of governance but important tactics of governmentality (Sokhi-Bulley 2011a, 2011b). The importance of this distinction resides in the observation that these new modes of governance are not simply *better* forms of governing, or more participative and neutral mechanisms, but rather – understood through the Foucaultian lens of governmentality – a form of power relation which creates and regulates the subjects and populations it purports to govern.

This chapter elaborates these arguments by examining the role of *the individual* in governance. By 'individual', I refer to the 'citizen' of the EU. In the EU context, the individual subject of rights is necessarily a citizen of the Union. Citizenship has 'a close connection with the language of rights and entitlement . . . [It is] grounded in a normative discourse of "civic inclusion", and . . . provides the framework within which to make many legal [here, rights] claims' (Stychin 2003: 7). Individuals, as actors in rights discourse, are of particular interest to this chapter because they, firstly, do not obviously fit under the label of 'expert'. Secondly, the 'expert' category encourages a false dichotomy of governor/governed, wherein the individual is more readily misidentified as 'the governed', the object rather than (also the) subject of government. Rather, and on my view, the individual in a governmentality of rights is a 'free agent' and has knowledge of, takes part in and accepts responsibility for, the modes of government. I seek to explain how the individual is involved in governing herself through rights and that the processes of governing are a form of governmentality, not only governance. I propose that governmentality has, contrary to being lessened, been increased and made more efficient by becoming more deeply ingrained in the structures and processes relating to rights, and by becoming less visible because it manifests itself in forms of authority less detectable than hierarchical forms of government. We are, in other words, *governing ourselves*, through rights – but doing it believing that we are in fact being *less* governed and moving *away* from government.

The objective of this chapter is, therefore, to demonstrate *how* individuals govern themselves through rights by examining the various processes whereby the individual interacts with the FRA. This observation is significant for three reasons. First, it brings to light that speaking of rights in an apolitical language of governance through the FRA allows the EU to present an unproblematic image of itself as a non-regulatory, virtuous international actor. Secondly, it conceals the power relations of governmentality that produce this identity *and* the identities of the subjects of rights on which it relies for its construction: that is, the 'ideal citizen' versus the 'victim'. Thirdly, so obscures the fact that these power relations are reflexive and ethical.[6] I problematize rights as a seemingly 'ideal' discourse of government since it both allows for the construction of the EU's human rights identity *and* enacts a new ethics whereby individuals regulate themselves under a supposed banner of 'governance' rather than government(ality).

Governmentality as a technology of the self

'Governmentality' can be understood as both the *process* of government (that is, as an 'art of government' – Foucault 2007: 205) and as a *methodology* (that is, as a 'rationality of government' – a way of thinking about the practice of government and hence of who or what is being governed, what governing is, whom or what can govern – Foucault 2007: 106). This chapter uses governmentality as a methodology to understand rights practices. As the process of government, governmentality describes processes concerned not with relations of sovereignty but rather with tactics and techniques used to regulate the conduct, or behaviour, of individuals.

The notion is not distinct from Foucault's earlier portrayals of power as discipline (Foucault 1991, 1998). Disciplinary power focused on how 'meticulous, often minute techniques . . . gradually led to the blueprint of a general method' (Foucault 1991: 138) – for example, the use of the timetable and the spatial distribution of cells in prisons as means of controlling activity led to the construction of the 'delinquent' as a 'subjected, used and transformed' docile body (Foucault 1991: 136). Foucault's studies on the prison focused also on how these techniques resulted in the creation of 'delinquency' – an abnormal, deviant category which was politically useful because it provided an undesirable label against which the ideal society was able to define and regulate itself. Foucault's later articulation of governmentality retains the disciplinary concern with minor tactics of control and with the ways in which the individual body is 'made' by the power relations rendered possible through forms of overt disciplinary organization. However, the scale of the target of power is maximized (from the individual to the population). Importantly, rather than the *body* of the individual, *space* becomes a primary modality of rule, along with the circulation of people, merchandise, air and so on, within that space. That is, the key issue is how a particular space becomes *governmentalized*, with how mutations in the technologies of power occur within a given (populated) space.

Nevertheless, despite this scalar move from the individual to the population, the individual's role in governmentality is key – for governmentality necessarily involves *self*-government. Questions of governmentality concern: 'How to govern oneself, how to be governed, by whom should we accept to be governed, how to be the best possible governor?' (Foucault 2007: 88) Thus governmentality is often described, using Colin Gordon's phrase, as 'the conduct of conduct' (Gordon 1991: 2) – that is, as an activity or practice that aims to shape, guide or affect the conduct of some person or persons. 'Conduct' (*conduite*) here refers to two things: it is 'the activity of conducting (*conduire*), of conduction (*la conduction*) if you like, but it is equally the way in which one conducts oneself (*se conduit*), lets oneself be conducted (*se laisse conduire*), is conducted (*est conduit*), and finally, in which one behaves (*se comporter*) as an effect of a form of conduct (*une conduit*)' (Foucault 2007: 193). It is therefore the activity of 'self on self' (Foucault 2010: 223–44) – a set of practices through which the subject behaves and has a relationship with itself, literally '*self*-government'.

The practices of self-government are what are referred to as 'technologies of the self', that is, activities 'which permit individuals to effect by their own means or with the help of others a certain number of operations on their own bodies and souls, thoughts, conduct, and a way of being, so as to transform themselves in order to attain a certain state of happiness, purity, wisdom, perfection or immortality' (Foucault 1988: 18). For example, the confession is a technology of the self: it requires absolute obedience to the spiritual director and examination of one's conscience. Other rituals of self-examination include the spiritual retreat, meditation, ritual purification and the interpretation of dreams (Hutton 1988: 133–4). The management of disease is interpreted by Nikolas Rose as a technology of the self – he explains, using the microcosm of web forums and chat rooms, that the practices undertaken in these fora of diary writing, reading, posting and replying to messages, are an exposure of experience and thoughts according to particular rules, norms, values and forms of authority (Rose 2007: 106–30). They allow the 'individual at risk' of disease actively and responsibly to participate actively and responsibly in the management of her own disease so as to better herself and her existence.

Technologies of the self therefore privilege the idea of the care of the self. 'The self', Foucault claimed, referred 'not [to] clothing, tools or possessions. It is to be found in the principle which uses these tools, a principle not of the body but of the soul. You have to worry about your soul – that is the principal activity of caring for yourself' (Foucault 1988: 25). The activity of 'self on self' (self-government) is not, however, a solitary but rather a social exercise centred upon 'the aesthetics of existence' (Foucault 2000a: 260). It consists of regulatory practices which the individual engages in not only to better herself but to exist in and to fit better into society. That is, the self acts on itself in order to have a better relationship with the world. Rights, I argue, are one of the regulatory practices in our contemporary society which incite and enjoin the work of the self on itself.[7] Rights, in Foucault's words, are one of the 'models that [the individual] finds in his [*sic*] culture and [which] are proposed, suggested and imposed on him by his culture, his society and his social group' (Foucault 2000b: 291).

It is interesting that Foucault saw a link between the care of the self and *ethics*. His idiosyncratic view of ethics was influenced by Greco-Roman philosophy to the extent that he saw ethics as the conscious practice of freedom (Foucault 2000a: 284).[8] Amongst in particular the Greeks, the concern with the self and the care of the self, he observes, was required 'for right conduct and the proper practice of freedom' (Foucault 2000a: 285). This was 'freedom' in the sense of not being a slave to the people around you, to those governing you, or to your own passions. The freedom of the individual was thus problematized as an ethical problem – but ethical in the sense of how it was then understood, as '*ēthos*' – that is, as a *way of being* and of *behaviour* that was, moreover, visible to others. A person's *ēthos* could therefore be observed in their clothing, appearance, gait and so forth. Whilst *ēthos* does imply a relationship to others, it is key for Foucault that the relationship with oneself is ontologically prior. Rose describes this as an 'ethopolitics' (Rose 2007: 18) – a politics of 'life itself', focused on how to 'control, manage, engineer, reshape and modulate the very vital capacity of human beings as living creatures' (Rose 2007: 3). Central to the arguments presented in this chapter is the understanding that technologies of the self represent a form of *ethical government* because the 'governors' and the 'governed' *regulate themselves* as they concern themselves with policing their own desires, aspirations, needs and lifestyles (through rights) in order to exist better in relation to others in society. The governor and the governed are thus aspects of the one actor. This duality relies on the freedom of the individual, which is central to governmentality.

Describing the government of the self as 'ethical' may be misleading. It is important to understand that directing action towards an aesthetics of existence always gestures both towards an autonomy and refinement of the self, *and* towards allowing governmental control. It is the very practices of care of the self that try to shape, guide and affect the desires, aspirations and needs of individuals. Rights are just such a practice. The key question for this chapter is, then, *what are* the practices of 'self on self' with respect to human rights in the EU context? And, moreover, *how* do rights operate as technologies of the self? Accordingly, the next section examines the functioning of the EU's new FRA as an institution that promotes and circulates some of these forms of ethical self-government through rights.

The individual as (lay)expert: producing the governmentable subject

Crucial to understanding self-government in the rights context is the point that the individual becomes not only an object (of regulation) but an active, educated and responsible subject – that is, an *expert* (in and of herself). I identify three elements that constitute individual expertise in the context of the EU's contemporary rights discourse. These are: interaction, knowledge and responsibility. The individual, as citizen, *interacts* with the FRA and thereby acquires *knowledge* not only of the FRA's processes and of rights, but also of the type of individual that the discourse says she is and can be (an 'ideal citizen'). Furthermore, interaction with the FRA engages individual *responsibility*.

Interaction: producing the active subject

The interaction of the citizen with the apparatuses of the FRA occurs through various processes, or 'tactics, techniques, [and] functionings' (Foucault 1991: 26), which form part of the general pattern of governmentality. The citizen is, first, involved in the socio-legal methods whereby the FRA collects information and data – for example, surveys. Surveys are important tactics of governmentality. The largest and most detailed example is the FRA's first (and largest) EU-wide Survey on Minorities and Discrimination: EU-MIDIS.[9] The FRA also gathers information and data for its thematic reports via surveys, enabling further contact between the individual and the Agency (Council Regulation (EC) 168/2007, art. 4(1)(f)).[10] For instance, in *Part II – The Social Situation* of the first thematic report on homophobia and discrimination on grounds of sexual orientation ('*Homophobia Report*') (FRA 2008, 2009a), one of the FRA's key publications to date, surveys were conducted at European and national level to assess attitudes towards Lesbian, Gay, Bisexual, Transgender (LGBT) people (FRA 2008: Section I.1). The surveys may involve face-to-face interviews – for instance, for the purposes of EU-MIDIS, a total of 23,500 immigrants and ethnic minority people were interviewed face to face during 2008 in all 27 Member States.[11]

A second example of the tactics of interaction with the FRA is the individual accessing it voluntarily and on her own initiative using the internet. The FRA recognizes a 'frequently asked question' (FAQ) to be: 'You have been discriminated against – can the FRA help you?'[12] It promises that 'FRA will make people more aware of their fundamental rights'. It is not empowered to deal itself with individual complaints but it can refer people to organizations in each Member State where individuals can go for 'help, advice and also support in legal matters'.[13] The FRA also recently announced that it has '3,000 fans now on Facebook'[14] and has also set up an official Twitter feed and YouTube channel.[15] It is using social media not only to raise awareness of fundamental rights and related challenges but to make itself as accessible as possible to the individual.[16]

The citizen, moreover, has access to all the FRA's products through the website and also through the FRA's InfoPortal,[17] described as a 'user-friendly information system' which provides free online access to the public. In this way the individual can access the FRA Newsletter[18] and its magazine, *Equal Voices*. In addition, she can sign up for content alerts of the former for increased ease of access and a continuous flow of information. The FRA produces several individual, user-friendly educational documents. One example is the eye-catching publication 'Circle of Rights'. At the centre of the circle are the words 'having the right to be yourself' and around the centre are the various rights which citizens might enjoy since the FRA is 'making these a reality'; for instance, 'being respected and looked after in your old age', 'being able to choose to believe in whatever you believe in' and 'living a free and dignified life'.[19] Another example is the colourful FRA booklet *The European Fundamental Rights Agency: An Introductory Guide*, which uses diagrams, pictures and biographies of key individuals to illustrate what the FRA is, why it was set up and how it operates.[20] The FRA also aims its publications and events at specific groups of individuals. For example, the *S'Cool Agenda* is targeted at young people.[21] It is published in three languages (English, French and German) for greater accessibility and acts as an awareness-raising tool to help young people to learn about fundamental rights issues in Europe through various activities (such as how to keep track of homework and a 'human rights temperature' test). The FRA recently published *Excursion to the Past – Teaching for the Future: A Handbook for Teachers*, which 'encourages national governments to better integrate education on the holocaust and human rights into their school curricula to reflect the significance of human rights in both the history and the future of the EU'.[22]

The interaction of the citizen with the FRA through these techniques (that is, surveys, interviews, accessing the FRA online) would appear to happen through relations of pastoral power. Foucault describes this as 'the power of the shepherd' (Foucault 2007: 125), a type of power that is exercised over a 'flock' rather than a territory and that is concerned with the welfare of the flock. The citizen is surrounded by a range of experts, including the FRA's structural expert bodies – that is, the four bodies of the Agency itself, the Management Board, Executive Board, Scientific Committee and Director (Council Regulation (EC) 168/2007, art. 11) – its national expert networks, RAXEN[23] and FRALEX,[24] and other national-level expert bodies (for example, national equality bodies, national human rights institutions). These experts are characterized as such by virtue of possessing 'expert knowledge' (Kennedy 2005: 17–18) concerning human rights and their implementation. This expertise is marked by a shared disciplinary sensibility and qualification. They represent the pastorate – the experts guide the individual and determine her conduct through prescribed modes of behaviour. However, despite expert involvement, the individual is expected to act for herself and interaction with the FRA actually conditions the individual of the FRA's rights discourse into herself *becoming an expert.* Relations of self-government mean the individual becomes a 'layexpert' (Rose 2007: 128) in the management of risk of rights violation because through the tactics of interaction with the FRA she acquires *knowledge* about rights and accepts *responsibility* for her rights status.

Knowledge and responsibility: producing the educated, responsible subject

Rose's example in the context of health care describes how the layexpert is constructed via the self-government of one's disease. By participating in web forums and chat rooms (tactics designed to encourage the individual to take part in managing her own disease), the individual at risk of disease is able to gain as much knowledge about the management of disease as possible and apply it to herself. Her aim in all this is to better her health and the quality of her life. Similarly, the citizen at risk of rights violation becomes a layexpert in the management of her rights status.

The citizen is educated as to – that is, acquires *knowledge* about – her rights in the process of being surveyed and the answers which citizens give are used to formulate reports containing statistics, opinions and policy outcomes that educate the population of the EU more broadly as to their rights. In fact, raising rights awareness is one issue that EU-MIDIS intended to bring to the attention of policymakers (FRA 2009b: 14). Where the citizen seeks out the FRA because she has experienced discrimination, she is advised to get in touch with either her national equality body or national human rights institution. The FRA's website contains enough information for the citizen to educate herself on the role of these bodies and gives details of how to contact these bodies within each of the Member States – listing telephone numbers, email addresses and websites. A 'Guide for Victims of Discrimination' also advises the citizen on how to act for herself, stressing '*you* can now take action' (emphasis added)[25] if you are a victim of discrimination, harassment or victimization. The guide can be interpreted as imposing a *responsibility* on the citizen, giving a 'to do' list under the heading: 'Get to know your legal system'. The emphasis is thus placed on the citizen acting for herself. The general sentiment is reminiscent of the tone of the governance discourse of the Commission – that 'we need to govern *ourselves* better, together' (Communication from the Commission 2002). The citizen may comment on the operation of the FRA by posting comments and suggestions.[26] The latest means of doing this has been via Facebook, through which the FRA encourages individuals to 'get recent updates and give us your feedback', and Twitter.[27]

By using technology in this way to converse with the FRA and to access information on rights, the citizen is operating as an 'e-citizen' (Morison 2010: 571). Technology here operates as a new tactic of governmentality that allows individuals to manage themselves and express their own needs. The relation of the layexpert to 'professional expert[ise]' (Morison 2010: 571) is carried out 'at a distance' (Rose 2000: 324). The lay and professional experts may not come into contact with each other (for instance, accessing the FRA via the internet does not allow for this – although interviews conducted for surveys, like EU-MIDIS, mean that the citizen comes into direct contact with the FRA experts at the localized, national level) but do work together, such that they are 'partners in prudence' (Rose 2000: 327), or 'partners in their own governance' (Morison 2010: 571). Citizens therefore not only educate themselves on the FRA and on their rights – gaining 'expert knowledge' – but the layexperts, moreover, become responsible for *educating each other* in the knowledge they have gained. They become 'experts by experience' (Rose 2007: 128). Moreover, education engages the responsibility of the citizen; not only do citizens become responsible for themselves but this responsibility is extended to the population.

Producing the 'ideal citizen': towards 'ideal government'?

Interaction with the FRA therefore creates a new type of European '*governmentable*' citizen (Foucault 2008: 295, emphasis added): a citizen that is at once an active, educated and responsible subject, as well as the object of government through rights. The responsibility assumed by individuals and the extent to which they (are expected to) educate themselves on rights implies that within the processes of interaction with the FRA there is an 'ethics of care' at work. The citizen comes to act upon herself within certain regimes of authority and knowledge, by means of technologies (here, rights) that are directed to self-improvement and preservation within a safe and secure society – that is, she strives to become the 'ideal citizen' with rights in contrast to the 'victim' (the minority or LGBT citizen), or 'most vulnerable victim' (the Roma or Muslim citizen), and to exist better within the safe and secure rights society of the EU.

The FRA gathers knowledge on the citizen during participation in surveys – EU-MIDIS, for example, asks for the respondent's gender, date of birth, religion, clothing preference (whether traditional dress is worn) and employment status, amongst other details. Moreover, the FRA is determined to have an answer – the instructions to the interviewers are to 'probe' the respondent if they are unwilling to give answers (FRA 2009c: 38–42). For instance, if the respondent is unwilling to give the interviewer their exact age, the instructions are to 'probe with listed categories' – that is, 16–19, 20–24, and so forth (FRA 2009c: 38). Certain details are noted without asking, such as place of residence and language proficiency of the respondent in the national language.[28] A 'leave-behind' information pack, containing a Gallup notification letter and a letter from the FRA (with the signature of senior officials), is also left with the individuals interviewed, given to hesitant contacts before a recall attempt is made, or left in mailboxes for potential respondents who are not at home. The citizen is disciplined to the extent that she becomes part of and produced by the FRA's discourse – she must respond within the boundaries set by the FRA, choosing from a list of already constructed scenarios or answers. The space of interaction is thus *managed*. The individual is disciplined into representing herself as either a 'minority' citizen according to the FRA (that is, what I describe here as a 'victim'/endangered category), or '*not* a minority' citizen. The questions create and reinforce the belief that the category of 'minority' is in danger and asks whether any such experiences of crime are frightening (for instance, the survey asks: 'do you think that [this incident/any of these incidents] IN THE LAST 12 MONTHS happened partly or completely because of your immigrant/minority background?' and 'during the last 5 years, have you been personally attacked in a way that REALLY frightened you?') (FRA 2009c: 23, 28, emphasis in original). This vulnerable, 'minority' category thus acquires an undesirable status amongst citizens and within the FRA's rights discourse. The *Homophobia Report* also indentifies a vulnerable, 'victim' category: the LGBT person, constructed also through managed interaction with the FRA. Part II of the *Homophobia Report* compiles data on homophobia and sexual discrimination using interviews and surveys, specifically for Chapter I.1 of the Report, entitled 'Attitudes towards LGBT people'. Here, quotations taken from LGBT persons suffering 'multiple discrimination' are highlighted in boxes – for example: 'Depending on which part of Berlin I go to, in one I get punched in the mouth because I'm a foreigner and in the other because I'm a queen' and '[i]t is really difficult sometimes being gay and having a disability, especially when it comes to accessibility . . . It is obviously quite difficult to become part of a community you can't access' (FRA 2009a: 4).

The (ethnic minority/LGBT) 'victim' is portrayed by the FRA as an unwanted, delinquent category within the EU's safe and secure society, and the victim should strive to seek help and aspire to the protection of her rights.[29] The 'victim' is a politically useful category (compare 'delinquency') since it defines a norm against which the safe and secure, victim-less, or 'ideal' rights society wants to define itself. In fact, the safe and secure rights society relies on the production of the 'victim'. The victim status is thus a political strategy, making society manageable by ensuring it is observed – such that 'victims' are identified and labelled through tactics of interaction with the FRA and then able to be kept separate from the rest of the rights-bearing population. The use of socio-legal methods to collect information and data in the form of statistics is also a significant tactic of governmentality – since statistics help to 'strengthen the fundamental rights architecture' (FRA 2010) of the EU, creating a solid, evidence-based foundation on which to build progress in EU human rights policy.

The tactics by which the FRA's discourse produces the 'victim' are thus not simply apolitical strategies of governance – they are rather political strategies of governmentality. Makau Mutua's metaphor of 'savage-victim-saviour' describes the political processes at work well: the construction of the 'saviour' (the FRA/EU as virtuous international human rights actor) is reliant on there being a 'victim' (the minority or LGBT citizen, for instance) and a 'savage' (the 'bad' Member State, for example, that does not show evidence of good human rights practice) (see Mutua 2002).[30] Note that the 'saviour' of course refers to the EU, and not only the FRA, as it is the political space of the EU that is governmentalized by rights. The victim is shown ways to better herself – she is given guidance on how to access organizations at her national level that will inform her of her rights and how the wrongs that she has suffered may be remedied.[31] She is also informed that steps are being taken to help potential victims of discrimination. She can feel reassured, furthermore, that the FRA is looking out for the best interests of what it sees as 'victims'. The individual is thus disciplined into self-reflection, into a conditioning, or 'taking care of' herself, so as to avoid the 'victim' label by the FRA's rights discourse.

The individual, moreover, also governs herself into producing a '*most vulnerable* victim' category. The results of EU-MIDIS include 'Data in Focus' reports which concentrate on providing statistics on the *most vulnerable* ethnic and religious minorities. The reports have focused, for instance, on the Roma and on Muslims (FRA 2009d, 2009e). The Roma were chosen as the first focus group since EU-MIDIS showed that, of all the groups surveyed (for example, Asians, Central and Eastern Europeans),[32] the Roma reported the highest levels of being discriminated against. On average 47 per cent of all respondents stated that they had been victims of discrimination based on their ethnicity in the previous 12 months.[33] The FRA therefore constructs a discourse through which the 'most vulnerable' citizens of the EU can be identified – in terms of their minority group and in terms of individuals belonging to the most vulnerable minority group. These are then constructed as 'the most vulnerable victims' of the FRA's rights discourse.

The normalization of the subject of rights as either a 'victim', 'most vulnerable victim' or 'ideal citizen' is made possible because the citizen as expert becomes characteristic of the whole *population* of the EU. This occurs despite the statistical reality that 'the citizen' does not proportionately represent the citizenry at large of the EU, and the inevitably low number of citizens that actually access the FRA to educate themselves on the forms of action they might take to counter a rights violation or to take part in voluntary or random surveys. The understanding behind representation of the population lies in the issue of whether the interaction of the citizen with the FRA must be *active*. Must the individual be *consciously* active in order to be an expert? In Rose's healthcare analogy, the subject is an active individual 'at risk' – that is, an individual suffering from disease, who consciously seeks medical advice and consciously educates herself on medical knowledge. I argue for something more radical. The citizen, I propose, is constructed as an expert by virtue of the FRA being a governmentalized space. The citizen becomes one of the nodes of experts in the FRA's structure. Therefore the citizen, first, has the *possibility* of active participation in the technologies of government. Secondly, and this is the crucial point, the citizen is *always-already* an expert because the governing structure of the FRA, its very discourse, assumes that she is. This is the result of a new authority of expertise that is to be found in the individual herself – a new relation to expertise, one that is representative of self-government. The possibility for active participation and the always-already determined nature of expertise allows for self-government of the citizen to be understood as a condition of the entire population of the EU. Furthermore, the form in which information concerning rights circulates within the FRA/EU is important. Information and data are communicated as statistics – these are important tactics of governmentality that make intelligible the human rights situation in the EU, thereby providing rights knowledge of the population as a whole (Sokhi-Bulley 2011a). The statistics gathered from the citizens who take part in EU-MIDIS, for instance, are used to represent the population of the EU at large.

Rights therefore represent a new ethics of government – where government means that individuals must 'take care of' themselves in order to exist better within the EU's rights society and avoid the 'victim' label. Could this be the ideal formulation for a human rights regime, the neoliberal 'dream of democracy' (Brown 1995: 5)?[34] It might be considered *ideal* because, first, government through rights is ethical in a Foucaultian sense, meaning that actors are always-already responsible for themselves. Secondly, actors therefore govern themselves, without coercion or the need for a coercive body. They do so believing that they are engaged in an 'aesthetics of existence' – gesturing towards autonomy and *less* government. Thirdly, rights protection and promotion is a direct consequence of this government and, finally, government reinforces the identity of the FRA as a human rights institution and of the EU as a virtuous, international human rights actor.

However, the power relations of governmentality which act upon and through individual freedom ensure that this aesthetics always harbours governmental control. In addition, a major flaw in this seemingly ideal model of government is that it does not encourage or facilitate critique of the system. Rather, it imprisons the critical voice within a 'plastic cage' in the name of emancipation. This image is used by Wendy Brown to describe a system that reproduces and regulates the injured subjects it would protect (Brown 1995: 23).[35] That it is plastic means that the cage is transparent to the ordinary eye and distressingly durable. It has been erected, moreover, in the name of equality and justice but, notwithstanding these good intentions, it ties, categorizes, marks and imposes a law of truth on the individual (Brown 1995: 28–9). The law of truth in this case is a regime of fundamental rights protection as defined by the FRA. This regime involves tactics like asking set questions of the individual (in surveys, for example) which invite a certain type of managed response, formulating an endangered 'victim' category, or through delimiting who the 'victim' can approach and the procedures through which this should happen in cases of discrimination. These are technologies of the self and are significant to observe because it reveals a (self-)governmentality through rights which not only disturbs but inverts the liberal tradition of rights – of rights against the state, or *against government*. With this caution in mind, we must ask: How far could government in the name of human rights go? What 'evils' might it perpetrate?

Conclusion

This chapter has explained how in the rights discourse of the EU, citizens, who by virtue of their citizenship can *benefit* from rights, actually *govern* themselves through these selfsame rights. Via the elements of interaction, knowledge and responsibility the individual citizen becomes a European governmentable subject: always-already an *expert* and so directly involved in the 'self on self' governing tactics and techniques that are taking place. I have demonstrated the strength of this model of government as its reflexivity and association with an 'ethics of care'. In other words, individuals engage (consciously or not) in self-government in an effort to 'better' themselves and to 'exist better' (as 'ideal citizens' in the EU) and, in so doing, they seek to define themselves within a determined regime of authority or expertise, fitting better into the EU's safe and secure rights society. The chapter has also considered the implications of human rights as technologies of the self, namely the resultant idea that the EU governance model of rights protection through the FRA is an 'ideal model of government' – one that protects rights at the same time as promoting an image of the EU as a virtuous international human rights actor. And yet, in so doing, I have also sought to identify a major flaw in this seemingly ideal model – namely the suppression of critique.

This now brings me to the several advantages of understanding rights as technologies of the self. First, this critical perspective promotes resistance to rights as governmentality through critique; we have, in other words, a 'right to question' (Foucault 1997: 32; Cadman 2010), the right and ability to resist regimes of government that govern in the name of values we are told we ought to aspire to for our own good. We are, after all, not passive, governed objects but rather active, educated and responsible partners, or 'empowered citizen-consumer[s]' (Morison 2010: 566), in a new governmental rationality, which I have suggested here is government of the self through the techniques of rights. Freedom, as I have previously outlined, is an essential part of governmentality: we accept the conditions of government by rights. This individual empowerment takes the form of resistance through critique. We ought therefore to ask: Who are the experts who govern? Who should they be? What identities are attached to the rights holder? How are these identities constructed, at the expense of labelling what groups within society as undesirable and under threat (ethnic minorities, religious minorities, LGBT persons, for example)? What counts as information and data? How is it managed, using what (socio-legal) techniques?

Secondly, recognizing rights as technologies of the self opens up actual strategies of resistance to the individual. For example, we might refuse to interact with the FRA in the sense that we might refuse to respond to surveys, questionnaires or to invitations for comment via the website, or we may act disruptively, responding incorrectly and frequently. These would be forms of individual resistance to and refusal of the position of the layexpert. Moreover, we might make more strategic use of rights in efforts to resist the 'ideal citizen' label. So, we may actively approach the FRA (through response to online questionnaires – for example, the FRA asked the individual for feedback on its new website through a questionnaire in 2009, entitled the 'FRA website survey'[36]) and respond beyond the managed parameters set by the Agency. That is, we can make uncalled for suggestions for change, or spoil the form. Individuals may also create their own networks, joining to form community organizations (or religious or ethnic minority persuasion), advocacy groups, or non-governmental organizations (NGOs) and demand to participate in the FRA's processes. The NGO can already be seen to be doing this. NGOs have a relationship of 'cooperation' with the FRA and engage with it through a cooperation network called the 'Fundamental Rights Platform' (Council Regulation (EC) 168/2007, art. 10). NGOs have suggested, successfully, that the Platform establish a permanent structure (the 'Advisory Panel') and have observer status at the meetings of the FRA's Management Board and Scientific Committee.[37] As actors in the discourse, we can therefore assert – through these strategies of resistance and critique, and as the NGO involvement in the FRA's discourse shows – that we want to be 'conducted differently, by other leaders (*conducteurs*)' (Foucault 2007: 194), that we do not want to be governed *like that*. Critique therefore empowers the European governmentable subject of rights in that it offers the possibility of '*not being governed quite so much*' (Foucault 1997: 29, emphasis added).

Finally, a governmentality critique is not nihilistic or pessimistic: it does not advocate an 'end of human rights' (Douzinas 2002). Nor does it reject the FRA. The project of human rights may have become institutionalized and compromised in the name of governance but human rights can be re-imagined by not assuming too much of them as given 'values':

> Let us speak it aloud, this *new challenge*: we need a *critique* of moral values, *for once the value of these values must be called into question* . . . One has taken the *value* of these 'values' as given, as a fact beyond all calling-into-questioning; until now no one has had not even the slightest doubt or hesitation ranking 'the good' as of higher value than 'the evil' . . . What? if the opposite were true? What? if a symptom of regression also lay in the 'good,' likewise a danger, a temptation, a poison, a narcotic through which perhaps the present were living *at the expense of the future*?
>
> (Nietzsche 1998: 5, emphasis in original)

A governmentality critique, such as that presented in this chapter, consequently urges (self-)reflection on our roles as governmentable subjects in (self-)government through rights. This, in turn, allows the project of rights to continue to offer the promise of *less government*. In the tradition of the growing body of work therefore, both in this collection and elsewhere,[38] that points to the value of Foucault's thought for key questions on law, power and rights, this chapter has sought to emphasize the usefulness of Foucault's concept and methodology of governmentality for understanding human rights law, and for appreciating the contribution of expert bodies and new institutions for human rights protection (like the FRA) to a governmentality of rights.

Notes

1 Joined cases C-402/05 and C-415/05 P *Yassin Abdullah Kadi and Al Barakat International Foundation v. Council and Commission* [2008] ECR I-06351.

2 'New Modes of Governance Project', an integrated project coordinated by the European University Institute and funded by the EU under its Sixth Framework Programme, 2004–2008 http://www.eu-newgov.org/index.asp (accessed 26 January 2007). See, further, Rosenau and Czempiel 1992.

3 I understand government *as* governmentality – that is, I look at the FRA/EU as a governmentalized space, wherein a distinction between government and governmentality is unnecessary since government is always *government(ality)*.

4 The 1960s saw the burgeoning of the jurisprudence of the ECJ, note for instance Case 29/69 *Stauder v. City of Ulm* [1969] ECR 419; Case 11/70 *Internationale Handelsgesellschaft mbH v. Einfuhr-und Vorratsstelle für Getreide und Futtermittel* [1970] ECR 1125; Case 4/73 *Nold v. Commission* [1974] ECR 491; Case 36/75 *Rutili v. Minister for the Interior* [1975] ECR 1219. A codification of the ECJ's case law occurred in 1992 in the form of art. 6 of the Treaty on European Union (TEU, Maastricht Treaty). Note new arts 2 and 6 TEU, consolidated version as amended by the Treaty of Lisbon [2010] OJ C 83, 30 March 2010.

5 Pursuant to Council Regulation (EC) 168/2007 of 15 February 2007 establishing a European Union Agency for Fundamental Rights [2007] OJ L 53/1.

6 Dean understands the mechanisms for active participation within the technologies of citizenship to be representative of 'reflexive government' – which he describes as sites of self-government, or the 'governing of government' (Dean 1999: 2). See, also, Dean 2007 for a strong argument distinguishing governmentality studies from theories of governance and globalization.

7 Other scholars (Brown 2002; Golder 2010; Orford 2007) too make the claim of rights being modes of subjectification.

8 For a range of more conventional understandings of 'ethics' see, for example, Singer 1994.

9 http://fra.europa.eu/fraWebsite/eu-midis/index_en.htm (accessed 2 September 2011).

10 Thematic reports cover analyses, research and surveys in the thematic areas of the FRA's Multi-Annual Framework and in response to requests from the European Parliament, the Council or the Commission.

11 In addition, 5,000 people from the majority population living in the same areas as minorities were interviewed in ten Member States, so as to allow for comparison of results. The survey used the same standardized questionnaire in all Member States, which is divided into eight categories, namely: general discrimination, rights awareness, discrimination experiences, experience of crime, corruption, police contact, customs and border control, and background information. The questionnaire consists of 150

questions and 300 variables (answers), taking into account what the FRA anticipated as all the possible answers people could give in response to the questions. Each interview lasted for between 20 minutes and one hour (FRA 2009b: 4).

12 http://194.30.12.221/fraWebsite/faq/faq_en.htm (accessed 2 September 2011).

13 http://194.30.12.221/fraWebsite/faq/faq_en.htm (accessed 2 September 2011).

14 http://fra.europa.eu/fraWebsite/news_and_events/news-archive/news-archive-2011/infocus11_0109_en.htm (accessed 3 May 2012).

15 http://twitter.com/#!/EURightsAgency; http://www.youtube.com/user/EUAgencyFRA (accessed 3 May 2012).

16 The FRA also invited individual comments and suggestions on its role and functions through its magazine, *Equal Voices*, which until recently was published every quarter.

17 http://194.30.12.221/fraWebsite/research/publications/publications_en.htm; http://www.facebook.com/fundamentalrights and http://infoportal.fra.europa.eu (accessed 2 September 2011).

18 http://fra.europa.eu/fraWebsite/news_and_events/newsletter/newsletter_en.htm (accessed 1 June 2010).

19 http://194.30.12.221/fraWebsite/attachments/FRA-10-101_disk_BAT_EN.pdf (accessed 29 June 2010). See also the 'Your rights' link http://194.30.12.221/fraWebsite/your_rights/your_rights_en.htm (accessed 2 September 2011), which includes 'real-life stories on discrimination'.

20 http://fra.europa.eu/fraWebsite/attachments/FRA-10-101_booklet_V5%20EN.pdf (accessed 29 June 2010).

21 For the 2010 version, see http://fra.europa.eu/fraWebsite/your_rights/materials/scool_agenda_ 2010_en.htm (accessed 1 August 2010).

22 http://fra.europa.eu/fraWebsite/attachments/Handbook-teachers-holocaust-education_EN.pdf (accessed 26 November 2010).

23 RAXEN refers to the groups of 27 National Focal Points (NFPs), present in each of the Member States, which report on racism, xenophobia and related intolerances. The first kick-off meeting of the NFPs of a new body, the FRA Research Network (FRANET). was announced on 12 September 2011 – this will work for both the FRA and the European Institute for Gender Equality (see http://fra.europa.eu/fraWebsite/news_and_events/2011-events/evt11_12sep_en.htm (accessed 22 September 2011).

24 FRALEX refers to the FRA's 'group of legal experts', who report on legal aspects of fundamental rights issues in all Member States.

25 http://ec.europa.eu/employment_social/fundamental_rights/pdf/public/factsheet2_en.pdf (accessed 20 March 2009).

26 The *Equal Voices* magazine, for example, welcomes comments and suggestions on forthcoming topics.

27 http://www.facebook.com/fundamentalrights (accessed 20 February 2011); http://twitter.com/#!/EURightsAgency (accessed 2 September 2011).

28 Here the instructions to the interviewer are 'note down the following details after interview, do not ask' (FRA 2009c: 42).

29 See, further, Foucault (1991) for his discussion of delinquency.

30 The FRA monitors 'good practice' by Member States in its annual reports. The latest annual report of 2011, though it adopts a new format and style to previous annual reports, nevertheless highlights initiatives that ought to be emulated by the Member States as 'Promising Practices' and 'Key Developments' (FRA 2011).

31 This is made apparent in the FAQ section of the FRA website, http://fra.europa.eu/fraWebsite/faq/faq_en.htm (accessed 2 September 2011).

32 For a full list, and definitions of the groups, see FRA 2009b.

33 For the seven Member States where the Roma were surveyed and with respect to nine different areas of discrimination (for example, at work, by healthcare personnel) (FRA 2009d: 4).

34 For more on how Foucault relates governmentality to neoliberalism, see Burchell 1991; Foucault 2007; Gordon 1991.
35 The image is taken from Max Weber's '*iron* cage of rationalisation and enslavement to bureaucratic soullessness'.
36 http://www.surveymonkey.com/s.aspx?sm=Kcd_2bGYOIyqG9qjcRgT_2bSCQ_3d_3d (accessed 3 March 2009).
37 http://194.30.12.221/fraWebsite/partners_networks/fundamental_rights_platform_frp/advisory-panel/advisory-panel_en.htm (accessed 1 August 2010).
38 See, further, Brown 1995, 2002; Golder 2010, 2011; Golder and Fitzpatrick 2009.

References

Brown, W. (1995) *States of Injury: Power and Freedom in Late Modernity*, Princeton, NJ: Princeton University Press

___ (2002) 'Suffering the Paradoxes of Rights', in W. Brown and J. Halley (eds) *Left Legalism/Left Critique*, Durham, NC: Duke University Press

Burchell, G. (1991) 'Peculiar Interests: Civil Society and Governing "The System of Natural Liberty"', in G. Burchell *et al.* (eds) *The Foucault Effect: Studies in Governmentality*, Chicago, IL: University of Chicago Press

Cadman, L. (2010) 'How (Not) To Be Governed: Foucault, Critique and the Political', *Environment and Planning D: Society and Space*, 28: 539–56

COM (2001) 428 final, Commission of the European Communities *European Governance: A White Paper*

COM (2002) 275 final, Communication from the Commission 'European Governance: Better Lawmaking'

COM (2004) 693 final, Communication from the Commission 'The Fundamental Rights Agency Public Consultation Document'

Dean, M. (1999) *Governmentality: Power and Rule in Modern Society*, London: Sage

___ (2007) *Governing Societies: Political Perspectives on Domestic and International Rule*, Maidenhead: Open University Press

de Búrca, G. (2010) 'The European Court of Justice and the International Legal Order after *Kadi*', *Harvard International Law Journal*, 51: 1–49

de Schutter, O. (2006–7) 'Fundamental Rights and the Transformation of Governance in the European Union', *Cambridge Yearbook on European Legal Studies*, 9: 133–75

___ (2007) 'The Added Value of the European Union Agency for Fundamental Rights', *Equal Voices*, 21: 27–30

Douzinas, C. (2002) *The End of Human Rights: Critical Legal Thought at the Turn of the Century*, Oxford: Hart

European Commission (2008) 'Proposal for a Council Directive on Implementing the Principle of Equal Treatment Between Persons Irrespective of Religion or Belief, Disability, Age or Sexual Orientation', COM (2008) 426 final

European Parliament (2009) Resolution on the Application of Directive 2004/38/EC on the Right of Citizens of the Union and their Family Members to Move and Reside Territory of Member States, INI/2008/2184

European Policy Evaluation Consortium (2005) 'Preparatory Study for Impact Assessment and Ex-Ante Evaluation of Fundamental Rights Agency: Analysis of Responses to Public Consultation', http://ec.europa.eu/justice/news/consulting_public/0011/analysis_written_contributions_en.pdf (accessed 25 April 2012)

European Union Agency for Fundamental Rights (FRA) (2008) *Homophobia and Discrimination on the Grounds of Sexual Orientation in the EU Member States: Part I – Legal Analysis*, http://www.fra.europa.eu/fraWebsite/material/pub/comparativestudy/FRA_hdgso_part1_en.pdf (accessed 2 May 2011)

___ (2009a) *Homophobia and Discrimination on the Grounds of Sexual Orientation in the EU Member States: Part II – The Social Situation*, http://fra.europa.eu/fraWebsite/research/publications/publications_per_year/2009/pub_cr_homophobia_p2_0309_en.htm (accessed 3 May 2012)

___ (2009b) 'EU-MIDIS at a Glance: Introduction to the FRA's EU-wide Discrimination Survey', http://fra.europa.eu/fraWebsite/eu-midis/eumidis_glance_en.htm (accessed 2 September 2011)

___ (2009c) 'EU-MIDIS European Union Minorities and Discrimination Survey: Questionnaire', http://fra.europa.eu/fraWebsite/eu-midis/index_en.htm (accessed 24 April 2009)

___ (2009d) *EU-MIDIS European Union Minorities and Discrimination Survey: Data in Focus Report: The Roma*, http://fra.europa.eu/fraWebsite/eu-midis/index_en.htm (accessed 2 September 2011)

___ (2009e) *EU-MIDIS European Union Minorities and Discrimination Survey: Data in Focus Report 2: Muslims*, http://fra.europa.eu/fraWebsite/eu-midis/index_en.htm (accessed 2 September 2011)

___ (2010) *National Human Rights Institutions in the EU Member States: Strengthening the Fundamental Rights Architecture in the EU I*, http://fra.europa.eu/fraWebsite/attachments/NHRI_en.pdf (accessed 2 May 2011)

___ (2011) *Fundamental Rights: Challenges and Achievements in 2010*, http://fra.europa.eu/fraWebsite/attachments/annual-report-2011_EN.pdf (accessed 14 September 2011)

Foucault, M. (1988) 'Technologies of the Self', in L. H. Martin *et al.* (eds) *Technologies of the Self: A Seminar with Michel Foucault*, Amherst, MA: The University of Massachusetts Press

___ (1991) *Discipline and Punish: The Birth of the Prison*, trans. A. Sheridan, Harmondsworth: Penguin

___ (1997) 'What is Critique?', in S. Lotringer and L. Hochroth (eds) *The Politics of Truth*, New York, NY: Semiotext(e)

___ (1998) *The History of Sexuality, Vol. 1: The Will To Knowledge*, trans. R. Hurley, Harmondsworth: Penguin

___ (2000a) 'On the Genealogy of Ethics: An Overview of Work in Progress', in P. Rabinow (ed.) *Essential Works of Foucault Vol. 1: Ethics*, London: Penguin

___ (2000b) 'The Ethics of the Concern for Self as a Practice of Freedom', in P. Rabinow (ed.) *Essential Works of Foucault Vol. 1: Ethics*, London: Penguin

___ (2005) *The Hermeneutics of the Subject: Lectures at the Collège de France, 1981–82*, trans. G. Burchell, New York, NY: Palgrave Macmillan

___ (2007) *Security, Territory, Population: Lectures at the Collège de France, 1977–78*, trans. G. Burchell, New York, NY: Palgrave Macmillan

___ (2008) *The Birth of Biopolitics: Lectures at the Collège de France, 1978–79*, trans. G. Burchell, New York, NY: Palgrave Macmillan

___ (2010) *The Government of Self and Others: Lectures at the Collège de France 1982–83*, trans. G. Burchell, Houndmills: Palgrave Macmillan

Golder, B. (2010) 'Foucault and the Unfinished Human of Rights', *Law, Culture and the Humanities* 6: 354–74

___ (2011) 'Foucault's Critical (Yet Ambivalent) Affirmation: Three Figures of Rights', *Social & Legal Studies*, 20: 283–312

Golder, B. and Fitzpatrick, P. (2009) *Foucault's Law*, Abingdon: Routledge

Gordon, C. (1991) 'Governmental Rationality: An Introduction', in G. Burchell, C. Gordon and P. Miller (eds) *The Foucault Effect: Studies in Governmentality*, Chicago, IL: University of Chicago Press

Hutton, P. (1988) 'Foucault, Freud, and the Technologies of the Self', in L. H. Martin *et al.* (eds) *Technologies of the Self: A Seminar with Michel Foucault*, Amherst, MA: The University of Massachusetts Press

Kennedy, D. (2005) 'Challenging the Expert Rule: The Politics of Global Governance', *Sydney Law Review*, 27: 5–28

Möllers, C. (2006) 'European Governance: Meaning and Value of a Concept', *Common Market Law Review*, 43: 313–36

Morison, J. (2003) 'Modernising Government and the E-Government Revolution: Technologies of Government and Technologies of Democracy', in N. Bamforth and P. Leyland (eds) *Public Law in a Multi-Layered Constitution*, Oxford: Hart

___ (2010) 'Gov 2.0: Towards a User Generated State?', *Modern Law Review*, 73: 551–77

Mutua, M. (2002) *Human Rights: A Political and Cultural Critique*, Philadelphia, PA: University of Pennsylvania

Nietzsche, F. (1998) *On the Genealogy of Morality*, trans. M. Clark and A. J. Swensen, London: Hackett

Orford, A. (2007) 'Bio-politics and the Tragic Subject of Human Rights', in E. Dauphinée and C. Masters (eds) *The Logics of Biopower and the War on Terror: Living, Dying, Surviving*, Basingstoke: Palgrave Macmillan

Rose, N. (1999) *Powers of Freedom: Reframing Political Thought*, Cambridge: Cambridge University Press

___ (2000) 'Government and Control', *British Journal of Criminology*, 40: 321–39

___ (2007) *The Politics of Life Itself: Biomedicine, Power, and Subjectivity in the Twenty-First Century*, Princeton, NJ: Princeton University Press

Rosenau, J. and Czempiel, E. (eds) (1992) *Governance Without Government: Order and Change in World Politics*, Cambridge: Cambridge University Press

Scott, J. and Trubek, D. (2002) 'Mind the Gap: Law and New Approaches to Governance in the European Union', *European Law Journal*, 8: 1–18

Sending, O. J. and Neumann, I. B. (2006) 'Governance to Governmentality: Analyzing NGOs, State and Power', *International Studies Quarterly*, 50: 651–72

Singer, P. (ed.) (1994) *Ethics*, Oxford: Oxford University Press

Sokhi-Bulley, B. (2011a) 'Governing (through) Rights: Statistics as Technologies of Governmentality', *Social & Legal Studies*, 20: 139–55

___ (2011b) 'Government(ality) by Experts: Human Rights as Governance', *Law and Critique*, 22: 251–71

Stychin, C. F. (2003) *Governing Sexuality: The Changing Politics of Citizenship and Law Reform*, Oxford: Hart

References to primary sources of law

Joined cases C-402/05 and C-415/05 P *Yassin Abdullah Kadi and Al Barakat International Foundation v. Council and Commission* [2008] ECR I-06351

Index

Lightning Source UK Ltd.
Milton Keynes UK
UKOW05f0936140517
301130UK00007B/60/P

9 780415 634137